Union with God in Christ

American Society of Missiology Monograph Series

Series Editor, James R. Krabill

The ASM Monograph Series provides a forum for publishing quality dissertations and studies in the field of missiology. Collaborating with Pickwick Publications—a division of Wipf and Stock Publishers of Eugene, Oregon—the American Society of Missiology selects high quality dissertations and other monographic studies that offer research materials in mission studies for scholars, mission and church leaders, and the academic community at large. The ASM seeks scholarly work for publication in the series that throws light on issues confronting Christian world mission in its cultural, social, historical, biblical, and theological dimensions.

Missiology is an academic field that brings together scholars whose professional training ranges from doctoral-level preparation in areas such as Scripture, history and sociology of religions, anthropology, theology, international relations, interreligious interchange, mission history, inculturation, and church law. The American Society of Missiology, which sponsors this series, is an ecumenical body drawing members from Independent and Ecumenical Protestant, Catholic, Orthodox, and other traditions. Members of the ASM are united by their commitment to reflect on and do scholarly work relating to both mission history and the present-day mission of the church. The ASM Monograph Series aims to publish works of exceptional merit on specialized topics, with particular attention given to work by younger scholars, the dissemination and publication of which is difficult under the economic pressures of standard publishing models.

Persons seeking information about the ASM or the guidelines for having their dissertations considered for publication in the ASM Monograph Series should consult the Society's website—www.asmweb.org.

Members of the ASM Monograph Committe who approved this book are:

Paul V. Kollman, University of Notre Dame
Roger Schroeder, Catholic Theological Union
Bonnie Sue Lewis, University of Dubuque Theological Seminary

RECENTLY PUBLISHED IN THE ASM MONOGRAPH SERIES

Chin, Clive S. *The Perception of Christianity as a Rational Religion in Singapore: A Missiological Analysis of Christian Conversion.*

Hubers, John. *I Am a Pilgrim, a Traveler, a Stranger: Exploring the Life and Mind of the First American Missionary to the Middle East, the Rev. Pliny Fisk (1792–1825).*

McGill, Jenny. *Religious Identity and Cultural Negotiation: Toward a Theology of Christian Identity in Migration.*

Union with God in Christ
Early Christian and Wesleyan Spirituality as an Approach to Islamic Mysticism

By Matthew Friedman

Foreword by A. H. Mathias Zahniser

American Society of Missiology Monograph Series vol. 32

◆PICKWICK *Publications* · Eugene, Oregon

UNION WITH GOD IN CHRIST
Early Christian and Wesleyan Spirituality as an Approach to Islamic Mysticism

American Society of Missiology Monograph Series 32

Copyright © 2017 Matthew Friedman. All rights reserved. Except for brief quotations in critical publications or reviews, no part of this book may be reproduced in any manner without prior written permission from the publisher. Write: Permissions, Wipf and Stock Publsihers, 199 W. 8th Ave., Suite 3, Eugene, OR 97401

Pickwick Publications
An Imprint of Wipf and Stock Publishers
199 W. 8th Ave., Suite 3
Eugene, OR 97401

www.wipfandstock.com

PAPERBACK ISBN: 978-1-4982-7838-6
HARDCOVER ISBN: 978-1-4982-7840-9
EBOOK ISBN: 978-1-4982-7839-3

Cataloging-in-Publication data:

Names: Friedman, Matthew. | Zahniser, A. H. Mathias (foreword)

Title: Union with God in Christ : early Christian and Wesleyan spirituality as an approach to Islamic mysticism / by Matthew Friedman, foreword by A. H. Mathias Zahniser.

Description: Eugene, OR : Pickwick Publications, 2017 | Series: American Society of Missiology Monograph Series 32 | Includes bibliographical references and index.

Identifiers: ISBN 978-1-4982-7838-6 (paperback) | ISBN 978-1-4982-7838-6 (hardcover) | ISBN 978-1-4982-7839-3 (ebook)

Subjects: LCSH: Sufism. | Spirituality—Methodist Church—History—18th century. | Spiritual life—Christianity. | Mysticism—Judiasm. | Christianity and other religions—Islam.

Classification: LCC BP172.5.O77 F7 2017 (print) | LCC BP172.5.O77 (ebook)

Manufactured in the U.S.A.   10/24/17

Contents

Permissions | vii
Foreword by A. H. Mathias Zahniser | ix
Acknowledgments | xiii

Introduction | 1

1. "Will You Not Discover The Lord In All This?":
   The Context of Ancient Jewish Mysticism | 22

2. "With Unveiled Faces": New Testament Response to Ascension and Vision Mysticism | 59

3. "That He Be Surrounded by God's Glory": Christian Interaction with Jewish and Hellenic Mysticism in Late Antiquity | 90

4. Union with God and Mission in the Theology of John Wesley | 111

5. Sufism: A Brief Overview | 145

6. ʿAlī Ibn ʿUthmān Al-Hujwīrī and Sharaf Al-Dīn Manerī | 194

7. Conclusion | 239

Bibliography | 261
General Index | 285

Permissions

Excerpts from Sharafuddin Maneri: The Hundred Letters, translated and introduced by Paul Jackson, SJ. Copyright © 1980 by Paulist Press, Inc. Paulist Press, Inc., New York/Mahwah, NJ. Reprinted by permission of Paulist Press, Inc. www.paulistpress.com

PHILO, VOL. IV, translated by F. H. Colson and G. H. Whitaker, Loeb Classical Library Volume 261, Cambridge, Mass.: Harvard University Press, First published 1932. Loeb Classical Library ® is a registered trademark of the President and Fellows of Harvard College.

PHILO, VOL. V, translated by F. H. Colson and G. H. Whitaker, Loeb Classical Library Volume 275, Cambridge, Mass.: Harvard University Press, First published 1934. Loeb Classical Library ® is a registered trademark of the President and Fellows of Harvard College.

All Scripture quotations, unless otherwise indicated, are taken from the Holy Bible, New International Version®, NIV®. Copyright ©1973, 1978, 1984, 2011 by Biblica, Inc.™ Used by permission of Zondervan. All rights reserved worldwide. www.zondervan.com The "NIV" and "New International Version" are trademarks registered in the United States Patent and Trademark Office by Biblica, Inc.™

Scripture quotations from The Revised Standard Version Bible, copyright © 1946, 1952, and 1971, and the New Revised Standard Version Bible, copyright © 1989 National Council of the Churches of Christ in the United States of America. Used by permission. All rights reserved worldwide.

Foreword

THE EVANGELIST MATTHEW BEGINS his gospel with *mission*: the centripetal mission of Gentile wise men from the East who, having exercised their cultural practice of star gazing, aided by those who know scripture, travel to Bethlehem to see the new child king of Israel (Matt 2:1–12). Matthew ends his gospel with *mission*: the now adult king Jesus, crucified and resurrected, commissions his disciples for centrifugal mission to "make disciples of all *nations*"—nations in the sense of ethnic communities (Matt 28:16–20).

In this book, *Union with God in Christ: Early Christian and Wesleyan Spirituality as an Approach to Islamic Mysticism*, Matthew Friedman helps twentieth-century disciples engage in centrifugal mission in a way that taps into the deep worldview of an ethnic community today. The Magi were looking at the heavens where God met them. Friedman understands that one cannot go anywhere where God is not involved already, using what people are interested in to draw them in a centripetal quest whose destination can only be explained through the story of Jesus the Messiah. This Matthew has found Muslims from the East looking for union with God. They are already on a path like that of the Magi that can lead to Jesus. His book represents a profound cooperation with a long divine engagement, the culmination of which is union with God in Christ.

It will accordingly help practitioners, teachers, and students of contextualization grasp what union with God means to Muslims with a mystical bent and how contextualization can avoid the superficial and syncretistic errors born of poor analysis and uninformed enthusiasm. In order to unveil the bridges available among communities involved in varying degrees of Islamic mysticism and to guide followers of Jesus in disciple making and community building among them, Friedman gleans from the experience of early Christians in dealing with communities influenced by Jewish and Hellenic mysticism. He gives special attention to New Testament literature—particularly, but not exclusively, the fourth gospel and the other writings of the Apostle John.

After a survey of Christian interaction with various mystical writings in late antiquity, including the Gospel of Thomas, Friedman zooms in on the *Homilies* of a fourth-century Syrian monk collected pseudonymously under the name Macarius of Egypt, whose critical interaction with the ascension and vision mysticism of his Jewish and Hellenic environment is particularly clear and relevant to the quest of Muslims for union with God. Furthermore, the monk's *Homilies* selected for careful evaluation by Friedman eventually contributed to the theology of John Wesley. Indeed, Friedman finds Wesleyan missiology a rich source for contextualizing the Christian gospel to satisfy any quest for union with God.

Of course, when followers of Jesus seek "to recognize what the Creator-Redeemer is doing in this world and try to do it with him,"[1] especially among adherents of another religious tradition or ideology, they must avoid compromising the Christian faith itself in the process. Friedman, aware of the possibility of debilitating syncretism, frames his analysis with the seminal work of the Scottish missiologist Andrew Walls, arguably the preeminent missiologist of our time. In a classic essay, "The Gospel as Prisoner and Liberator of Culture," Walls identifies two principles that must always be kept in mind in contextualization: "the indigenizing principle," that faithful Christians must always experience their faith as relevant and reliable within their own culture; and "the pilgrim principle," that faith in Christ will always result in tension with their society and culture: "there will be rubs and frictions—not from the adoption of a new culture, but from the transformation of the mind toward that of Christ."[2] These principles have been validated by much research and experience; Friedman applies them adroitly throughout the book, but especially to the exemplary Sufi writings of the Afghani ʿAlī ibn ʿUthmān al-Jullābī al-Hujwīrī (d. AD 1073) and the Bihari Indian, Sharaf al-Dīn Manerī (d. AD 1381). He examines these thinkers who have influenced contemporary Muslims seeking union with God in the light of Christian parallels in scripture, early and subsequent Christian tradition, reason and experience.

---

1. Taylor, *Go Between God*, 37, 39.
2. Walls, *Missionary Movement in History*, 8.

Two additional features of Friedman's approach to contextualizing Christian faith and practice in a Muslim Sufi community make the book you have in your hands very valuable indeed: the thoroughness of his research—he leaves no stone unturned—and the fact of his own engagement with what God is already doing in one such community.

> Lord, you beat in our hearts and thrive in every cell of our bodies. All that we are leaps for delight. Wherever we go, we know we shall find you there. Amen.[3]

A. H. Mathias Zahniser
John Wesley Beeson Professor of Christian Mission emeritus
Asbury Theological Seminary, Wilmore, Kentucky
Currently, Scholar in Residence
Greenville College, Greenville, Illinois

---

3. Wyes, *From Shore to Shore*, 92.

Acknowledgments

REFLECTING BACK ON THE journey that has in some ways culminated, and in other ways commenced, with this project, I find that I have so much for which to be grateful to so many.

I am grateful to my long-patient wife Chandra and our son Eli for their grace and endurance during the many, many hours that I spent researching and writing this manuscript, and for their support and love along the way. I can also be thankful for parents who gave me a love of learning and a continual curiousity.

I am grateful for those who walked with me in through classes, research and careful mentoring. Special thanks goes especially to my dissertation supervisor, Lalsangkima Pachuau, for his theological wisdom, and for his attention to ensuring that the fine details of this project were all in their proper place. I likewise wish to thank A. H. Mathias Zahniser, for both affirming and challenging me as I worked through the complex and interconnected worlds of Jewish, Christian and Islamic mysticism. Though not officially on my "committee," Dale F. Walker was also very helpful in providing numerous suggestions; as a "walking bibliography," he often pointed me to sources that I might otherwise never have found. I am proud to be able to refer to each of you not only as mentors, but as friends. I am also so very thankful for the opportunity to have served as teaching assistant under not only Dr. Pachuau and Dr. Walker, but also under Steve Seamands and Ruth Anne Reese.

I am grateful for other professors from whom I have learned both formally in classes, as well as informally in discussions, over coffee, and with as much laughter as furrowed brows deep in thought: In addition to the aforementioned, George Hunter, Eunice Irwin, Steve Ybarrola, W. Jay Moon, Kevin Kinghorn, Art McPhee, Terry Muck, Howard Snyder, and Lawrence Wood.

I am grateful to those congregations and individual friends, too many to name, whose support over the years in South Asia and in North America made this research possible. I want to particularly express my gratitude for the encouragement and openheartedness of Dan and Cynthia Strull and Olive Tree Congregation, Raul and Mary Nassar, and Walter and Jeryl Buehler in North Jersey.

I will always be grateful for those who shared my journey in South Asia and beyond, and who share in this story and in the working out of what it may mean to walk with Jesus in a context in which Islamic mysticism is frequently encountered. In addition to colleagues on the ground, I also appreciated the advocacy of Steve Cochrane and others toward an ethos of developing "scholar-practitioners" who pursue academic research, but also seek to connect this with their own field experience, following models from the past such as the great W. H. T. Gairdner of Cairo.

I give special thanks to J. Dudley Woodberry, who first demonstrated to me that serious intellectual engagement and devout love for Jesus could be brought together with seamless intergrity, and for the introduction to Islamic mysticism from which I benefited in his classroom.

I also am grateful for the friendship and occasional nudging of Phil Parshall, from whose writings I first learned of engagement with the context of Islamic mysticism in print. I later discovered a graceful man of God behind the pen.

Greg Livingstone has given my family and I much encouragement over the years, as he has to many as a kind of "father figure" for all who share our particular focus.

I am grateful for colleagues and students at Kingswood University and Asbury Theological Seminary; at Oak Hills Christian College, where I taught for four years, and in training programs around the world.

Above all, I am thankful for the grace of God which I have discovered in Yeshua the Messiah, the Word within God's Essence, and the Spirit of God in whose grace I am carried along and transformed into his image, being brought into deepening union with the Beloved.

Introduction

BACKGROUND OF THE PROBLEM

HENRY MARTYN (1781–1812) WAS an early Anglican missionary with a focus on the Muslims, first in India, and then in the final stage of his short life in Persia. It was in Persia that he wrote of interacting with Sūfīs, the mystics of Islam, and he made a curiously hopeful comment regarding this special kind of Muslims, recording in his journal:

> These Soofies are quite the methodists of the East.[1] They delight in everything Christian, except in being exclusive. From these. . . you will perceive the first Persian church will be formed, judging after the manner of men. [sic][2]

Martyn saw a hunger for God in the Sūfīs which is what we can understand him to be referring to here. In reflecting on Martyn's observations here, it would be worthwhile to investigate an approach to these "Methodists of the East" in light of some of the spiritual and missiological principles of early Methodism and some of the Patristic sources which parallel and in some ways contributed to the development of the classic Wesleyan understanding of sanctification as union with God in Christ. These seem as well to have parallels with some of the same themes in early Sūfī thought. It is in view of these parallels that we will explore the

---

1. It is worth noting that in the early nineteenth-century context in which Martyn was writing, referring to Sūfīs as "Methodists" of the East was probably something akin to the analogy more common today in suggesting that Sūfīs are rather like the "Pentecostals of the Muslim World." See Jenkins, "Sufi Rising," and Morin, "Sufism and 'the Beloved,'" 1.

2. Martyn, *Journal and Letters*, 2.383.

possibility of applying in the Sūfī context the insights of the early Church's interaction with particularly the context of Jewish mysticism.

We have had an interest in Sufism for a number of years. As we have lived in the midst of communities of spiritually curious, mystically-inclined Muslim people, we have sought to engage in dialogue as well as mission among a population with a particularly strong inclination towards mysticism, and among whom even those not formally initiated into a Sūfī *tarīqa*[3] (order) are influenced by the philosophy and practices of Islamic mysticism. We have had the privilege of interacting with and learning from both those among the common people, as well as educated Sūfī teachers. We have found there to often be a great deal of openness to discussion about matters of faith, especially of themes which have some level of parallel in Sufism and Christian faith. Moreover, we have found that it has been fruitful and rewarding to integrate Sūfī terminology and concepts into our witness among Sūfīs, both in terms of our own interaction with those who have not yet entered into covenant faith in Jesus, as well as in the context of teaching and discipleship of those who have entered into faith in him.

These discoveries have driven us to deepen our understanding of the roots and background of Sufism. Some of the reading and research we have done up until now on Sūfī thought and practice has introduced the suggestion that the development of early Sufism was impacted Muslim interaction with Christian monastic communities.[4] Early Islam was influenced by interaction with both Jewish and Christian faith, and even the Qur'an itself includes evidence of having emerged in a milieu in which these were embedded. Thus it is written in Q 5:82b, "thou wilt surely find that, of all people, they who say, 'Behold, we are Christians,' come closest to feeling affection for those who believe [in this divine writ]: this is

---

3. The Sūfī *tarīqa* is a brotherhood or order of people, men and sometimes women, too, who are initiated into a path (the literal meaning of *tarīqa*) for the purpose of spiritual advancement, usually under the guidance of a spiritual director, or *walī* (Arabic) or *pīr* (Persian). Please note that for the sake of simplicity, we have chosen to avoid using diacritical subdots in our transliteration of words from Arabic and Hebrew (such as *tarīqa*, which would have a dot under the initial "t"), though we will use macrons where appropriate.

4. This has been affirmed, for example, by Tor Andrae in his *In the Garden of Myrtles* and Margaret Smith in *Studies in Early Mysticism in the Near and Middle*. More recent scholarship such as that of Annemarie Schimmel has affirmed some of this, while cautioning against overstating the influence of Christian monastic spirituality upon Sūfī development; see Schimmel, *Mystical Dimensions*, 10.

so because there are priests and monks among them, and because these are not given to arrogance."[5] Muslim scholar Mahmoud Ayoub expresses his own yearning for a rediscovery of this earlier Christian tradition by Christians themselves, when he writes,

> It is my conviction that Christianity began to lose its power of sanctification as it lost its Eastern home and character. It was in this Eastern piety and spiritual dynamism of the holy desert fathers that Islam was born and nourished. It was not dogma but holiness, victory against demonic spirits of uncleanness, which spoke to the needs of men and women. We dismiss as a bit of Eastern superstition that Jesus cast out unclean spirits. Yet it was this piety of healing and sanctification, whose ultimate source Jesus was, that played an important role in the life of the society of the ancient Near East, and that can once again rejuvenate the materialistic society of our world today.[6]

This familiarity with and admiration of monastic life is illustrated even more strikingly in the heart of the Muslim faith, in the Qur'ān itself. Q 24:35–37 reads:

> God is the Light of the heavens and the earth. The parable of His light is, as it were, that of a niche containing a lamp; the lamp is [enclosed] in glass, the glass [shining] like a radiant star: [a lamp] lit from a blessed tree—an olive-tree that is neither of the east nor of the west the oil whereof [is so bright that it] would well-nigh give light [of itself] even though fire had not touched it: light upon light! God guides unto His light him that wills [to be guided]; and [to this end] God propounds parables unto men, since God [alone] has full knowledge of all things. In the houses [of worship] which God has allowed to be raised so that His name be remembered in them, there [are such as] extol His limitless glory at morn and evening, people whom neither [worldly] commerce nor striving after gain can divert from the remembrance of God, and from constancy in prayer, and from charity: [people] who are filled with fear [at the thought] of the Day On which all hearts and eyes will be convulsed.

---

5. Unless otherwise noted, all references from the Qur'ān will be from the Asad translation: Asad, *The Message of the Qur'ān*. Since there are several other editions and printings of this particular translation, we will only cite the Sūrah (chapter) and verse reference, following Egyptian versification.

6. Ayoub, A *Muslim View of Christianity*, 77.

4 Union with God in Christ

In an earlier generation, Richard Bell recognized that this passage, with its description of a lamp in a wall-niche as a metaphor for God's presence, may very well be a description of monks in a monastery or desert cell.[7] Not surprisingly, even as many of the monks in places thus described sought to walk in union with God, this passage has been a point of departure for Sūfī speculation on the nature of God and of ascending union with him.[8] This is a crucial passage of the Qur'ān for many Sūfīs, and has been the subject of both devotion and much philosophical speculation.

Part of the question for us relates, for example, to how one can respond to what is referred to as the "light verse" of the Qur'ān above, and what follows immediately afterwards. While we believe that we share with the Sūfīs a common metaphysical understanding of God in the most general sense, nonetheless, the Judeo-Christian Scriptures make it clear that in common with all humankind, we also share a need to be united with Him *in Christ*. How can this gap be bridged? One avenue which we will explore begins with a passage in the Pauline epistles which almost seems to be a Christological answer to the sentiment expressed above from the Qur'ān.

> [W]hen one turns to the Lord, the veil is removed. Now the Lord is the Spirit, and where the Spirit of the Lord is, there is freedom. And all of us, with unveiled faces, seeing the glory of the Lord as though reflected in a mirror, are being transformed into the same image from one degree of glory to another; for this comes from the Lord, the Spirit.... And even if our gospel is veiled, it is veiled to those who are perishing. In their case the god of this world has blinded the minds of the unbelievers, to keep them from seeing the light of the gospel of the glory of Christ, who is the image of God. For we do not proclaim ourselves; we proclaim Jesus Christ as Lord and ourselves as your slaves for Jesus' sake. For it is the God who said, "Let light shine out of darkness," who has shone in our hearts to give the light of the knowledge of the glory of God in the face of Jesus Christ. But we have this treasure in clay jars, so that it may be made clear that this extraordinary power belongs to God and does not come from us. (2 Cor 3:16–18; 4:3–7 NRSV)

---

7. Bell, *Origin of Islam*, 115–16.

8. See especially Ghazzali, *Mishkât Al-Anwar*, Kalābādhī, *The Doctrine of the Sūfīs*, 11, with a story citing this very passage.

This passage seems potentially powerful in the context of Sufism, even without much further elaboration: It takes the yearning for the light of God and focuses it on Messiah Jesus.

It was this very passage which was the focal point of the writings of fourth-century Syrian writer Macarius-Symeon in his own understanding of a Christ-focused, Holy Spirit-empowered union with God. One Orthodox writer, Alexander Golitzin,[9] goes so far as to suggest that the "whole Macarian corpus is like an extended meditation on this scriptural passage" (that is, 2 Cor 3:7—4:7), bringing together "all the essentials of what he wants to say to his monks," and from there demonstrates how this passage contains so many of the classic contrasts relating to themes of "change, alteration, or transfiguration . . . which occurs in the Christian soul through the indwelling Spirit, and of the glory (*doxa*) of God in which the soul and ultimately the body are called to share."[10]

By way of example, some scholars have noticed that in the first of his "spiritual homilies," Macarius-Symeon seems to be interacting with the early Jewish mystical tradition of the *Merkavah*, meditations on the throne-chariot of God based primarily on the opening vision of Ezekiel in the first chapter. Following the overview of Ezekiel's vision, Macarius-Symeon begins seeking to explain it in the language of *theosis*[11] which one finds again and again throughout the *Homilies*. Here he says, that Ezekiel saw that mystery which

> was that of the soul, that was to receive her Lord, and to become a throne of glory for Him. For the soul that is privileged to be in communion with the Spirit of His light, and is irradiated by the beauty of the unspeakable glory of Him who has prepared her to be a seat and a dwelling for Himself, becomes all light, all face, all eye; and there is no part of her that is not full of the spiritual eyes of light. That is to say, there is no part of her darkened, but she is all throughout wrought into light and spirit, and is full of eyes all over, and has no such thing as a back part, but in every direction is face forward, with the unspeakable beauty of the glory of the light of Christ mounted and riding upon her. As the sun is of one likeness all over, without any part behind or inferior, but is all glorified with light throughout, and is, indeed,

---

9. Retired Marquette University professor Alexander Golitzin is a noted scholar in ancient Eastern Christian and Jewish mysticism.

10. Golitzin, "Christianity as Transfiguration," 133.

11. Sometimes literally translated "divinization," it is meant to convey the broader idea of union with God.

all light, with no difference between the parts, or as fire, the very light of the fire, is alike all over, having in it no first or last, or greater or less, so also the soul that is perfectly irradiated by the unspeakable beauty of the glory of the light of the face of Christ, and is perfectly in communion with the Holy Spirit, and is privileged to be the dwelling-place and throne of God, becomes all eye, all light, all face, all glory, all spirit, being made so by Christ, who drives, and guides, and carries, and bears her about, and graces and adorns her thus with spiritual beauty.[12]

Macarius-Symeon seems here to be connecting the *Merkavah* tradition with an explanatory principle of sorts in the form of the aforementioned passage in 2 Corinthians, in this case particularly 4:6.

Another, similar theme which we will examine concerns suggestions made by scholars such as April D. DeConick[13] and the aforementioned Alexander Golitzin in regard to this interaction with "vision" or "ascension" mysticism. They have asserted that this provides the context for many of the statements in John's Gospel regarding Jesus as being the representation of the vision of God. In John 14:3–7, for example, Jesus is making clear that the "way of ascent," that is, to the Father and into the throne room of God himself, is not, and indeed, cannot, be through self-effort or self-knowledge: It is only through entering into a relationship of faith in Jesus. Having in effect earlier attacked the ascension enterprise in John 3:13 ("No one has ascended into heaven except he who descended from heaven, the Son of Man"), here he comforts his disciples by informing them that, while they cannot follow him in their own strength (13:36), they shall later join him; indeed, "rooms" will be prepared for them in Jesus' "Father's house" (14:2–3). Thus, the hope of the *hekhalōt*, or heavenly palaces, and of the *Merkavah* tradition, of not merely visiting, but *abiding* with God, seems to be understood as finding its fulfillment in Jesus.[14]

Thus a key element in the following research relates to the manner in which both the author of John's Gospel and other relevant passages in the New Testament and Macarius-Symeon interact with this theme of Jewish *Merkavah* mysticism. Particular attention is paid to whether writings such as these may provide material for developing an approach

---

12. Homily 1.2; Macarius, *Fifty Spiritual Homilies*, 2.

13. April D. DeConick is a professor and historian of early Jewish and Christian thought at Rice University in Texas, particularly noted for several volumes published on the Gospel of Thomas.

14. DeConick, *Voices of the Mystics*, 124.

for the Sūfī context, which contains some elements in common with that of early Jewish mysticism.

Having examined examples of the biblical and Syrian Christian interaction with these traditions, we will now move on to consider the writings of John Wesley and others in the early Wesleyan Methodist tradition, *noting in particular the parallel themes of union with God* in Wesley's writings and those of the Syrian mystics, especially the writings of Macarius-Symeon.[15] As will be discussed in greater detail in the fourth chapter, Wesley's interacted critically and programmatically with the Macarian *Homilies*, other early Christian writings, as well as Anglican and Continental thinkers whose writings also contained a focus on the theme of union with God. As we will observe, Wesley's contribution to this understanding of union with God was to emphasize both the communal element of how God's grace meets us, and, importantly for us, the manner in which our union with God is meant to transform us individually and corporately in such a way that we seek bless others missionally, both in terms of loving service and proclamation of the Gospel.

In the eleventh century CE, several important Islamic thinkers developed works which were designed to present a vision of Sufism which brought the adherent into a deep connection with God, yet remaining rooted in the Islamic tradition. A significant number of studies have already been done concerning particularly two of these who wrote in Arabic, Abū Hāmid al-Ghazālī (d. 1111) and Abū'l-Qāsim al-Qushayrī (d.1072). Two relatively lesser-known Sūfī figures whose writings we will examine as part of this research are the eleventh-century Persian Sūfī writer and historian 'Alī bin 'Uthmān al Jullābī al Hujwīrī and the thirteenth-century Indian Sūfī figure Sharaf al-Dīn Manerī.[16] Both left writings which reflect a more "sober" idea of Sūfī union with God, and which have been and continue to be influential in the lives of Indian Sūfīs. Hujwīrī's *Kashful Mahjūb* ("Unveiling the Veiled")[17] is the oldest

---

15. Indeed, John Wesley included his own edited version of the *Fifty Homilies* (whittled down to twenty-two) in the first volume of his *Christian Library*. Robert S. Brightman notes that "Wesley's edition was compiled by the use of an editorial blue pencil" on the 1721 translation of the Macarian *Homilies* published by Thomas Haywood. See Brightman, "Gregory of Nyssa and John Wesley," 230.

16. We are here following the convention of writing out the saint's name in proper Arabic form, although in context of South Asia, it would be pronounced "Sharafuddin."

17. The primary edited text in Persian is that of V. A. Zhukovsky (*Kashf al-Mahjūb*, 1957). Zhukovsky's edited text was originally published in St. Petersburg in 1899, rather than Leningrad in 1926, as others have noted. See Mojaddedi, "Kaŝf al-Mahjūb

Sūfī writing in the Persian language, and Manerī's *Maktubat-i Sadī* ("The Hundred Letters"),[18] also originally written in Persian, has circulated widely in South Asia. The former is more of a history and encyclopedia of classic Sufism; the latter more of a manual for Sūfī practice. Both, we believe, will prove to be of value in this study.

Potential areas of commonality which we've found especially intriguing are expressions of mysticism focused on the theme of union with God, including the restoration of the image of God in which humankind was created, but which has become corrupted through sin. This theme of union with God is central to the broader subject of mysticism, and will be key in our own examination to follow. An important element of this

---

of Hojvirī," 665. While the standard translation of this work into English is the Nicholson translation al-Hujwīrī, *Revelation of the Mystery* (using here the 1999 reprint by Pir Press, including an added foreword by Carl W. Ernst), there is one other important translation in print: That of Maulana Wahid Baksh Rabbani, including a commentary (*Kashful Mahjub*). We will generally cite the Nicholson translation, but will occasionally use Rabbani's translation instead. As he explains within the Kashf itself, Hujwīrī's other works have been lost (see Hujwīrī, *Revelation*, 2; also Nicholson, "Preface to *Revelation of the Mystery*," xv–xvi).

18. C. A. Storey wrote that editions of the Persian of the *Maktūbāt-i Sadī* were published in Arrah, India in 1870 and Lucknow in 1885 (see Storey, *Persian Literature*, 1049 n. 2); curiously, Paul Jackson, the translator of the English translation, places these translations in Kanpur and Lahore; see Jackson, "Introduction to *The Hundred Letters*," 3. The primary English translation of the Maktūbāt-i Sadī is the Jackson-translated *Hundred Letters*; Jackson explains that for this translation he utilized a manuscript of the the *Maktūbāt-i Sadī* dating from "before the reign of Mughal Emperor Akbar (1556–1605) and now belonging to the Khuda Baksh Oriental Public Library, Patna" [Bihar, India] (Jackson, "Introduction to *The Hundred Letters*," 3). Jackson also utilized the aforementioned nineteenth century published editions, and an Urdu translation done in 1973. In addition to this English translation, there is also an older translation of a number of the letters done by Bhaijnath Singh and published as *Letters from a Sufi Teacher*, as well as selections from Manerī's writings translated by Bruce B. Lawrence and published in *Notes from a Distant Flute*, 72–78. Manerī's additional correspondence has also been influential, most notably the *Maktūbāt-i Do Sadī* ("Another Hundred Letters"); this has also been translated into English by Paul Jackson as *In Quest of God*. Jackson mentions a translation of the first forty letters of the *Maktūbāt-i Sadī* in Bengali in 1976 (Jackson, "Introduction to *The Hundred Letters*," 3); more recent translations in Bengali of both the *Maktūbāt-i Sadī* (2007) and the *Maktūbāt-i Do Sadī* (2011) have been done by A. K. M. Fajlur Rahman Munshi and published in Dhaka by Bangladesh Taj Company, Ltd. Finally, it has been noted that "No other saint of Medieval India has inspired as many *malfūzāt*" [recorded discourses of a Muslim saint] as has Manerī, with Manerī's discourses having been the subject of no less than nine collections of *malfūzāt* (Lawrence, *Notes from a Distant Flute*, 76–77). An English translation done more recently by Paul Jackson of some selections of Manerī's *malfūzāt*, *A Mine of Meaning*, is a valuable and useful study.

study involves differentiating between different understandings of union with God. The late German scholar Annemarie Schimmel, in her own study of Sūfī thought, referred to two broad categories of mysticism: the "Mysticism of Personality" focused on the relationship of the Lover and the Beloved, and in which the distinction is maintained between creature and Creator, as well as the "Mysticism of Infinity," more characteristic of the mystical speculations of Plotinus and Ibn 'Arabi's idea of *wahdat al wujūd*, and in which the devotee sees her goal as being one of the effacement of her personality as she dissolves into the Absolute like a drop into the ocean. Though these can often be entwined with one another *in situ*, in this study we will nonetheless focus more on the former type of mysticism, recognizing even as Schimmel does that it is more compatible with the idea of creation *ex nihilo* found in both the Bible as well as the Qur'ān.[19] Of course, it would be too broad to examine every area in which the writers of Scripture, the early Church and the early Methodists interacted in this manner with their religio-cultural context. We will therefore be especially looking at the classical elements of *ascension, vision,* and *transformation* which have been examined especially by Alan F. Segal, and found in various mystical traditions.[20]

Expressions of longing for union with God in Sufism has some significant parallels with similar aspirations expressed by early Christian writers, including Macarius-Symeon.[21] The late scholar of Islam, Tor Andrae[22] considered the closeness with which Sufism can come towards a

---

19. Schimmel, *Mystical Dimensions*, 5–6.

20. On this tripartite schema, see Segal, "Paul and the Beginning of Jewish Mysticism," 97.

21. "Macarius-Symeon" is the one who John Wesley and others prior to the twentieth century knew as "Macarius the Egyptian," and who modern scholars have now believe was likely a Syrian monk. This was originally noted in Dörries, *Symeon von Mesopotamien*, 7–8; See also Plested, *The Macarian Legacy*, 12–16, and Golitzin, "Christianity as Transfiguration," 148 n. 5. Although the name of Symeon of Mesopotamia appears on some of the manuscripts of the Macarian corpus; see George A. Maloney, "Introduction and Notes," 7. The most recent scholarship has not been able to conclude that he was the author of these writings, as there is very little known about Symeon to begin with; see Plested, *The Macarian Legacy*, 16. Possibly because of associations which came to be formed between the Macarian corpus and the Messalians, who were considered heretical, these writings were attributed to a widely-revered early Church figure as a means of protecting their circulation (Maloney, Introduction and Notes," 9).

22. Tor Andrae was a twentieth-century scholar of Islam, whose expertise and published work included an examination of some of the Jewish and Christian roots of

yearning for a genuinely Christian understanding of the idea of union with God found in the teaching of *theosis*:

> One who corresponds to the ideal thus described has attained union with God. This is the real meaning of the "disappearance," *fanā'*, a concept that has been compared, somewhat rashly, to the Buddhist concept of *nirvāna*. . . . To the Sūfī, the disappearance of the self has a meaning no different, in principle, than it has to the Apostle Paul, when he says: ". . . it is no longer I who live, but Christ who lives in me" (Gal 2:20). Sūfī mysticism uses the term *baqā'*, "abiding." "Disappearance" is to disappear in God through God. "Abiding" is to live with God.[23]

Henry Martyn may very well have referred to the Persian Sūfīs with whom he was interacting as "Methodists of the East" because of what he perceived to be their enthusiasm. In view of a Sūfī understanding of union with God and possible parallels with early Christian and Wesleyan understandings of this central theme, Martyn may have been closer to the truth than he realized at the time. Consider that John Wesley himself wrote in the "question and answer" section of *A Plain Account of Christian Perfection*, "True humility is one kind of self-annihilation; and this is the center of all virtues."[24] As we will describe in our fourth chapter, John Wesley's understanding of union with God was influenced by both his reading of early Christian writers, as well as parallel thinking on this subject in Continental and Anglican theology in and in the century prior to Wesley. Wesley doesn't merely reflect earlier ideas of union with God, however; we will observe that he seeks both to express it in a manner which dovetails with his Reformational understanding of salvation by grace through faith, as well as expands and clarifies this idea of union from one of personal mysticism to a communal and missional ideal.

In this research, we focus on the more devotional, "wise" mysticism,[25] since it is not only more faithful from a biblical perspective, but also more congruent with the kind of vision for union with God shared by those who shaped the early Wesleyan tradition. Moreover, this distinction between acceptable and unacceptable varieties of mysticism will be part of

---

Islam, as well as of the life and influence of Prophet Muhammad.

23. Andrae, *Garden*, 123–24.

24. John Wesley, *Plain Account*, Q. 38, A. 3.

25. To use a turn of phrase from Wesley colleague John Fletcher's essay, "An Evangelical Mysticism," *Works*, 4.7–13.

helping to understand how John Wesley and his colleagues interacted with and critically applied the heritage of early Christian faith.

STATEMENT OF THE PROBLEM AND THEORETICAL FRAMEWORK

Central to Sūfī thought and practice is the desire and search to be united with God in a manner which often involves ascension and vision mysticism. There appear to be potential parallels with Sūfī thought in ancient Jewish and Christian mysticism which had some influence on the development of Sūfī tradition, beliefs, and practices. What, then, can be learned from the manner in which early Christian thought interacted with ancient ascension and vision mysticism which may prove to be of value for the Sūfī context? What might be gleaned in particular from the New Testament writings, especially those of John's Gospel, and the writings of Macarius-Symeon for this purpose? How might the theology of Wesley on these parallel themes of union with God strengthen the *missional* and *communal* elements of this theology? What elements within the writings of more orthodox Sūfīs themselves may provide wisdom for developing an approach which will interact with this desire and search for union with God which remains rooted in the Scriptural tradition?

Scottish missiologist Andrew F. Walls, in an essay, "The Gospel as Prisoner and Liberator of Culture,"[26] described two crucial elements in the entry and integration of the gospel message and the life of Jesus into a given cultural setting. In the first of these, the "indigenizing principle," the gospel is understood to be integrated with the life and thought forms of a given society, where the church which becomes "a place to feel at home." He notes that the spiritual reality for those who have become a "new creation" by joining themselves to Christ by faith does not mean that they start or continue life in a vacuum, or that their minds are a blank tablet. It has been formed by their culture and history, and since God has accepted them as they are, their Christian mind will continue to be influenced by what it was before. This is as true for groups as for individuals.[27]

Walls does not stop with the crucial importance of *indigenizing*, but rather holds this principle in tension with another, equally central idea,

---

26. Walls, *Missionary Movement in History*, 3–15.
27. Ibid., 8.

the "pilgrim principle." Here the "Christ-following 'pilgrim'" finds that this principle

> whispers to him that he has no abiding city and that to be faithful to Christ will put him out of step with his society; for that society never existed . . . which could absorb the word of Christ painlessly into its system . . . there will be rubs and frictions—not from the adoption of a new culture, but from the transformation of the mind towards that of Christ.[28]

Without both of these two principles, the *indigenizing* principle which "associates Christians with the *particulars* of their culture and group"[29] and the *pilgrim* principle, which brings a *universalizing* element into the life of a community of believers as they enter into a common salvation history with the faithful throughout the ages, the gospel ultimately risks losing its power and/or its relevance. The gospel must become "local" to such an extent that its message and *life* are no longer regarded wholly foreign. Yet because it is the *Gospel*, not merely the good news in terms of *kerygma* but the impartation of the very life of God into individual believers and communities, it must also be able to speak prophetically into these same contexts, that nothing hinders the full integration of this Life with every element in a given society—including its philosophy regarding its connection with God's own self.

In this dissertation, I explore Jewish, Christian, and Muslim primary and secondary sources that engage with a mysticism of union with God, interpreting them in accordance with Walls' two principles. I tested the hypothesis that these principles would both be at work in these three religious traditions. The positive outcome of this research makes it reasonable that biblical Christian faith can flourish among Sūfī Muslims without compromising its essential faith and practice.

Here we will uncover the parallels between the mysticism of *union* with God and abiding in God in Sufism and in the writings of the early Christian community, including both the New Testament scriptural witness and the Syrian tradition as expressed in Macarius-Symeon. We will also examine how John Wesley and his colleagues critically appropriated this heritage, developing a "wise mysticism," an expression of union with God in the "mysticism of personality" stream, remained the focus. The manner in which Wesley developed this often inwardly-focused mystical

---

28. Ibid.
29. Ibid., 9.

tradition in such a manner that the inward union spilled over proactively into reaching out to others. We will examine how this development can facilitate dialogue in the context of the genuine spiritual longing which so many Sūfīs have for God. How can this be met so as to bear witness to the ultimate fulfillment of this longing to be found in union with God as he has revealed himself in Christ?

One element which will be a focus in what is to follow is a critical approach to the elements of ascension, vision and transformation found in the mysticism of many different traditions, including early Jewish mysticism. Howard A. Snyder has noted four elements of Wesleyan spirituality, focused on the *image of God* in humankind, the *prevenient grace* of God, salvation as *healing*, and *sanctification*[30]—which can be understood as both intertwined with one another as well as collectively representing the reality of *transformation* in the mystical "process" described by Segal. We will examine the presence of these same elements not only in Wesley, but also in the early Christian writings and the Sūfī context, too. Each element in this Wesleyan theology of mission connects with an element of union with God in the Patristic (and Sūfī) writings. For example, the idea of the need for union with and participation in God in what has often been described as *theosis* is connected with the recognition that the Image of God in humankind has been damaged and needs to be healed.[31] It is only by God's gracious presence that we are drawn and empowered to respond to God, and to live in a manner which reflects his transforming power.[32] Moreover, it is by his sanctifying power, this very grace, that we are transformed increasingly into his likeness.[33] Will these parallels be helpful in the development of an approach to the Sūfī community? The problem is to develop a framework, a theology of mission, which can facilitate and guide this process—guide it in such a way that it facilitates not only witness in terms of evangelization of Sūfīs who have not yet come to faith in Jesus, but a more holistic model which will continue to

---

30. Snyder, "The Missional Flavor," 62–73; see also an earlier version of these principles in Snyder, "Wesleyan Theology of Mission?" In the more recent version of these cited above, Snyder adds a fifth element of what he sees as a "Wesleyan theology of mission," that of the "restoration of all things" and an emphasis on "creation care" (see Snyder, "Missional Flavor," 69–71). Though affirming the importance of this theme, it is less relevant for our discussion here, and so will not be given emphasis in the fourth chapter, on which the focus is on the John Wesley.

31. Athanasius, *On the Incarnation*, 17–19

32. Lossky, *Mystical Theology*, 86–90.

33. Maddox, *Responsible Grace*, 179–91.

use these Ṣūfī elements in discipleship and the ongoing life of the emerging faith community.

In summary, the research problem and process for this project can be understood as follows:

1. We will analyze the context of ascension, vision and transformation mysticism of ancient Jewish and Hellenic traditions, according to the contextualizing principles elucidated by Andrew Walls: the indigenizing and pilgrim principles.

2. We will then examine the manner in which the New Testament writings, particularly, but not exclusively, the Johannine writings, interacted contextually, yet critically, with this stream of mystical thought and practices, again utilizing Walls' the indigenizing and pilgrim principles.

3. Next, we will analyze the writings of fourth-century Syrian writer, Macarius-Symeon, once again observing the manner in which he uses these same indigenizing and pilgrim principles in further interaction with both Jewish and Hellenic ascension, vision and transformation mysticism, with an increasing focus on the theme of union with God.

4. We will then examine how John Wesley and his colleagues appropriated this heritage of interaction, both from early Christian writers such as Macarius-Symeon, as well as via the Anglican and Pietist traditions which had also been developing a theme of union with God, particularly as this is expressed in the four intertwined themes of *prevenient grace, humankind created in God's image, salvation as healing,* and *sanctification.*

5. Then we will compare these results with the contextualization in a mystical setting of ascension, vision and transformation revealed in the classical Ṣūfī Muslim writings, particularly those of ʿAlī ibn ʿUthmān al-Jullābī al-Hujwīrī and Sharaf al-Dīn Manerī in accordance with these same Walls' principles of contextualization. We will seek to uncover parallels between the mysticism of *union* with God and abiding in God in Sufism and in the writings of the early Christian as well as John Wesley and his colleagues.

6. We will then suggest the implications this analysis has for contextualizing Christianity in Ṣūfī communities. Our thesis is that parallels with concepts of union with God in classical Sufism will show that

the manner in which the early Christian community interacted contextually and critically with the milieu of ancient mysticism, John Wesley's appropriation of this interaction, and parallels within the Sūfī traditions themselves can be applied in the development of a fruitful theology of mission.

It is hoped that what has been developed in this project can be understood as an exercise in Andrew Walls' *translation principle* of the expression of the Gospel into the language, structures and forms of a receptor culture.[34] Using the metaphors of *incarnation* as well as *conversion*, Walls explains *translation* as involving

> the attempt to explain the meaning of the source from the resources of, and within the working system of, the receptor language. Something new is brought into the language, but that new element can only be comprehended by means of and in terms of the pre-existing language and its conventions. In the process that language and its system is effectively expanded, put to new use; but the translated element from the source language has also, in a sense, been expanded by translation; the receptor language has a dynamic of its own and takes the new material to realms it never touched in the source language. Similarly, conversion implies the use of existing structures, the "turning" of those structures to new directions, the application of new material and standards to a system of thought and conduct already in place and functioning. It is not about substitution, the replacing of something old by something new, but about transformation, the turning of the already existing to new account.[35]

The conclusion will be demonstrated to be a synthesis faithful to the biblical witness of the findings of the first three studies into a fruitful theology of mission for various Sūfī contexts. It is important to emphasize that while such a study would necessarily need to be modified according to each *specific* Sūfī context, this will hopefully be able to provide a *basis* from which workers in the field as well as the academy may begin this process.

---

34. Please note that this is not to be confused with the idea which Stephen Bevans expresses as a *translation model* in his *Models of Contextual Theology*, 37–53.

35. Walls, *Missionary Movement*, 28

DELIMITATIONS

Sūfī theology is a vast field, and it would be virtually impossible to cover every element of Sūfī thought in a study of this size. We will therefore limit this study to the elements of union with God, focusing on the fourfold elements of what Howard Snyder described as a "Wesleyan Theology of Mission." Within the rubric of a Wesleyan theology of mission, We also include Wesley's adaptation of the Anglican emphasis on the "means of grace"—for which parallels are to be noted in the Sūfī context as well. While in our examination of early Christian writings we will be focusing on those of Macarius-Symeon, we will also include material from other writers—but only as they interact with the Macarian tradition. Similarly, while we will include relevant quotes from other Sūfī figures of the period such as Ghazālī and Qushayrī, especially in my fifth chapter introducing the context of Sufism, in this study we will focus my efforts on the writings of Hujwīrī and Manerī, whose writings then provide the focus of the sixth chapter.

DEFINITIONS OF KEY TERMS

- *Allāh*, God: In this context, it would be worth noting briefly that there has been an ongoing discussion regarding the question of whether *Allāh*, the Arabic name for God in Islam (though used by people of all religious traditions speaking in Arabic), is the same as the God worshiped by Christians. Thus, in this discussion, the question could be framed as, "With Whom do the Sūfīs seek union?" Writing in the opening pages of his recent *The Mission and Death of Jesus in Christianity and Islam*, A. H. Mathias Zahniser straightforwardly asserts that "Muslims and Christians worship the same God."[36] Citing the published dialogue of Badru D. Kateregga and David W. Shenk,[37] he notes that while both parties had much on which they could agree on the identity of the one God, in spite of diverging on issues such as the Sonship of Christ. They could "agree on the subject of the one God," while at the same time maintaining robust differences regarding certain predicates concerning the one God.[38]

---

36. Zahniser, *Mission*, 3.
37. Kateregga and Shenk, *A Muslim and a Christian in Dialogue*.
38. Zahniser, *Mission*, 30–31.

The same idea could hold with regard to those in other faith traditions. For example, consider the tradition of Rabbinic Judaism which was emerging in the same period as the early Christian tradition.[39] These gradually developed different understandings of the predicates of God, and these views grew wider apart over time, particularly as Judaism continued to develop, often in a hostile Christian environment. Perhaps the best example of this is in Moses ben Maimon's (Maimonides') twelfth-century Jewish creed, where he reformulated the *Shemaʿ* (based on Deut 6:4) with a reading replacing the original Hebrew word *ekhād* ("one," but which can admit a compound unity) with *yakhīd* (absolute unity).[40] This changes a key predicate about the very nature of God. Does this then mean that one needed to communicate (then, or now) with Jewish people in a manner which precisely clarifies that we somehow worship another God, apart from them? Or would it rather likely be more fruitful if we begin with the understanding they have, recognize the commonalities, and build upon them. Ultimately, we would suggest that we *should* start with the metaphysical reality that we *are*, in fact, worshiping the same Deity, but seek to help our Sūfī friends to grow in their understanding in the predicates; more, to grow *together* with them in a continually deeper understanding in which Sūfī believers may have insights into the *translation* (in the sense used by Andrew Walls) of the biblical tradition in this area which will be of help to the wider body of Messiah's people.[41]

- *Mysticism* as a word is connected with the *mysterious*, the unknown, but in this context is related specifically to the idea of contact with that which is transcendent, the Real or Absolute. Rudolf Otto, in his influential *The Idea of the Holy*, coined the term *numinous*[42] to

---

39. Amy-Jill Levine suggests that, rather than the traditional "mother-daughter" relationship often posited for Judaism and Christianity, it might be more helpful to view the relationship more as "siblings fighting over the parents' legacy." See Levine, *Misunderstood Jew*, 5.

40. Peterson, *Everlasting Tradition*, 22.

41. Affirming that the Muslims metaphysically seek to approach the same God with whom we are in relationship, let me add as well that, *soteriologically*, Sūfīs and other Muslims ultimately must also approach God as He is revealed in Messiah Jesus, even as would, again, ultimately be the case with those in the Jewish community from the comparison above.

42. Although Paul Tillich observed that this term was actually *reintroduced* by Otto, having earlier been used by John Calvin in his *Institutes*. See Tillich, *Christian Thought*, 263. We owe this observation to Lalsangkima Pachuau. Of course, Christian use of *numen* goes back at least as far as Augustine's letters; e.g., Letter 17, "To

describe the experience of awe in the presence of the *holy* or *sacred*.[43] William James, in his *Varieties of Religious Experience*, enumerates four elements of what he considers mystical experience: *ineffability*, or the inexpressibility of the experience in normal terms; *noetic quality*, or the sense of great insight having been gained in the experience; *transiency*, or the unsustainable nature of mystic states; and *passivity*, or the idea that the state is something which is happening *to* the person having the experience, that the will of the person having the experience is somehow held under the influence of something else.[44]

Gershom Scholem moves this closer to the idea of mysticism as personal experience of God. Having quoted Thomas Aquinas' definition of mysticism as "*cogito dei experimentalis*," or "knowledge of God through experience," he goes on to note that,

> He leans heavily, like many mystics before and after him, on the words of the Psalmist (Psalm xxxiv, 9): "Oh taste and see that the Lord is good." It is this tasting and seeing, however spiritualized it may become, that the genuine mystic desires. His attitude is determined by the fundamental experience of the inner self which enters into immediate contact with God or the metaphysical Reality. What forms the essence of this experience, and how it is to be adequately described—that is the great riddle which the mystics themselves, no less than the historians, have tried to solve.[45]

April D. DeConick offers a good working definition of what is meant by *mysticism*, suggesting that *mysticism* is not a word which occurs in the ancient primary sources, but is what she describes as an *etic* term referring to "a tradition ... centered on the belief that *a person directly, immediately and before death can experience the divine, either as a rapture experience or one solicited by a particular praxis.*"[46] To this we would add Jarl E. Fossum's brief definition vis-à-vis the apocalyptic tradition, which is so intertwined with mysticism in this discussion. Fossum notes that "Mysticism is 'vertical' apocalypticism ... dealing with the mysteries of

---

Maximus" 17:5. See Augustine, *Works*, 6.41 and 6.41 n. 1.

43. Otto, *Idea of the Holy*, 6–7, 13.
44. James, *Varieties*, 380–81.
45. Scholem, *Major Trends*, 4.
46. DeConick, "Early Jewish and Christian Mysticism," 2, emphasis in the original.

the heavenly world and the ways in which man can gain knowledge of those mysteries."[47] Similarly, Mircea Eliade, referring to this idea of spiritual ascent more generally, noted that the one "who ascends by mounting the steps of a sanctuary or the ritual ladder that leads to the sky ceases to be a man; in one way or another, he shares in the divine condition."[48] This is the understanding which we are seeking to bear in mind in this chapter, and indeed, in this project as a whole, connected with the elements of ascension, vision and transformation.

- *Tasawwuf*, commonly translated "Sufism," and some key related terms: The term *tasawwuf*, or Sufism, has been explained in various ways, but most scholars agree that the term is derived from the Arabic word *sūf*, or wool, referring to the woolen clothing worn in ascetic simplicity by the earliest generation of Sūfīs.[49] They developed a path of illumination which Annemarie Schimmel compares with the classic Christian division of the *via purgativa*, the *via contemplativa* and the *via illuminata*; the respective terms in Sufism (varying, of course, according to context) are an ascending path of *sharīʿa*, or the law of Islam, *tarīqa*, or the path, and finally then *haqīqa*, or realization of the truth (or sometimes *maʿrifa*, or gnosis in the sense of mystical knowledge).[50] A kind of parallel understanding of the path to salvation in Sufism involves devotion to a *walī* or *shaikh* (Arabic) or *pīr* (Persian), a high level spiritual director/saint, devotion to whom is meant to be an aid towards the eventual goal of union with God. Because of the fairly strong Neoplatonic element in much of Sufism, this idea of union can often be conceptualized more as *henôsis* than as the more Christian-devotional *theosis*, and the exercises meant to move towards that goal can end up being conceptualized more as *theurgy*.[51] That having been said, the "guided path" (which is generally a complement to the description above, not an alternative) is conceptualized as system of ascending into union with God through progressive union with one's own *pīr* (*fanā fīʾsh-shaykh*), sometimes through this into union with the Prophet Muhammad

---

47. Fossum, *Image of the Invisible God*, 1.
48. Eliade, *Sacred*, 119.
49. Schimmel, *Mystical Dimensions*, 14.
50. Ibid., 98–99.

51. The term *theurgy* conveys the idea of rituals which are designed to bring the adept into union with the One (*Hen*). In chapter 1, we will describe James R. Davila's understanding of *shamanism*, which corresponds broadly to the idea of *theurgy*.

(*fanā fi'r-rasūl*) and finally through these stages somehow reaching for union with God (*fanā fī Allāh*).[52]

- *Theosis* is the Greek word most commonly used by the writers of the early Church to refer to the idea of union with God in Christ. The theology behind this has varied over the centuries, but in orthodox Christian circles has been differentiated in various ways from the idea of *henôsis*, union with the "Hen" or the One in Neoplatonic religious philosophy which generally entails "a creative partnership with God, realized through theurgic rituals that raise the soul up to the level of divine demiurgic power."[53]

SIGNIFICANCE OF THIS RESEARCH

In describing the potential significance of this research, consider a religious context in which Islamic mysticism is a crucial part of the spiritual lives of those for whom this is home. The author of this dissertation wrote the following description of his own visit to a local celebration which he was privileged to attend in one such location in South Asia:

> The air virtually crackled with energy in the large hall of the *mazār*, or tomb, of the *pīr* whose departure had taken place only a decade or so before. Tonight was the '*urs*[54] of Hazrat Mahmūd al-Haqq Siddīqī, and judging by the sheer volume of sandals deposited at the entry to the tomb complex, the place was packed. Walking into the complex in the company of my guide, I saw hundreds of people sitting closely together, eyes bright in anticipation and excitement of the evening's events. In contrast to the mosque down the street, here there were women as well as men, heads covered for modesty's sake, and seating separated by gender, but the presence of so many women at an Islamic gathering was almost jarring.
>
> The proceedings began with prayers, and announcements, and a bit of preaching by local speakers of varying capabilities. Following this, however, one by one, mostly younger men began to arise and sing *ghazals*, devotional songs in honor of the *pīr*. There was a bit of a hush as one young man, Mohib, his wispy beard as thin as his body, arose before the gathered crowd and

---

52. Schimmel, *Mystical Dimensions*, 216.
53. Moore, "'Likeness to God."
54. The death anniversary of a Muslim saint; literally the "wedding" of that saint's soul with God, the Beloved.

opened what looked like a school boy's notebook. In a voice so strong it seemed to shake the building as well as the crowd, he began to sing an Urdu *ghazal* of his own composition. As his song reached vocal or rhetorical heights, the crowd would erupt with cries of *wāh! wāh!* urging him on. His *ghazal* concluded with a description of what the singer imagined to have been the scene as the departed *pīr* arrived in heaven, and is received by the Prophet Muhammad himself: "*Behold, Muhammad! Come, welcome your friend!*" and the place burst with energy, men and women together once more shouting their approval of the song and singer, and of the *pīr* of whom he sang.

We recently met a couple who had been fruitfully engaged in mission in a Muslim context for over a year. They were young, full of energy and zeal to share the message of God's transforming love in Christ with people with whom they interacted in their community on a daily basis. They spoke of their plan: to return to their country of service and relocate to a remote area of their country, an area which is a key center for Sufism in their entire region. In considering the future work of this young couple, we also, more broadly, think about many others like them, the *next* and upcoming wave of mission to the Muslim world. How might they be better prepared to tackle the issues of not just how to appropriately *evangelize* in the context of a Sūfī society, but to effectively partner with God in the work of the Kingdom of God in a network of *discipleship* of families and individuals, of men and women, of young people and older people. It is our hope that this study will provide a useful tool for engaging in discipleship and community-building in settings such as those represented by my short description of the *'urs* celebration with which we began the final section of this introduction. It is thus also our own hope that this will provide not only an impetus to others who would seek to engage the Sūfī context on the ground, but that others in academic circles would build further upon the conclusions of this research, and seek to apply the results of this project in communities all over the world in which Islamic mysticism is a key part of the local milieu.

1

"Will You Not Discover The Lord In All This?"
The Context of Ancient Jewish Mysticism

> And, when the happy soul holds out the sacred goblet of its own reason, who is it that pours into it the holy cupfuls of true gladness, but the Word, the Cup-bearer of God and Master of the feast, who is also none other than the draught which he pours—his own self free from all dilution, the delight, the sweetening, the exhilaration, the merriment, the ambrosian drug (to take for our own use the poet's terms) whose medicine gives joy and gladness? (Philo of Alexandria, *On Dreams* 2.249)[1]

INTRODUCTION

EARLY CHRISTIAN FAITH DID not develop independently of a human social and religious context, but emerged into a first-century world with a number of competing versions of Jewish and Hellenic religion and spirituality in the first-century Levant. Part of this milieu included movements which involved processes of seeking to ascend through the heavens, to achieve the vision of deity (or, in some cases, deities) enthroned, and to be transformed and empowered by this experience.

My intention in this chapter is to examine this context, and to gain wisdom concerning how the 100 BCE to the 100 CE Jewish communities

---

1. Philo, v. 555. In this chapter, with the exception of the initial instance, quotations from the *Loeb* edition will be referenced with "Philo" and the volume and page number. Other translations used will have fuller references.

interacted within this context. We will thus seek in this first chapter to introduce the context of ascension, vision and transformation mysticism itself, and to observe how some Jewish thinkers parsed between what was "wise" and what was "unhealthy" mysticism. This will be relevant for understanding Walls' *indigenous* principle in the Hellenic and Jewish communities outlined in this chapter; there will also necessarily be elements reflective of Walls' *pilgrim* principle in which Jewish writers such as Philo interact critically within their Hellenic context. One reason for which this is important is that in this period, both Christian faith and Rabbinic Judaism were to begin to emerge from within Second Temple Judaism. Note that Alan F. Segal describes the relationship between the two faiths as "Rebecca's children," one of "siblings" rather than a "mother-daughter" relationship.[2]

THE ASCENSION TRADITION OF VISION MYSTICISM

> It was Ezekiel who saw the vision of glory, which God showed him above the chariot of the cherubim. (Ben Sirach 49:8, NRSV)

It is worth repeating from the introduction that we are giving primacy to what Annemarie Schimmel referred to as the "mysticism of personality," the idea which maintains the distinction between the Creator and the created devotee, over the "mysticism of infinity," which tends to blur these distinctions.[3] This was well-illustrated many years ago by the Indian mystic, Sadhu Sundar Singh, who wrote,

> We have been created in the image of God. Our destiny is to be restored into that image. God came to us in the Master to restore us to God's divine nature. In this way, the Master transforms us into flames of spiritual fire. To become spiritual fire means to become like God. Even the smallest flame of fire is fire and has all the qualities of fire. This does not mean that our spirit is God's spirit, as some pantheists and philosophers suppose.

---

2. See Segal, *Rebecca's Children*.

3. Schimmel, *Mystical Dimensions*, 5–6. Let me note here that we recognize the immense value of studies of mysticism which have focused on the psychological perspective of such religious experience, such as James' *Varieties of Religious Experience*, the more recent Pilch, *Flights of the Soul*, and those focused on the social influences on mystical experience, such as Durkheim's *The Elementary Forms of Religious Life*. Nonetheless, we are writing here with an assumption that while there can clearly be either or both psychological and sociological factors involved in mystical experience, there is also a spiritual element which transcends these.

We are not fragments of God's spirit. We are not God. God is distinct from us, but our souls can only find peace in oneness with God.

A sponge lies in the water and the water fills the sponge, but the water is not the sponge and the sponge is not the water. It is the same when I immerse myself in God. God fills my heart and I am in complete union with God, but I am not God and God is not I. We are distinct though not separate.[4]

ASCENSION AND VISION MYSTICISM IN HELLENIC (AND SYRO-PERSIAN) CULTURE

The concept of mystical ascension, where an adept ascends, usually by means of spiritual exercises,[5] into the heavenly realms, is very ancient and is found in numerous religious traditions.[6] Most seem to involve ecstatic performance, some are initiated by rituals involving a narcotic or hallucinogen.[7]

There are some rather early allusions to ecstatic ascension experience in Greco-Roman literature, such as the famous dream of Scipio in Cicero's *Republic*,[8] as well as the chariot vision of the soul ascending the heavens in Plato's *Phaedrus*.[9] This became more fully developed in the

---

4. Singh, *Wisdom*, 112–13. Sundar Singh also claimed to have experienced visions of Jesus, one example of which is recounted in Merkur, "Unitive Experiences," 134–35. See also Streeter and Appasamy, *The Sadhu*.

5. James R. Davila distinguishes mystical ascent which has union and intimacy with God as its goal from what he considers "shamanism," which may also involve such ascent (or descent), but has as its goal "esoteric knowledge and power" (Davila, "The Hekhalōt Literature," 771). Like Mircea Eliade before him (Eliade, *Shamanism*, 4–5), he distinguishes "shamanism" from "magic" (Davila, "Shamanism," 772). He goes on to give examples of shamanistic techniques such as "various forms of isolation and self-denial, such as fasting, solitary confinement, celibacy, dietary and purity restrictions, and protracted prayer" (Davila, *Descenders*, 46). Significantly, Davila classifies Hekhalōt/Merkavah ascent (early Jewish beliefs and practices discussed below) as shamanistic rather than mystical, noting (in an echo of Gershom Scholem) that "there is no thought of mystical union. God is nearly as remote in the heavenly throne room as he is on earth" (Davila, "Shamanism," 772). See also Scholem, *Major Trends*, 55.

6. Tommasi, "Ascension," 1:518.

7. Ibid., 1.519.

8. Cicero, *The Republic*, 86–94; see as well Tommasi, 1.521.

9. Plato, *Phaedrus*, 26–29; see also DeConick, *Voices*, 43. This imagery may also have had influence on the Jewish mystical literature, where the *Hekhalōt Rabbati* notes one of the angels "brings you in a whirlwind, and he places you in a wagon of light"

Hermetic writings.[10] Dan Merkur writes that while Hermeticism "had its origin in age-old practices of Egyptian magic,"[11] its philosophical system can be understood as an attempt to develop a rationale for their theurgical practices. He also notes that in addition to various influences of a Hellenic nature on Hermetic philosophy (e.g., Platonic, Aristotelian, Pythagorean, Stoic), Jewish thought also played a role in its development.[12] In Hermeticism, then, one is ultimately to be illuminated in the process of ascent to the deity, shedding the mortal "sheath" of the body and journeying towards divinization.[13] This process of illumination was understood to be accomplished through ascetic disciplines in which the passions are overcome,[14] and towards an experience of being divinized through being "born again."[15] The *Corpus Hermeticum* states, "Thus, unless you make yourself equal to god, you cannot understand god; like is understood by like" (*Corpus Hermeticum* 11.19–20).[16] In Hermeticism, this idea of union with a deity who was understood primarily as "Mind," a "God whose thought was the universe," ultimately seems to have been motivated by a desire for the acquisition of power for the purpose of working magic.[17]

There has also been a fair bit of debate regarding ascension accounts from ancient Syro-Persian (rather than, or in addition to, Hellenic) sources,[18] and their possible influence upon early Jewish ascension

---

(Gruenwald, *Apocalyptic and Merkavah*, 121). As will be noted later, this image in Phaedrus was used both independently as well as in conjunction with Ezekiel's vision in Ezek 1 in the writings of later Christian figures. See also Golitzin, "Christianity as Transfiguration,140 & 152, n. 74, as well as in *Ode* 38.1–3 of the *Odes of Solomon*, 109.

10. The *Corpus Hermeticum* is now understood to have been composed in late antiquity (roughly 250–750 CE) rather than in ancient times. See Copenhaver, *Hermetica*, i.

11. Merkur, "Stages of Ascension," 80.
12. Ibid., 81.
13. DeConick, *Voices*, 46.
14. Merkur, "Stages of Ascension," 84.
15. DeConick, *Voices*, 49.
16. Copenhaver, *Hermetica*, 41; quoted in Merkur, "Stages of Ascension," 85.
17. Merkur, "Stages of Ascension," 90.
18. See Bousset, "Himmelsreise," 136–69, 229–73; the author sees the roots of the idea of the soul's ascension in Zoroastrian traditions. He specifically cites the example of the Enoch literature in the Jewish tradition.

mysticism, particularly the more ancient Jewish literature and accounts associated with the name of the antediluvian figure of Enoch.[19]

Pierre Grelot, for example, argued for a Babylonian geographic background in 1 Enoch, noting similarities with the epic of Gilgemesh.[20] More recently, Helge Kvanvig published a monograph on this topic entitled *Roots of Apocalyptic: The Mesopotamian Background of the Enoch Figure and of the Son of Man*,[21] in which he argues that both the biblical Enoch figure and the later apocalyptic writings associated with his name were greatly influenced by rather ancient Syro-Persian antecedents. This has been cautiously critiqued by others such as John J. Collins.[22] He recognizes some similarities while also observing some significant differences between Syro-Persian and ancient Jewish apocalyptic.[23] Collins elsewhere suggests that:

> the genesis of the genre apocalypse in Judaism remains uncertain. There are obvious lines of continuity with prophetic visions, but also with Babylonian dream interpretation....The relationship between Jewish and Persian apocalypses remains in dispute, but at present the evidence does not permit us to rule out a genetic connection there.[24]

Other writers in the discussion have included George W. E. Nickelsburg,[25] T. Francis Glasson,[26] and Guy G. Stroumsa,[27] who see Hellenic, rather than Persian influence. All three of these writers have noted possible parallels with Greek *nekyia* literature. This literary form focuses on journeys to the underworld realms of the dead found in particularly in the Pythagorian tradition, emphasizing "Orpheus's *katabasis eis Aidou*."[28] While recognizing these Persian and Hellenic influences,

---

19. "More ancient" in reference especially to sections of 1 Enoch which are understood to be from the first century BCE and earlier.

20. Grelot, "Géographie Mythique," 33–69.

21. Kvanvig, *Roots of Apocalyptic*.

22. John J. Collins is a scholar of early Judaism and the Dead Sea Scrolls, and teaches Old Testament at Yale Divinity School.

23. Collins, "Place of Apocalypticism," 542–544.

24. Collins, "Genre, Ideology and Social Movements," 21.

25. Nickelsburg, *Jewish Literature*, 54; 66 n. 27.

26. Glasson, *Greek Influence*, 8–19, 81–85.

27. Stroumsa, "Mystical Descents," 139–154.

28. "Descent to Hades;" the basic idea of this literature involving descriptions of descent into the underworld, where reward and punishment is given according to

Glasson concludes optimistically, suggesting that "as far as the Bible is concerned the fundamental element of divine revelation is not affected. For the outer garment, whether a Greek chlamys or a goodly Babylonish mantle, was always shared to the living body of truth."[29] Glasson seems, by this, to be indicating contextualization rather than syncretism as the fruit of this interaction with these traditions. As we progress here, we will observe the degree to which this held true as this interaction continued past the era of the writing of the Hebrew Scriptures themselves, and into the emerging Jewish traditions.

The above brings in some possible indicators of the influence of Hellenic and/or Syro-Persian influence on the development of Jewish apocalyptic, especially of the ascension and vision variety. There are other writers who seem to stretch the parallels further than available evidence may bear.[30] A relevant question to raise as we turn to look at the Jewish apocalyptic texts themselves would be whether they might represent a syncretism with the Hellenic/Syro-Persian influences which were pervasive in the ancient Near East, and what the response to these developments was within both the emerging Christian movement and the emerging Rabbinic Jewish movement.

JEWISH ASCENSION AND VISION MYSTICISM IN THE APOCALYPTIC LITERATURE

Jewish mysticism of ascension and the throne vision of God is centered especially on the vision described in Ezek 1 of the *kāvōd YHWH*, or glory of God, seated above his wheeled throne (Ezek 1:26–28). This was later referred to as the *Merkavah*, or throne-chariot of God, going back at least to 1 Chron 28:18, in the description of the items in the inner sanctum of the Temple, and in the tradition to Ben Sirach 49:8 quoted as the heading of the second section of this chapter.[31] Early on, the *Merkavah* tradition

---

deeds good or evil done on earth, and an eventual "return of the soul to the divine realm" (Glasson, *Greek Influence*, 28).

29. Glasson, *Greek Influence*, 84–85.

30. See, for example, Abusch, "Ascent to the Stars," 15–39, in which Abusch attempts to compare some visionary elements and sentences from ancient Babylonian *Maqlû* texts of magical incantations with the wording from Isaiah's vision in Isa 6. The latter can hardly be considered a depiction of a magical incantation or of a theurgical attempt to summon the deity; rather, the prophet is summoned! See also Idel, *Ascensions*, 24–25.

31. See Gruenwald, *Apocalyptic and Merkavah*, 74–75, incl. n. 6.

was particularly grounded in a rather esoteric exegesis, which is also encountered early on in Christian exegesis, and, as we shall see, in Muslim exegesis of the Qur'ān.[32] It was focused on passages such as Ezek 1, as well as Exod 24 and 33,[33] Isa 6, Ezek 8, 10, 40–48, and Dan 7, all of which included visions of God or of his glory.[34] Other mystical passages from the Hebrew Scriptures which include an element of theophany, such as the prophet Micaiah's vision in 1 Kgs 22:19, and Elijah's being taken up in a "chariot of fire" in 2 Kgs 2:11, also played a role in the development of this tradition.[35] The enthronement passage in Psalm 110, so central to the development of early Christology, is used in surprisingly few of the documents connected with the *Merkavah* tradition.[36]

Moshe Idel takes a rather skeptical view of the degree to which such ascension elements are actually present in the Hebrew Scriptures, including the passages cited above. His analysis is worth quoting at length on this point, in part because of the question which we raised above: Do such elements represent a syncretistic accretion, or are they an "organic" development from within the Scriptural tradition itself? Idel notes the theme of ascension mysticism and the Scriptures:

> A survey of the history of the ascent to heaven in Judaism, however, reveals a rather interesting difference: in the earliest descriptions, the founding figures, the patriarchs and Moses are never portrayed as ascending to and entering a totally different realm for the sake of a *rendez-vous* with the divine. In the Bible it is God who reveals himself by coming down to the recipients of the divine message rather than by bringing the messenger to his realm in order to receive it. In other words, the biblical

---

32. See Böwering, "Medieval Sūfī Qurʾān Exegesis," 353, in which the author compares the differentiation between the "literal" and "spiritual" senses of what the sacred text says in the earlier Jewish and Christian as well as Muslim traditions.

33. Interestingly, the Hebrew word in Exod 33:19 is not *kāvōd*, but *tūv*, which can be translated as "glory," but can also mean "goodness" or "beauty." The LXX translates both words with the same word, *doxa*. See Ramm, *Them He Glorified*, 20. This dichotomization of the God's "glory" and his "beauty" later turn up in Sūfī language of God as *jalāl* and *jamāl*.

34. DeConick, *Voices*, 51–53; see also Gruenwald, *Apocalyptic and Merkavah*, 29–31, which has a somewhat expanded list.

35. Eskola, *Messiah*, 66.

36. Eskola, *Messiah*, 78–79 & 157. It should be noted, however, that Psalm 110 *did* later play a decisive part in the development of what Richard Bauckham refers to as a "Christology of divine identity," which was crucial to the interaction with ascension and vision mysticism. See Bauckham, *Jesus and the God of Israel*, 173–76.

apprehension of the revelation is based upon the assumption that man as a psychosomatic entity cannot transcend his mundane situation and penetrate the divine realm, while God is able to adapt himself, and perhaps also his message, to human capacity. While the way down is open, the way up is basically closed. The ascents of Elijah and perhaps of Enoch are presented in the Bible as initiated not by men, but rather by God. In more concrete terms, Moses is portrayed in the biblical texts as climbing a mountain in order to receive the Torah, while God, for his part, descends upon the same mountain. The human remains human and is not radically transformed by his reception of the divine message. Man may temporarily touch the divine who descends for the sake of revelation, but this does not indicate an ontic transformation of his personality. Moses remains a man, despite the luminous face he is attributed, and he remains mortal despite his extraordinary experience of direct conversation with and gift of the Torah from God.[37]

Of course, Itamar Gruenwald recognizes that, in spite of the clear opposition to such things in Jewish Scripture, shamanistic practices were widespread enough both among the common people and the elite rabbinic authorities as to actually be more or less taken for granted within the *Hekhalōt* literature.[38] Ithamar Gruenwald also looks at the Hebrew Scriptures on the topic of ascent (notably in Ps 115:16, Prove 30:4, Deut 30:12, Isa 14:12–15, Ezek 28:12–19, and especially poignantly, Gen 11:4), and finds that "attempts to rise too high are condemned as blasphemous acts."[39] The emphasis in the Scriptures is on God's taking the initiative in such encounters, and also that God is more flexible than humans in the presentation of his message. Idel sees such encounters in the Hebrew Scriptures as relating to God's revelation, but he also observes that the degree of transformation is limited in this schema. We will return below to the Jewish (especially Rabbinic Jewish) response to this ascension mysticism and its rationale.

Alan F. Segal describes three elements in the literature of the period which characterize this early Jewish mysticism.[40] He refers to the first of these as *angelophany*, or the "vision of a principal angelic mediator," who

---

37. Idel, *Ascensions*, 24.
38. Gruenwald, *Apocalyptic and Merkavah*, 108–9.
39. Gruenwald, *Apocalypticism to Gnosticism*, 20.
40. Segal, "Paul and the Beginning," 97.

"carries the name of God or somehow participates in God's divinity."[41] This connects with vision mysticism, with the desire to see God (or his representative) enthroned, as Ezekiel is described as having seen in his opening vision in Ezek 1. To be sure, Segal is ambiguous (as are the Scriptures) regarding the degree to which the "angelic" beings thus depicted share in the divine identity; this will be an important element in the discussion below. The second element Segal describes is that of *transformation*, the mystic or figure described is "transformed or subsumed into the mediator figure," sometimes including on some level the idea of deification.[42] Finally, there is the element of *ascent*, of a journey into the heavens during this life.[43] Indeed, Segal feels that he sees each of these features in Paul's account in 2 Cor 12:1–5.[44] Craig Keener, though, has noted on this passage that although "Paul sought intimacy with Christ, . . . he may not have "sought" visions per se; he was 'caught up.'"[45] For now, we can note that each of these three elements is part of the context of those engaged in this early Jewish apocalyptic mysticism, and can be understood as representing a real desire to draw close to God. As will be described later, however, Segal demonstrates quite effectively that the way in which Paul interacts with and speaks the language of Jewish mysticism connects the Jewish mystical tradition directly into his conversion experience and the manner in which he explains the meaning of life in Christ.

The earliest account of ascension mysticism in Jewish literature outside the Scriptures is thought to be in 1 Enoch, parts of which are believed to date back to as early as the third century BCE.[46] The earliest part is believed to be the first thirty-six chapters, which are referred to as

---

41. Ibid.

42. The meaning assigned to the idea of "deification" depends greatly upon the context, and will be discussed more in detail later on. It can refer to transformation on some level into the likeness of deity, or being subsumed into deity itself.

43. Segal, "Paul and the Beginning," 97. Note that while we have placed these three elements in the order "vision," "transformation," and "ascent," these will often be described in the order of "ascent/descent," "vision," and "transformation."

44. Ibid., 108–9.

45. Keener, *1–2 Corinthians*, 238.

46. See Tommasi, "Ascension," 1.522; see also Himmelfarb, "The Practice of Ascent," 130. Another brief account of throne ascension mysticism is found in the "Testament of Levi," chapter 5, part of the "Testament of the Twelve Patriarchs." Fragments of the Testament of Levi have been found in Qumran Cave 4, although there are also clear Christian interpolations in the book as well. See Kee, "Testaments of the Twelve Patriarchs," 789–90.

"The Book of the Watchers."[47] An important section of this text depicts Enoch, having risen to heaven in a vision, entering what is apparently the terrifying palace of God. Finally he is brought before the "Great Glory" in an account which seems to bear the "flavor" of Ezekiel's vision:

> And I observed and saw inside it a lofty throne—its appearance was like crystal, and its wheels like the shining sun; and (I heard?) the voice of the cherubim; and from beneath the throne were issuing streams of flaming fire. It was difficult to look at it. And the Great Glory was sitting upon it—as for his gown, which was shining more brightly than the sun, it was whiter than any snow. None of the angels was able to come in and see the face of the Excellent and Glorious One; and no one of the flesh can see him—the flaming fire was round about him, and a great fire stood before him. No one could come near to him from among those that surrounded the tens of millions (that stood) before him. He needed no counsel, but the most holy ones who are near him neither go far away at night nor move away from him. Until then I was prostrate on my face covered and trembling. And the Lord called me with his own mouth and said to me, "Come near to me, Enoch, and to my holy Word." And he lifted me up and brought me near to the gate, but I (continued) to look down with my face. (1 Enoch 14:18–25)[48]

George W. E. Nickelsburg recognizes not only that the account of Enoch's ascension "is especially beholden to Ezekiel 1–2 and to the account of that prophet's tour of the eschatological temple in Ezekiel 40–48," but also that "these chapters mark an important transitional point at which the tradition about Ezekiel's throne vision is moving in the direction of later Jewish mysticism."[49] In this text, it can be observed that the prophet, Enoch, comes into the anteroom of God's house, and finally enters the throne room itself, all of which is described in some detail. The supremacy of the prophet above even the angels (who, unlike Enoch, are not invited into God's presence) is evident as God prepares to give him a message of judgment to deliver. The account is similar not only to that of Ezekiel, but also to that of Isaiah and Daniel in the passages noted above. As Gershom Scholem wrote in his seminal *Major Trends in Jewish Mysticism*, this throne-mysticism's:

47. First categorized by Milik, "Littérature Hénoquique," 334; see also Isaac, "Enoch," 7.

48. Isaac, 21.

49. Nickelsburg, *Jewish Literature*, 53.

essence is not absorbed in contemplation of God's true nature, but perception of His appearance on the throne, as described by Ezekiel, and the cognition of the mysteries of the celestial throne-world. The throne-world is to the Jewish mystic what the *pleroma*, the "fullness"…is to the Hellenistic and early Christian mystics of the period who appear in the history of religion under the names of Gnostics and Hermetics.[50]

Moshe Idel later expressed agreement with Scholem on the connections between *Merkavah* and Gnosticism, though he suggested that rather than the Gnostics having influenced the Jewish tradition, Jewish influence was brought to bear upon Gnosticism![51]

Ithamar Gruenwald also offered a brief study of the connections, or at least some apparent similarities, between the Jewish *Merkavah* and Gnosticism. He concluded that any connection between the two, especially at this early period, was limited to Gnostic borrowing from the Jewish tradition, rather than vice-versa.[52] Significantly, he suggests that even where he does see some overlap in two of the *Nag Hammadi* texts, *The Hypostasis of the Archons* and another work referred to as *On the Origin of the World*,[53] he sees something other than syncretism, asserting that

> These writings used the Jewish material to polemicize against an accepted—Jewish or Christian—understanding of Scripture. The inversion of values—the *Umdeutung*—as maintained in the Gnostic writings was not a neutral practice with no special aim in view, but a pointed polemic against the Jews, and even more so against the early Christians who had a good Jewish schooling.[54]

This is a crucial insight, because it provides an example of one side in a debate in this period seeking to use the language of their opponents in their own discourse. This is a crucial element of our own analysis.

---

50. Scholem, *Major Trends*, 44. Scholem later offered a more comprehensive look at what he considered Jewish borrowing from Gnostic sources which publicly emerged in medieval Kabbalah in his *Jewish Gnosticism*.

51. Idel, *Kabbalah*, 116.

52. Gruenwald, *From Apocalypticism to Gnosticism*, 204, and thus in partial agreement with Idel, though P. S. Alexander has noted that Gruenwald "represents in general a negative reaction to Scholem's central thesis that Merkavah Mysticism may be defined as Rabbinic Gnosticism" (Alexander, "Merkavah Mysticism," 1).

53. Gruenwald, *From Apocalypticism to Gnosticism*, 193.

54. Ibid., 195.

"Will You Not Discover The Lord In All This?"   33

Scholem makes the startling statement that at this early stage, even in the midst of mystical ecstasy, the adept "knows nothing of divine immanence; the infinite gulf between the soul and God the King on His throne is not . . . bridged."[55] His continuing assertion regarding the nature of this early Jewish mysticism becomes still more surprising:

> Not only is there for the mystic no divine immanence, there is also almost no love of God. What there is of love in the relationship between the Jewish mystic and his God belongs to a much later period and has nothing to do with our present subject. Ecstasy there was, and this fundamental experience must have been a source of religious inspiration, but we find no trace of a mystical union between the soul and God. . . ..The mystic who in his ecstasy has passed through all the gates, braved all the dangers, now stands before the throne; he sees and hears—but that is all.[56]

As we will see, this particular focus on acquiring knowledge of the divine through mystical vision, yet somehow devoid of the love of God and indeed of true relationship with him, is one of the areas in which we observe the Christian tradition challenging the *Merkavah* system, yet doing so using images and vocabulary from within *Merkavah* discourse.[57] To take up the terminology used by James R. Davila, it would seem that at this point, what is present in this idea of *Merkavah* is less *mysticism* as such than *shamanism*.[58] This is where the early Christian tradition had to be sure to understand at what point the *indigenous* principle segued into

---

55. Scholem, *Major Trends*, 55.

56. Ibid., 55–56.

57. A more relational and love-focused idea of mysticism and union with God, referred to as "*devekūt*," developed within Judaism later in movements such as medieval Hasidism. See Scholem, *Major Trends*, 95–96.

58. Davila, "Hekhalōt Literature and Shamanism," 771, though an argument in favor of using the term "magic" can be found in Swartz, *Mystical Prayer*, 3 n. 7. Worth adding to this is a quote from Peter Schäfer (using *magic* where Davila is using *shamanism*). He notes that, "The world view which informs these texts is thus one which is deeply magical. The authors of the Hekhalot literature believed in the power of magic and attempted to integrate magic into Judaism" (Schäfer, *Hekhalot-Studien*, 290). Gruenwald similarly has suggested that "A short paraphrase of the whole of the *Hekhalōt* literature . . . would always begin: What is the mystic expected to do if he wants to bring about a certain mystical experience" (Gruenwald, *From Apocalypticism to Gnosticism*, 99–100), followed by a list of these ritual "techniques" which were regarded as efficacious toward that end.

a *pilgrim* principle, introducing a biblical and prophetic tension into the interaction.

JEWISH ASCENSION AND VISION MYSTICISM IN THE DEAD SEA SCROLLS

Another source of early, pre-Christian Jewish mystical thought has been the documents which were discovered at Qumran beginning in 1947, which have come to be known as the Dead Sea Scrolls. These are widely understood to have been produced by the Essenes. Their library included texts displaying clear connections with the kind of thought which developed into *Merkavah*. These connections are made, for example, in lines from the *Songs of the Sabbath Sacrifice* such as,

> The cherubim lie prostrate before him and bless when they arise. The voice of divine silence is heard, and there is the uproar of excitement when they raise their wings, the voice of a divine silence. They bless the image of the throne-chariot (which is) above the vault of the cherubim, and they sing [the splen]dor of the shining vault (which is) beneath his seat of his glory. (4Q405, frags. 20–21–22).[59]

As has already been noted, the primary exegetical focus of the *Merkavah* texts was Ezekiel's vision in the first chapter of the book which bears his name. Ezekiel was a priest (Ezek 1:3), as the members of the Qumran community may have been. Focusing on the *Shirot 'Olat Hashabat* (Songs of the Sabbath Sacrifice), Elior proposes that these *Merkavah*-related compositions from Qumran may well be "the missing link between the priest-prophet Ezekiel and the foundation of the biblical chariot tradition, on one side, and the *Hekhalōt*[60] literature chariot tradition, on the other side."[61] She sees three consistent characteristics in the Sabbath Songs which make the connection between the *Merkavah* tradition and the priestly tradition: 1) the clear connection between these songs and Ezekiel's vision, 2) the depiction of angels and cherubim fulfilling priestly duties in the heavenly sanctuary, and finally, 3) the

---

59. García Martínez and Watson, *The Dead Sea Scrolls*, 429; see also Elior, "Mystical Traditions," 83.

60. Literally, "palaces," because of the focus on passing through the "palaces" of God and the angelic beings in the heavenly realms in the ascent of the adept.

61. Elior, "Mystical Traditions," 87.

chronological structure of the Songs which connects them to the priestly solar calendar described in 1 Enoch 74.[62]

Beyond these descriptions of the content of the *Shirot*, Jey Kanagaraj extends the discussion to question the purpose of this liturgy. Recognizing that the community at Qumran very likely combined the heavenly and earthly priesthood, the community sought to worship *along with* the angels, who were believed to be performing the rituals of the Temple cult in the heavenly Temple.[63] Kanagaraj believes that this demonstrates that in their contemplation of the *Merkavah* and the *Hekhalōt*, the members of the Qumran community sought mystical knowledge through their experiences.[64] While acknowledging this element, however, it is important to note along with Gruenwald that what "originally were the hymns of the angels have become theurgical incantations which help the mystic to achieve his goal."[65] Michael Swartz,[66] looking specifically at the (third-fifth century CE) *Ma'aseh Merkavah*, suggests that "the text underwent a process of evolution from a collection of prayers to be recited in community with the heavenly hosts, to a prescription for the active cultivation of the individual's ascent to and vision of the upper realm—that is, an evolution from liturgy to theurgy."[67]

Connected with this, and perhaps *beyond* this, Alan F. Segal quotes a section of the translation of 4QM[a] of the Dead Sea Scrolls done by the late Morton Smith. Smith sought to actually connect the world of Second Temple Judaism and even Jesus himself with magic techniques and practices.[68] While some of these ideas are problematic in terms of interpretation of the Gospel accounts of Jesus, this translation cited by Segal may nonetheless point to a degree of interaction with vision and

---

62. Ibid, 90–93; also Isaac, "Enoch," 53–54.

63. Kanagaraj, 'Mysticism,' 96–97. See also Tuell, "Divine Presence," 110–14. Tuell suggests that the book of Ezekiel itself, particularly chs. 40–42, as a kind of "verbal icon" functioning as a "window into heavenly reality" (Tuell, "Divine Presence," 110) in much the same way as a visual icon is meant to function for many in the Eastern and Oriental Orthodox traditions.

64. Kanagaraj, 'Mysticism,' 97.

65. Gruenwald, *Apocalyptic and Merkavah*, 152.

66. Michael Swartz is a scholar of ancient Jewish magic and mysticism, and currently teaches at The Ohio State University.

67. Swartz, *Mystical Prayer*, 5.

68. See Morton Smith, *Jesus the Magician*, 124.

ascension mysticism in the context of the Qumran community. Smith's translation reads,

> [El Elyon gave me a seat among] those perfect forever,
> A mighty throne in the congregation of the gods. (Heb. *bny elohim*).
> None of the kings of the east shall sit in it
> And their nobles shall not [come near it].
> No Edomite shall be like me in glory.
> And none shall be exalted save me, nor shall come against me.
> For I have taken my seat in the [congregation] of the heavens,
> And none [find fault with me].
> I shall be reckoned with gods
> And established in the holy congregation. (4QM^a)[69]

Here as well there is an element not only of ascent, but of transformation. Questions remain, however—Segal suggests that "they must have achieved this through some rite of translation and transmutation"[70] It would seem that, *if* Smith is correct on this point, this may also be an element which was actually challenged by the early Christian movement.

Finally, in an essay published in *The Historical Jesus in Context*, Peter Flint offered translations of some Dead Sea Scrolls passages demonstrating themes which seem to run parallel with the New Testament.[71] One passage contains a possible foreshadowing of how the kind of mysticism described by Segal might have elicited a pre-Christian (first century BCE) response which remained grounded in the Scriptural tradition. More intriguing still is that it connects this with a concept of the Messiah which closely resembles that found in the Gospels; indeed, this particular Qumran text (4Q521, frag. 2 col. 2) has been rather tellingly entitled, "The Messianic Apocalypse":

> [For the hea]vens and the earth will listen to his Messiah (or, anointed one) [and all t]hat is in them shall not stray from the commandments of the holy ones.
>
> Strengthen yourselves, you seekers of the Lord, in his service!

---

69. Smith, "4QM^a," 184; see also Segal, "Paul and the Beginning," 118–19 n. 22. For another, quite similar translation of this text, see García and Watson, *Dead Sea Scrolls*, 118 (frag. 11, col. 1). 4QM^a is also called 4QWar Scroll or 4Q491; see García Martínez and Watson, *Dead Sea Scrolls*, 115.

70. Ibid., 119 n. 22.

71. Flint, "Jesus and the Dead Sea Scrolls," 110–31.

> Will you not discover the Lord in this, all you who hope in their heart?
>
> For the Lord will bestow care on the pious, and he will call the righteous by name;
>
> And over the poor in spirit he will hover,[72] and he will renew the faithful with his strength.
>
> For he will honor the pious upon the throne of an (or: the) eternal kingdom,
>
> Setting captives free, opening the eyes of the blind, lifting up those who are bo[wed down].[73]
>
> And for[ev]er will I cling [to] those who [ho]pe in his mercy [...];
>
> And the fru[it of...] will not be delayed for anyone;
>
> And the Lord will perform glorious things which have not existed, just as he s[aid].
>
> For he will heal the wounded,[74] he will make the dead live, he will bring good news to the poor;[75]
>
> And he will [...the...]. He will lead with care the uprooted ones, and he will make the hungry rich.[76]

This is a remarkable passage which seems to promise those who are "pious" that they will sit upon a throne in an (or the) eternal kingdom. In the degree of context afforded by this brief translated passage, this appears to be in connection not with a detailed schema of ascent technique, but with reference to the action of a promised Messiah for those who follow him. There may very well be too little here to conclusively consider this a foreshadowing of the New Testament response to ascension mysticism, but it nonetheless remains an intriguing example.

---

72. In a personal conversation, Dr. Dale Walker pointed out that the word translated "hover" here is from the same Hebrew root as the word used in Gen 1:2 for what the Spirit is doing.

73. Flint, the translator of and commentator on this passage, includes reference here in brackets to Ps 146:7–8 and Isa 58:6 and 61:1 (Flint, "Jesus and the Dead Sea Scrolls," 119).

74. Flint adds, "lit. pierced"

75. Isa 61:1 again

76. Flint, "Jesus and the Dead Sea Scrolls," 119. For another translation of this passage, see García Martínez and Watson, *Dead Sea Scrolls*, 394.

PHILO AND ASCENSION/VISION MYSTICISM[77]

Philo of Alexandria stands apart as a unique thinker, one who bridged the Jewish and Hellenic worlds in the period roughly coinciding with that of the Apostles themselves. From a prominent family in the large Jewish community of Alexandria, as his writings make plain, he was trained in Platonic philosophy, though there is certainly Stoic influence also evident in his writings. Moreover, he was prominent enough to have been chosen to lead a Jewish delegation to Emperor Gaius Caligula, following a deadly pogrom against the Jews in Alexandria in 39 CE.[78]

There are many important aspects to Philo's theological writings and philosophy, but for the purpose of this study we will take a brief look at two of these: Philo's view of Scripture, and the motif of ascension and other elements of mysticism in his writings, especially those surrounding his use of the term and concept of *Logos*. We will especially examine the manner in which Philo interacted with both the Hellenic context in which he wrote, as well as his own interaction with the ascension motif. Can Philo be understood as using an *indigenous* principle in his own context with regard to his Platonic mode of expression, and yet maintaining a "*pilgrim*-like" faithfulness to the Scriptures?

Philo is often regarded as a forerunner of the sort of allegorical exegesis which came to be associated with Alexandria, especially in the Christian tradition.[79] Yet as much as his writings came to be associated with allegorical interpretation, this was by no means to the exclusion of a plainer or more literal reading of the text.[80] Philo desired to use allegory to present what he felt was a *deeper* interpretation of the sacred text:[81]

> This is our explanation, but those who merely follow the outward and obvious think that we have at this point a reference to the origin of the Greek and barbarian languages. I would not censure such persons, for perhaps the truth is with them also. Still I would exhort them not to halt there, but to press on to allegorical interpretations and to recognize that the letter is to the oracle but as the shadow to the substance and that the higher

---

77. In Runia, "Review of *The Works of Philo*," Runia expresses his preference for the *Loeb Classical Editions* translation done by F. H. Colson & G. H. Whitaker and published 1929–1953 over the earlier Yonge translation.

78. Runia, "Philo," 78.

79. Hall, *Reading Scripture*, 127–28.

80. Schiffman, *Text to Tradition*, 96.

81. Carmichael, *Story of Creation*, 36.

values therein revealed are what really and truly exist. (*The Confusion of Tongues* 28:190)[82]

He expands elsewhere on the analogy of the body and his understanding of scripture, suggesting that even as the soul is housed in the body, thus must the body also be maintained in order to also maintain the soul:[83]

> We should look on all these outward observances as resembling the body, and their inner meanings as resembling the soul. It follows that, exactly as we have to take thought for the body, because it is the abode of the soul, so we must pay heed to the letter of the laws. If we keep and observe these, we shall gain a clearer conception of those things of which these are the symbols; and besides that we shall not incur the censure of the many and the charges they are sure to bring against us. (*The Migration of Abraham*, 16:93)[84]

This also dovetails with what was noted more recently by Stefan Nordgaard Svendsen concerning Philo's manner of allegorical exegesis. Importantly, he sums up Philo's view of the relationship between a literal and an allegorical reading as that the "allegorical meanings must be seen as abstract rational structures *within* the literal meanings," and goes on to assert that "literal meanings should not be conceived as arbitrary representations, but rather as *manifestations* of their allegorical counterparts."[85] On one level, this may seem to be very Platonic: the ideal, abstract allegorical meaning is made manifest in the world of phenomena on the literal level with flesh-and-blood examples. Philo is not merely being swallowed whole by his Platonic context; he is interacting with it critically and modifying the manner in which Plato viewed the relationship between the transcendent world and the world of phenomenological existence. Svendsen explains:

> In a way that would have struck Plato as heresy, Philo describes the world of transcendence, not only as the paradigm behind the construction of the world, but also as an active and dynamic force that pervades the physical world—as an ideal and

---

82. Philo, iv.113, 115.
83. Kelly, *Doctrines*, 8–9.
84. Philo iv. 93.
85. Svendsen, "Allegory Transformed," 51.

conceptual structure that exists and operates *within* the world of matter.[86]

This theme of the relationship between a literal and an allegorical understanding of scripture will be examined more closely in later chapters more focused on mystical exegesis of sacred texts.

With regard to Philo's writing on what is understood as the "mystical" tradition, we can look at it with a modified version of Segal's elements noted earlier: Those of *vision* of the Deity or the Deity's representative, of *transformation* and finally of *ascent*. While elements of all three seem to be present in Philo's writings, they can at times be clearly referring to mystical experience, but at other times to a more allegorical or intellectual idea of the meaning of the terms used. For example, the following is from Philo's treatise *On the Embassy to Gaius*, and certainly carries some of the language of ascension which has been encountered elsewhere:

> . . .souls which have soared above[87] all that is created and have been schooled to see the uncreated and divine, the primal good,
>
> More excellent than the excellent,
>
> More blessed than blessedness,
>
> More happy than happiness itself,
>
> And any perfection there may be greater than these.
>
> (*On the Embassy to Gaius* 1.5)[88]

The context of this particular treatise is Philo seeking to understand or explain the providence of God in the midst of persecution such as that which had just recently taken place in Alexandria.[89] Peder Borgen examined this, observing a contrast between what he called "proper ascent" and contrasting it with "illegitimate invasion." Concerning the latter, and in contrast with the specifically *Jewish* kind of ascent described above, he speaks (without actually naming Gaius Caligula) of one who has ascended through bloodshed over the Senate, the "equestrian order" or knights, and finally over his own family,[90] but finally "he claimed to

---

86. Ibid., 36.

87. The translator notes that the Greek term used here, *hyperkupsasai*, literally means, "put one's head over." Borgen, *Hellenistic Judaism*, 294.

88. Borgen, *Hellenistic Judaism*, 294.

89. Ibid., 295.

90. Ibid., 300–6.

remain no more within the limits of human nature, but soared above[91] them desiring to be thought a god" (*On the Embassy to Gaius* 11:75).[92]

Philo contrasts Gaius Caligula's "invasion" with the ascent accounts of the various prophets, such as Abraham and Aaron, and culminating in the ascent of Moses. While Borgen recognizes that the ascents of the former of these are understood as something like more of the "qualities and abilities the mind needs in the ascent,"[93] in Philo, Moses' ascension is of a rather distinct quality. In response to Moses' entreaty in Exod 33:13 that God reveal himself, Philo interprets God's reply as

> Know yourself, then, and do not be led away by impulses and desires beyond your capacity, nor let yearning for the unobtainable uplift and carry you off your feet, for of the obtainable nothing shall be denied you. (*The Special Laws* 1:44)[94]

Borgen describes this response as a "polemic against illegitimate invasion," that "neither God nor his powers can be apprehended in their essence"[95] In another of the treatises which touches on this same interaction between Moses and God, this idea of God's ineffability (even to Moses) is similarly emphasized, as Philo writes,

> Moses who, as the divine oracles tell us, entered into the darknessa (Ex. xx.21), by which figure they indicate existence invisible and incorporeal, searched everywhere and into everything in his desire to see clearly and plainly Him, the object of our much yearning, Who alone is good. And when there was no sign of finding aught, not even any semblance of what he hoped for, in despair of learning from others, he took refuge with the Object of his search Itself and prayed in these words: "Reveal Thyself to me that I may see Thee with knowledge" (Ex. xxxiii.13). And yet he fails to gain his object. To know what lies below the Existent, things material and immaterial alike, is a most ample gift even for the best sort among mortals, as God judges, for we read, "Thou shalt see what is behind Me, but My face thou shalt not see" (*ibid.* 23). It means that all below the

---

91. Significantly, the same Greek term used in 1:5 and noted above is also used here in a similar manner; the parallel seems to indicate a contrast between the two "ascents" described.

92. Borgen, *Hellenistic Judaism*, 301.

93. Ibid., 304.

94. Ibid., 296.

95. Ibid.

Existent, things material and immaterial alike, are available to apprehension even if they are not all actually apprehended as yet, but He alone by His very nature cannot be seen. (*On the Change of Names* 7–9)[96]

Sandmel similarly sees Philo's mysticism as a rational or "philosophical" mysticism, suggesting that in this he does not

> mean only that Philo utilizes philosophy, as obviously he did. Rather, Philo was not an intuitive mystic, as I believe Paul was. Philo was given to meditation and contemplation, and his sense of union with God is at all times controlled or even determined by his broad knowledge and his rationalism. His own experience of "seeing the divine vision" is always expressed against such a background.[97]

Indeed, as Borgen notes,[98] in the subsequent passage of what constitutes Philo's commentary on Moses' conversation with God, Moses requests to at least see God's *glory*. He has God respond that while his essence is incomprehensible, even that which *can* be understood can only be comprehended by the one of "mind at its purest" (*The Special Laws* 1:46):[99]

> But I readily and with right goodwill will admit you to a share of what is attainable. That means that I bid you come and contemplate the universe and its contents, a spectacle apprehended not by the eye of the body but by the unsleeping eyes of the mind. (*The Special Laws* 1:49)[100]

The Philo material examined thus far doesn't sound all that different from Sandmel's more "rationalist" perspective. Yet Philo seems to go far beyond this idea into something more, especially in the case of Moses. That Moses is understood to have ascended to see God, perhaps from the mountaintop, "into the darkness" (Exod 20:21), is clear from Philo's writings on him, and moreover is understood as a *model* for others to follow:

> Again, was not the joy of his partnership with the Father and Maker of all magnified also by the honour of being deemed

---

96. Philo v. 145–47.
97. Sandmel, *Philo*, 124.
98. Borgen, *Hellenistic Judaism*, 296.
99. Philo vii. 125.
100. Ibid., 127.

worthy to bear the same title? For he was named god and king of the whole nation, and entered, we are told, into the darkness where God was, that into the unseen, invisible, incorporeal and archetypal essence of existing things. Thus he beheld what is hidden from the sight of mortal nature, and, in himself and his life displayed for all to see, he was set before us, like some well-wrought picture, a piece of work beautiful and godlike, a model for those who are willing to copy it. (*On the Life of Moses, Book 1* 28:158–159)[101]

Philo here sees a connection between genuinely mystical experience and the manner in which this is meant to have a practical effect in the life of the one who seeks to "ascend" (in this case, to "take the perfect appearance of virtue").[102] One noteworthy element in the above is that this seems to bridge to some degree a gap between Sandmel's idea of seeing Philo's mysticism as purely intellectual, and the polar opposite of seeing these descriptions as purely mystical experience.

Kanagaraj observes that in Philo's writings, the idea of ascension is linked with the divine vision of God.[103] As has been noted above, God is understood by Philo as unknowable in his essence, utterly transcendent.[104] He is revealed to humankind, however, in the Word, or *Logos*, which reveals "the face of God (or of Being) as it is turned to created reality," on one level and "aspect of the divine nature," yet on another "the *Logos* is treated as a *hypostasis*; i.e., a self-subsistent theological entity that is at least to some degree independent of God himself."[105] He is referred to by a number of divine or semi-divine titles, often of various types within the same passage. For example, in his treatise *On the Confusion of Tongues*, Philo describes the *Logos* as follows:

> But if there be any as yet unfit to be called a Son of God, let him press to take his place under God's First-born, the Word, who holds the eldership among the angels, their ruler as it were. And many names are his, for he is called, "the Beginning," and

101. Philo vi. 357, 359.

102. See also Segal, "Risen Christ," 312; Segal sees this as an account of ascension mysticism in Philo. He finds it especially noteworthy that in this passage, Moses is referred to as a "partner" of God (*koinōnon*); this same term in a rabbinic context (*šwtp*) later comes to "be understood as heresy by the rabbis" (Segal, "Risen Christ," 312), and carries echoes as well in the idea of ascribing "partners" to God in Islam (*širk*).

103. Kanagaraj, '*Mysticism*', 72.

104. Winston, "Was Philo a Mystic," 15.

105. Runia, "Philo," 81–82.

the Name of God, and His Word, and the Man after His image, and "he that sees," that is Israel. (*On the Confusion of Tongues* 28:146)[106]

Philo gives the *Logos* many different titles, and as Runia notes, he isn't consistent in the manner in which he describes the properties and identity of the Word.[107] There is certainly an element of Stoic philosophy involved behind the idea of the *Logos*[108] although Runia suggests that this is actually closer to the Platonic idea of the "World-Soul."[109] At the same time, scholars have sought to understand not merely the possible *Hellenic* influence on Philo's use of *Logos*, but also the *Jewish* use of the term and concept.

The connection between Philo's *Logos* and the *Memra* of the *Targums* has been a subject of discussion for a good century. The *Targums* were the Aramaic paraphrases of the Hebrew Scriptures, written from at least the Second Temple era and into the *Tannaitic* period.[110] Within the *Targums*, the *Memra* is "the 'Word,' in the sense of the creative or directive word or speech of God manifesting His power in the world of matter or mind; a term used especially in the *Targum* as a substitute for 'the Lord.'"[111] There are indeed numerous examples of the striking manner in which the *Memra*, or "Word of the Lord," is substituted in the *Targums* for the Tetragrammaton in the text of the Hebrew Scriptures. One of the more striking examples is in the Exodus account, where both the text as well as the Jewish tradition itself are emphatic that it was not merely an angel who redeemed Israel from the bondage of Egypt, but the Lord himself. It is that much more remarkable, then, when we find how *Targum Pseudo-Jonathan* reads Exod 12:29, paraphrasing the Hebrew as, "In the middle of the night of the fifteenth (of Nisan), the *Memra of the Lord* slew

---

106. Philo iv. 89, 91.

107. Runia, "Philo," 81.

108. E.g., the term *Logos* itself. Svendsen notes that "even though he consistently deployed Stoic terminology, he represented a move away from Stoic philosophy rather than an approximation toward it" (Svendsen, "Allegory Transformed," 32 n. 77).

109. Runia, "Philo," 81.

110. The "*Tannaim*" were the early Rabbinic sages whose ideas are found in the Mishna. The period runs roughly from that of Hillel and Shemai and their disciples to that of Judah ha-Nasi, from 10 CE to 220 CE (see Bacher, Lauterbach, Jacobs and Ginzberg, "*Tannaim* and Amoraim," 12.49.

111. Kohler, "Memra," 8.464–865.

all the firstborn in the land of Egypt."¹¹² The upshot of this is that the use of the "Word of the Lord" to designate some sort of *hypostasis* of God has a Jewish as well as Hellenic background, and Philo is, in reality, synthesizing these in a continuation of what was likely an effort to explain how the transcendent God could be understood as so clearly encountering humankind in such a personal manner.¹¹³

The connection in Philo's writings between the *Merkavah* and the ascension concept noted in his *Logos* figure has been recognized at least as far back as Kohler¹¹⁴ and Toy, et al.,¹¹⁵ and has more recently been briefly discussed by Jey Kanagaraj.¹¹⁶ Indeed, in a passage describing the ark, Philo writes that,

> The Divine Word, Who is high above all these, has not been visibly portrayed, being like to no one of the objects of sense. Nay, He is Himself the Image of God, chiefest of all Beings intellectually perceived, placed nearest, with no intervening distance, to the Alone truly Existent One. For we read: "I will talk with thee from above the Mercy-seat, between the two Cherubim" (Ex. xxv.21), words which shew that *while the Word is the charioteer of the Powers*, He Who talks is seated in the chariot, giving

---

112. McNamara, *Targum Neofiti*, 193. See also Gieschen,. *Angelomorphic Christology*, 113. Alan F. Segal gives a very brief overview of this in his *Two Powers in Heaven* noting G. F. Moore's (1922) opposition to the identification of *Memra* and Philo's *Logos* (Moore, *Tannaim*, and G. H. Box (1932–1933) coming out in favor of the idea (Box, "Intermediation," 103–119); see Segal, *Two Powers in Heaven*, 132–33, n. 1. More recently, Daniel Boyarin similarly quotes (and challenges) C. K. Barrett's (1978) commentary on John on this topic (Barrett, *The Gospel According to St. John*, where Barrett asserts that, "*Memra* is a blind alley in the study of the biblical background of John's Logos doctrine" (Boyarin, "The Gospel of the *Memra*," 248, n. 19.

113. In citing Targumic and other Rabbinic material regarding which there is no consensus on dates, we are following Craig Keener in his preference for casting a "wide net" for sources, even when there may not be unambiguous "proof" of pre-Christian dating for the sources named (Keener, *The Gospel of John*, 1:194). Keener challenges the connection with the *memra* as possibly too late and isolated a concept, but finds a similar idea in other Jewish concepts of the period in the personified Word as Wisdom or Torah, It can also be noted that Samuel Sandmel wrote that the *Targums* were "engaging in euphemism" and that the "connection between *memra* and *logos*, if any, is at most very tenuous" (Sandmel, *Philo*, 156). An overview of the discussion over the course of the twentieth and early twenty-first centuries, along with a defense of the position of *memra* as part of the background to *logos* in John's prologue, is found in McNamara, *Targum and Testament Revisited*, 153–65.

114. Kohler, "Merkabah," 8.500.

115. Toy, Siegfried and Lauterbach, "Philo Judæus," 10.13.

116. Kanagaraj, *"Mysticism,"* 72–73.

directions to the charioteer for the right wielding of the reigns of the Universe.[117]

Indeed, Moshe Idel suggests parallels between Philo's description of the *Logos* and what is stated of the glorified angel Metatron in the *Hekhalōt*[118] literature:

> Some of the more general characteristics of the *Logos* are reminiscent of those of Metatron, e.g., its basic function as an hypostatization of God. On the other hand, the salvific nature of union with the *Logos* is also found in a variety of Jewish traditions in connection with Metatron. Like this angel, the *Logos* is described as the ruler of the world and the angel of the divine face. The *Logos* may also be identified with a Messianic figure.[119]

What of the final key aspect of early Jewish mysticism noted by Segal? As has already been observed, the elements of ascent to God's presence and theophany, or vision of God, certainly seem to be present in Philo's writings. Earlier scholars such as Kaufmann as well as the more recent Kanagaraj have published remarks on connections between these elements in Philo and similar themes in the *Merkavah* writings. Is the element of *transformation* found in Philo's writings? Certainly; we have already noted Philo's understanding of Moses' ascension on Sinai involved Moses' being transformed in some ways, which was held by Philo as an example or model for others (e.g., as in the passage in *A Treatise on the Life of Moses, Book 1* 28:158 cited above).

One element which Philo connects with this idea of transformation, and also seems to imply an indwelling in a manner echoing some passages in John's Gospel is that of the *Logos* as the nourishing bread of life and as the "Cupbearer of God." This chapter opened with the latter quoted image, which is particularly startling in that the *Logos* pours out *himself* to the "happy soul."[120] Another similar passage which depicts the

---

117. Philo v.65; see also Urban and Henry, "Does Philo Explain John 8:56–58?," 175.

118. Metatron is a high angel mentioned in Talmud and in the pseudopigraphical *3 Enoch*, a work also known as *Sepher Hekhalōt* and dated variously from the 2nd to 6th centuries CE (Odeberg, "Introduction," 23–43). In the *Sepher Hekhalōt*, Rabbi Ishmael ascends to Heaven and encounters the high angel Metatron. Metatron is depicted as the transformed Enoch, who is now the "Prince of the Presence" and the "Lesser YHWH" (3 Enoch 9–15; Tommasi, "Ascension," 1.522).

119. Idel, *Messianic Mystics*, 342 n. 51.

120. Philo, *On Dreams* 2:249; Philo v.555. This seems to be echoed in John 7:35.

Logos as a nourishing stream or as the bread in the wilderness is found in *On Flight and Finding*:

> When they sought what it is that nourished the soul (for, as Moses says, they "knew not what it was")(Exod. xvi. 15), they became learners and found it to be a saying of God, that is the Divine Word, from which all kinds of instruction and wisdom flow in perpetual stream. This is the heavenly nourishment, and it is indicated as such in the sacred records, when the First Cause in his own person says, "Lo, it is I that am raining upon you bread out of the heaven" (*ibid.* 4); for in very deed God drops from above the ethereal wisdom upon minds which are by nature apt and take delight in Contemplation; and they see it and taste it and are filled with pleasure, being fully aware of what they feel, but wholly ignorant of the cause which produced the feeling. So they inquire, "What is this" (*ibid.* 15) which has a nature making it sweeter than honey and whiter than snow? And they will be taught by the seer that "This is the bread, which the Lord hath given them to eat" (*ibid.* 15). Tell me, then, of what kind the bread is. "This saying," he says, "which the Lord ordained" (*ibid.* 16). This Divine ordinance fills the soul that has a vision alike with light and sweetness, flashing forth the radiance of truth, and with the honeyed grace of persuasion imparting sweetness to those who hunger and thirst after nobility of character. (*On Flight and Finding* 137–39)[121]

Here, Philo seems to be truly describing not merely transformation, but an understanding of transformation intertwined with genuine relationship with God. That is to say (using Davila's terminology again) that Philo is clearly moving the Jewish ascent and vision mysticism beyond a *shamanistic* understanding to one of a more relational *mysticism*. Philo appears to be interacting with the Scriptures and the prevalent ideas of Jewish and Hellenic mysticism of the day to push the idea more into one of loving relationship with God through the Logos. As such, it seems to me that he is implementing Walls' principles: Using the (*indigenous*) language and ideas of both the Platonic and Jewish elements of his milieu, while at the same time going beyond these and challenging what he would see as the inadequacies of the current understandings of ascent, vision and transformation (which would be more of the *pilgrim* idea).

---

121. Philo v. 83, 85. Again, this seems to be echoed in Jesus' discourse on himself as the "bread from heaven" in John 6:35–58.

One more element of ecstatic mysticism which we encounter in Philo, and which we will encounter later on in both Christian and Sūfī texts, is the idea which Philo expresses as *sober intoxication*. In the following passage from *On the Creation of the World*, this idea of spiritual ecstasy and heavenly ascent are combined into a rather dramatic narrative.

> Again, when on soaring wing it has contemplated the atmosphere and all its phases, it is borne yet higher to the ether and the circuit of heaven, and is whirled round with the dances of planets and fixed stars, in accordance with the laws of perfect music, following that love of wisdom which guides its steps. And so, carrying its gaze beyond the confines of all substance discernible by sense, it comes to a point at which it reaches out after the intelligible world, and on descrying in that world, sights of surpassing loveliness, even the patterns and the originals of the things of sense which it saw here, it is seized by a sober intoxication, like those filled with Corybantic frenzy, and is inspired, possessed by a longing far other than theirs and a nobler desire. Wafted by this to the topmost arch of the things perceptible to mind, it seems to be on its way to the Great King Himself; but, amid its longing to see Him, pure and untempered rays of concentrated light stream forth like a torrent, so that by its gleams the eye of the understanding is dazzled. (*On the Creation of the World*, 70–71)[122]

What is behind this, ecstatic ascension and visionary experience for Philo? David Winston has observed that "this longed-for experience can come only after long and arduous preparations."[123]

Winston goes on, however, to note Philo's ambivalence regarding an ascetic regime, and seems to advocate extremes neither of indulgence nor of deprivation.[124] He concludes that "like any good Platonist, Philo would much prefer to dispense with material reality and the human body that constitutes an inseparable part of it. As a philosophical realist, however, he must accept it and, on occasion, justify its existence within the divine scheme of things."[125] We wonder if, rather than mere "philosophical realism," what perhaps mitigates this is Philo's attachment to the Jewish tradition. In regard to this element of ascension and ecstatic vision, it is thus

---

122. Philo i.55, 57. David Winston notes a parallel here with Plato's *Phaedrus* 249C, regarding the flight of the soul (Winston, "Introduction," 358 n. 340).

123. Winston, "Introduction," 30.

124. Ibid., 31.

125. Ibid., 32.

unclear to what extent Philo may be advocating something more along the lines of shamanism in the sense in which we are using the term here, though his language seems to lend itself to that speculation. As noted earlier, however, we will find ourselves encountering the idea of *sober intoxication* again later on, sometimes with a rather different means of explaining what this is.

It should also be noted that Alan Segal has pointed out that Philo writes in one instance that the kind of language used in Scripture which speaks of God in human terms is actually meant to communicate to the *hoi polloi*, while the more allegorical conceptions in scripture are meant for the educated or enlightened.[126] This really returns the discussion to the whole question of literal vs. allegorical interpretation of the text in Philo. Earlier, we noted that for Philo, there was a clear interdependency of these modes of understanding of the text. While in places Philo is emphatic regarding the *Logos* in terms which amount to a view equating the *Logos* with a kind of *demiurge* figure, Philo also at times sees the anthropomorphism in scripture as a kind of pedagogical tool for those who are not sufficiently enlightened to grasp pure monotheism. Thus in a discussion regarding the idea of "two powers" in heaven, Philo suggests that

> the sacred word ever entertaining holier and more august conceptions of Him that is, yet at the same time longing to provide instruction and teaching for the life of those who lack wisdom, likened God to man, not however, to any particular man. For this reason it has ascribed to Him face, hands, feet, mouth, voice, wrath and indignation, and, over and beyond these, weapons, entrances and exits, movements up and down and all ways, and in following this general principle in its language it is concerned not with truth, but with the profit accruing to its pupils...For it is something to be thankful for if they can be taught self-control by the terror held over them by these means. Broadly speaking the lines taken throughout the Law are these two only, one that which keeps truth in view and so provides the thought "God is not as a man" (Num. xxiii. 19), the other that which keeps in view the ways of thinking of the duller folk, of whom it is said,

---

126. Segal, *Two Powers*, 159–61; see also idem, "*Rebecca's Children*," 154–55. Segal later notes that both Justin and Trypho, his Jewish interlocutor, use language similar to that used by Philo here (citing Justin's *Dialogue with Trypho* 56). Segal suggests that Trypho actually is willing to accept that the angel mentioned in Gen 19:24 as the "Lord who rained down fire from the Lord" is divine, but disputes that this hypostasis of sorts can be identified with the Messiah (Segal, *Rebecca's Children*, 159–60).

"the Lord God shall chasten thee, as if a man should chasten his son" (Deut. viii. 5). (*On Dreams* 1:234–35, 237)[127]

In spite of the above, however, Segal goes on to quote other passages from Philo which seem to indicate an ultimate goal of *divinization* by means of the *Logos*, which is understood not merely as an entity, but as a *place*. Thus, Segal quotes Philo's *Questions and Answers in Exodus* on the *theophany* in Exod 24:11–12:

> What is the meaning of the words, "Come up to Me to the mountain and be there"? This signifies that a holy soul is divinized by ascending not to the air to the ether or to heaven (which is higher than all) but to a region above the heavens, and beyond the world where there is no place but God. And He determines the stability of the removal by saying "be there"....[128]

Segal concludes by following this with the observation that the "highest purpose of man is to perceive the face of God or the *Logos*. In this way, one sees God in all His power. This is the meaning of the Sinai theophany."[129] Between Philo's apparent elitism reflected in the earlier quote, and this expression of the potential for union with God on some level by means of the *Logos*, there is certainly a significant amount of ambiguity of the meaning of both *Logos* and of these ideas of transformation in the writings of Philo.

Philo's writings and philosophy are thus an integration of Hellenic and Jewish ideas. While deeply immersed in Platonic thought, with some clear influence from Stoicism too, Philo is, from a perspective of a Scripturally-grounded Judaism, interacting critically with both his Hellenic and Jewish-mystical context. Philo appears to be seeking to maintain something like Walls' tension between an *indigenous* principle and a *pilgrim* principle. Pratap Chandra Gine, writing on Philo's use of terms relating to the "law" (*nómos*), concluded that while Philo was "highly acculturated" in terms of his Hellenism, he nonetheless "used his acculturation to present Judaism as a universal religion," acting as an "evangelical apologist" (!).[130] Philo displays a fair amount of ambiguity, however: There is an idea of mysticism for the elite who can achieve the ascent, but also elements for the common people who require some sort

---

127. Philo v. 421–23.
128. Philo Supplement II.82, quoted in Segal, *Two Powers*, 172.
129. Segal, *Two Powers*, 172.
130. Gine, Νομος *in Context*, 74–75.

of anthropomorphism in order to attain to the more "pure" monotheism of the better educated.

THE RABBINIC JEWISH RESPONSE TO ASCENSION MYSTICISM

Before we turn to the response to this form of early Jewish ascension and vision mysticism found in the New Testament and the early Christian tradition in the next chapter, we will look at one other element of their context: the response of the emerging Rabbinic Jewish movement to many of the same features of the religio-social landscape described above. In the following chapter, we will observe areas of convergence as well as divergence with the Christian witness as found in the New Testament, although much of the response to ascension and vision mysticism was formulated with this very Christian movement in view, emerging in roughly the same period.

While we have observed the response to vision and ascension mysticism in the early Christian movement, it is also important to note that some of the *Tannaim*[131] responded with polemics against speculation regarding the ascent of Enoch (as well as that of Moses). In an ironic twist, the Rabbinic response was apparently motivated, at least in part, by debate with the early Christian movement.[132] Enoch was denigrated by some of the *Tannaim* as "a repentant sinner who did not ascend to heaven."

According to Abraham Joshua Heschel, in the understanding of some (though by no means all) of these *Tannaim*, the Christians:

> formulated two basic articles of faith: (1) God or the *Logos* descended from heaven, took on flesh, and became human; (2) Jesus rose from the dead and ascended to heaven. The second dogma served as a basis for and proof of the first. As John put

---

131. On the *Tannaim*, early Jewish Rabbinic authorities from approximately 10–220 CE, see 58 n. 109.

132. It is important to note here that the response of the *Tannaim* should not be understood as "the Jewish response" to ascension mysticism, simply because there were, at this point, a number of expressions of Judaism, including the community of those following Jesus. Indeed, Martha Himmelfarb describes the *Tannaim* in this early period as "a small elite ... even in Palestine their influence was not widespread." (Himmelfarb, "Parting of the Ways," 50, 59 n. 14; see also Neusner, *Evidence from the Mishnah*, 3–5).

it, "No one ever ascended to heaven except the one who came down from heaven" (John 3:13).[133]

This seems quite accurate as a brief description of how the faith of the early Jesus community would have been understood and expressed, especially within this context of ascension mysticism. Heschel further suggested, however, that a belief in the ascension of *Jesus* was *based* in some manner on the ascension of Enoch. He asserts that the "disciples of Jesus regarded the ascent of Enoch to heaven in his lifetime as of supreme importance. Perhaps for this reason the Sages of Israel insisted that Enoch died a natural death."[134] Gruenwald suggests as well that the later idea of the transformation of Enoch into the angel Metatron, notably found in *Sefer Hekhalōt/3 Enoch*, may actually have also been a polemical attempt to provide an alternate ascended super-human who is transformed into an *angelic* rather than *divine* figure.[135] Heschel's commentator Gordon Tucker seeks to explain this by speculating that "Enoch was, for Christians, a paradigm of ascent to heaven, just as Isaac was the paradigm for the sacrifice of the beloved son."[136]

Another surprising element in this vein is the criticism by some *Tannaim* not only of Enoch's ascension, but also that of *Moses*. Itamar Gruenwald cites a passage in the *Mechiltā de-Rabbi Ishmael* in which Rabbi Yose, commenting on Ps 115:16, "The heavens are the Lord's heavens, but the earth he has given to the children of man." Yose insists that, "Neither did Moses and Elijah ascend to heaven nor did the Divine Glory (*Kavod*) descend to the earth."[137] Heschel thus cites Rabbi Yose's[138] opposition to any idea of ascension to heaven, recognizing that Yose sought to

> set hard and fast boundaries between the exalted divinity and unworthy humankind. We learn the thrust of his thought from the polemics he directed against both central Christian dogmas:

---

133. Heschel, *Heavenly Torah*, 349.

134. Ibid. On rabbinic polemics concerning the Enoch tradition vis-à-vis the Christian tradition.

135. Gruenwald, *Apacalyptic and Merkavah Mysticism*, 199–201

136. Gordon. Tucker, Commentary to *Heavenly Torah*, 350 n. 21.

137. Horovitz and Rabin, eds., *Mekhiltā de-Rabbi Ishmael*, 217; quoted in Gruenwald, *Apocalyptic and Merkavah*, 93.

138. Rabbi Yose Ben Halafta was a Tanna (teacher) from the second-century CE, who was a disciple of Rabbi Akiva. See Schechter and Seligsohn, "Jose Ben Halafta," 7. 241–42.

the ascent of mortals to heaven and the descent of the divine Glory (or *Logos*) to earth.[139]

Thus Yose stood opposed to the idea of any human having ascended to heaven, whether Enoch, Moses, or even Elijah. On this point, Heschel quotes Yose as correcting Rabbi Akiva on this point, making it clear that in his own view, as well as that of the ancient *Tanna* Rabbi Yose, that this was neither standard teaching among the people nor was Moses' ascent affirmed by any of the *Tannaim* prior to Rabbi Akiva.[140]

Of course, none of this is to suggest that the *Tannaim* were not conversant with the *Merkavah* tradition, but more that there was a great amount of caution attached to study of the mystical tradition. *Mishnah Hagigah*, for example, contains a significant section focused on explanations of as well as warnings concerning study of the *Ma'aseh Bereshit* as well as *Ma'aseh Merkavah* traditions. It is to this that we will now turn in examining another aspect of the early rabbinic response to *Merkavah* mysticism. The section begins with *Mishnah Hagigah* 2:1,[141] warning that "They do not expound upon the laws of prohibited relationships before three persons, the Works of Creation [*Ma'aseh Bereshit*] before two, or the Chariot [*Ma'aseh Merkavah*] before one, unless he was a sage and understands of his own knowledge;"[142] the kind of shamanism connected with these traditions was a subject which was considered potentially dangerous. One image which this brings to mind is of the story from *Hagigah* 2:1 of the *Talmud*, illustrating the above warning, in which a child in his teacher's home reading Ezekiel realized the meaning of *hashmal* in Ezek 1:27,[143] and was consumed by fire.[144] Meditating on the *Merkavah* could be dangerous as well as glorious! In its original context, Ezekiel used *hashmal* in 1:4 to describe his initial vision of the *Merkavah*, and later

---

139. Heschel, *Heavenly Torah*, 350.

140. Ibid., 350–51.

141. That is, the 2nd chapter of *Mishna* tractate *Hagigah*, section 1.

142. Neusner, *Hagigah*, 43; note also Gruenwald, *Apocalyptic and Merkavah*, 75.

143. *Hashmal* is the word which has been variously translated into English as "glowing metal" (NIV), "gleaming bronze" (RSV) and "gleaming amber" (NRSV); in modern Hebrew, it refers to electricity. Daniel Bodi presents a convincing case that it is related to a term in Akkadian, *elmēšu*, which was used to refer most likely to the shining quality of amber stone (Bodi, *The Book of Ezekiel and the Poem of Ezra*, 82–94; see also Halperin, *Faces of the Chariot*, 4 n. 7). See also Gruenwald, "Nature and Origins," 47.

144. Neusner, *Hagigah*, 52–53; see also Scholem, *Kabbalah*, 373.

in 1:27 in describing the climax of his vision.[145] Moreover, in addition to *hashmal*, there is also the element of God's fiery presence among the *hayyōt*, the living creatures, in 1:14–15, described in terms of "lightning" (*barak/bazak*).

At Qumran, *hashmal* is also used in a fragment from the *Songs of the Sabbath Sacrifice* in the Dead Sea Scrolls 4Q405, fragments 20–22, column 2, line 10, which reads in part, "Like the appearance of fire (are) the spirits of holiest holiness round about, the appearance of streams of fire like electrum [*hashmal*]."[146] Similarly, 1Q29 and 4Q376 include a fragment which has been entitled, "Liturgy of Three Tongues of Fire," in which the "tongues of fire" are described as "shining" with what appears to be a related word (*hashemali, hashemalot*), and described in connection with the sacrificial liturgy.[147] This idea of "tongues of fire" in the presence of God also shows up in the Greek text of 1 Enoch 14:9, which states that Enoch saw "a wall which is built of white marble and surrounded by tongues of fire."[148]

The rabbinic speculation found especially in *Hagigah* on the subject of the *Merkavah* and in particular with regard to the term *hashmal*, can thus be understood as interacting on some level with this earlier tradition as found at Qumran and in the Enoch writings. Thus, in the Talmud, the speculation moves from the story of the unfortunate boy consumed by *hashmal* to consideration of possible meanings of the term itself. In view of the above emphasis on what appears to be interaction between the presence of God's power and glory with the idea of this presence being associated with the power and beauty of fire. Thus, the question at the end of *Hagigah* 2:1 (folio 13, side a), "What is the meaning of *hashmal*?" is answered at the beginning of folio 13, side b, by Rabbi Yehuda, who says it is an acronym of the Hebrew phrase "Living creatures talking fire" (*hayyōt esh mamelelot*).[149] Later on, this element finds its way into the speculative *Merkavah* writings. In a version of *Hekhalōt Rabbati* called

---

145. Halperin, *Faces of the Chariot*, 4 n. 7.

146. Newsom, *Songs of the Sabbath Sacrifice*, 95.

147. See Parry and Tov, *Parabiblical Texts*, 98–105; see also Gruenwald, *Apocalypticism to Gnosticism*, 138. Menzies, "Pre-Lukan Occurances," 44–55, sees possible connections between this Qumran fragment and Acts 2:3, a theme which will be explored more in the following chapter.

148. Isaacs, "Enoch," 20; see also Gruenwald, *Apocalyptic and Merkavah*, 32.

149. Neusner, *Hagigah*, 53. See also DeConick, *Seek to See Him*, 107 n. 27, and Lieb, *The Visionary Mode*, 95–96.

by the alternate name *Pirkei Hekhalōt* (third to fifth century), bridges in the heavenly realms are described as connected with growing chains composed of "tongues of fire,"[150] and *Hekhalōt* fragments from the Cairo Geniza have been found reading, "And the *Hashmal* is singing before you."[151] Moreover, *Maʿaseh Merkavah* has Akiva describing how each *hekhal* is populated by thousands of *Merkavot of fire* singing hymns of praise.[152]

Finally, it may also be appropriate to note in this context the famous account of *Pardes* found in slightly varying versions in Talmud and Medieval writings, of the four rabbis who ascended to heaven. Samson Levey quotes and translates the version of this story found in *Hagigah* 2:3–4:

> Four entered *PRDS*, Ben Azzai and Ben Zoma, Aher and R. Akiba. Ben Azzai caught a glimpse and died. Concerning him the Scripture says, "Precious in the eyes of the Lord is the death of his faithful ones (hasidim)" (Ps 116:15). Ben Zoma caught a glimpse and was smitten. Concerning him Scripture says, "If you have found honey eat only as much as you need" (Prov 25:16). Aher caught a glimpse and mutilated the plants. Concerning him Scripture says, "Do not let your mouth cause your body to sin" (Eccl 5:5). R. Akiba emerged in peace. Concerning him Scripture says, "Take me along! We would run after you!" (Song of Songs 1:4).[153]

While the discussion of this passage usually centers on the idea of ascension and its dangers, Samson Levey posited an alternate explanation: That this was an "encoded" account of what happened to four rabbis who investigated the claims of the Christian tradition, or *Paradosis*.[154] In Levey's view, Ben Azzai may have dabbled in Christianity, but turned back, Ben Zoma actually became a Judeo-Christian, Aher turned from his faith altogether and sought to negatively impact the next generation of Jewish youth, and only Akiba made it through the study with his faith

---

150. Blumenthal, *Understanding Jewish Mysticism*, 56.

151. Gruenwald, *Apocalyptic and Merkavah*, 77 n. 13. Still later, the writer of *Masekhet Hekhalōt*, *hashmal* is explained as meaning "378 kinds of light," providing the numerical value of *hashmal* according to *gematria*, or Jewish numerology (Gruenwald, *Apocalyptic and Merkavah*, 209, including n. 3).

152. Swartz, *Mystical Prayer*, 74–75; also his translation at 231–32.

153. Levey, "Akiba," 334–35; see also Neusner, *Hagigah*, 60–66.

154. Levey, "Akiba," 334.

fully intact.¹⁵⁵ As an aside, Gruenwald also speculates on possible parallels between the language here of *pardes* as mystical language which Paul is using in the passage in 2 Cor 12:1–4, in which he alludes to an ascension experience.¹⁵⁶

As has already been demonstrated, however, this view of ascension in general, and particularly that of Moses, *was* actually taught by Philo of Alexandria. Given this context of antagonism and perhaps fear, David Halperin's observations regarding textual variants in some of the manuscripts of Philo's writings seem to make sense. Citing a 1967 study by Dominique Barthélemy on Origen's connections with the Jews of his day,¹⁵⁷ Halperin observes that these variants seem to bear evidence of "deliberate 'corrections' of the writings of the Alexandrian Jewish philosopher, designed to bring them into harmony with rabbinic Judaism and to eliminate bits of aid and comfort that they might provide to Christianity."¹⁵⁸ The conjecture is that Origen may actually have served to "reintroduce" the Jewish community of Caesarea to Philo's writings, and that it was there, in a milieu in which Origen was interacting on some level with the Jewish community, that this particular response to what was assumed to be Christian-friendly elements in Philo's writings was apparently censored.¹⁵⁹

The irony of the above reaction will become increasingly apparent in the next chapter, as we examine the interaction with vision and ascension mysticism within the early Christian movement, especially as reflected in the writings of the New Testament. At the same time, it is not necessarily unreasonable to assume that a crucial concern was not merely a polemic against Christian or other "sectarian" inroads, but also with regard to what was understood as a faithful understanding and portrayal of the meaning of such apprehension of God in the Hebrew Scriptures. we earlier quoted Moshe Idel at length concerning this,¹⁶⁰ because his focus here may very well represent a point on which the *Tannaim* and the writers of the New Testament were actually in agreement. The passage previously quoted continues, with Idel asserting:

155. Ibid., 335–36.
156. Gruenwald, *Apocalyptic and Merkavah*, 91.
157. Cited as Barthélemy, "Est-ce Hoshaya Rabba qui cesura le 'Commentaire Allegorique'?," 140–73. See Halperin, *Faces of the Chariot*, 575.
158. Halperin, *Faces of the Chariot*, 325–26.
159. Ibid., 326.
160. See above, 28–29.

In other words, divine theophany—the revelation of the divine personality, especially the divine will—is the constituting moment of biblical Judaism, not an apotheotic experience of an individual mystic. This does not mean that apotheosis or the ascent on high is unknown to biblical Judaism. In fact, the succinct descriptions of the translations of Enoch and Elijah constitute forms of apotheosis, but they remain a tiny minority in the vast biblical literature.[161]

Thus the response from the Rabbinic Jewish movement was in some ways hostile—indeed, sometimes directly so, as they sought to distinguish themselves from what was then a still viable Jewish Christian movement, especially over concerns regarding what Alan Segal refers to as "two powers in heaven." It was this idea which the rabbis perhaps saw as reaching its fruition in the development of Christian faith, which didn't merely acknowledge, but sought to *worship* the "second power."[162]

This part of the Rabbinic response appears, however, to have included a degree of confusion between the more gnosis-centered Christian movements which posited a self-powered ascent, and what emerged as the Christian consensus which understood any such ascent as empowered and initiated by God.

Up until now, we have examined the Hellenic and Jewish mystical context in which some early Jewish writers were seeking to build a faithful, yet contextual expression of mysticism, while others seemed to lean toward a syncretistic shamanism. Swartz, examining *Ma'aseh Merkavah* from a different perspective, nonetheless concludes with what he understands to have been a "fundamental step in the history of Jewish mysticism," focusing on the "point at which the visionaries of ancient Judaism attributed their visions not to Divine initiation, as in prophetic and apocalyptic texts, but to their own efforts to cultivate the ascent with God's blessing but without His direct intervention."[163] Swartz goes on to locate this development after the destruction of the Second Temple, but it

---

161. Idel, *Ascensions*, 24–25. Gruenwald also makes brief note of what he refers to as "non-Merkavah mysticism," which (even in later redactions in rabbinic writings) contain not merely elements of apotheosis, but of anthropomorphic ideas of God himself. Thus the *Mechiltā de-Rabbi Ishmael* on Exod 17:6 reads, "God told him (=Moses): wherever you find a place with the imprint of a man's foot, there I am in front of you!" (Horovitz and Rabin, *Mechiltā de-Rabbi Ishmael*, 175; quoted in Gruenwald, *Apocalyptic and Merkavah*, 73 n. 1.).

162. Segal, "Paul and the Beginning," 112–13; see also Segal, *Two Powers*, 68–73.

163. Swartz, *Mystical Prayer*, 28.

seems to me that this has earlier roots, as indicated in our earlier examination of the writings from Qumran.

We examined how Philo seems, in at least a preliminary manner, to be engaging Walls' *indigenous* and *pilgrim* principles in maintaining a tension between contextual relevance in his Judeo-Hellenic context and faithfulness to the tradition, and moreover pushing the context itself in a way towards intimacy with the Almighty.

Finally, we also briefly examined the response to many of these same elements by Rabbinic Judaism which was emerging at roughly the same time as the Christian movement. The sages probed the teachings of those who had concluded that this Jesus who had been crucified and who they claimed had risen from the grave was the Messiah. There they concluded that this movement, particularly the element of the worship of Jesus, didn't fit their *own* understanding of an "indigenous" principle. Yet at the same time, we observed that the Rabbinic movement itself appropriated and participated in ascension and vision mysticism in the *Merkavah* and *Hekhalōt* and practices associated with these.

In the following chapter, we will observe whether, and how, the early Christian movement interacted with anthropocentric shamanism, and how some of the New Testament writings may reflect a response. How did the tension between *indigenous* and *pilgrim* principles play out in the very writings which became foundational for the Christian faith?

2

"With Unveiled Faces"

New Testament Response to Ascension and Vision Mysticism

THE CHRISTIAN RESPONSE TO VISION MYSTICISM IN THE NEW TESTAMENT

WE WILL NOW EXAMINE how the writers of the New Testament interacted with their religio-social context. Given the above information regarding how the process of *ascension, vision,* and *transformation* was often understood in the Judeo-Hellenic context in the first century, how do these writings portray the response as evaluated in light of Walls' *indigenous* principle and *pilgrim* principle. To what extent did the writers utilize the language and thought forms of this mystical framework. How did it shape their message, and how did their message speak back into this context prophetically and critically?

In this chapter, we will seek to provide a response to these questions, as we examine a brief overview of how the Scriptures actually respond to *ascension, vision* and *transformation* mysticism. we will examine how an understanding was strengthened which moved more clearly away from an earlier, shamanistic framework towards a more genuinely mystical framework centered on the life, death and resurrection of Jesus, and the empowering grace and presence of the Holy Spirit. In this brief overview, we will focus on several passages in John's Gospel, in the writings of Paul, in Second Peter, and in Revelation. In the following chapter, we will briefly look at how particularly one Syrian monk, Macarius-Symeon, interacted with vision and ascension mysticism in general, and particularly the *Merkavah* tradition. In each of these cases, it can be demonstrated that the solution is nearly always Christological, re-framing the issue at hand by placing Jesus at the center as the Incarnate, crucified and risen Savior of humankind.

THE GOSPEL OF JOHN

In John's Gospel, we observe several passages which can be understood as interacting with ascension and vision mysticism. These passages interact with the religio-historical context and the opposing view as represented in our point of discourse regarding salvation critically *within* the context.

The first passage which we will examine, John 14:3–28, is an important part of Jesus' conversation with his disciples centered around the word *hodos*, "the way."[1] DeConick here cites the understanding of Rudolph Bultmann concerning the meaning of *hodos*, that "when the soul separates from the body, it journeys to the sacred realm often guided by a superior being."[2] She presents examples representing this in the early Judeo-Christian *Odes of Solomon*, Philo of Alexandria, and in the *Corpus Hermetica*.[3] Yet here, Jesus is telling his disciples that, rather than "the way" being a technique of ascension or some theurgical or shamanistic practice, he is himself the embodiment of the way; it is through him, and *only* through him, that the Father can be reached.[4] Alternatively, Keener suggests that

> A cupbearer or some other high official could control access to a king's presence, but out of affection the king might waive this obstacle for his young son or grandson. In turn, this child might receive whatever gifts he requested for his friends (cf. 14:13–14).

---

1. DeConick, *Voices*, 69–73.

2. Bültmann, *Gospel of John*, 630; quoted in DeConick, *Voices*, 69.

3. DeConick, *Voices*, 69–72; but as has been noted by Charlesworth, the *Odes of Solomon* really have the closest connections with the theology and even words of John's Gospel.

4. DeConick, *Voices*, 73. See also Keener, *Gospel of John*, 2:940, where he acknowledges this viewpoint, though Keener examines other meanings for "way" in this text. It seems to me that Kanagaraj also makes a convincing case here for interaction with ascension mysticism. See Kanagaraj, '*Mysticism*', 209. That having been noted, however, Keener's presentation of an alternative idea of what this can mean in terms of mediation and access is worth repeating here:

The idea here includes access (though it involves more, namely, remaining in his presence, 14:23), but also the access becomes direct in Jesus, no longer mediated through him at one remove (14:17; 16:26–27).[5]

While John's use of "the way" in this passage may indicate a co-opting of sorts of the language of ascension by Jesus, there is another important point to underline here: When Jesus refers to himself as "the way," "the truth" and "the life," aside from using the language of ascension traditions, he is also referring to himself by names which would be understood as attributes of God.[6] The same could be said for most of the "I am" statements in John; Jesus is stating that he has God's prerogatives. This connects to and challenges the *Merkavah* accounts. The *Merkavah* accounts do include elements of glorified humans who have been made into angels, most famously Enoch's transformation into the angel Metatron, who is "called by the name of [his] Creator" (3 Enoch 14:1).[7] Nonetheless, as Bauckham has pointed out, other figures in *Merkavah* literature, even those who are given to be enthroned, such as Moses in the account of Ezekiel the Tragedian as well as Enoch-Metatron, do not, as does Jesus, receive the worship of all creation, including angelic worship.[8]

The above elements, *especially* the worship given to and received by Jesus, point to Jesus as *Logos* being not merely the image of God, but being within God's very essence. As has been noted earlier, Philo referred to the *Logos* using words which seem to imply something of a borderline idea of deity, a *demiurge*, who is given the run of the universe, given God's utter transcendence as understood by both Philo and the Middle Platonic context in which he wrote.[9] As will be seen below regarding Phil 2:6–11, but is also evident in John and Revelation, the understanding of the Suffering Servant passages in Isaiah as interpreted in the New Testament

---

5. Keener, *Gospel of John*, 2.940.

6. See Grillmeier, *Christ in Christian Tradition*, 26–27; though see also Keener, *The Gospel of John*, 2.943.

7. Odeberg, , tr., *3 Enoch*, 40, though we hasten to add here that the account in *3 Enoch*, or *Sefer Hekhalōt* is fairly late, and the only one of the Enoch accounts to present him as transformed into Metatron. See Gruenwald, *Apocalyptic and Merkavah*, 197–200, incl. 197 n. 11.

8. Bauckham, *Jesus and the God of Israel*, 166–69; 171–72; 178–81.

9. There has been some speculation that even Jesus' fairly radical statements in John 8:56–58 may have connections with Philo's interpretation of Abraham's vision of the *Logos*; see also Urban and Henry, "Before Abraham was, I Am."

presents a direct challenge to the idea found in Philo that the revelation of the divine *Logos* is merely a stepping stone of sorts en route to a more abstract understanding of God. Recall how Philo noted in *On Dreams* that a presentation of God communicating in a human-like or angelic form is actually meant to aid the unenlightened *hoi polloi* to understand something, at least, about God. Citing texts such as John 12:23 and John 13:31–32, Bauckham demonstrates that this not merely reveal God's love for us in his sacrifice. Far from being some sort of lower stepping-stone en route to higher and more abstract enlightenment, God is revealed for who God truly is in the crucifixion itself.[10] In a passage of soaring beauty, Bauckham asserts that:

> Jesus and his story are intrinsic to the divine identity. The history of Jesus, his humiliation and his exaltation, is the unique act of God's self-giving, in which he demonstrates his deity to the world by accomplishing salvation for the world. In the words of the Johannine Prologue, through Jesus Christ, grace and truth *happened*—the divine self-giving occurred in full reality—and in this way the glory of the God whom no one has ever seen was revealed (John 1:14–18). In this act of self-giving God is most truly himself and defines himself for the world.[11]

Moreover, Jesus is making clear that the "way of ascent," that is, to the Father and into the throne room of God himself, is not, and indeed, cannot, be through self-effort or self-knowledge: It is only through entering into a relationship of faith in Jesus. Having in effect earlier attacked the ascension enterprise in John 3:13 ("No one has ascended to heaven except he who descended from heaven, the Son of Man"),[12] here he comforts his disciples by informing them that, while they cannot follow him in their own strength (13:36b), they shall later join him, indeed, "rooms" will be prepared for them in Jesus' "Father's house" (14:2–3). Thus, the hope of the *Hekhalōt*, of not merely visiting, but *abiding* with God, is understood as fulfilled in Jesus.[13] Moreover, James Charlesworth

---

10. Bauckham, *Jesus and the God of Israel*, 41–51. James L. Price recognized this as well, writing that in "his whole life, in his rejection, suffering and death, Jesus manifests the divine power and glory." (Price, "Light from Qumran," 31).

11. Bauckham, *Jesus and the God of Israel*, 51.

12. See Keener, *Gospel of John*, 1:168, 206, 563, as well as DeConick, *Voices*, 34–40 and Kanagaraj, 'Mysticism', 195–201.

13. DeConick, *Voices*, 124. Raymond E. Brown also ties this into the Hebrew Scriptures, noting, "In Deut 1.33 God says that He will go before Israel in *the way* to choose

has also noted that when Jesus describes himself as the "truth" in 14:6, not only is truth "personified as the Saviour," but, citing the statement in the *Odes of Solomon* that the truth "became for me a haven of salvation" (38:3),[14] Charlesworth notes that this may refer as well to the eternal dwelling-place.

Another interesting interaction with regard to the element of *transformation* is found with Jesus' famous statement to Nicodemus in the same passage, "Unless a man is born again, he cannot see the kingdom of God" (3:3). There is a parallel here with a statement in the *Hekhalōt Rabbati*, in what is referred to as the *Sar-Torah* area of this writing: In this passage, Rabbi Yishma'el is grieving at his inability to recall what he has been studying of Torah. He is instructed in the use of one of the theurgic prayers by Rabbi Nehunya ben Ha-Qanah, and then notes that "he felt himself as if born anew and 'everyday it seemed to me as if I was standing before the Throne of the Glory.'"[15] Gruenwald, who quotes this, suggests that this theurgic practice is seen as a *replacement* of sorts for the ascent. While it was noted in the previous chapter that the language of spiritual rebirth was found in the Hermetic tradition, Keener notes a number of Rabbinic sources in which this language was found, especially with regard to proselytes to Judaism.[16]

In connection with the context of ascension and vision mysticism, it is with this in mind that we need to examine the next several passages. If a key goal of vision mysticism is a vision of the glorified figure enthroned in the highest heaven, then in the following phrases, Jesus can be understood as pointing to himself as the legitimate fulfillment of this desire. He says in 14:7-11,

> If you really know me, you will know my Father as well. From now on, you do know him and have seen him." Philip said, "Lord, show us the Father and that will be enough for us." Jesus answered: "Don't you know me, Philip, even after I have been among you such a long time? Anyone who has seen me has seen the Father. How can you say, 'Show us the Father'? Don't you

---

for them a *place*; Deut 1:29 reads, 'Do not be in dread or afraid of them'—a command not unlike Jesus' 'Do not let your hearts be troubled'" (Brown, *Gospel According to John*, 2.625).

14. See Charlesworth, *Earliest Christian Hymnbook*, 109, as well as Charlesworth, *Critical Reflections on the Odes of Solomon*, 219.

15. Gruenwald, *Apocalyptic and Merkavah*, 179-80.

16. Keener, *Gospel of John*, 1:542-44.

believe that I am in the Father, and that the Father is in me? The words I say to you I do not speak on my own authority. Rather, it is the Father, living in me, who is doing his work. Believe me when I say that I am in the Father and the Father is in me; or at least believe on the evidence of the works themselves."

To see Jesus is to see the Father; this carries with it the idea of Jesus being related to the *kāvōd*, the glorious image of God, the view of which was understood to be the splendor[17] of the *Merkavah* vision.[18] Thus it is that much more startling when Jesus is actually using for himself variations of the word translated "glory." In the Greek New Testament, this word is *doxa*—the word used in the LXX to translate *kāvōd*. In the words of Alexander Golitzin, "*kāvōd* and its Greek equivalent are, put simply, the biblical terms of choice for theophany."[19] The use of this language seems to culminate in John 17:5, where Jesus prays, "And now, Father, glorify me in your presence with the *glory I had with you before the world began.*"[20] This emphasis is found in Jesus' words on not only his glorification, but in combination with his pre-existence.[21] Moreover, this ontological unity which Jesus has with the Father, manifesting his glory, is the basis on which the very community of God is established. James L. Price writes that

> It is only because Jesus and God are one, that Jesus' words and work are constitutive of the eschatological community. The unity that God wills for the disciples of Jesus is therefore grounded upon the unity of God the Father and his only Son, a unity sustained in love.[22]

As we noted in the previous chapter, the pattern of ancient mysticism was one of *ascension, vision* and *transformation,* with the latter of these often, in the classic sources, including empowerment to perform works of power. This also is addressed in the subsequent section of John

---

17. Or "presence."

18. Keener (*Gospel of John*, 2.944–945) sees a request for a theophany in Philip's question.

19. Golitzin, "Christianity as Transfiguration," 138. See also the Greek text of 1 Enoch 14:20, where the one who Enoch observes seated upon the heavenly throne is described as "The Great Glory" (*he doxa megale*) (Gruenwald, *Apocalyptic and Merkavah*, 35).

20. Emphasis mine.

21. DeConick, *Voices*, 111–17.

22. Price, "Qumran and Johannine Theology," 37.

14, where having already gone through parallels to ascension and vision, Jesus tells his disciples,

> Truly, truly, I say to you, whoever believes in me will also do the works that I do; and greater works than these will he do, because I am going to the Father. Whatever you ask in my name, this I will do, that the Father may be glorified in the Son. If you ask me anything in my name, I will do it. (John 14:12–14)

This is essentially the very *goal* of ancient Jewish mysticism (and often of shamanism generally): to be enabled to do works of power, by acquisition of knowledge of the secret, powerful name of God.[23] Here Jesus makes it clear that it will be *his* name in which the disciples are thus empowered, though Brown also alludes to the idea here that Jesus' "in my name" could be another way of saying, "in union with me."[24] This stands as a contrast to the more shamanistic ideas of developing one's own power, and a focus on the power itself rather than on relationship. Keener insists that "magical use [of Jesus' name] is hardly in view here;" we wonder, however, if this may be in part a *response* to such practices (as we have observed is the case with other elements in this chapter). Note that along with *power* we find the idea of loving *relationship*, an element which was absent from traditional mysticism in this period. It may be helpful to cite the example of Paul vis-à-vis the "sons of Sceva" in Acts 19:11–20; Paul was enabled to do "extraordinary miracles," not because he had mastered the use of Jesus' name as a power word of some kind, but because of his relationship with God in Christ. The attempt by the "sons of Sceva" to use Jesus' name as a power word backfires spectacularly in this passage, and the narrative perhaps is meant to serve as a warning against such attempts.

Another area of contrast demonstrated between John's Gospel and the earliest Jewish mysticism is with regard to the degree of connection enjoyed by the adherent with the enthroned *glory* of God. In contrast with Gershom Scholem's earlier quote concerning the lack of love, and indeed, of *relationship* beyond one merely of power in the early *Merkavah* tradition,[25] here we observe both relationship and power in the love which Jesus proclaims for his disciples in John 13:34–35. This is all the more significant for its having quickly followed a statement of

---

23. See Keener, *Gospel of John*, 947–48.
24. Brown, *Gospel According to John*, 2.622.
25. Scholem, *Major Trends*, 55.

glorification, of *doxa*. The very majesty which seems to make the Almighty that much more distant in the early *Merkavah* tradition actually leads *into* a statement of love for, as well as among, the disciples.[26] This is what A. H. Mathias Zahniser calls an understanding of God as the "intimate ultimate."[27]

This becomes even clearer as we examine the subsequent section, in which the themes of love and obedience predominate within the context of the promise of the Holy Spirit's indwelling in the believers, and in the believing community. In verses 15, 21 and 23, Jesus repeats that love for him will express itself in obedience to him, and that this obedience (and thus loyalty to him) is rewarded by a greater level of intimacy with God in him and his Spirit. Jesus promises that the Holy Spirit will live within the believers (14:17), that Jesus will "manifest himself" to them (14:21), and that he and the Father will "come to him and make our home with him" (14:23). Gregory the Great (6th century) captured something of the wonder of this in his comments on this passage, when he wrote,

> Consider, dearly beloved, how great this solemnity is that commemorates the coming of God as a guest in our hearts. If some rich and powerful friend were to enter your home, you would quickly clean the entire house for fear of offending your friend's eyes when he entered. Let anyone who is preparing his inner house for God cleanse away the dirt of his evil deeds. . .[28]

This brings in an important question, however: On the one hand, it can appear that we are to obey Jesus' commands in order to grow in intimacy with God and in the depth of his presence. On the other hand, apart from union with him, we "can do nothing" (John 15:5). How does this empowered obedience and union with God in Christ work? Keener responds:

> Does this imply that for John the Spirit can be earned?. . .Clearly for John the Spirit is not simply merited; apart from Jesus' presence, the disciples can do nothing (15:5), and the Spirit is received through faith (7:39). At the same time, the Spirit comes only to the disciples, to those committed to Jesus (14:17); those

---

26. Kanagaraj, '*Mysticism*', 26.
27. Zahniser, *Symbol and Ceremony*, 10.
28. Gregory the Great, *Forty Gospel Homilies*, 237.

who obey (14:15) receive greater power for obedience (14:16–17), moving in a cycle of ever deeper spiritual maturation.[29]

The picture, implied in the quote from Gregory, is like that of the relationship between a peasant and a king. In 14:2–3, Jesus is like a king who promises a peasant that he will bring him to live in his palace, a hope which brings joy, but which remains in the future. Later, however, the same king (Jesus) informs the peasant that he will come and stay in the peasant's house—an honor indeed! Empowered by the love expressed by the king, the peasant seeks to ensure that his house is in condition for a visit by the king himself.

In contrast, then, with the ascension and vision mysticism which seem to feature a striving for purity in order to achieve the vision of God, Jesus offers not only grace and mercy to those who believe in him, becoming his disciples, but also *empowers* those who have been joined to him to fulfill his commands. Thus, even when the Jesus as the *kāvōd* departs and is no longer physically *seen*, the spiritual presence of the *kāvōd* is nonetheless with his followers, empowering and guiding us. Indeed, Jey Kanagaraj quotes T. L. Brodie, who notes that the "language of mutual seeing" in the Paraclete passages in John 14:15–26 and 16:5–15 develops from a "language of mutual abiding" in John 15:4–10.[30] Kanagaraj continues, observing that "unless the Spirit first confronts and guides the disciples, one cannot see Jesus, that is, one cannot have 'an inner sense of the human face of God.'"[31] Again, the vision of the *kāvōd*, which had become available to the believers during Jesus' earthly lifetime, continues to be available to those who are joined by faith to Jesus.

Finally, Christopher Rowland noted Peter's declaration that Jesus was a "righteous angel" in Logion 13 of *Thomas*, and wonders if Peter's confession of Jesus as "the holy one of God" is something of an answering statement to this.[32] In the *Gospel of Thomas*, this is followed up with the

---

29. Keener, *Gospel of John*, 2.952.

30. Brodie, *Gospel According to John*, 494; quoted in Kanagaraj, 'Mysticism', 267.

31. Kanagaraj, 'Mysticism', 267.

32. Rowland, *Open Heaven*, 501 n. 45. Importantly, however, most modern scholars would challenge the idea that *Thomas* is a first century work to which *John* could have been responding (see for example Perrin, *Other Gospel*, 48–49, as well as 114 n. 26, where Perrin indicates that it is *Thomas* which is attempting to respond polemically to the Gospel of John, rather than vice-versa). We do think, however, that these ideas likely predated *Thomas*, and relate to some of the anthropocentric trends which we have observed in some streams of early Jewish mysticism.

disciple Thomas being taken aside and told three secrets by Jesus, and Thomas being told by Jesus that if he repeated them, Thomas "will pick up stones and throw them at me; a fire will come out of the stones and burn you up."[33] Contrast this with the setting of Peter's statement in the John passage. Jesus has just spoken out a deep mystery regarding "eating his flesh and drinking his blood" (6:43–59), and as a result has been deserted by a number of those who had been following him. In the midst of his discourse, moreover, he has included statements challenging vision mysticism ("not that anyone has seen the Father except he who is from God; he has seen the Father," 6:46) as well as ascension mysticism:

> Do you take offense at this? Then what if you were to see the Son of Man ascending to where he was before? It is the Spirit who gives life; the flesh is no help at all. The words that I have spoken to you are spirit and life. (6:61–63)

In view of the above analysis, John's Gospel actually seems to point towards Jesus *meeting* the very desires which Alan Segal enumerated as central to early Jewish mysticism. Jesus is presented as the solution to the questions and desires represented by vision and ascension mysticism, as well as a corrective to what the author of John would have recognized as misperceptions concerning the means of entering into empowering as well as loving relationship with the Almighty. This also perhaps brings clarity to the ambiguity concerning the nature of the *Logos* in Philo's writings, as well as the focus concerning the interaction of the *Logos* with the phenomenal world. This is not to suggest that John is responding *directly* to Philo, but rather both are drawing from a common source of speculation present in their age.[34] We think it is also fair to suggest that John is not merely challenging, but is also clarifying this idea of the *Logos* as well as building on and past it. While Philo acknowledges that the *Logos* is God's means of interacting with the created world, the author of John goes further and presents the *Logos* as having *materially* entered the phenomenal world in order to bring redemption to it.[35] This is precisely where John's Gospel maintains the tension between the *indigenous* principle and the *pilgrim* principle: Having engaged deeply with the Judeo-Hellenic context, the writer of John can then express what needs to be addressed critically and prophetically. In effect, part of the answer which

---

33. Lambdin, *Gospel of Thomas*, 128.
34. Kanagaraj, 'Mysticism', 299.
35. Ibid.

John's Gospel provides to the practice of attempted shamanistic *ascension* to emphasize that the only true means of *ascent* is through union with the Jesus, the one who *descended*.

REVELATION

Although there has been so very much to mine from John's Gospel, we must also examine similar themes in the apocalyptic book of Revelation, as well as in just two of the many examples of such interaction with ascension and vision mysticism in other parts of the New Testament.

Revelation lends itself to apocalyptic speculation, and there are a number of connection points which can be described between Revelation and the *Merkavah* writings. We will focus in particular on the throne room/Temple visions in chapters 4 and 5, moving strikingly into chapter 7 as well. The parallels between this passage in Revelation and Ezekiel's vision, especially the version of it in the Targum of Ezekiel, are particularly strong. David Halperin sees both texts (Revelation and the Ezekiel Targum) as having emerged from what he refers to as a "*merkabah* exegesis;"[36] or the "hymnic tradition, whose development we can now begin to trace to the synagogue."[37]

The writer of Revelation begins the chapter with an exclamation that he saw a "door standing open in heaven" (4:1a). Gruenwald sees a parallel here with the description in Ezek 1:1 that "the heavens were opened."[38] When a heavenly voice (what the Jewish tradition refers to as a *bat qōl*) invites him to "Come up here" (4:1b), the writer suddenly finds himself "in the Spirit" (4:2), before the heavenly throne, and begins to describe the scene in the throne room before him. It is important to note

---

36. Halperin, *Faces of the Chariot*, 37; see also Afzal, "Wheels of Time," 1.469.

37. Halperin, *Faces of the Chariot*, 87. The connections between Revelation and the Targum of Ezekiel are more than this, as Samson H. Levey has pointed out in the introduction to his translation of the Ezekiel Targum. He notes that Ezek 48:35b in the Targum reads, "And the name of the city shall be designated from the day that he makes his Shekinah rest upon it, 'The Lord is there'" (Levey, *Targum of Ezekiel*, 6).

38. Gruenwald, *Apocalyptic and Merkavah*, 63; see also Kanagaraj, 145, who points to parallels with this language to *Testament of Levi* 5:1 and *Ascension of Isaiah* 6:6 and the initiation of the "first stage of his entry into heaven;" and Aune, *Revelation*, 1.270, where he connects this with a parallel in the *Testament of Abraham* 10:12, "and immediately a voice came from heaven," and where Aune later observes (importantly, for our discussion) that "it is *God* who opens the heavenly door for John." He also sees a close parallel on this with 1 Enoch 14:14b–15, "I saw in my vision, and behold another door was opened before me" (Aune, *Revelation*, 1.280).

here that the writer doesn't explain the means by which the writer arrived in the throne room to be granted his heavenly vision;[39] his sudden shift to heaven seems to have been more on God's initiative than based on anything the seer did shamanistically.

I see possible parallels here with the *Shirot 'Olah HaShabbat* (4Q 405) in a manner which fits in here with our analysis. It has been suggested that Paul's rebuke of those who insist on "asceticism and worship of angels, going on in detail about visions, puffed up without reason by his sensuous mind" (Col 2:18) are corrected not only because of their failure to hold "fast to the Head," but because of their pride and elitism in regard to who is sufficiently "pure" to worship with the angels.[40] Another possibility arises if the underlying Greek is understood to be objective rather than subjective genitive, possibly engaged in a syncretistic worshiping of (rather than merely with) angels.[41] Indeed, Francis notes that a primary element of worshiping *with* the angels could very well have slipped into a secondary, derivative worship directed *to* the angels.[42] On the other hand, but still relevant for our analysis here, Crispin Fletcher-Louis has suggested that what is at issue in the *Shirot* itself is neither worship directed at angels nor with angels. Rather, he posits the songs as a form of "ritualized ascent" in the sense of a liturgy in which the participants are divinized or of "angelomorphic transformation."[43] Alan Segal had suggested that the Qumran mystics "must have achieved this unity through

---

39. Gruenwald, *Apocalyptic and Merkavah*, 64.

40. Variations of this view are held or alluded to in Francis, "Humility and Angelic Worship," 176–81; Rowland, "Apocalyptic Visions," 74–78; Evans, "Colossian Mystics," 96–205, and the case laid out by Sappington in *Revelation and Redemption at Colossae*, 19–22, 150–228. Modern analyses of all views invariably trace the discussion to Lightfoot, *Letters to the Colossians and to Philemon*, 73–113, and Lightfoot's analysis of specifically Essene influence from 115–179.

41. Clinton E. Arnold presents a fairly strong argument for an objective reading indicating worship *of* angels in *The Colossian Syncretism*, 96–98; following the earlier stance of Bruce, *Epistles to the Colossians, to Philemon, and to the Ephesians*, 17–26, 117–122. Both writers suggest connections with the later developments of *Merkavah*. A monograph by Richard E. DeMaris has taken a similar stance, though suggests more Hellenic as well as Jewish influence in this context; see his *Colossian Controversy*, 58–97.

42. Francis, "Humility and Angelic Worship," 179.

43. Fletcher-Louis, "Heavenly Ascent or Incarnational Presence?," 1.367–99.

some rite of translation and transmutation,"[44] and asks as well whether Wisdom of Solomon 5:5[45] may also have connections with this tradition.[46]

Vis-à-vis this section of Revelation, however, the crucial point remains that of elitism. Thus Rowland's recognition that Paul is "warning the Colossians about those who would attempt to distinguish between believers, accepting some and disqualifying others"[47] is central to part of what we see happening in this section of Revelation. Part of it involves the question of who can ascend to the heavens and view the divine worship and receive and reveal the mystery.

Halperin sees the whole scene in these two chapters as taking place in the heavenly Temple, concluding that the twenty-four elders in chapter 4 represent "the twenty-four courses of priests and Temple singers" mentioned in 1 Chr 24–25.[48] William H. Brownlee, by contrast, sees the twenty-four elders as a kind of "heavenly Sanhedrin."[49] It is interesting that the elders are depicted as being seated upon twenty-four thrones (Rev 4:4); while neither these elders nor their thrones appear in the Ezekiel 1 vision which parallels Rev. 4, we find it interesting that the *Shirot 'Olah HaShabbat* in 4Q405 describe *Merkavot Kəvodo*, or "glorious thrones."[50] The later *Ma'aseh Merkavah* also speaks of "thousands upon thousands of heavenly chariots in each of the heavenly palaces which are said to give praise to God."[51] As was noted earlier, this element of multiple *Merkavōt* is repeated in the later *Ma'aseh Merkavah*, with thousands of flaming *Merkavōt* singing hymns of praise at each *hekhal*.[52] Ford sees a connection here (and in chapter 5; see below) with the passage in Exod 24:9–11, describing Moses, Aaron and his sons, and the seventy elders of Israel ascending Sinai and experiencing a vision of God.[53] There is

44. Segal, "Risen Christ," 308.

45. Wisdom of Solomon 5:5 reads, "Why have they been numbered among the children of God? And why is their lot among the saints?" (NRSV).

46. Segal, "Risen Christ," 308.

47. Rowland, "Apocalyptic Visions," 74.

48. Ibid., 89.

49. Brownlee, *Ezekiel 1–19*, 17.

50 Newsom, *Songs of the Sabbath Sacrifice*, 92–95.

51. Gruenwald *Apocalyptic and Merkavah*, 184.

52. In addition to what was cited in the previous chapter, see also Swartz, *Mystical Prayer*, 21.

53. Ford, *Revelation*, 76; Aune also notices the connection with Exod 24:9–11, but also recognizes a similar connection with Isa 24:23 (Aune, *Revelation*, 1.287–288).

also a possible connection between the elders and a passage in *Hekhalōt Rabbati*; Gruenwald takes note of a passage in *Hekhalōt Rabbati* 11 in which the Angel of the Countenance "crowns each of the living creatures" [the *hayyōt*] with multiple thousands of crowns; in the following chapter, when "the Living Creatures see that God is, so-to-speak, angry with the People of Israel, they untie their 'crowns' and beat them upon the ground asking forgiveness for the People of Israel."[54] Aune cites the first century *Apocalypse of Zephaniah* A, as quoted in Clement of Alexandria's *Stromata* 5.11.77, in which the scene described resembles that here in Rev 4.[55] The *Zephaniah* fragment reads,

> And a spirit took me and brought me up into the fifth heaven. And I saw angels who are called "lords," and the diadem was set upon them in the Holy Spirit, and the throne of each of them was sevenfold more brilliant than the light of the rising sun. And they were dwelling in the temples of salvation and singing hymns to the ineffable most high God.[56]

Although there are certainly differences here (e.g., the "lords" are described as angels, the fifth heaven), it seems that the vision described in Rev 4 fits in clearly with the ancient Jewish milieu. Indeed, other theories include the aforementioned correspondence to the twenty-four orders of priests,[57] the "twelve tribes of Israel plus the Twelve Apostles, together constituting the new people of God,"[58] and curiously, with the traditional number of Jewish prophets who authored the books of the Hebrew Scriptures.[59]

---

54. Gruenwald, *Apocalyptic and Merkavah*, 160; Bauckham describes this act by the "elders" as acknowledgement that "their authority is wholly derivative from God's. He alone is to be worshiped as the source of all power and authority" See Bauckham, *Book of Revelation*, 34. Aune cites the *Mekhilta de Rabbi Ishmael* 3:81 as describing a heavenly *bêt din šel šāmayyim* corresponding to the earthly *bêt din*, or "court of judgment" (Aune, *Revelation*, 1.290).

55. Aune, *Revelation*, 1.290.

56. Wintermute, "Apocalypse of Zephaniah," 508.

57. See above, 71.

58. Aune, *Revelation*, 1.314.

59. Aune (*Revelation*, 1.291–292) cites Talmud tractate *Baba Batra* 14b–15a on this point, as well as the commentary of Victorinus on Rev 4:3, which takes this view. See Neusner, *Baba Batra*, 55–56, and Victorinus, "Commentary on the Apocalypse of the Blessed John," 348.

It is in chapter 5 that we see the first of two decisive shifts: The "Slaughtered Lamb" appears, bearing the same "sevenfold Spirit of God"[60] that was represented before the throne in the previous chapter (4:5). He is declared "worthy" to open the sealed scroll (5:5, 7), and as the Lamb receives the scroll, the worship which has been offered before the throne of God is now offered to the Lamb, with language which echoes the praises offered to the enthroned God in the previous chapter (4:11), the Lamb is now praised for having redeemed humankind with his own sacrificial death (5:9-10),[61] and the song of praise expanding beyond the *hayyōt* and the elders to the hosts of heaven (5:11-12) and the whole of creation (5:13) before it returns to that of the *hayyōt* and the elders as the chapter concludes (5:14).[62] It is crucial to point out that here the slaughtered Lamb, representing Jesus, clearly has that which is only the prerogative of God: the Lamb is "in the midst of the throne" (5:6), and receives the worship of the angels as well as the *hayyōt*, related to the creatures who were found in Ezekiel's original vision[63] (as well as to those in Isa 6:2) and the elders, and "ten thousand times ten thousand" angels, with eventually all creation thus worshiping the Lamb in ever-widening circles (5:11-14).[64] As Bauckham notes, however, the writer of Revelation is careful to demonstrate that the worship of the Lamb in 5:8-12 leads into worship of God and the Lamb (5:13); the Lamb is *included within* the monotheistic worship of the one God.[65] Bauckham reinforces this principle in pointing out how elsewhere in Revelation the writer uses a singular verb (in

---

60. Kanagaraj ('*Mysticism*', 147) notes that the "seven eyes of Christ, being reminiscent of the seven eyes of Yahweh which run through the whole earth (Zech. 4:10), indicate that he shares the omniscience as well as the omnipotence of God." See also Charles, *Revelation of St. John*, 1.142-43. Aune also notes the fairly obvious comparison with the seven-branched *menorah* (Aune, *Revelation*, 1.295).

61. Indeed, as Sophie Laws points out, this ransom-death and lamb imagery recalls connections with the Passover event in Exodus. She cites not only Exod 12:46 and the related John 19:6, but also John the Baptist's exclamation in John 1:29, 36. She adds Paul's words in 1 Cor 5:7, and 1 Pet 1:19. See Laws, *In the Light of the Lamb*, 29.

62. Noteworthy in 4:6 and 4:8 is mention of the *hayyōt*'s being "full of eyes" as in Ezek 1:18 and 10:12; this idea of beings (including *ophanim*, or the heavenly creatures represented by the wheels in Ezek 1:15-18) has been subject to many interpretations (see Aune, *Revelation*, 1.297-98). For our purposes, we find the most intriguing to be the idea expressed in Macarius-Symeon of these representing "light" and the glory of God in Christ in Homily 1.2 (Macarius, *Homilies*, 2). See more on this in chapter 3.

63. Kanagaraj, '*Mysticism*', 146.

64. Bauckham, *Revelation*, 33-34, 41, 60-61.

65. Ibid., 60-62.

11:15) and singular pronouns (in 22:3–4 and 6:17) to describe God and Christ together.[66] Interestingly, Aune recognizes here a parallel with *Odes of Solomon* 23, which seems to reflect elements found both here as well as in some of the *Merkavah* texts noted in the previous chapter, though Aune denies any *direct* connection between these two passages.[67]

Bauckham has noted strong parallels between Rev 5 in particular and the *kenosis* hymn in Paul's letter to the Philippians in 2:9–11, emphasizing especially the worship received by the *crucified* Lamb, as well as the language used in this worship (sourced, perhaps, from Isa 45:23).[68] Moreover, Brownlee points out the similarities between the revelatory scroll as described in Ezek 2:9–10, with writing on the front and back, and that in Rev 5:1. The difference, of course, is that in the latter, the scroll is sealed, but the seals can be opened (and the scroll's contents revealed) only by Christ, the Lamb of God as depicted in the rest of this chapter. Later on, in 19:13, he is referred to as the Word of God (who can reveal the fullness of the word given?), and this, too, is connected with the sacrificial blood into which his robe has been dipped.[69]

Aune points out here both connections with the *Christus Victor* motif,[70] of Christ's victory through his death and resurrection, and this very much demonstrates in effect the combining of his declaration as the "Lion of the tribe of Judah" and the as well as the fact that "the Aramaic term *zĕkā'* means *both* 'to conquer' and 'to be worthy.'"[71] Various scholars have attempted to demonstrate the lamb as being a metaphor for leadership, or as a metaphor of sacrifice.[72] It seems to me however, that *both* elements are central to an understanding of the character and nature of

---

66. Ibid.

67. Aune, *Revelation*, 1.329–30, and Charlesworth, *Earliest Christian Hymnbook*, 67–70.

68. Bauckham, *Jesus and the God of Israel*, 198. Indeed, the *Isaiah Targum* reads for the previous verse, Isa 45:22, "Turn to my *Memra* [Word] and be saved, all those at the ends of the earth! For I am God, and there is no other" (Chilton, *The Isaiah Targum*, 91). See also Ronning, *The Jewish Targums and John's Logos Theology*, 247.

69. Brownlee, *Ezekiel 1–19*, 17.

70. Aune, *Revelation*, 1.349, citing Aulén, *Christus Victor*, 4. For a comprehensive view, see also Boyd, *God at War*, esp. 238–68.

71. Aune, *Revelation*, 1.349, citing Levy, *Wörterbuch über die Talmudim und Midraschim*, 1.534–35; Dalman, *Handwörterbuch*, 128; and Bauernfiend, "Nikao ktl," 4.943 n. 6. For more on possible Semitic influences and elements in the Greek text of Revelation, see Beale, *Revelation*, 103–5.

72. A survey of these is found in Aune, *Revelation* 1.368–73.

God's Messiah. Moreover, rather than being discrete, separate elements of his identity, we discover that they are *intertwined*. G. B. Caird made note of the paradox in the identity of God in Christ, the Lion of Judah, worshiped as the slaughtered Lamb. He describes what may have been the surprise of the Jewish author of Revelation:

> The Old Testament leads John to expect a Messiah who will be the Lion of Judah, but the facts of the gospel present him with a Lamb bearing the marks of slaughter (v.5–6). The Old Testament predicts the smashing of the nations with an iron bar, but the only weapon the Lamb wields is his own Cross and the martyrdom of his followers (ii.27, xxii.5, xix.15). The seven Spirits of God can be let loose into the world only as the eyes of the Lamb (i.4, iii.1, iv.5, v.6).[73]

This resonates with Bauckham's perspective, which is worth quoting at length with regard to the *kenosis* hymn in Phil 2:6–11. Similar to his observations regarding John's Gospel, this passage expresses the manner in which the crucifixion actually reveals something concerning the very nature of God, and seems reflected in Caird's observations, too. Here Bauckham insists that the Philippians passage

> amounts to a Christological statement of the identity of God. The exaltation of Christ to participation in the unique divine sovereignty shows him to be included in the unique divine identity. But, since the exalted Christ is first the humiliated Christ, since indeed it is *because* of his self-abnegation that he is exalted, his humiliation belongs to the identity of God as truly as his exaltation does. The identity of God—who God is—is revealed as much in self-abasement and service as it is in exaltation and rule.[74]

So far, what we have here is that, contrary to the philosophy confronted in Colossae by Paul, John is *lifted* to heaven (as opposed to shamanistically lifting himself), where he views the eternal worship in chapter 4. In chapter 5, John observes the dilemma that no one is worthy to open the scroll and reveal the mystery contained therein, and in the midst of his grief, observes the titanic shift in the heavens as the slaughtered Lamb enters and is included in the worship of the one on the

---

73. Caird, *Commentary on the Revelation*, 292–93; see also Gieschen, "The Lamb (Not the Man)," 227, and 430 n. 23.

74. Bauckham, *Jesus and the God of Israel*, 45.

throne. Why is he included? He is found "worthy" to open the scroll and reveal the mystery. Why is he found worthy? He is found worthy because he was slain, and with his bloody sacrifice, he

> ...ransomed people for God
> from every tribe and language and people and nation,
> and...made them a kingdom and priests to our God,
> and they shall reign on the earth. (5:9b-10)

Aune suggests that this depicts the *investiture* of the Lamb, as opposed to the enthronement or commissioning, defining "investiture" as "the act of establishing someone in office or the ratification of the office that someone already holds informally."[75] and that it is an "adaptation of Dan 7 and Ezek 1-2, and by analogy with the investiture features of other visions of the heavenly court, particularly 1 Kgs 22 and Isa 6."[76] Indeed, Aune sees especially the parallels between the language of universal dominion of the Son of Man in Dan 7:14 and 18 and of the Lamb in Rev 5:9b-10.[77] An important *difference* between these, however, is that this dominion is not merely that of the Lamb, but that those who follow him "from every tribe and language and people and nation" are made into "a kingdom and priests to our God" (language which Aune recognizes as reflecting Exod 19:6),[78] who shall "reign on the earth"—Jesus' investiture is thus understood to segue into the idea of his followers being granted authority because of their union with him, what Aune describes as "participation in the reign of God."[79] As we shall see below, this idea turns up as well in Eph 2:6.

Following the Lamb's opening of the seals in chapter 6, chapter 7 is focused on those from Israel (7:3-8) and the very multitude from "every nation, and all tribes, peoples and languages" (7:9) which the Lamb had "ransomed with his blood," innumerable in number, and worshiping "God, who sits on the throne" (7:10) as well as the "Lamb in the midst

---

75. Aune, *Revelation*, 1.336.
76. Ibid.
77. Ibid., 1.337.
78. Ibid.
79 Ibid., 1.362. There is a parallel in regard to this idea of participating in Christ's reign between 5:10 and the earlier 2:26-27 on the promise of authority, and 3:21, "The one who conquers, I will grant him to sit with me on my throne, as I also conquered and sat down with my Father on his throne" (both possibly alluding to Matt 19:28). Bauckham sees this statement in 3:21 as anticipatory of chapter 5 as a whole. See Bauckham, *The Climax of Prophecy*, 6, as well as Osborne, *Revelation*, 214.

of the throne" (7:17).⁸⁰ Important to this passage is the connection made with God's promise to Abraham of his descendents being "innumerable;"⁸¹ here this promise is regarded as fulfilled in his *ingrafted* as well as *natural* descendants.⁸² In a possible reification of John 1:14, as well as an allusion to Ezek 37:27, Rev 7:15b reads that "the one who sits on the throne will shelter them;" he will both shelter and protect, as well as live among the multitude of his people.⁸³ Within this is a possible allusion to the idea of Jesus as the *Shekinah*, God's glorious presence with the people of Israel in the desert, and connected with the desert tabernacle of God's very presence dwelling in the midst of his people.⁸⁴ Echoing his earlier-cited comments on the meaning of Jesus' incarnation in Philippians, Bauckham concludes that that when "the slaughtered Lamb is seen 'in the midst of' the divine throne in heaven (5:6; cf. 7:17), the meaning is that Christ's sacrificial death *belongs to the way God rules the world*."⁸⁵ Indeed, as Gieschen explains, the combination of Jesus depicted as "Glorified Man" and as the "Slaughtered Lamb" serves to unite two key aspects of an understanding of his identity for those who follow him. He notes that, "the glorified man scenes provide the reader/hearer with a Christology that depicts the risen Christ in continuity with previous theophanies of YHWH, while the exalted lamb scenes provide a Christology that accents Jesus' humanity, atoning sacrificial death, resurrection victory, and authoritative status as universal ruler."⁸⁶

In Rev 4–5 and 7, then, it can be noted that while the writer is certainly speaking in (and likely experiencing) the language of apocalyptic literature and mystical ascent to and vision of heaven such as seems to be described in the *Shirot 'Olah HaShabbat* and critically challenged by Col 2:18,⁸⁷ these passages address this milieu critically and Christologically as well. John's heavenly journey is God-initiated, and as noted above, he

---

80. See Bauckham, *Book of Revelation*, 77–78.
81. E.g., Gen 15:5, 17:4, 22:17. See Aune, *Revelation*, 2.466.
82. Cf. Rom 11:17–24.
83. Osborne, *Revelation*, 328–29.
84. Ibid.
85. Bauckham, *Book of Revelation*, 64; emphasis in the original.
86. Gieschen, "The Lamb (Not the Man)," 228.
87. See above 70–71. Indeed, in describing the context of the initial part of the heavenly ascent and throne-room vision, Bauckham notes that "there is nothing in chapter 4 which could not have been written by a non-Christian Jewish visionary" See Bauckham, *Book of Revelation*, 32.

observes and participates in the shift in which the Slaughtered Lamb receives the praise due to God, *including the praise of the angels who are so central to both the milieu of the* Shirot *and the likely opponents addressed in Col 2:18.* Moreover, the scene moves into the spectacle of the innumerable multitudes of the ransomed. In contrast with the elitism of the Colossian opponents, this multitude from every nation are worshiping God and his Lamb as "a kingdom and priests"—the very aspiration of the sectarians. This is then graciously fulfilled by God through the sacrificial death of the Lamb, which also demonstrates a central element of God's own character. Thus, we can observe that in Revelation, the writer is "indigenously" speaking the very language of ascension/vision/transformation mysticism, yet rather than following this down the shamanistic path in which it could often lead, the writer refocuses the language Christologically. He speaks prophetically of the Messiah who is the Lamb of God, and who ransoms not only the elite, but all of the nations.

IN THE PENTECOST ACCOUNT OF ACTS 2:1–4

In the account of the descent of the Holy Spirit in Acts 2, there are elements, particularly related to *fire*, which seem to reflect back on the context of *Merkavah* visions and the discussions related to them.

The main verse to which we refer in this passage concerns the visual phenomena which were described in the account of the Holy Spirit's descent:

> When the day of Pentecost arrived, they were all together in one place. And suddenly there came from heaven a sound like a mighty rushing wind, and it filled the entire house where they were sitting. And divided tongues as of fire appeared to them and rested on each one of them. And they were all filled with the Holy Spirit and began to speak in other tongues as the Spirit gave them utterance.

What were the "tongues of fire" which were seen resting upon each of the disciples? Gary Gilbert cites Exodus (the burning bush in 3:2, the pillar of fire in 14:24, and the fire on Mt. Sinai at the Lord's descent in 19:18) and Isaiah (literally referring to a *lashon esh*, tongue of fire, in 5:24), as well as the passage in 1 Enoch 14:8–25 cited in the previous chapter,[88] noting that tongues of fire as well as fire generally are symbolic of "divine presence."[89] Craig Keener suggests that this presence is one of "eschatological judgment," a "reminder of the fire to be unleashed in God's vengeance at the end of the age."[90] Blaine Charette likewise observes that "this remarkable phenomenon also points to the judgment that comes upon those within Israel who refuse to listen to what God is saying through this and the other eschatological events that are centered in Jesus."[91]

The above may well be part of what Luke is getting at, indeed, what God seeks to reveal in the Pentecost event in Acts 2, and in particular in the "tongues of fire" described in Acts 2:3. It seems to me, however, that Menzies makes the connections with ancient Jewish mysticism to understand what is happening here; he sees this as an "inverted Merkavah," asserting,

> A visionary does not take a trip to heaven in order to experience a taste of the divine glory. Instead, a bit of heaven comes down to earth. Whether upon the high priest, as in Three Tongues of Fire, or upon all who were in the house, as in Acts 2:2, the divine glory is received passively and yet is experienced directly, in a manner that is apparent to others. This is the primary significance of the tongues of fire.[92]

It seems to me that this connects as well with some of the descriptions of the heavenly realms, and even comports with the cryptic suggestion concerning the meaning of Ezekiel's *hashmal* quoted in the previous

---

88. See above, 31.

89. Gilbert, "Acts of the Apostles," 201. See also Menzies, "Pre-Lukan,"29–33, 55 n. 85, where the author lays out a case for the phrase "tongue of fire" being awkward in Greek, so much so that the LXX doesn't render this literally, thus implying that the term as used in Acts 2:3 is a semitism referring back to a Jewish source. He cites as well Isa 30:27–28, which reads that the Lord's "tongue is a consuming fire" (Menzies, "Pre-Lukan Occurances,"34). At the same time, Hellenic influence within the Jewish context at the time cannot be ignored either, thus Pieter W. van der Horst provides a list of Hellenic parallels to the presence of the divine being expressed in wind and fire, including fire alighting on the head in a list of Greek and Latin texts by Iamblichus, Homer, Euripides Cicero and others. Van der Horst, "Hellenistic Parallels," 49–50. See also DeConick, *Seek to See Him*, 111 n. 37, where the author makes note of the connection between fire in early Jewish ascension and vision mysticism and fire as a metaphor.

90. Keener, *The Spirit*, 193.

91. Charette, "'Tongues as of Fire,'" 174.

92. Menzies, "Pre-Lukan," 58.

chapter from *Hagigah* 2:1.[93] There it was suggested that *hashmal* can be understood as an acronym of *hayyōt esh mamelelot*. It also brings to mind the depiction in *Ma'aseh Merkavah* which has Akiva describing how each *hekhal* is populated by thousands of *Merkavot of fire* singing hymns of praise.[94] Indeed, Macarius-Symeon, the fourth-century Syrian whose writings interact with this context of early Jewish mysticism (and whose writings will be more closely examined in the following chapter), seems to combine the emphasis of judgment and of empowering presence:

> There is indeed a burning of the Spirit, which burns hearts into flame. The immaterial divine fire his the effect of enlightening souls and trying them, like unalloyed gold in the furnace, but of consuming iniquity, like thorns or stubble; for our God is a consuming fire,[95] taking vengeance on them that know Him not in flaming fire, and on them that obey not His gospel.[96] It was this fire that worked in the apostles, when they spoke with fiery tongues.[97]

One more element worth noting here as well is the interplay here between unity and individualism. On the one hand, Acts 2 begins with a statement of unity: "When the day of Pentecost arrived, they were all together in one place" (2:1), yet in a real sense, they are each still individuals. As the Holy Spirit's presence enters the picture, John D. Zizoulas explains that

> the individualization of human existence which results in division and separation is not transformed into existence in communion where the otherness of persons ("on each of them separately," Acts 2:3) is identical with communion within a body ... Christ's existence is applied to our historical existence not *in abstracto* or individualistically, but in and through a community. This community is formed from out of ordinary existence, through a radical conversion from individualism to personhood ...[98]

---

93. See above 53–55.
94. Swartz, *Mystical Prayer*, 74–75; also his translation at 231–32.
95. Heb 12:29
96. 2 Thess 1:8
97. *Homily* 25.9; Macarius, *Homilies*, 183
98. Zizoulas, *Being as Communion*, 112–13.

In this passage, then we can observe that once again, Luke is utilizing the language of ancient Jewish ascension-vision mysticism, but turning it on its head in what Menzies rightly refers to as an "inverted" *Merkavah*: rather than devotees ascending through spiritual exercises or rituals, the Holy Spirit *descends* (even as Jesus was depicted as having done in the Johannine writings examined above). They *see* the manifestation of God's presence in the "tongues of fire," and they are decisively *transformed* by their encounter with the Holy Spirit, not only inwardly, but in a manner as to bear witness to the very God who has empowered and transformed them. The *language* (and to an extent the goals) of the *Merkavah* are by and large preserved in a manner which is deeply *indigenous*, yet they are also addressed prophetically in line with the *pilgrim* principle: The initiative and power belong to God, for God's own purposes.[99]

2 PETER 1

One of the most crucial passages in the New Testament addressing Segal's element of *transformation* in the mystical process is 2 Pet 1:4. It is perhaps the most frequently cited passage in the early Christian writings concerning union with God, or *theosis,* in the Scriptures. It is the only writing known in antiquity (apart from other writings quoting this verse) which uses the phrase "partakers of the divine nature."[100] That said, it has been noted that there is some interaction going on here in 2 Peter with a context of Hellenic as well as apocalyptic Judaism, as well as with the Middle Platonic and Stoic context among the Greeks, and with which the Hellenic Jewish context had some fairly strong connections.[101] The question here, however, is with regard to the nature of 2 Peter's interaction with its context.

The first question which arises is with regard to the nature of this "partaking of the divine nature." Ernst Käsemann felt this statement was

---

99. While too late to have the same importance as the above-cited texts, there are some interesting parallels in the *Zohar* to the Acts 2 event. Wolfson, "Forms of Visionary Ascent, 209–35, speaks of the "gathering of mystics to expound the mysteries of Torah" on Pentecost as a "collective experience of union with the Presence" (Ibid., 213). In the *Zohar*, the *Shekinah*, the feminine aspect of God, the bride, unites with the Holy One on Pentecost. Speaking of those devout mystics who stayed awake through the night, it is said that they are "to be crowned by the *Shekinah* in the night and by the Holy One and the *Shekinah* during the wedding ceremony of the day" (Ibid., 213–14 n. 21).

100. Starr, "2 Peter 1:4," 88.

101. Ibid., 85–86.

an indication of Hellenic paganism having entered into the Christian faith early on, and is indeed concerned that what is here reflected is an anthropocentric rather than Christocentric idea of the gospel and union with God.[102] Käsemann was concerned that this passage in 2 Peter was evidence of a "relapse of Christianity into Hellenistic dualism,"[103] understanding this passage to refer to *apotheosis*, the Greco-Roman idea of "migration from humanity to deity,"[104] the kind of idea which referred to the "deification of emperors and heroes."[105] James Starr, however, challenges Käsemann's assertion. Starr demonstrates that, far from an uncritical syncretism with the Hellenic context, it is rather *confronting* the idea of *apotheosis*.

Both Starr and Stephen Finlan note that there is certainly *interaction* with the Hellenic context in 2 Peter. Finlan observes, for example, that 2 Pet 1:4 uses the same word for lust (or "earthly cravings"), *epithymia*, which is found in Plato to denote the "lowest level of a human being,"[106] and the word for "divine," *theios* is also a common term in the writings of Middle Platonism. The idea in Middle Platonism is that as one seeks to put away corruption and walk in virtue, imitating God, one works her way into deification.[107] Moreover, the list of virtues in 2 Pet 1:5–7 is reminiscent of the Stoic emphasis on the practice of virtue as a rational response to reason.[108] Finlan recognizes that the terms used in this passage are rare in the LXX, but common in Greek moralizing literature," yet significantly, the list begins with "faith" and ends with "love," distinctly Christian virtues.[109]

Henry Fischel, commenting on the use of Greco-Roman rhetoric in the Tannaitic period, referred to this literary device as *sorites* (or *climax* or *graditio*), which he defines as "a set of statements which proceed, step by step, through the force of logic or reliance upon a succession of indisputable facts, to a climactic conclusion, each statement picking up the last key word (or key phrase) of the preceding one."[110] Fischel, as well as

102. Käsemann, "Christian Eschatology," 184–85.
103. Ibid., 180.
104. Starr, "2 Peter 1:4," 81.
105. Finlan, "Second Peter's Notion," 32.
106. Ibid., 33.
107. Ibid., 34.
108. Ibid., 36–37.
109. Ibid., 38.
110. Fischel, "Sorites," 119; quoted in Bauckham, *Jude, 2 Peter*, 175. Dr. Dale

Bauckham, has noted that this device, while originating in Greco-Roman literature, also found its way into Jewish literature, as indeed these cultural settings can hardly be thought of as having been somehow sealed off from one another in this period. Thus Bauckham cites other New Testament examples such as that of Paul in Rom 5:3–5, and in 2 Cor 8:7, as well as of Jas 1:15.[111] There are also Hellenistic *Jewish* examples such as the *sorites* in Wisdom 6:17–20,[112] as well as traditional Tannaitic Jewish examples such as the opening of the *Pirke Avōt*.[113] The use of such Hellenistic terminology and rhetorical form can thus be understood to be on a continuum from Hellenistic Judaism which was already adapting to its environment. Bauckham recognizes that, "our author uses his Hellenistic terminology with some care and skill, so that a Christian content controls it;"[114] and responding directly to Käsemann, insists that the "Greek aspiration for immortality was not simply denied, but taken up and critically fulfilled by the gospel of the resurrection . . . .[the] task of translating the gospel into terms appropriate to a new cultural milieu was (and has always continued to be) essential to the church's missionary role."[115] We can observe how the author of 2 Peter is seen to be effectively employing both Walls' indigenous principle as well as his pilgrim principle.

Starr also sees the connections here with Hellenistic Judaism, giving the example of 4 Maccabees 18:3, "Those who gave over their bodies in suffering for the sake of piety were deemed worthy to share in a divine inheritance."[116] Starr contrasts 4 Maccabees, in which reason as an "*innate* human capacity" simply needs to be trained properly in order to conquer the passions and develop virtue, with the 2 Peter passage.[117] This dovetails with the basic Platonic idea that ultimately, "virtue is the *means* of achieving incorruption/immortality, and exercising the reason develops virtue."[118]

Walker refers to these as "ladders of virtues."

111. Bauckham, *Jude, 2 Peter*, 175–76.
112. Fischel, "Sorites," 133.
113. Ibid., 119.
114. Bauckham, *Jude, 2 Peter*, 153.
115. Ibid., 183.
116. Starr, "2 Peter 1:4," 85; see also Bauckham, *Jude, 2 Peter*, 177–78.
117. Starr, "2 Peter 1:4," 85–86.
118. Ibid., 88.

This is where the contrast between the more anthropocentric idea of *apotheosis* and what is actually being asserted in 2 Pet 1:4 is most marked, especially when taken in the context of the chapter as a whole. Rather, 2 Pet 1 begins with having obtained faith "through the righteousness of God and our Savior Jesus Christ," and that his "divine power has given us all things that are needful for life and godliness" through knowledge of God and Christ, who have called us by his "own glory and perfection." It is through the promises and power of God that we are enabled to become "sharers in the divine nature," and it is in having *obtained this*, and *only then*, that the writer now begins to speak of escaping corruption and lustful passions and goes on to the list of virtues referred to above. The key difference, then, is that although 2 Peter uses language which would be familiar to those who had been involved in Middle Platonism and/or Stoicism, the central point is one of *contrast*: The virtue is not the *means* of obtaining *theosis*, but rather is the *fruit* of having been joined to God; he "gives the whole matter a new frame of reference, namely, the knowledge of Christ rather than innate divine reason. Sharing in divine nature is not something 2 Peter's readers *achieve* but something they *receive* as a result of their knowledge of Christ."[119] Bauckham underlines this more Jewish grounding in 2 Pet 1:4, noting that to "become in this sense, 'divine' is, of course, for these Jewish writers the gift of God's grace, not attainable on human initiative alone."[120] Thus, while again interacting deeply, *indigenously*, with the Judeo-Hellenic context, the writer of 2 Peter is also speaking as a prophetic *pilgrim* into that context by actually setting elements of the context on their head, so to speak. It is worth considering, especially in light of 2 Cor 3:18 and patristic use of this passage, that here as well (2 Pet 1:3), God is calling the faithful to his "glory" (*doxa*).

---

119. Ibid.

120. Bauckham, *Jude, 2 Peter*, 180–81. It's important to note here, however, that Bauckham also expresses doubt as to 2 Pet 1:4 expressing, in its historical context, the idea of "participation in the life or essence of God himself, but to the gift of 'godlike' immortality" (Bauckham, *Jude, 2 Peter*, 180–81, 193), though he does allow for the possibility of a connection here with Paul's words in Rom 8:11 and 1 Cor 15:42–53, expressing the "Pauline concept of the Christian's participation in the Holy Spirit" (Bauckham, *Jude, 2 Peter*, 181).

IN THE PAULINE WRITINGS

Segal sees the concept of Christ as the *image* and *glory* of God as being quite central to Paul's understanding of the intertwined issues of the vision of God and transformation. The idea of the "glory" of God as related to *theosis* is more central to passages such as 2 Cor 3:8—4:6, indeed in several places in the context of these verses, the theme of glory is repeated. The word *katoptrízomai* in 2 Cor 3:18 can be translated as beholding or reflecting,[121] and in either case, whether beholding or reflecting, the emphasis in the text is ultimately with regard to being transformed (*metamorphóomai*) into the image beheld/reflected. Segal observes that, "For Paul, as for the earliest Jewish mystics, to be privileged enough to see the Kabod or Glory of God is a prologue to transformation into His image."[122]

As has been noted earlier, April DeConick has written on the connections and contrasts between this vision mysticism, in which the devotee is attempting to ascend through the heavens by means of one's piety or *theurgic* (or shamanistic) exercises, and the response of John's Gospel, in which the vision of God *in Christ* is given as a gracious gift. This 2 Corinthians passage in effect links into DeConick's discussion on Thomasine vision mysticism and the Johannine response with the transforming vision of God in Christ being granted as a gift to those who have joined themselves to Christ by faith. Robert Rakestraw affirms this, writing that,

> Pauline teaching supports much that is emphasized by theosis theologians. Paul writes that Christians, "who with unveiled faces all reflect the Lord's glory, are being transformed into his likeness with ever-increasing glory, which comes from the Lord, who is the Spirit" (2 Cor 3:17–18). The Christian who experiences this transformation develops a remarkable God-given assurance that she is actually thinking the thoughts of God, doing the works of God, and at times even speaking the words of God. These energies and ministries of God in the Christian yielded to her Lord are the natural outcome of the life of God in the soul.[123]

Segal has another insight which needs to be folded into this idea of Christian mysticism in Paul's writings:

---

121. A metaphor perhaps related, as Finlan notes, to the production of "highly reflective bronze mirrors" in Corinth in that period. See Finlan, "*Theosis* in Paul," 76.

122. Segal, "Paul and the Beginning," 111.

123. Rakestraw, "Becoming Like God," 267.

> the mystical experience of conversion is not only with the *risen* Christ but with the *crucified* Christ. . .By being transformed by Christ, one is not simply made immortal, given the power to remain deathless. Rather, one still experiences death as Christ did and, like him, survives death for heavenly enthronement.[124]

This last point is crucial, and alludes to the earlier point about how the crucifixion of Christ as the Glory and Word of God made flesh communicates something vital not only about how much God loves us, but about the depth of God's humility as intrinsic to his very nature. Being transformed into his likeness and united with him involves us as well, being conformed to his suffering and death as well as to his resurrection (Phil 3:10), as we observed above in Rev 3:21 and 5:10.[125] It is this which also provides the necessary link between Christ enthroned (Eph 1:20) and his people thus graciously enthroned with him (Eph 2:6).[126] As Andrew T. Lincoln explains, Eph 1:20 contains an allusion to the frequently-quoted enthronement psalm (Psalm 110),[127] and moves from there into a declaration that not only is the Messiah seated at the Father's right hand in the heavenly places, but he also has authority "far above all rule and authority and power and dominion, and above every name that is named, not only in this age but also in the one to come" (1:21), that is, above all other earthly and heavenly powers.[128] What this means for those who have been joined in union with the Messiah is that, having been *incorporated* into Christ, "what God did for Christ he did at the same time for believers."[129] The previous verse (2:5) and the first part of 2:6 make it clear that this is preceded by our having died and been raised with Christ.[130] Lincoln notes that believers are said to share in the glory of Christ's resurrection, though he also points out that the phrase "at his right hand" in 1:20 is not repeated in 2:6, since Christ's "position in the heavenly realm and his relationship to God are unique."[131] This actually serves to under-

---

124. Segal, "Paul and the Beginning," 114.

125. See Segal, "Conversion and Universalism," 165.

126. 2 Tim 2:12 also reflects this idea.

127. Lincoln, *Ephesians*, 61–62. It should be noted that there are many scholars who have questioned the Pauline authorship of Ephesians.

128. Ibid., 62–65.

129. Ibid., 105.

130. Perhaps a parallel with Col 3:1–3 (Lincoln, *Ephesians*, 106), as well as a potential allusion to baptism (Ibid., 109).

131. Ibid., 108–9.

line the important distinction between Christ and those in union with him and the believers' dependence upon him, and reinforces the central idea of Christocentricity in our idea of union with God in Christ.

It has been suggested that 2 Cor 3:7—4:6 is a kind of Pauline *midrash* on Exod 34:29–35,[132] seeking to explain it in Messianic terms. The key term used here is *glory*, for which Paul uses the Greek term, *doxa*, used to translate the Hebrew *kāvōd* in the LXX. While some scholars have interpreted the veil which Moses wore to conceal the glory on his face as a Pauline polemic against the law itself,[133] we can lean more toward what Martin refers to as the "obverse side of this negative assessment of the OT as seen in Luke 24:45, 46 where the disciples 'minds' were opened (and no longer obtuse and they can then see the OT as full of messianic prefigurations (cf. Luke 24:27, 32)."[134] For this passage, the key to the removal of the veil of misunderstanding and for beginning to walk in the freedom of the Spirit is a turning to the Lord (2 Cor 3:16). In something of a word-play, the expression "turns to the Lord" (*epistrephein pros Kyrion*) replaces the phrase the LXX uses in Exod 34:34, which states that Moses "used to go in" (*eiseporeueto*, imperfect tense).[135] Here Paul is using a term for repentance (and perhaps familiar in Hellenic Judaism) found in several passages in the LXX.[136] In this view, a central theme here would be gaining true understanding of the meaning of the *Torah* in the process of turning to and being united by faith with the Messiah, who removes the "veil" of our own obstinacy and enables us to see rightly in him. Moreover, this is stated using the very terminology which would have been quite understandable to the non-Jewish audience, yet would actually serve as an example of the indigenous principle in terms of the language used. The pilgrim principle appears here not only in the Christocentricity of the passage itself, but importantly, in the use of the passive voice: thus "*the* Lord is the agent of the veil's removal."[137] This culminates

---

132. McNamara, *Targum and Testament*, 170–73; and Martin, *2 Corinthians*, 70.

133. E.g., Martin, *2 Corinthians*, 69, suggesting that what is being done away with is the "glory of the Old Testament."

134. Ibid.

135. Keeping in mind that the context of the verse in Exodus states that whenever "Moses went in before the Lord to speak with him, he would remove the veil." See Martin, *2 Corinthians*, 70.

136. Furnish, *II Corinthians*, 211. Furnish provides LXX references including Deut 4:30, 2 Chron 24:19 and 30:9, Ps 21(22):27, Isa 19:22 and Ben Sirah 5:7.

137. Furnish, *II Corinthians*, 212.

in the final verse of the chapter (3:18) in which the now unveiled believer is effectively in the place of Moses, beholding the Lord's glory in the Messiah and undergoing a Spirit-empowered transformation into his image.[138] The believer thus completes the connection with the indigenous *ascension, vision* and *transformation* motif.

Keener, interacting with Timothy B. Savage's notes on the glory of Christ in the 2 Cor 3:7—4:6 passage has also observed a point-by-point parallel between those "blinded by the god of this age" in 2 Cor 4:4 and those who have been "enlightened," in a sense culminating the "veiling" and "unveiling" imagery of the previous passage in 3:7–18.[139]

4:4	4:6
The god	God
Of this age	Who shines light from darkness
Has blinded	Has shined
The minds of unbelievers	Our hearts
Lest should shine	For (*pros*)
The light of the gospel	The light of the knowledge
Of Christ's glory	Of God's glory
Who is God's image	In the face of Jesus Christ

Savage describes parallels between Paul's language here and the LXX version of Isa 60, using the same image of eschatological glory (*doxa*), made that much more striking by Paul's using this parallel to equate God's glory with Christ's glory.[140] Savage continues on this theme, citing *Pesikta Rabbati* 36:2, which reads, "Then the Holy One, blessed be He, will brighten the light of the king Messiah and of Israel, whilst all the nations of the earth will be in darkness—in gross darkness—and they shall walk, all of them, by the light of the Messiah and of Israel, as it is said *And nations shall walk at thy light, and kings at the brightness of thy rising* (Isa 60:3)."[141]

---

138. A case for 2 Cor 3:18 as an example of *theosis* theology in Paul is made by Litwa, "2 Cor 3:18 and its Implications for *Theosis*," 117–33.

139. Keener, *1–2 Corinthians*, 173, and Savage, *Power Through Weakness*, 127–28.

140. Savage, *Power Through Weakness*, 128.

141. Ibid.; *Pesikta Rabbati* 36:2; Braude, *Pesikta Rabbati*, 2.682. Savage also cites *Pesikta Rabbati* 36:1 and 37:1.

This had a powerful effect on a fourth-century Syrian monk, who most scholars now refer to as Macarius-Symeon. As we move toward the third chapter which will focus on the Macarian writings, it is worth quoting Golitzin in regard to Macarius-Symeon again, in that Golitzin recognizes that the "whole Macarian corpus is like an extended meditation on" this passage in 2 Cor 3:7—4:6, demonstrating in this passage the themes of contrast in regard to themes of "change, alteration, or transfiguration . . . which occurs in the Christian soul through the indwelling Spirit, and of the glory (*doxa*) of God in which the soul and ultimately the body are called to share."[142] We will examine in the following chapter how the *Homilies* of Macarius-Symeon, appear more to be speaking missionally into the context of Jewish and Hellenic Shamanism.

In this chapter, we examined several sections of the New Testament, looking for evidence of interaction with ascension, vision and transformation mysticism. In John's Gospel, we found a number of instances in which the text seems to stand as a Christocentric contrast to this sense of mysticism, that only in union with Christ, who *descended* from the heavenly realm, can one hope to ascend. In Revelation, we see the system of seeking to ascend in order to be empowered through the shamanistic process is turned upon its head, with the seer brought up into heaven by God's initiative and power, rather than his own. In the narrative of the Pentecost event in Acts 2, the fire of the divine presence descends and is seen upon, and supernaturally empowering, the disciples of Christ. The passage in 2 Pet 1 discusses not only *participation* in God, but that as we participate in God, our lives should rightly be transformed into displaying God-empowered virtue in the manner in which we live. Finally, we see in the 2 Cor 3–4 passage that in Christ we are unveiled, and not only may receive the inner "vision" of Christ, but we are thus *transformed* into his image.

---

142. Golitzin, "Christianity as Transfiguration," 133.

3

"That He Be Surrounded by God's Glory"
Christian Interaction with Jewish and Hellenic Mysticism in Late Antiquity

> [T]he soul that is perfectly irradiated by the unspeakable beauty of the glory of the light of the face of Christ, and is perfectly in communion with the Holy Spirit, and is privileged to be the dwelling-place and throne of God, becomes all eye, all light, all face, all glory, all spirit, being made so by Christ, who drives, and guides, and carries, and bears her about, and graces and adorns her thus with spiritual beauty; for it says, the hand of a man was under the Cherubim, because He it is that is carried upon her and directs her.
>
> Macarius-Symeon, *Homily* 1.2b[1]

IN THE FIRST CHAPTER, we examined some of the ancient beliefs and practices associated with Jewish and Hellenic mysticism. In the second chapter, we then looked at how the authors of the New Testament writings interacted with this material. We have sought to understand how these inspired writers interacted with their context in a manner which maintained a balance between what Andrew Walls terms the *indigenous* principle of integrating with a local context, and the *pilgrim* principle in which the gospel speaks prophetically into the local context. In this chapter, we will examine how these themes continued to be developed over the next several centuries of Christian interaction with these contexts.

---

1. Macarius, *Homilies*, 2.

Was there continuity with the kind of interaction which was observed in the New Testament writings themselves? Moreover, in what manner did those in the Christian communities continue to develop this interaction—particularly those in the Syrian and Semitic East?

Concerning the years following the initial expansion of the Christian faith outside of its Jewish cradle in Judea and Galilee, much attention has often been focused on the regions within the Roman Empire, which provided the setting for much of Luke's narrative in Acts. The community of faith in Christ also continued to spread in the other direction, toward the East, among both Jewish and Gentile communities. How did the issues of Christian interaction with ascension and vision mysticism play out in this context? In this chapter, we will focus on the writings of a fourth-century Syrian monastic whose writings were circulated pseudonymously under the name of Macarius. These writings demonstrate a significant degree of critical interaction with these same themes of mysticism. In view of Walls' *indigenous* and *pilgrim* principles, we will seek to observe how the believing community in this area and time period interacted with their religious and cultural environment. The Macarian *Homilies* are a good choice on which to focus this part of the study, in part because this critical interaction with the wider Jewish and Hellenic mystical milieu seems particularly clear.

Another reason is that the Macarian *Homilies*, especially the second collection of fifty in the widest circulation, had both a direct and indirect influence on the theology of theology of John Wesley. Not only did he read the *Homilies* himself (and distribute his own revision of them as part of the required reading for his preachers), but Wesley also likewise included (in the same volume) a revision of proto-Pietist Johann Arndt's *True Christianity*. Arndt was a German Reformer who had memorized the Macarian *Homilies*. Arndt's writings were a vital part of the process which birthed the Pietist movement on the European Continent.

MACARIUS-SYMEON

We will focus this chapter with an examination of these themes in the fourth-century writings which were distributed under the name of "Macarius of Egypt." For many years, these have been recognized as actually having been written in the Syrian East, by a monk who has sometimes been identified with the Messalian tradition.[2] This monk is often referred

2. On the question of Macarius-Symeon's identification with the Messalian

to in scholarly circles as "Macarius-Symeon," due to possible connections between this writer and a figure from the period named Symeon of Mesopotamia;[3] he is also sometimes referred to as "Pseudo-Macarius." The collections of writings which come down to us include four interrelated collections of homilies, three of which have been published in critical editions.[4] For our purposes, most of our observations will be focused on the most well-known writings in collection II, the "Fifty Spiritual Homilies," as well as the *Epistola Magna*, or Great Letter.[5] These integrate many of the same Semitic and Hellenic themes of ascension, vision and transformation which we have already briefly observed in the previous chapter in the *Gospel of Thomas*. As has been briefly noted, the Macarian *Homilies* also had an impact on the development of the traditions of Pietism and Methodism, and galvanized a vision of personal and corporate holiness in action, the hallmark of Wesleyan thought.[6]

Several writers have noticed parallels in the Macarian *Homilies* with the *Gospel of Thomas*, and it is to this theme we will now turn. We will observe the degree to which the writer of the Macarian *Homilies* interacts with the language and the themes represented in his milieu *indigenously*, and to what extent the writer may be using these in part as a platform from which to bring the prophetic, *pilgrim* challenges the gospel would present to the broader society.

---

sectarians, and his location within the Syrian milieu generally, see especially the monograph by Stewart, *'Working the Earth of the Heart'*.

3. See above, 9 n. 21.

4. The critical edition of collection I, which also included the Great Letter, is Berthold, ed., *Makarios/Symeon*; that of collection II is Dörries, Klostermann and Kroeger, eds., *Die 50 Geistlichen Homilien des Makarios*, and of collection III is Klostermann and Berthold, *Neue Homilien eds Makarios/Symeon*. As the writings in collection IV are entirely found within collection I, no one has yet undertaken a critical edition of these. See also Maloney, "Introduction," 5–6, and Golitzin "Christianity as Transfiguration," 148 n. 4.

5. Except where noted, we will refer to the A. J. Mason translation, published in 1921. I have made some adjustments to this, such as replacing the more archaic "Holy Ghost" with the more commonly used "Holy Spirit."

6. Marcus Plested notes that "The Macarian writings are one of the principal fountainheads of the Christian ascetic and mystical tradition" (Plested, *Macarian Legacy*, 1); Plested recounts this through the influence the Macarian writings had on the Eastern tradition, through "Mark the Monk, Diadochus of Photis, Maximus the Confessor, Symeon the New Theologian, and Gregory Palamas" (Plested, *Macarian Legacy*, 1).

Dom Aelred Baker, for example, examined the parallels between *Thomas* Logion 27 and Macarian *Homily* 35, both of which touch on the theme of the Sabbath. Logion 27 reads,

> "If you do not fast as regards the world, you will not find the kingdom. If you do not observe the Sabbath as a Sabbath, you will not see the father."[7]

Connected as it is in *Thomas* with the theme of fasting, this appears to be part of the broader general theme of encratic practices[8] which form part of the emphasis in much of *Thomas*, and Baker suggests that this theme is shared by Macarius-Symeon in the parallel passage on Sabbath in *Homily* 35,[9] where the author writes that the "the soul to which it has been granted to be set free from base and foul thoughts both keeps true sabbath and enjoys true rest, being idle and at leisure so far as the works of darkness are concerned. There, in the typical sabbath, although they rested in bodily fashion, their souls were in bondage to wickednesses and sins. This, the true sabbath, is true rest, the soul being idle and cleansed from the suggestions of Satan, and resting in the eternal rest and joy of the Lord."[10]

On the one hand, Baker is clearly correct in observing that Macarius-Symeon is, like the author of *Thomas* Logion 27, interpreting the Sabbath spiritually. Macarian *Homily* 35, however, doesn't really seem to be about fasting, or even about asceticism generally. As Maloney recognizes by placing this reference in brackets in his translation, the Sabbath theme here seems to parallel Matt 11:28 and Heb 4:11, which speak of entering into Christ's rest, and the rest of grace. Similarly, Macarius-Symeon concludes the *Homily*, to "serve God out of a pure heart, and celebrate the feast of the Holy Spirit."[11] While Macarius-Symeon, like other monastics of the period, sometimes exhorts his readers toward ascetic practices, this seems rather to be an encouragement to walk in holiness by means of the empowering, sanctifying grace of the Holy Spirit. Thus he writes, in *Homily* 26.10b,

---

7. Lambdin, *Gospel of Thomas*, 121.
8. *Encratics* were radical ascetics who forbade marriage.
9. Baker, "Pseudo-Macarius and the Gospel of Thomas," 220–21.
10. *Homily* 35.1, Macarius, *Homilies*, 246.
11. Ibid., 247.

> If no moisture comes from above, the husbandman has no profit from his tilling of the ground. So is it with the spiritual world. There are two factors to be taken into consideration. The man must cultivate with a will the ground of his heart, and labour upon it for God requires the man's labour and toil and travail. But unless clouds of heaven make their appearance from above, and showers of grace, the husbandman does not profit by his toil.[12]

For Macarius-Symeon, God's grace is primary as well as preliminary, and can never be merited or earned. There is nonetheless an element of synergy, of a necessary response of turning toward God in Christ, even such a response understood as empowered by God.[13]

Gilles Quispel also seeks to find parallels between the *Gospel of Thomas* and the Macarian writings, though in one instance, at least, there is a slight difference between the Coptic text of *Thomas* and that of the Greek fragment from Oxyrinchus which Quispel quotes. He suggests, for example, a parallel to the Macarian *Great Letter*, where Jaeger's Greek text includes the term *anapauómenoi sumbasileúsomen*,[14] which may be translated, "peacefully reigning with God in the Kingdom." He compares this with the Greek of *P. Oxy 654*, 2[15] in Logion 2.1–4, which DeConick translates as,

> [Jesus said], "Whoever seeks should not cease [seeking until] he finds. And when he finds, [he will be amazed. And] when he is [amazed,] he will be king. And [once he is a king,] he will rest.[16]

It's certainly possible that Macarius-Symeon is here consciously using language from *Thomas*, though it's also possible that he is using the language and themes in New Testament passages such as Matt 11:28, Eph 2:6 and 2 Tim 2:12, which also speak of reigning and rest. In the case of both *Thomas* and of Macarius, there is a real sense of rest in both the

---

12. Ibid., 190.

13. See also Maloney, "Introduction and Notes," 282 n. 72.

14. Quispel, "The Syrian Thomas and the Syrian Macarius," 118; see also Jaeger, *Gregory of Nyssa and Macarius*, 291.

15. Quispel, "The Syrian Thomas and the Syrian Macarius," 118; DeConick, *The Original Gospel of Thomas*, 48, places the quote in P. Oxy. 654.5–9.

16. DeConick, *Original Gospel of Thomas*, 48. DeConick notes that the Coptic version of this passage reads, "he will be a king ruling over everything," but she considers this to be a later modification, noting that the Greek agrees with the theme of rest in Logion 90 (DeConick, *Original Gospel of Thomas*, 49).

eschatological sense, and perhaps the sense of rest and reigning with God in Christ even now.

Gospel of Thomas Logion 11 concludes with Jesus saying, "On the day when you were one, you became two, When you are two, what will you do?"[17] DeConick connected this with the encratic theme of returning to an androgynous ideal of prelapsarian Adam through ascetic exercises. It is interesting, therefore, to examine a passage in Macarius-Symeon with similar wording, but which the writer takes in a very different direction.

In *Homily* 15.22, Macarius-Symeon writes:

> If a man loves God, then God also mingles His love with him. Once trusted by man, He adds to him the trust of heaven, and the man becomes a twofold being. Whatever part of yourself you offer to Him, He mingles with your soul a like part of His own, that all that you do may be purely done, and your love pure and your prayer pure. Great is the dignity of man. See how mighty are the heaven and the earth, the sun and the moon; but the Lord was not pleased to rest in them, but in man only. Man, therefore, is of more value than all created things I may venture to say, not only than visible creatures, but invisible likewise, even than the *ministering spirits*.[18] . . . But you are for this reason after the image and likeness of God.[19]

What Macarius-Symeon is describing here is the idea of the presence of God's Spirit entering and empowering one who is moving closer in relationship with him. Note here especially the emphasis on humankind's having been created in the image and likeness of God in the context of a discussion on union with him. The encratic theme of uniting the genders within a person in the asexual sense is replaced by the ideal of union of human people with God through the presence of his Spirit.

This same idea of union with God in connection with the restoration of the image of God is a theme found elsewhere in the *Homilies*. We can observe this, for example, in the very first *Homily* described in the beginning of this section in the context of a discussion of the fall of Adam and of transformation by the power of the Holy Spirit. Moreover, as noted earlier, the broader context of the first *Homily* is an adaptation of the schema of ascension, vision and transformation to the life of the

---

17. DeConick. *Original Gospel of Thomas*, 78.

18. Heb 1:14.

19. *Homily* 15.22; Macarius, *Homilies*, 116–17, slightly altered for language, emphasis mine.

follower of Jesus who is entering into union with Christ. There, the metaphor is of the human soul becoming the throne of God.[20] In parts 7 and 8 of the same *Homily*, there is a discussion of how the soul is affected by rebellion against God, and, conversely, by union with God. In the first instance, Macarius-Symeon recounts that Adam

> was sold, or sold himself, to the devil, and the evil one put on his soul like a garment—his soul, that fair creation, which God had fashioned after His own image...For this reason, the soul is called the body of the darkness of wickedness as long as the darkness of sin is in it, because there it lives to the evil world of darkness, and is there held fast.[21]

Macarius-Symeon describes God's solution to the soul's enmeshment in darkness as being a rescue operation via the crucifixion, "This was the purpose of the Lord's coming, that He might cast them out, and recover His own house and temple."[22] He goes on to explain that in coming to faith in God in Christ, the human soul is "On the other hand, the soul which has believed God, and has been rescued from sin, and done to death out of the life of darkness, and has received the light of the Holy Spirit as its life, and by that means has come to life indeed, spends its existence in the same for ever after, because it is there held fast by the light of the Godhead.",[23] and concludes that

> Whichever the soul, then, is mixed with, it is thence-forward united with the same in the motions of the will. Either it has the light of God within it, and lives in the same, in all virtues, and belongs to the light of rest, or it has the darkness of sin, and meets with condemnation.... Let us therefore pray that we ourselves may be slain through His power, and die to the world of the wickedness of darkness, and that the spirit of sin may be destroyed in us, and that we may put on and receive the soul of the heavenly Spirit, and be translated from the wickedness of darkness into the light of Christ, and may rest in life through world after world.[24]

---

20. *Homily* 1.2; Macarius, *Homilies*, 2.
21. *Homily* 1.7a; Macarius, *Homilies*, 6–7.
22. *Homily* 1.7b; Macarius, *Homilies*, 7.
23. *Homily* 1.7c; Macarius, *Homilies*, 7.
24. *Homily* 1.8a, 9a; Macarius, *Homilies*, 7–8.

According to Macarius-Symeon, then, by being joined with Christ by faith in his death and life, the soul is both freed *from* the powers of darkness which would "put it on like a garment," and freed *to* put on the heavenly Spirit, being renewed in God's image and empowered by his gracious presence. This is a theme which is repeated over and over again throughout the *Homilies*, the theme of transforming union with God.

Indeed, this combination of use of the metaphors of ascension, vision and transformation, combined with an emphasis on the image of God in humankind restored in Christ by the power of the Holy Spirit is a particularly strong theme in the following *Homily* 2.3b-5. Macarius-Symeon is very clearly speaking indigenously, but focuses everything back on Christ and the empowering presence of the Holy Spirit. More than merely using indigenous language to challenge a system which needed to be corrected, Macarius-Symeon is using very beautiful, poetic language to describe a way forward into union with God. Thus, in an allusion to Ps 55:6, he encourages his readers to "beseech God that he bestow upon us the *wings of a dove,* even of the Holy Spirit, that we may fly to him and be at rest and that He would separate and make to cease from our souls and bodies, that evil wind,[25] which is the sin that dwelleth in the members of our souls and bodies. None but He can do it. . . . In like manner there is a day of light and a divine wind of the Holy Spirit, which blows and refreshes the souls that are in the day of the light of God."[26] The Spirit of God, Macarius-Symeon writes, "recreates" those in union with him, so that

> all who have put off the old man, which is from beneath the earth all whom Jesus has stripped of the clothing of the kingdom of darkness have put on the new and heavenly man, Jesus Christ, once more corresponding, eyes to eyes, ears to ears, head to head, to be all pure, and wearing the heavenly image..
>
> The Lord has clothed them with the clothing of the kingdom of ineffable light, the clothing of faith, hope, charity, of joy, peace, goodness, kindness, and all the other divine and living clothing of the light of life, of inexpressible rest [*anapaúseos*],[27] that,

---

25. Noting the word play, of course, as "wind" would be the same word as "spirit" in the Syriac (*ruha*) which was likely the first language of the writer of the *Homilies*. See Brock, *Syriac Tradition*, 91.

26. *Homily* 2.3b-4a; Macarius, *Homilies*, 13-14. Burns quotes a similar passage from *Homilies* Collection I.48.6,9; Burns, "Divine Ecstasy," 318.

27. Dörries, et al., *Die 50 Geistlichen Homilien des Makarios*, 19.

> as God Himself is love, and joy, and peace, and kindness, and goodness, so the new man may be through grace.[28]

Here then we find the idea of ascension and vision in a metaphoric sense of being brought to God. That is one of the crucial differences between writers such as what we observe here in Macarius-Symeon and the more shamanistically-oriented Jewish and Hellenic writers: the idea of "being brought" rather than working one's way up; of being *given* Holy Spirit-empowered "wings," even if metaphorically.[29] Burns describes the dynamic as involving

> The goal of the flight of the soul is into a "heavenly frame of thought," and it is here that Ps-Macarius locates the activity of the divine within man. That is, in this present age God's grace teaches the mind to fly and releases the soul into the presence of God through prayer. . . . The result of flight is therefore not only entering into the presence of God but the removal of the "evil wind of sin" that is evident within the body. This, as noted above, is accomplished by the sacrifice of Christ and the sprinkling of His Blood, and actuated by prayer. This prayer is directed by the Spirit, and the soul is transformed by grace.[30]

This is emphasized repeatedly in the Macarian writings, that those who would approach the Almighty are dependent upon his strength and initiative to do so, yet the cooperation of the devotee is required. Moreover, this carries with it the theme of participation in the Holy Spirit's activity, of his transforming, sanctifying power;[31] as Macarius-Symeon writes that these devotees are, "truly sharers [participators] of the secrets of the heavenly King,"[32] engaged in "the mystical, ineffable fellowship of [participation in] the heavenly King [or kingdom]."[33]

28. *Homily* 2.4b–5; Macarius, *Homilies*, 14–15.

29. Of course, metaphorical as this may be on one level, Macarius-Symeon also understands this eschatologically too, for he writes in *Homily* 5.11, "When God created Adam, He did not provide him with bodily wings, like the birds, but He had designed for him the wings of the Holy Spirit, those wings which He purposes to give him at the resurrection, to lift him up and catch him away whithersoever the Spirit pleases which holy souls even now are privileged to have, and fly up in mind to the heavenly frame of thought." (Macarius, *Homilies*, 54).

30. Burns, "Divine Ecstasy," 318–19.

31. See 2 Pet 1:4 as well as *Homily* 5.12 (Pseudo-Macarius, *Fifty Spiritual Homilies*, 75).

32. *Homily* 17.2; Macarius, *Homilies*, 143; see also Burns, "Divine Ecstasy," 322.

33. *Homily* 4.15; Macarius, *Homilies*, 56; amended slightly.

In our introduction, we mentioned briefly how Alexander Golitzin has sought to build upon the connection between early Jewish mysticism and the *Homilies*. Golitzin observes, for example, that the first of the fifty *Homilies* in the second collection is focused on the *Merkavah* vision in Ezek 1, but reinterpreted with a Christological focus through the "lens" of Paul's mystical passage in 2 Cor 3:7—4:6.[34]

Golitzin is not the first scholar to notice this, however. A century ago Joseph Stoffels noted the similarities in Macarius-Symeon and that of the mystical tradition of the *Merkavah* speculation on Ezekiel's vision, describing how the first of Macarius-Symeon's *Homilies* opens with a description of Ezekiel's vision and "reads like a programme of his mystical faith."[35] Following the overview of Ezekiel's vision, Macarius-Symeon begins seeking to explain it in the language of union with God which one finds again and again throughout the *Homilies*. Here he says,

> The mystery which he beheld was that of the soul, that was to receive her Lord, and to become a throne of glory for Him. For the soul that is privileged to be in communion with the Spirit of His light, and is irradiated by the beauty of the unspeakable glory of Him who has prepared her to be a seat and a dwelling for Himself, becomes all light, all face, all eye; and there is no part of her that is not full of the spiritual eyes of light. That is to say, there is no part of her darkened, but she is all throughout wrought into light and spirit, and is full of eyes all over, and has no such thing as a back part, but in every direction is face forward, with the unspeakable beauty of the glory of the light of Christ . . . so also the soul that is perfectly irradiated by the unspeakable beauty of the glory of the light of the face of Christ, and is perfectly in communion with [participator in] the Holy Spirit.[36]

Here Macarius-Symeon connects the *Merkavah* tradition with an explanatory principle of sorts in the form of the aforementioned passage in 2 Corinthians, in this case particularly verse 4:6. Indeed, the connections enable Golitzin to feel confident enough to write that, "the soteriology of deification also emerges in a light at once more 'Jewish,' and so more in obvious continuity with the revelation accorded Israel."[37] Indeed, the language of 2 Cor 4:6 shows up in a number of places, and connects

---

34. See also the quotations to this effect from Golitzin in our Introduction (5).
35. Stoffels, *Die Mystiche Theologie*, 79; cited in Scholem, *Major Trends*, 79.
36. *Homily* 1.2; Macarius, *Homilies*, 1–2.
37. Golitzin "Review of *Holiness: Rabbinic Judaism*," 462.

this idea of the *doxa*, the glory of God, with the removal of the dark veil on the heart (which also brings in the language of 2 Cor 3:17-18).[38] In another passage, Macarius-Symeon writes,

> When man first transgressed the commandment, the devil covered the soul all over with a covering of darkness. Then grace comes, and wholly removes the veil, so that the soul, now cleared, and regaining its proper nature, created without blemish and clear, continually beholds clearly with its clear eyes the glory of the true light and the true sun of righteousness l beaming in the heart itself.[39]

Thus the grace of God brings transforming union, granting the soul the spiritual vision of God.

Golitzin's further explanation of the Semitic elements in the Macarian *Homilies*, as an understanding of this background, deepens an already rich vault of spiritual insight. Golitzin continues to pursue the theme of God's glorious presence, which echoes in other Patristic writers of the era:

> I should like, though, to underline what I take to be the *Homilies'* particular emphasis on the Old Testamental motifs of the promised land and holy city, Jerusalem, and of the tabernacle and temple as the place of God's abiding. Christ is the reality of these images. He is the heavenly fatherland and the celestial city, the place of God's presence and — to borrow an expression from the *Targumim*, since I think the traditions the latter represent are close to Macarius' own heart — the "glory of the *Shekinah*" which dwells there and fills all with light. This presence or abiding, the literal sense of *Shekinah*, which comes to the Christian through baptism and the gift of the Holy Spirit, renders the soul in its turn the city and temple of God, at least in potential.[40]

This *Shekinah* imagery of God's glorious presence, a concept which began in the Jewish *Targumim* and Rabbinic writings, Golitzin says, was absorbed into Christian writing in Syriac. Golitzin has noted this theme, for example, in Ephrem the Syrian's *Paradise Hymns*, in which

---

38. See similar language in *Homily* 14.2: "And when he tastes the goodness of the Lord, and delights in the fruits of the Spirit, and the veil of darkness is taken away, and the light of Christ shines upon him and works in him in joy unspeakable, then is he, fully satisfied, having the Lord with him in great affection" (Macarius, *Homilies*, 102).

39. *Homily* 17.3b; Macarius, *Homilies*, 143.

40. Golitzin, "Christianity as Transfiguration," 133.

the *Shekinah* is "identified with the Presence enthroned at the Tree of Life and visible atop Sinai."[41] Though Macarius-Symeon was not unique among early Christian writers in this,[42] Golitzin finds significance in his use of the word *doxa* to express this "glory" of God:

> What is surely more significant about Macarius' use of *doxa* is that term's long-standing use in Greek-speaking Jewish and Christian traditions as the translation of the Hebrew *kabod* YHWH, such as, for example, in such texts of the Septuagint as Exodus 24 and 33–34, Numbers 12:8 (where *doxa* translates the divine form, *temunah*, in the context of the *visio dei*)... *Kavod* and its Greek equivalent are, put simply, the biblical terms of choice for theophany.
>
> What is at work in Macarius' use of *doxa* is therefore a persistent and conscious interiorization of the biblical glory tradition, of theophany.[43]

Importantly, Macarius-Symeon utilizes this language of glory and union to express how this will impact the way the devotee lives and thinks. Thus in the *Great Letter*, he writes that it

> is necessary that a man of God should also live in the divine tabernacle and should place his abode on the holy mountain of the most pure divinity in order that God not only completely surrounds him, but that he be surrounded by God's glory, which never allows him to be brought under the power of the darkness of passions.[44]

In the understanding of the writer of the *Great Letter*, then, God's *glory* is to be experienced by devotees, that they themselves are reckoned to have entered into the tabernacle (as did Moses), but more, that this should be reflected in a life which is being progressively delivered from the internal power of darkness.

In the previous section we also observed how the theme of God's presence and power as *fire* was a recurring theme in the Jewish ascension and vision writings as well as in writings such as *Thomas* and the *Odes*. This continues in the Macarian writings as well, often within the context

---

41. Ibid., 150–51 n. 29.

42. Golitzin lists, for example, Evagrius, Augustine and Cyril of Alexandria (Golitzin, "Christianity as Transfiguration," 138).

43. Golitzin, "Christianity as Transfiguration," 138.

44. Pseudo-Macarius, *Fifty Spiritual Homilies and the Great Letter*, 253.

of very creative metaphors. For example, in *Homily* 11, there is a discussion of idolatry and the manner in which the fire itself was said to have fashioned the golden calf.[45] From there the author moves to the account of the three young men in the furnace,[46] who "received in themselves the fire of God, and worshiped the Lord in truth."[47] Comparing these with his audience, he moves from there to state that, "so now faithful souls receive that divine and heavenly fire, in this world, in secret; and that fire forms a heavenly image upon their humanity."[48] He goes on to state:

> Christians in like manner have that heavenly fire for their [food]. That is their pleasure. That cleanses, and washes, and sanctifies their heart. That brings them to increase. That is their air and their life. . . . If it has not that divine fire for [food] and drink and [clothing], and cleansing of heart and sanctification of soul, it is taken by the evil spirits and demolished.(!)[49]

The *fire* of the presence of God's Spirit is depicted here as not only the source of sustenance, but also of spiritual protection. Considering the emphasis on the motif of the victory of Christ over the powers of darkness as a central theme in Christian theology for the first millennium of the Church, this is a powerful statement and warning.

In the Macarian writings, there are places in which this theme of *fire* is combined with another theme: The theme of drinking and intoxication as a spiritual metaphor, or to use Philo's term again, *sober intoxication*. Thus in *Homily* 8, we find Macarius-Symeon using both of these illustrations:

> Sometimes the fire flames out and kindles more vehemently; at other times more gently and mildly. The light that it gives kindles up at times and shines with unusual brightness; at others it abates and burns low. The lamp is always burning and shining, but when it is specially trimmed, it kindles up with intoxication of the love of God ; and then again by God's dispensation it gives in, and though the light is .always there, it is comparatively dull.

---

45. That is, according to Aaron's explanation to Moses in the account of Exod 32:24.

46. Dan 3:19–25.

47. *Homily* 11.2b; Macarius, *Homilies*, 80.

48. Ibid.

49. *Homily* 14.5; Macarius, *Homilies*, 103–104. slightly modified. On the theme of the protection and "arming" provided by the Spirit of the Lord, see also *Homily* 23.2b.

Another while, the light shining in the heart disclosed the inner, deeper, hidden light, so that the man, swallowed up in the sweetness of the contemplation, was no longer master of himself, but was like a fool or a barbarian to this world by reason of the surpassing love and sweetness, by reason of the hidden mysteries ; so that the man for that season was set at liberty, and came to perfect measures, and was pure and free from sin.[50]

This idea of sober intoxication is only referred to once in the Macarian writings, where he speaks of the "deep sober intoxication, caused by the Spirit, just as the body is said to be intoxicated by wine.[51] Although this is understood to be an ecstatic rather than a continual experience,[52] there is yet a sense in which this is understood as part of the journey of union with God in Christ. It is nonetheless recognized that to remain in a constant state of spiritual intoxication would leave a person unable to interact with or serve others by proclamation or service; were that the case, the devotee would "only to sit in a corner, aloft and intoxicated."[53] It is apparently crucial to alternate between a sense of union which is more ecstatic and one which is more "sober."[54]

Importantly, Macarius-Symeon regards this experience of "intoxication" not merely as ecstatic, spiritual and emotional experience. This also has an ethical dimension: "sober drunkenness" is meant to free the devotee from the power of sin. The end of the passage quoted above, for example, from *Homily* 8.3b contains echoes of 2 Cor 3:18, describing the resulting influence on the person's life as one of imparting liberty, purity and freedom from sin.

An important element of the theme of transformation in the Macarian writings is that of the grace of God. Western Evangelicals idea of grace tends to be overwhelmingly, if not exclusively, on the idea of grace as *unmerited favor*. The idea of grace in Macarius-Symeon widens out from this, especially for our purposes here, to include the theme of the work of the uncreated presence of God's Spirit. On the one hand, there are numerous examples of God's grace in the "legal" sense, with, for example, the metaphor of the beautiful maiden who takes a husband mired

50. *Homily* 8.2b & 3b, Macarius, *Homilies,* 66.

51. Macarius-Symeon, *Homilies* Collection I, *Homily* 63.6, Burns, "Divine Ecstasy," 312.

52. Burns, "Divine Ecstasy," 312.

53. *Homily* 8.4, Macarius, *Homilies,* 67.

54. *Homily* 8.5a, Pseudo-Macarius, *Fifty Spiritual Homilies,* 82.

in poverty.⁵⁵ Beyond (yet in conjunction with) this legal sense of grace, we also find throughout the *Homilies* the sense of grace as God's working presence. Macarius-Symeon describes the working of God's grace in the devotee, that

> Like a bee secretly forming her comb in the hive, grace secretly forms in hearts the love of herself, and changes them from bitterness to sweetness, from roughness to smoothness. As a silversmith and engraver, engraving a plate, partly covers up the various little animals that he is cutting, but when he has finished, displays it flashing with the light.⁵⁶

Another key theme and metaphor for transformation in the Macarian writings is that of *healing*, of salvation involving not only justification in the legal sense, but healing from the damage sin has done to the soul and restoration to its proper state. This is a common theme throughout the writings of the early church, and Macarius-Symeon utilized it as well. Thus we find him describing Christ as the one who came for those who had need of salvation "that He might convert them to Himself, and heal those that believe Him He is merciful, and quickening, curing the maladies that were incurable, working deliverance for those who call upon Him and turn to Him,."⁵⁷ Here he speaks of healing in this sense, alongside other metaphors of conversion and redemption; healing of the soul is understood to be part of the broader "package" involved in salvation and transformation. We see as well the love and dignity of his approach to the devotee as spiritual healer. This is well-illustrated in the following "parable" Macarius-Symeon presents to us:

> Suppose there were an emperor, and he were to find a man in want and suffering, and were not ashamed of him, but treated his wounds with healing medicines, and brought him into his palace, and clothed him with the purple and the diadem, and made him partaker of the royal table ; even so Christ the heavenly King came to suffering man and healed him, and made him partaker of the royal table, and this without putting constraint upon his will, but by persuasion He sets him in such honour.⁵⁸

---

55. *Homily* 7.1b; Macarius, *Homilies*, 61. See also *Homily* 11.10b, where the homilist has Christ say, "I paid the debts of Adam, when I was crucified and descended into hell" (Macarius, *Homilies*, 85).

56. *Homily* 16.7; Macarius, *Homilies*, 137.

57. *Homily* 4.27; Macarius, *Homilies*, 36.

58. *Homily* 15.30b; Macarius, *Homilies*, 121.

Here again the theme of healing connects with both the grace of God in Christ and with union with Christ, resulting in our elevation to the very palace (*hekhāl*) of the Almighty; a subtle connection with the theme of ascension. God brings us healing not just in order to make us "well," but with a greater aim in mind—to bring us into the *family*. Another parable in *Homily* 25 reflects this, though with a rather different application. It describes a battle between God and the devil and their respective angels over a person's soul. Macarius-Symeon notes that in the case of the illustration, just as a father sending his child along a dangerous route would provide "remedies and antidotes, in order that if the venomous creatures or dragons attack him he may give them his remedy and kill them," even so, the "heavenly remedy, the healing and antidote of the soul . . . may kill the poisonous beasts of unclean spirits."[59] This is a surprising use of the healing metaphor, but it makes it clear that for Macarius-Symeon, spiritual healing includes an element of deliverance. Importantly, we can observe here an element of *synergism*: the power is God's ("gives him remedies and antidotes"), but there is a certain amount of responsibility assumed on the part of the devotee to appropriate this ("he may give them his remedy").

Not only is healing for the soul from the ravages of sin and deliverance from spiritual evil part of the understanding of this element of salvation, but Macarius-Symeon touches on the element of healing of the physical body. Note how he connects these two elements:

> Do you believe, then, that your soul is receiving healing at Christ's hand from the eternal wounds which with men are incurable, the wounds of the passions of sin, for the sake of which healing the Lord also came hither, that He might now cure the souls of the faithful of those incurable wounds, and cleanse them from the foulness of the leprosy of evil, He, the only true physician and healer? . . . For if you believed the eternal, irremediable wounds of the immortal soul, and its disorders of evil, to be cured by Christ, you would have believed Him able to cure also the temporary disorders and maladies of the body.[60]

Thus for Macarius-Symeon, the spiritual healing which heals us from sin and delivers us from the powers of darkness could spill over into physical healing of the body as well. At the same time, it should be noted

---

59. *Homily* 26.24; Macarius, *Homilies*, 197.
60. *Homily* 48.3b-4; Macarius, *Homilies*, 302.

that in Macarius-Symeon's understanding of physical healing, medicines and herbs are "for the weak and unbelieving … men of the world and to all who are without, for solace, and healing, and care of the body, and permitted them to be used by those who could not yet entrust themselves wholly to God," while those who are truly a "stranger to the world" should rely on Christ's power for healing.[61] While we would resist the idea that there is something necessarily deficient about those who utilize medicine while trusting God as the ultimate source of healing, it is still noteworthy that Macarius-Symeon did recognize the reality of physical healing by the power of God.

A theme which is highlighted in the Macarian *Homilies* is that of the relationship between the believer (or, again, the community of believers) and the Lord being expressed through the metaphors of Lover and Beloved, as well as those of Bridegroom and Bride. It is crucial to emphasize this, since it was an element that was missing from the more shamanistically-oriented ascension and vision mysticism of early Judaism, yet is found very strongly represented in the Johannine writings as well as elsewhere in the New Testament. Moreover, this idea of a Lover-Beloved relationship between those who follow Jesus and their Lord is also intertwined with the idea of union with God, or *theosis*, which becomes such a central theme in monastic writers such as Macarius-Symeon. As we will see later on, this theme also developed into a key focus of Islamic mysticism, emerging within similar geographical and cultural areas.

One of the most beautiful passages in the Macarian writings with this focus is found in the *Great Letter* of Macarius-Symeon, in which he connects the soul's espousal to Christ with the description of a bride adorned in her jewels in Isa 61.10.

> For such a soul, wounded by love for Christ, dies to any other desire in order, I speak boldly, to possess the most beautiful intellectual and mystical communion with Christ according to the immortal quality of divinizing fellowship. Truly, such a soul is blessed and happy, when conquered by spiritual passion, it has become worthily espoused to God the Word. Let her say, "My soul will exalt in the Lord, who has clothed me in garments of salvation and has wrapped me in the cloak of integrity like a bridegroom wearing his crown, like a bride adorned in her jewels." For the King of Glory, ardently desiring her beauty, has deigned to regard her, not only as the temple of God, but also as

---

61. *Homily* 48.6; Macarius, *Homilies*, 302–3.

the daughter of the king and also the queen. Indeed, she is the temple of God, since she is inhabited by the Holy Spirit. She is also the daughter of the king since she has been adopted by the Father of lights. She is also queen as endowed with divinity of the glory of the Only-Begotten Son.[62]

In the passage above, there is a deep sense of anticipation of union with the Lord, an element echoing, for example, similar mystical love poetry such as that found in *Ode 3* of the *Odes of Solomon*. There is expressed here not only a sense of being taken up and transformed, but once again a sense of *participation*,[63] of being taken into the very family of the King! Even the idea of the soul as *queen* seems to contain echoes of the idea of the believers' participatory enthronement hinted at in Eph 2:6. This same imagery is found in the concluding section of *Homily* 47 as well, in this case more focused on a process of gradual transformation of the soul, folding in as well the theme of healing. Macarius-Symeon writes,

> For God desired to have communion with her, and espoused her to Himself as the King's bride, and He cleanses her from pollution, and washing her makes her bright from her blackness and her shame, and quickens her out of the state of death, and heals her of her shattered condition, and gives her peace, reconciling her enmity. For creature though she is, she has been espoused as bride to the King's Son; and by His own power God receives her to Himself, gradually accommodating Himself to her changes, until He has increased her with His own increase. For He stretches her out and lengthens her to an endless and immeasurable increase, until she becomes a bride without blemish and worthy of Him. First he begets her within Himself, and increases her through Himself, until she receives the full-grown measure of His love. For being Himself a perfect Bridegroom, He takes her as a perfect bride into the holy, mystical, undefiled fellowship of marriage; and then she reigns with Him to endless ages.[64]

---

62. *Great Letter*; Pseudo-Macarius, *Fifty Spiritual Homilies and the Great Letter*, 257.

63. On the theme of participation, see also *Homily* 15.35, where the homilist writes of the one who has been "for such a one is deified [that is, made a 'participator'], and made a son of God, receiving the heavenly stamp upon his soul." (Macarius, *Homilies*, 123).

64. *Homily* 47.17; Macarius, *Homilies*, 298–99.

As was the case with the previous passage from the *Homilies*, this passage concludes with the assertion that, having entered into union with him, the soul of the devotee will reign with Christ, the Bridegroom, for eternity.

What ultimately does this mean? Does this begin to blur the lines of identity with God, to indeed veer over into the kind of territory found in some of the logia in *Thomas*? On the one hand, consider what Macarius-Symeon writes concerning *perichoresis* (interpenetration) in the mystical union with God:

> For when the soul arrives at the perfection of the Spirit, perfectly cleansed from passion, -and united and mingled with the Spirit Paraclete by that unspeakable communion, and is permitted to become spirit itself in mixture with the Spirit, then it is made all light, all eyev all spirit, all joy, all rest, all gladness, all love, all compassion, all goodness and loving-kindness. As in the bottom of the sea a stone is encompassed on every side by water, so these men, mingled in every way with the Spirit, are made like Christ, having in themselves the virtues of the power of the Spirit unalterably, being faultless and spotless and pure within and without.[65]

Similarly, Macarius-Symeon is emphatic that this isn't simply an advanced option for those who would follow Jesus, but insists that this is the basic understanding and goal of Christian life. He writes that

> The soul which really believes Christ must be changed and altered from its present evil condition to a new condition which is good, and from its present lowly nature into another nature which is divine, and be itself made new by the power of the Holy Spirit.[66]

Macarius-Symeon, is, however, careful to explain (elsewhere) how human personality, as such, remains, and this type of explanation may help further discipleship as well as avoid confusion. He writes that

> all are plunged in light and fire, and changed, and yet are not, as some say, resolved and turned into fire, with nothing of their

---

65. *Homily* 18.10; Macarius, *Homilies*, 156. Haywood's 1721 translation reads "So are these every way Drench'd with the Holy Spirit, are made like to Christ himself, possessing unalterably within themselves the Vertues of the Power of the Spirit, being Blameles within *and without*, being Spotles and Pure" ("Macarius the Egyptian," *Primitive Morality*, 282).

66. *Homily* 44.5; Macarius, *Homilies*, 277.

natural substance left. Peter is Peter, and Paul is Paul, and Philip is Philip. Each one remains in his own nature and personality, though filled with the Spirit.[67]

This seems to contain something of an echo of the idea Sadhu Sundar Singh communicated as cited in the first chapter of this dissertation from a very different time and place, of union with God being like a "sponge" becoming immersed in the water rather than a "drop" being obliterated as it is merged into the ocean. It also reminds one of Annemarie Schimmel's description of the "mysticism of personality." Macarius-Symeon is speaking in robustly indigenous language, but the core of what he has to say remains rooted in the biblical "pilgrim" element of the faith, and of the new creation as described in 2 Cor 5:17–21 and 1 Cor 15:44–49 regarding our redemption in union with the Second Adam. It is in relationship with our heavenly Bridegroom (as described so beautifully by Macarius-Symeon above) that we are empowered to say, along with Paul, the words of Gal 2:20: "I have been crucified with Christ. It is no longer I who live, but Christ who lives in me. And the life I now live in the flesh I live by faith in the Son of God, who loved me and gave himself for me."

In recognizing that Macarius-Symeon was writing in an idiom which included a strong element of Neo-Platonism, Burns affirmed that Macarius-Symeon was seeking to communicate in a manner "understandable to his direct audience."[68] In this, and using Walls' terminology, Macarius-Symeon wrote in a highly *indigenous* way, incorporating images and language from both Jewish and Hellenic streams of mystical thought, and yet utilizing these to the end of forging a *pilgrim* theology of mystical encounter of union with the divine, deeply integrated with and rooted in his understanding of the scriptures. Macarius-Symeon used imagery from earlier Syrian literature as well as from earlier Jewish material, imagery of fire and of glory, and of spiritual intoxication. The Macarian writings evidence an interaction with the mystical themes of ascension, vision and transformation, yet, as in the case of the *Odes*, always centered Christologically and pneumatologically: the *visio dei* is to be found in the descended and ascended Christ, and it is by his Spirit given that we are transformed into his likeness. Macarius-Symeon depicts this transformation is depicted in a variety of ways, often using recurring themes of the uncreated presence of the grace of God, of our being made and remade

---

67. *Homily* 15.10; Macarius, *Homilies*, 110.
68. Burns, "Divine Ecstasy," 320.

into his image, of the healing of our spiritual sickness and malaise, and of sanctifying union which transforms our outward manner of life as our inner person is also transformed. In the following chapter, we will observe how these very themes, including these hallmarks of transformation, were taken up by John Wesley and his colleagues.

4

Union with God and Mission in the Theology of John Wesley

> *Come in, come in, thou heavenly Guest!*
> *Nor hence again remove;*
> *But sup with me, and let the feast*
> *Be everlasting love.*[1]
>
> —Charles Wesley (1707–1788)

INTRODUCTION

IN THE PREVIOUS CHAPTERS, we examined the beliefs and practices of early Jewish and Hellenic mysticism, and the tripartite schema described by Alan Segal of ascension, vision and transformation which served as their framework. Using James Davila's terminology, we recognized these as forms of *shamanism* rather than *mysticism* proper, since both the means and the ends were generally anthropocentric. We also sought to examine the interaction of these emerging traditions with early Judaism and the early Jesus movement. The latter was examined first by observing the elements of this ascension and vision mysticism in the light of the New Testament writings, and then moved on to the fourth-century writings of Macarius-Symeon, especially the *Fifty Spiritual Homilies* of the second collection of his writings. As we noted in the previous chap-

---

1. Charles Wesley, "Saviour of All, to Thee We Bow," second verse; quoted with slight variation in John Wesley, "The Scripture Way of Salvation," 3.18.

ter, these interacted in a manner which was contextual, reflecting what Andrew Walls has referred to as the *indigenous* principle, but also reflected Walls' *pilgrim* principle, in that while the elements of ascension, vision and transformation were present, the anthropocentric expression of these was challenged by viewing them in a manner which was deeply Christocentric and dependent upon the power of grace in the presence of the Holy Spirit.

Moreover, in the Macarian writings in particular, we observed that the idea of transformation was expressed in the intertwined elements of the empowerment through the uncreated grace of God in the presence of the Holy Spirit, of the restoration of the soul into the fullness of the image of God, of salvation expressed, in part, through the metaphor of healing of the soul from sin and the demonic, and finally, in union with God which includes both an element of deep mystical Lover-Beloved communion as well as the sanctifying power which flows from this union and enables a transformed inner life and is expressed in personal holiness.

In common with many other Anglican thinkers of the late seventeenth and early eighteenth century, both John and Charles Wesley were conversant with and influenced by some of the writings of early Christianity.[2] There were a number of other more contemporary sources, too, including Anglican, Catholic and Pietist writings, which also seem to have had an influence on these developments in Wesley's theology, and through which he received many of the same ideas regarding *theosis*, union with God in Christ, in second-hand form.[3] It's important to note that Kenneth Collins in particular cautions against the untenable position that Wesley was somehow influenced by the *Eastern Orthodox Church* (which should be distinguished from the early Church itself). Collins also rightly critiques the idea that Wesley is somehow simply

---

2. This is in no way to imply that the patristic writings were the sole influence on the development of Wesleyan theology, including Wesley's distinctive understanding of sanctification. Apart from figures in the patristic East such as Macarius-Symeon on whom we have focused here, there have been other patristic figures from the West, such as Augustine, whose writings had an influence on Wesley, as well as the secondary influence via the revival of patristic studies in the early eighteenth century. Perhaps the most comprehensive study undertaken in examination of the Anglican interaction with the patristic writings vis-à-vis Wesley is found in Anderson, *Clement of Alexandria.*.

3. On the diversity of theological influences on Wesley, see Collins, "John Wesley's Critical Appropriation," 69–90, and Heitzenrater, "John Wesley's Reading," 30–31.

"channeling" the theology of the early Christian writers with which he was acquainted. Collins notes, for example, the influence of Lancelot Andrewes in shaping the Anglican approach to the utilization of the writings of the early Christians.[4] While we would affirm (with Collins) that Wesley's theology seems to have been genuinely influenced by his reading of the early Christians, for our purposes, it is *more* important to note that the ideas of union with God which we find in Wesley are sourced from Wesley's reading of early Church, Anglican *and* Continental writers—for it is the theology of union with God which is itself primary here, rather than the particular historic source.

For example, as Collins has noted the importance of the influence of Lancelot Andrewes on the Anglican milieu of the period just preceeding Wesley, it's worth briefly quoting Andrewes 1606 Whit-Sunday sermon on Acts 2:1–4, in which he asserts that, "Whereby, as before He of ours, so now we of His are made partakers. He clothed with our flesh, and we invested with His Spirit. The great promise of the Old Testament accomplished, that He should partake our human nature; and the great and precious promise of the New, that we should be *consortes divinæ naturæ*, "partake His divine nature," both are this day accomplished."[5]

An example is the case of German theologian Johann Arndt. Arndt read and *memorized* the Macarian *Homilies*,[6] and these had a direct influence on the themes of his classic *True Christianity*. This volume was also read by John Wesley and his colleagues in the first generation of Methodist leadership. Arndt main idea was that if people have genuinely entered into relationship with God in Christ, this should be evident in both their spirituality as well as in their manner of life. Arndt was seeking to combat an antinomian tendency which had arisen in view of an overemphasis on doctrinal polemics, as well as an overbearing degree of influence of state authority on the Church (in this case, particularly

---

4. Collins, "John Wesley's Critical Appropriation," 74.

5. Andrewes, *Ninety-Six Sermons*, 109.

6. See Arndt, *True Christianity*, as well as Plested, *Macarian Legacy*, 1–2 n. 2. Note as well that not only did Wesley publish his own redaction of the Macarian *Homilies*, in the same, very first volume of his *Christian Library* he published extracts from the first four books of Arndt's *True Christianity*; see Arndt, *An Extract*. Interestingly (and perhaps a tad ironically), Wesley did not include excerpts from Arndt's *fifth* book within the original *True Christianity* (Arndt, *True Christianity*, 243–72), in which the primary focus is upon the theme of union with God in Christ. See also Peter Erb, Introduction to *True Christianity*, 7–8.

the Lutheran Church in the German states).⁷ *True Christianity* went through many editions in German, and had a great deal of influence on its own. It also had an influential role in the life of Philipp Jakob Spener, whose *Pia Desideria* had a key role in the initiation of the Pietist movement which was a key influence on Wesley's theology of union with God.⁸ While there is no evidence that Wesley read *Pia Desideria*, it is part of the broader milieu of continental Pietism which was also a key influence on Wesley—a milieu which had itself been influenced by the writings of early Christian faith on union with God.

Wesley sought to critically fold this understanding into his own teaching regarding justification, sanctification and the ultimate goal of those who walk in union with God in Christ. As we shall observe, this was integrated by the early Methodists into a theology of mission in which this union with God is meant to be lived out individually and in community in a manner in which the God's ultimate purpose in mission is extended in witness to the entire world.

Beginning in modern times with Albert C. Outler, a number of writers in the past forty-five years have sought to examine how the writings of some of these ancient figures in antiquity may have had an influence on the views of the leaders of early Methodism on this topic, and how the concept of *theosis* may have contributed to the Wesleyan idea of sanctification.⁹ Outler wrote in the introduction to his *John Wesley* that he believed that Wesley had acquired his concept of devotion and perfection from Gregory of Nyssa by way of "Macarius the Egyptian."¹⁰ As Ted Campbell has traced the conversation,¹¹ he notes that Outler, Campbell's

---

7. Tappert, Introduction to *Pia Desideria*, 3–9. See also Collins' excellent introduction to both Arndt and the Pietist movement and its influence on Wesley in Collins, "Early German Pietism," esp. 24–32.

8. Spener's *Pia Desideria* was originally written as a preface to a collection of Arndt's works (Tappert, Introduction to *Pia Desideria*, 14–15). In this brief work, Spener presented and summarized his own views of the necessity for personal holiness and genuine, living relationship with God. In addition to Spener's plea for holiness, he also added a key missiological concern to his argument: a concern regarding the impact the ungodly life of professing Christians was having on the Jewish population in Europe. "Christians today," Spener feared, "not only throw away their own salvation but also hinder the salvation of Jews and other unbelievers (which they should promote and bring about) by the most harmful offenses" (Spener, *Pia Desideria*, 68).

9. Outler, "Introduction to *John Wesley*," 9–10.

10. Outler, "Introduction to *John Wesley*," 9 n. 26.

11. Campbell, "Back to the Future," 5–16.

friend and mentor, hoped that Campbell would be able to "confirm his suspicion that Wesley's doctrine of sanctification was in essence that of ancient Eastern Christian asceticism."[12] Following his research, however, Campbell ultimately concluded that, "What I discovered about Wesley's use of Christian antiquity . . . was the selectivity *he* employed in choosing (and editing) historical materials as he saw their relevance to the eighteenth-century Revival."[13] Perhaps this is a case in which Wesley was correctly engaging in the work of discernment in sifting the "gold from the dross" of ancient traditions,[14] attempting to extract what he considered to be helpful to his people while taking care as to what got passed on. More recently, Kenneth J. Collins has asserted that, in spite of Wesley's having included his own redaction of the Macarian *Homilies* in his "Christian Library," he valued the Macarian corpus primarily for its *hamartiology* and understanding of remaining sin in the life of the believer, rather than the themes of union with God. While we would assert that the parallels between Wesley and the Macarian *Homilies* goes beyond *hamartiology*, we would nonetheless affirm with Collins that Wesley's interaction with all of his sources was done with an eye toward his understanding of a "biblical idiom."[15]

It is thus particularly interesting that, although Campbell suggested that Wesley actually omitted "references to the ascetic life and the notion of *theosis*,"[16] when we read Wesley's own edition of *Homily* 19 of the *Fifty Homilies*, we can observe that here, at least, he retained a rather clear reference to the transforming nature of union with God:

> It behooveth therefore the soul that truly believeth in CHRIST, *to be changed from her present nature into another nature, which is Divine*, and to be wrought new herself through the power of the

---

12. Campbell, *Christian Antiquity*, x.

13. Campbell, "Back to the Future," 15. Of course, it has also been noted that Wesley edited virtually everything from *any* source; see See Christensen, "Energy of Love," 221.

14. Tuttle, *Mysticism*, 126.

15. Collins, *Theological Journey*, 199.

16. Campbell, *Christian Antiquity*, x. Kenneth J. Collins makes this assertion as well in Collins, *Theological Journey*, 199. In the latter reference, Collins seems to understand that Wesley's substitution of *sanctification* for *theosis* somehow negates the latter in favor of the former. As we will see below, however, Christensen, while recognizing that Wesley is building his theology of sanctification upon a foundation of early Christian *theosis*, is also providing a clarification and corrective from his eighteenth-century Anglican perspective.

Holy Spirit. And to obtain this, will be allowed to us who believe and love him in truth, and walk in all his holy commandments.[17]

The perspective offered by Howard Snyder seems to represent a balanced understanding of Wesley's interaction with and appropriation of Macarius-Symeon, which takes into account the other influences in Wesley's own studies:

> I do not claim that Wesley simply "took over" this set of ideas from Macarius. Some of them he encountered elsewhere; some undoubtedly came to him through his own extensive study of Scripture; some were already present in the Anglican tradition; some were points of emphasis in the Pietist writings Wesley read (e.g., Arndt's *True Christianity* with its emphasis on the restoration of the image of God and the priority of love). But it is clear that the complex ideas on perfection Wesley taught were at key points strikingly similar to those taught by. . . Macarius and that these ideas had a particularly strong appeal to Wesley and therefore made a distinctive contribution to his doctrine of perfection.[18]

It seems to me that Snyder has the strongest perspective on the historic connection between the idea of union with God in the writings of ancient eastern Christians and Wesley. Kenneth Collins himself seems to recognize this when he observes not only the Wesley's appropriation of "insights of such eastern theologians as Pseudo-Macarius and Ephrem Syrus," but that "Wesley had *already* considered the participation motif (redemption entails participation in the life of God)" in the writings of other Continental and Anglican figures.[19] Wesley and his colleagues read and interacted with the fathers' writings *critically*, correcting concepts where they were unclear, and using terminology which they felt was less likely to lead to confusion.

When, for example, Wesley read in Clement of Alexandria's *Stromata* regarding *theosis* and the character of a "true Gnostic" (in the sense that Clement was seeking to speak to *his* Alexandrian context), Wesley

---

17. "Macarius of Egypt," 19.4, emphasis mine. Note that *Homily* 19 in Wesley's revised Macarian corpus is the equivalent of *Homily* 44 in the original Macarian corpus. See Lee, *New Creation*, 235 n. 99 for this particular *Homily*, and numerous notes from 230–40.

18. Snyder, "Wesley and Macarius," 59.

19. Collins, *Shape of Grace*, 195.

adjusted that with which he was interacting in Clement. Michael J. Christensen affirms that,

> For Wesley, we are justified and sanctified by "faith filled with the energy of love" (not by works nor by gnosis). We enjoy *communion* with God as creatures, but not *union* with God as equals. We may become *like* God, Wesley hopes and prays, but we do not become divine! Thus, when Wesley appropriates Clement's gnostic vision, he "corrects" the assertion of *gnosis* as the means to perfection.[20]

Christensen thus recognizes that these ideas contributed to the distinctly Wesleyan teaching of sanctification. He goes on to suggest that "what Wesley envisioned as Christian perfection, holiness, or entire sanctification is theologically dependent upon earlier versions of *theosis*."[21]

In the same manner, John Wesley and his colleagues sought to distinguish between a healthy, scripturally-based idea of union with God and what they saw as an unhealthy, speculative mysticism. John Fletcher, considered John Wesley's heir apparent until his untimely death from tuberculosis, wrote on this crucial distinction in an essay entitled, "An Evangelical Mysticism." Here he presents what he calls a "wise mysticism," which Fletcher describes as "glowing with Divine wisdom, and shedding luminous rays on the most profound truths . . . and which cautiously penetrates the bark or veil of religion to sound its depths." He then contrasts this with an "extravagant" or "frivolous" mysticism, "by which violence is done to sound criticism, in quitting, without reason, the literal sense of the Scriptures."[22]

The distinction which Fletcher was seeking to describe is related to the kind of pantheistic mysticism in which individuality is lost and we "dissolve into oneness with God" (as well as perhaps the idea of merely philosophical speculation), compared with the idea in which the personality continues and the distinction between the Creator and the creature is maintained.

While we can and should take seriously the refinements made to the tradition of *theosis* by John Wesley, we believe that Christensen is correct when he exhorts us to "read Wesley *with his sources*, and not simply read back into ancient sources Wesley's distinctive eighteenth-century vision

---

20. Christensen, "Christian Perfection," 222.
21. Ibid., 226.
22. Fletcher, "An Evangelical Mysticism," 4:9.

of perfection or programmatic agenda of reform."²³ Christensen goes beyond this, however, and exhorts his reader to seek to interact with these sources in a manner effective in our modern context,

> Such a reformulation would incorporate the best of John Wesley's theological refinements and improvements on the ancient doctrine of *theosis* (i.e., appropriation by faith not by works or knowledge, inward assurance over perpetual seeking, accessibility in this earthly life), while fully appreciating the Eastern emphasis on "therapeutic" soteriology with its biblical affirmation of original humanity and original blessing. In so doing, we may arrive at a . . . vision of *theosis* as part of the essential quest for human wholeness and completion of the new creation in Christ.²⁴

One of Wesley's important contributions to the discussion was his ability to hold in tension issues such as the importance of sanctification and a healing model of salvation without abandoning the reality of justification by grace through faith which is so clearly rooted in the Scriptural witness.

ON UNION WITH GOD

How can this understanding of union with God be integrated into a healthy mysticism which also bears witness to the gospel's reality? It is here as well that John Wesley offers some wisdom through his theological emphases, as well as in the way these emphases are meant to have an impact not only on the individual believer and the believing community, but on the world.

In Howard Snyder's 2009 essay on the "Missional Flavor of John Wesley's Theology," he describes the theological undergirding for mission which emerged out of some of the central themes in Wesley's theology. For Snyder, these themes, which he looks at as elements of a missional theology, include the image of God in humankind, reflected less directly throughout creation, a therapeutic view of salvation as healing (though without denying other elements of justification), God's prevenient grace which both empowers and draws all people to himself, and the Holy Spirit empowered process of Christian perfecting, also referred to as

---

23. Christensen, "Christian Perfection," 223.
24. Ibid., 227.

sanctification.²⁵ In practice, these are actually intertwined with one another; thus, the therapeutic theme is frequently expressed as the healing and restoration of the image of God, empowered by his grace, and ultimately moving towards further realization in the process of Holy Spirit-empowered perfecting. As may be noticed from the previous chapter, these four themes all found expression as well in the earlier writings of Macarius-Symeon, so there is a certain degree of continuity with these from antiquity. Significantly, these themes can also be recognized as components of Segal's element of *transformation* central to the discussion in the previous chapters; Wesley is here continuing an earlier theme of rooting what are ordinarily mystical goals in the biblical witness. As we will see, Wesley and his colleagues applied these themes in their own theology and teaching, making them particularly practical both internally for personal and communal transformation as well as for an outward focus in proclamation and service.

Wesley clearly believed that there would be an effect on the evangelization of humankind based on the state of Christians' lives and communities. If the nations were going to be impacted by the Gospel, it would be because they saw it being lived out and could observe the *glory* of God among Christian people—that is to say, if they could see a God-empowered *theosis* bringing healing and restoration to those who claimed to follow Jesus, walking in the fullness of the image of God, they would respond to the drawing of the prevenient grace of God and joyfully come to faith in Jesus. Thus, in his sermon on "The General Spread of the Gospel,"²⁶ Wesley begins with what is essentially an account of the lost state of the peoples and nations of the world, beginning with those he considers to be the farthest from God, exemplified for him among the tribal peoples of the South Pacific islands.²⁷ From there he moves on

25. Snyder, "Missional Flavor."

26. This sermon dates from 1783. Other recent writings which cite this sermon in a missional context include Muck, "Third Moment of Muslim Witness," 83–95; Muck, "Eighteenth-Century Contributions," 93–101; and Walls, "World Parish to World Church," 138–150. It is similar in some ways with William Carey's more famous (though later) *Enquiry*, though without Carey's rather extensive statistics. It is also reminiscent of Thomas Coke's 1783 *A Plan of the Society for the Establishment of Missions among the Heathens* (which Coke's biographer informs us was done without Wesley's blessing) as well as the 1785 *Address to the Pious and Benevolent* which he did under Wesley's blessing; on this see Vickers, "Introduction to *The Journals of Dr. Thomas Coke*," 7.

27. John Wesley, "The General Spread of the Gospel," 1–2.

to the Muslims, and from there to the state of the Christian community in non-Western lands,[28] to describe even the failings of those who consider themselves Christian in the West among Roman Catholics as well as Protestants.[29]

Wesley describes what he sees as the "problem" of the unevangelized, and, crucially, made it clear that a key element of the problem is the terrible example of the lives of those who claim to be Christians. For example, later in the sermon, Wesley describes the complaints voiced by Native Americans concerning the encroaching Colonial settlers; they ask in what manner is it that the Christians' lives are better than theirs. Wesley notes accusations from Hindu people in what would now be of one part of south India. He quotes them as listing the sins of the Christians in their area, concluding with "Christians are devils! I will not become a Christian!"[30]

Wesley sees the global spread of the revival of the gospel as the solution, in spite of the apparent human impossibility of the situation.[31] He reminds his readers of the transforming power of the gospel itself,[32] and offers a picture of the transformation of lives which God had been accomplishing in the midst of the Methodist movement up until that point.[33] As those who have been "Christian" for generations actually begin to live out the faith to which they claim to be adherents, it will have an effect on others.[34] Interestingly, he presents this spread in precisely the reverse order in which he had earlier discussed the state of the world. Wesley perceives that the *primary* element preventing Muslims, "heathens" and others from coming to Christ is the corrupt lifestyle of Christians. Thus, as Christians begin actually to live as Christ meant for them to live, Muslims and others will begin coming to faith in Jesus. Wesley writes,

> The grand stumbling-block being thus happily removed out of the way, namely, the lives of the Christians, the Mahometans (*sic*) will look upon them with other eyes, and begin to give

28. Ibid., 3–6.
29. Ibid., 7.
30. Ibid., 22. The actual quote in Wesley's sermon is, "Christian man take my wife: Christian man much drunk: Christian man kill man! Devil-Christian! Me no Christian."
31. John Wesley, "The General Spread of the Gospel," 8–9.
32. Ibid., 10–12.
33. Ibid., 13–15.
34. Ibid., 16–21.

attention to their words. And as their words will be clothed with divine energy, attended with the demonstration of the Spirit and of power, those of them that fear God will soon take knowledge of the Spirit whereby Christians speak. They will "receive with meekness the engrafted word," and will bring forth fruit with patience.[35]

He goes on to express a hope in the gospel's spread to those he refers to as "heathen,"[36] and finally, ultimately one might say, to the Jewish people, who must wait until the "fullness of the Gentiles be come in."[37] For Wesley, then, the evangelization of the nations of the world depends upon Christian holiness and sanctification. If Christians are living as they are meant to, and indeed, scripturally speaking, empowered to, those outside the community of Christ will be drawn in.

In his essay entitled "General Observations on the Redemption of Mankind by Jesus Christ," John Fletcher also saw clearly the degree of light which had been received by, for example, the Muslims, to be a kind of *preparatio evangelii*, preparatory for them, as well as perhaps for others in the lands of other religious traditions in which Islam had spread. For example, having described some of the exalted statements in the Qur'ān and Sunnah concerning Jesus, Fletcher goes on to assert that, in spite of the distortions of the Qur'ān concerning Christian faith,

> yet it admits enough of our doctrines to overthrow idolatry, and the external empire of Satan upon earth; insomuch that in Africa and India, Mohammedanism prepares idolaters for the reception of Christianity: and secondly to nourish our hope, that the Mohammedans, who have already such exalted notions of Jesus Christ, will embrace the Gospel, when the great scandals of the Christian Churches shall be done away... (*sic*)[38]

Thus Fletcher seems ultimately to lean in the direction of seeing the light the nations have already received as *preparatory* to their receiving the gospel in its fullness. Here he echoes Wesley's sentiments in "The General Spread of the Gospel" that this may be connected with the spread

---

35. Ibid., 21.
36. Ibid., 22–24.
37. Ibid., 25.
38. Fletcher, *Works*, 4.227. This positive view of Islam as a potential *preparatio evangelii* was shared, for example, by W. H. T. Temple Gairdner in his contribution to a 1915 consultation on mission in the Muslim context. See Gairdner, "First Study," 32, as well as Bennett, "Dialogue," 235 n. 102.

of the revival in the churches, that is, that they would be demonstratively walking in the fullness of what is relationship with God.

This is significant for our study on a number of levels. As was the case in the earlier writings we examined, the inner life of those who were walking in progressively deeper union with God was to be expressed in outward expressions of a transformed life. As we saw in Macarius-Symeon, while he affirmed a strong element of "sober intoxication," of ecstatic union with God, he also recognized that this could not be maintained indefinitely, but must ultimately be integrated with a sober, abiding union which is expressed in service to God and to other people. Macarius-Symeon's *Homily* 8.4–5a touches on this, and Wesley notices this *Homily*, rendering it in his own redaction,

> And one that is rich in grace, at all times, by night and by day, continues in a perfect state, free and pure, ever captivated with love, and elevated to God. But if a man should have these things always present before him, he would not be able to undertake—the dispensation of the word. Neither could he bear to hear, or have any concern for himself or the morrow; but purely to sit in a corner in a state of elevation: so that the perfect degree of all has not been given, that a man may be in a capacity to attend the care of the brethren, and the ministration of the word.[39]

Another element we see here is the recognition that God, by means of prevenient grace, is active in drawing all peoples to himself, and using truth even within other religious systems (most notably Islam) as part of his drawing and preparatory process. We will see more on this below, when we turn to the discussion of the element of prevenient grace.

THE IMAGE OF GOD IN HUMANKIND

> We, lastly, have daily opportunities of knowing, if Christianity be of God, then of how glorious a privilege are they thought worthy who persuade others to accept its benefits. Seeing when the author of it "cometh in the clouds of heaven," they who have saved others from sin and its attendant death "shall shine as the brightness of the firmament"; they who have *reprinted the image of God on many souls* "as the stars for ever"![40]

---

39. *Homily* 5.3–4; "Macarius of Egypt," 1819,

40. John Wesley, "The Image of God," 4.2, emphasis mine (Sermon dates from 1730).

Union with God and Mission in the Theology of John Wesley

What did Wesley mean by humankind created in the image of God? Wesley's sermon on "The General Deliverance" provides a concise explanation of his understanding of this. Wesley describes humans as having been created in God's image, in the "likeness of his Creator,"[41] which he describes as being "endued with *understanding* . . . with a *will* . . . with *liberty*."[42] Wesley thus connected his idea of human freedom of will and the creation of humankind in God's image.

Intriguingly, however, he also describes the lower creatures with the *same* attributes: *understanding, will,* and *liberty*.[43] "What then makes the barrier between men and brutes?" Wesley asks rhetorically. He answers that humans are "capable of God," whereas the lower creatures are not.[44] What does it mean to Wesley to be "capable of God"? He later concisely states that he is referring to a capability of "knowing, loving and enjoying the Author of their being,"[45] thus distinguishing not only the difference between human and animal nature, but as well what is to be, in effect, the end to which this capability is employed. Wesley is also conveying a warning, that those who neither know, love, nor enjoy their Creator essentially degrade themselves into beasts, as they avoid that which chiefly distinguishes humans from beasts.[46]

In his sermon on "The End of Christ's Coming," Wesley notes, as he has done earlier, the creation of humans in both what he describes as the *natural* image of God, that is, the earlier mentioned three-fold elements of *understanding, will,* and *liberty*, or free will.[47] He adds, however, that humankind was additionally created in the *moral* image of God, walking in "righteousness and true holiness."[48] It was this latter element which was lost at the fall, with the fearful consequences described by Wesley as

> The life of God was extinguished in his soul. The glory departed from him. He lost the whole moral image of God, righteousness

---

41. John Wesley, "The General Deliverance," 1.1. (Sermon dates from 1781)
42. Ibid.
43. Ibid., 1.4.
44. Ibid., 1.5.
45. Ibid., 3.6, see also Snyder, "Missional Flavor," 63.
46. John Wesley, "The General Deliverance," 3.11; see also Macarius-Symeon's *Homily* 25.3, Macarius, *Homilies*, 179–180.
47. John Wesley. "The End of Christ's Coming," 1.3–4. (Sermon dates from 1758).
48. Ibid., 1.7.

and true holiness. He was unholy; he was unhappy; he was full of sin, full of guilt and tormenting fears.[49]

Wesley's colleague and one-time designated successor John Fletcher had a particularly Trinitarian understanding of humankind created in God's image. He addressed this in his essay on this topic, "Remarks on the Trinity," that touches more directly on several of the Wesleyan themes which we am examining here. The original context of the essay involved answering some of the arguments of important eighteenth-century Deist spokesman, Joseph Priestly. How did this understanding of God's nature, he questioned, help to promote "morality and piety"?[50]

> . . . God, by the manifestation of his sanctifying Spirit, has re-established his image in their souls. Then the Trinity being clearly revealed, God is adored in spirit and in truth, with a zeal like that which burned in the bosoms of the primitive Christians; then men begin to love and help each other with a charity which the world never saw before . . .

> . . . And it should be remembered, that faith in the Father, Son and Holy Spirit, of which we speak, is the gift of God, Eph. ii, 8, and not the word of a nurse, or the dictate of a catechist. It is a Divine energy, which is "the substance of things hoped for, a cordial demonstration of things not seen;" for we believe with the heart unto righteousness, before we can make confession with the mouth unto salvation.[51]

We see here that John Fletcher took Wesley's understanding of the Trinity and expanded upon it, extrapolating it into the practical application of life in connection with God in Christ, and empowered by the Holy Spirit. Here we see the themes of the image of God in humans, the path of Christian perfection, and prevenient grace integrated with an understanding of the Trinity, which Wesley described in his related sermon on the Trinity as an essential of the faith.[52] This connection between renewal in the image of God and Christian perfection, or sanctification, was also expressed more concisely in Wesley's *Plain Account of Christian Perfection*, when the answer to the catechetical question, "What is it to be *sanc-*

---

49. Ibid., 1.10.
50. Fletcher, "Remarks on the Trinity," *Works*, 4.44.
51. Ibid., 4.45–46
52. John Wesley, "On the Trinity," 18; Wesley states, for example, "Therefore, I do not see how it is possible for any to have vital religion who denies that these Three are one." (Sermon dates from 1773).

tified?" is given as "To be renewed in the image of God, in "righteousness and true holiness."[53] Moreover, Wesley's brief comments on 2 Pet 1:4, the very verse which is a key touchstone for teaching on union with and participation in God, reflect this same idea. Regarding being "partakers of the divine nature," he explains that this refers to "being renewed in the image of God, and having communion with him, so as to dwell in God, and God in you."[54]

That God created humankind in his image is thus an important theme in the writings of John Wesley. It relates to his understanding of salvation, even as it did for the early church writers. Randy Maddox explains that Western and Eastern anthropology and view of the fall of humankind developed along different lines. Maddox views the Western view as being that humans were created "in a complete and perfect state—the epitome of what God intended them to be,"[55] with God's will being understood as for them to simply remain in that state. By contrast, the Eastern view understood that even at creation, while Adam and Eve were originally sinless, they were nonetheless *incomplete*—humankind was meant to grow from bearing the image of God ("the universal human potential for life in God") into the likeness of God, which was understood as the process of "progressive realization of that possibility."[56] This is the idea behind the process referred to as *theosis*, or divinization, involving *participation* in the life of God by women and men in worship, prayer, and partaking of the sacraments,[57] as well as in ascetical practices.[58]

Wesley integrated these ideas into his own anthropology, allowing for a degree of synergism between the empowering grace of God and the human responsibility to respond to that gracious empowering in

---

53. John Wesley, *Plain Account of Christian Perfection*, 17.

54. John Wesley, *Explanatory Notes*, 2 Pet 1:4.

55. Maddox, *Responsible*, 65. Note, however, that even Augustine in his *Enchiridion* says that, "God judged it better to bring good out of evil than not to permit any evil to exist." See Augustine, *Enchiridion*, viii. 27.

56. Ibid., 66.

57. Ibid.

58. See especially Lossky, *Mystical Theology*, 18. Here Lossky's description of Eastern Orthodox monasticism (meant to lead towards *theosis*) as being "exclusively contemplative" is held in contrast with the "secular" (married) clergy and the laymen, who may legitimately "occupy themselves with social activities or other outside work" (Lossky, *Mystical Theology*, 17–18). This highly quietistic idea of ascetic practice is a precise example the sort of ideas which Wesley sought to divest from his own appropriation of early Church practice (Campbell, *Christian Antiquity*, x).

faith and in flowing with his purposes "in the transformation of their lives."[59] We can see this element of synergism even in his redaction of Macarius-Symeon's 25th *Homily*, evoking the same passage in 2 Pet 1:4, "He therefore that is desirous to be made partaker of the Divine glory, ought, with an insatiable affection, with his whole heart and strength, night and day to seek help from God."[60] Importantly, we can observe here that Macarius-Symeon, and Wesley as his "editor," are not proposing an anthropocentric model of achieving divine glory, but rather are exhorting the reader to continually "seek help from God."

Wesley did not *jettison* the Western juridical model, but *merged* with it the more Eastern idea of a healing or therapeutic idea of salvation.[61] This meant that Wesley's anthropology was more optimistic than that of the pure Western model based on that of Augustine. It is important to emphasize here that Wesley nonetheless understood that even approaching God for salvation (with its attendant goal of the restoration of the divine image) required the empowerment of the grace of God.[62] Rooted in this understanding, witness can also proceed in a manner which acknowledges the legal as well as moral fall of humankind, while seeing the goal of salvation ultimately not only in re-setting the juridical ledger, but in the ongoing spiritual restoration of humankind into the likeness for which they were actually created. Note that here as well as elsewhere, there is a fairly strong degree of overlap with the theme of salvation as healing, which we will examine more directly in section below on this topic.

Interestingly, in regard to the fall of Adam, and consequently of humankind, Wesley makes the somewhat startling remark that

> we may gain infinitely more than we have lost. We may now attain both higher degrees of holiness and higher degrees of glory than it would have been possible for us to attain if Adam had not sinned. For if Adam had not sinned, the Son of God had not died . . . there would have been no place for love to God the Redeemer: this could have had no being. The highest glory and

---

59 Maddox, *Responsible*, 39.

60. *Homily* 13.2; "Macarius of Egypt," equivalent to *Homily* 25.3; Pseudo-Macarius, *Fifty Spiritual Homilies*, 160. See also Young, "Inner Struggle," 163.

61. Maddox, *Responsible*, 66–67.

62. Snyder, *Radical Wesley*, 144.

joy of saints on earth and saints in heaven, Christ crucified, had been wanting.[63]

Consider here again Richard Bauckham's words echoing this idea, that God's suffering and love as revealed in the Messiah's suffering and love is intrinsic to who God *is*, and extends our understanding of God's character in a way otherwise impossible. Bauckham describes how the death of Jesus "reveals who God is. What it means to be God in God's sovereignty and glory appears in the self-humiliation of the one who serves. . . . Because God is who God is in his gracious self-giving, God's identity, we can say, is not simply revealed but enacted in the event of salvation for the world which the service and self-humiliation of his Son accomplishes."[64]

Another element of the theme of the image of God is the manner in which a recognition of humanity in God's image enables us to understand human dignity and justice more deeply. Although Snyder notes that Wesley's concern about this area was *more* than the recognition of and full restoration of the image of God in people,[65] Wesley's view clearly includes this. *Because* people are created in the image of God, we are meant to interact with them in a manner which affirms this, and pursue relationship with them in such a way as to reflect Christ's heart for them regardless of their economic status or perceived spiritual state. This is one of the reasons for Wesley's frustration in sermons such as "On God's Vineyard"[66] and "Causes of the Inefficiency of Christianity."[67] Wesley notices the growing lack of concern for the poor among the members of the Methodist community as their diligence has enabled them to increase in wealth and stature. Of course, this is due not only to the intrinsic value which Wesley places on people, but also because for Wesley, the evangelistic power of the Methodist revival was centered precisely in the fact that a good percentage of Methodists were actively seeking to live out their faith. Indeed, as noted earlier in our brief examination of "The General Spread of the Gospel," Wesley describes both how the gospel's dissemination is hindered by the hypocrisy of Christians, as well as how

63. John Wesley, "On the Fall of Man," 2.10.
64. Bauckham, *Jesus and the God of Israel*, 50.
65. Snyder, "Missional Flavor," 66–67.
66. John Wesley, "On God's Vineyard," 5.3–4. (Sermon dated 1779).
67. John Wesley, "Causes of the Inefficiency of Christianity," 8–11. (Sermon dated 1789).

Christians living out their faith will be what enables the gospel to spread to all peoples in the world.

In practice, Wesley's focus on the poor came to the fore especially (and famously) in the work at Bristol among the coal miners of Kingswood. George Whitefield was preaching to thousands—at times, reportedly tens of thousands—and he invited Wesley to join him. In spite of some initial opposition from his brother Charles (as well as John's own reluctance), John Wesley went and not only preached, but quickly began the work of organizing those coming to faith into societies which could care for them and help them to continue their spiritual growth and discipleship.[68] Moreover, he also sought to utilize the evident gifting some of these simple people had "for exhortation and preaching," and sought to train them in an ongoing manner and to send them out with the message of the gospel themselves.[69] Importantly, Wesley "adopted and adapted forms to keep the sheep folded and growing,"[70] seeking what would be most practical in deepening as well as expanding discipleship partly through developing leaders among the poverty-stricken believers themselves.[71]

This work among the poor was not, of course, limited to *kerygma*, but also included a strong element of *diakonia*: in preaching to the coal miners, for example, Wesley was "touching those most cruelly victimized by industrialization,"[72] and in addition to the Word preached, the word was lived out in Wesley's actions. Snyder writes that Wesley "opened free dispensaries, set up a kind of credit union, and established schools and orphanages" and "worked tirelessly for their spiritual and material welfare."[73] Wesley also sought to include "creative economic alternatives,"[74] demonstrating an understanding of the need to differentiate between disastrous circumstances requiring *relief* and those best served by *development*. Of course, for Wesley, as in the scriptures, the key dynamic enabling this to work together was *love*: "the love of God and of all mankind, flowing

---

68. Snyder, *Radical Wesley*, 32–33.
69. Ibid., 34.
70. Ibid., 38.
71. Ibid., 53.
72. Ibid., 86.
73. Ibid.
74. Ibid., 87.

from faith in Jesus Christ, and producing . . . every right disposition of heart, toward God and toward man."[75]

How this played out in the waning years of Wesley's life and those following his death represented a somewhat uneven record. For example, Wesley was adamantly opposed to slavery, and sought to inculcate this understanding into the Methodist societies; David Hempton describes Wesley as "the first English religious figure of real significance to denounce slavery."[76]

Early on in his ministry, one finds this reflected, for example, in the journals of Thomas Coke.[77] Coke came to the newly independent United States shortly after the American Revolution. His initial encounters with African-Americans were presented in a sometimes condescending, but sometimes admiring manner. For example, Coke glowingly, but quite sincerely, described Francis Asbury's colleague Harry Hosier as "one of the best preachers in the world!"[78] Note that everywhere he went, whether he was formally preaching or traveling, Coke sought and used opportunities to share the message of the gospel with others; this is important to bear in mind in the midst of what Coke recorded following these above initial anecdotes. Coke made a preaching tour of several weeks into the American South, and it is here that he began to preach against the institution of slavery wherever he went,[79] asking slave owners to emancipate their slaves. Some did so; others resisted and some even threatened violence. Coke and Asbury eventually sought and obtained audience with the newly elected President George Washington to convince him to sign a petition against slavery.[80] In the event, in spite of a sympathetic hear-

---

75. Ibid., 88.

76. Hempton, *Methodism*, 41.

77. Interestingly, in common with Henry Martyn, another Anglican missionary of the period with Methodist connections who went to Bengal, Coke had been impacted by the lives of both John Fletcher and David Brainerd. "O that I may follow him as he followed Christ!" Coke exclaims in his journal concerning Fletcher (Coke, *Journals*, 28), even as Martyn exclaimed "Why cannot I be like Fletcher and Brainerd?. . . Is anything too hard for the Lord?" (Martyn, *Journal and Letters*, 1.452). Clinton Bennett acknowledges Martyn's Methodist connections, although he missed Martyn's devotion to John Fletcher in addition to his devotion to the writings of David Brainerd. Bennett also missed the connection which Martyn drew with the Sūfīs in "Dialogue," 196–204, 239.

78. Coke, *Journals*, 37.

79. Ibid., 53–64.

80. Ibid., 63–64.

ing, they were unable to convince President Washington to sign their petition. Part of their commitment to justice in this case, would likely have emerged in part from the view of humankind created in God's image, and of the opportunity for *all* of humankind to be restored into the fullness of that divine image.[81] Importantly, this represents a very Wesleyan element which integrates the theme of union with God and praxis in the community. While acknowledging the theme of *theosis*, Wesley and his colleagues nonetheless had little use for a mysticism which would result in a merely inward-looking quietism.

Finally, we can observe in his introductory remarks to his extracts from the Macarian *Homilies*, Wesley's description of what he saw represented in the Macarian writings included recognition of both the themes of restoration of the image of God and the theme of union with God. He writes that

> There is visibly to be distinguished in our author, a rich, sublime, and noble vein of piety, but that perfectly serious, sober, and unaffected; natural and lively, but sedate and deep withal. Whatever he insists upon is essential, is durable, is necessary. What he continually labors to cultivate in himself and others is, the real life of GOD in the heart and soul, that kingdom of GOD, which consists in righteousness, and peace, and joy in the Holy Ghost. He is ever quickening and stirring up his audience, endeavoring to kindle in them a steady zeal, an earnest desire, and inflamed ambition, to recover that Divine image we were made in; to be made conformable to CHRIST our Head; to be daily sensible more and more of our living union with him as such; and discovering it, as, occasion requires, in all the genuine fruits of an holy life and conversation, in such a victorious faith as overcomes the world, and working by love, is ever fulfilling the whole law of GOD, He seems indeed never to be easy, but either in the height, or breadth, or length of Divine love, or at least in the depths of humility.[82]

As we noted above, then, Wesley took up this theme of the recovery of the divine image which he observed in the Macarian *Homilies* (and

---

81. Later, however, the commitment to an anti-slavery stance sadly began to wane, particularly in the South (Hempton, *Methodism*, 106–8), and even in the North, African-American church members were often treated as second-class citizens in the kingdom of God, as was illustrated by Frederick Douglass' account of attending a Methodist church in New Bedford (Hempton, *Methodism*, 105–6).

82. John Wesley, "Of Macarius," *A Christian Library*, vol. 1, 1.

elsewhere), but then sought to take what was a largely *centripetal* theme in the monastic *Homilies* and bring to them a *centrifugal* focus in proclamation and service, including working for justice for those who have suffered oppression.[83]

SALVATION AS HEALING

Another area which has relevance for applying the patristic understanding of *theosis* as sanctification and perfection to the work of discipleship is the idea of salvation having a soul-healing, therapeutic dimension.[84] Randy Maddox points out that the dominant understanding of salvation in the Christian East is therapeutic rather than juridical, but, importantly, Wesley seems to have been able to *integrate* these in his own approach.[85] Wesley understood grace as referring to *both* the deifying, empowering, uncreated presence of the Holy Spirit *and* pardon from sin and justification.[86]

This theme of Christ as the healer of the soul is also found in Wesley's redaction of the Macarian *Homilies*. In fact, he integrates the themes of the Incarnation, the Crucifixion and Christ as sacrificial Lamb of God as well as the "true Physician" in the following passage:

> Moses came, but was not able to give perfect health. The priests, the gifts, tithes, new-moons, washings, sacrifices, whole burnt-offerings, and every other branch of righteousness, were punctually observed under the law; and yet the soul could not be healed, and cleansed from the impure fountain of sinful thoughts. Neither could all its righteousness avail any thing, till such time as the Savior came himself, the true Physician, who healeth freely—who gave himself a ransom for the race of mankind. He alone wrought the great and saving redemption, and cure of the soul: he it was that set it free from the state of bondage, and brought it out of darkness, having glorified it with his own light. He has dried up the fountain of unclean thoughts;

---

83. It's nonetheless important to observe here that while these themes of proclamation and service were not a central theme of the Macarian *Homilies*, on the ground, the Syrian monastic movement was vigorously missional. They traveled widely in proclamation and service, establishing communities of faith in Jesus in Central Asia, India and China. See Colless, trans. and introduction, *The Wisdom of the Pearlers*, 1–2, and Moffett, *Christianity in Asia*, 100–1.

84. Maddox, *Responsible*, 229.

85. Ibid., 67.

86. Ibid., 199.

for "behold," says the Scripture, "the Lamb of GOD, which takes away the sin of the world!" Its own medicines out of the earth, that is, its own righteous actions, were not able to heal it of so great a plague. But by the heavenly and Divine nature, the gift of the Holy Spirit, was man capable of recovering health, being purified in his heart by the Holy Ghost. Let us therefore have faith in him, and come to him in truth, that he may speedily perform his healing operation within us: for he has promised to "give to them that ask him, his Holy Spirit; and to open to them that knock; and to be found of them that seek him:" and he that promised cannot lie.[87]

A therapeutic view of salvation, as the healing of the soul, often in connection with the restoration of the image of God, is thus one which Wesley shares with the writers of early Christian faith. Snyder notes on this that people "are guilty for their acts of sin, but actual sin betrays the deeper problem of the moral disease that alienates people from God, from themselves and each other, and from the earth."[88] A number of the hymns and poems of the early Methodist Church illustrate this, such as the fourth verse of "The Good Samaritan."

> Savior of my soul draw nigh,
> In mercy haste to me,
> At the point of death I lie,
> And cannot come to thee;
> Now thy kind relief afford,
> The wine and oil of grace pour in;
> Good Physician, speak the word,
> And heal my soul of sin.[89]

In his early sermon on "The Image of God," Wesley is already focused on the theme of the creation of humankind in God's image, the loss of that image, and the restoration and healing of that image which has been an important thread through much of what has been examined until now. As before, Wesley uses the language of healing to describe the need of those who have not yet entered into faith in Christ—"how extremely pitiable their condition is who are insensible of their innate

---

87. *Homily* 12.7–8; "Macarius the Egyptian;" equivalent of *Homily* 20.6; Macarius, *Homilies*, 151–66.

88. Snyder, "Missional Flavor," 65.

89. Charles Wesley, "Woe is Me! What Tongue Can Tell," fourth verse.

disease, or refuse the only cure of it."[90] Indeed, Wesley proceeds to explain how the only "cure" for the natural corruption of humankind is Christ. "Our business it is to know in particular that we are all originally foolish and vicious, and that there is no truth in our whole religion more absolutely necessary to be known than this . . . if man be naturally corrupt, then Christianity is of God; seeing that . . . 'there is no other God which can deliver after this sort' from that corruption."[91] While we have already noted that Wesley's anthropology is positive overall, he does not deny the reality that the grace of God must animate humankind in a manner which people are incapable of receiving without divine assistance.

In his sermon on "The Mystery of Iniquity," Wesley focuses more sharply on the healing metaphor for salvation, and then hones a very prophetic message concerning the perils (for individuals, for the church, and for the nations) of purely nominal Christian faith. Towards the beginning, he demonstrates his synthesis of legal and therapeutic understandings of the atonement (combined with the earlier discussed theme of the restoration of the image of God in humankind), in one breath quoting 1 John 2:2 on Jesus' being "the propitiation for the sins of the whole world," and in the next breath describing Jesus as "the great Physician, who by his almighty Spirit should heal the sickness of their souls, and restore them not only to the favor but to the 'image of God wherein they were created.'"[92]

Like Wesley, Athanasius of Alexandria presented a balanced, "integrated" view of the atonement which integrated a healing understanding with one which included the legal metaphor which was predominant in much of Western Christendom. In his *On the Incarnation of the Word of God*, Athanasius famously stated that, "He indeed, assumed humanity that we might become God,"[93] a statement which for our purposes can be understood as pointing to both the already-discussed image of God in humankind, and the theme of sanctification. In this same work one can find statements affirming a legal substitution idea of the Atonement. For example, in 2.8, Athanasius writes,

> Thus, taking a body like our own, because all our bodies were liable to the corruption of death, He surrendered His body to

90. John Wesley, "The Image of God," 4.1.
91. Ibid., 4.2.
92. John Wesley, "The Mystery of Iniquity," 2.
93. Athanasius, *On the Incarnation*, 8.54.

death instead of all, and offered it to the Father. This He did out of sheer love for us, so that in His death all might die, and the law of death thereby be abolished because, having fulfilled in His body that for which it was appointed, it was thereafter voided of its power for men.[94]

Wesley's thinking on this is rather like what we find in Athanasius, who, like Macarius-Symeon, affirms a therapeutic idea of the Atonement, recognizing that this is not contradictory to an understanding of Jesus taking on the penalty of death on our behalf, but these rather are complimentary emphases. Athanasius asserts that,

But once man was in existence, and things that were, not things that were not, demanded to be healed, it followed as a matter of course that the Healer and Savior should align Himself with those things that existed already, in order to heal the existing evil. For that reason, therefore, He was made man, and used the body as His human instrument.[95]

Thus, when Wesley sought to express these emphases in the same work, he was really just following the precedent of the early Christian writers, as well as simply noting different facets of the atonement described in the scriptures themselves. Certainly from the perspective of a theology of mission, both understandings, as well as the connected element of the restoration of the lost (or perhaps, broken) image of God in humankind are crucial and central.

In Wesley's redaction of Macarian *Homily* 44 (19 in Wesley's version), he compares the scourge of sin with the ugliness of leprosy, and makes it clear that it is only Christ who, as the Shepherd, can bring healing to the one who comes to him. He writes,

For as the shepherd can heal a diseased sheep, and keep him from the wolves; so the true Shepherd is able to heal the sheep that was lost, even man from the leprosy of sin. . . .. After the same manner, CHRIST, the true high-priest of good things to come, in condescension to leprous souls, enters into the tabernacle of their body, takes care of their disorders, and healeth them.[96]

---

94. Ibid., 2.8.

95. Ibid., 7.44.

96. *Homily* 19.3–4; "Macarius of Egypt;" equivalent to *Homily* 44.3–4; Macarius, *Homilies*, 276–77.

Union with God and Mission in the Theology of John Wesley

John Fletcher expanded on this in a similar manner, combining the theme of healing, including the metaphor of sin as "leprosy" found in Macarius-Symeon, with that of the restoration of the image of God. Like Wesley above, he stresses the importance of the recognition of the depth of human need and corruption, and that indeed those who "do not sufficiently feel their sins and miseries"[97] can't adequately come to Jesus, who calls "sinners to repentance."[98] Notice how Fletcher combines these themes in what follows:

> Nevertheless, the time will come, when, if you harden not your heart, you shall feel your danger and disease; when you shall be as much charmed with submission to Jesus Christ as Naaman, the leprous general, was in submitting to the venerable prophet; when you shall feel that in order to find health of soul and a foretaste of eternal life, you must know the only true God, and Jesus Christ whom he hath sent, John xvii, 3. For regeneration, without which none can see the kingdom of heaven, is nothing more than the re-establishing the soul in that happy state, when impressed with the image of God, she has not only the life of the Father, as her principle of life, but also the light of the Son to illuminate her understanding, and the love of the "Holy Spirit" to regulate her will.[99]

Wesley and Fletcher thus both sought to ground their therapeutic understanding of salvation in the biblical text, and in synthesis with other models of salvation and the atonement. Moreover, this is also an element of the mystical *transformation* part of the process of union with God in Christ: Rather than just providing atonement for the purpose of legal forgiveness, Christ brings healing and deliverance to the souls of those who come to him.

THE PREVENIENT GRACE OF GOD

One of the elements frequently observed in Wesley's theology is that of *prevenient grace*, essentially the pervasive, uncreated presence of the Holy Spirit found throughout creation, drawing people to turn towards God. Wesley describes the operation of grace in terms of "preventing" (in modern English, *prevenient*) grace, in which this same Holy Spirit draws

---

97. Fletcher, "The Three Principles," *Works*, 4.232.
98. Ibid.
99. Ibid.

us to himself, then "convincing grace" (that is, the grace of repentance) which leads us to justification by grace through faith. This salvation, Wesley informs us, consists of "two grand branches, justification and sanctification. By justification we are saved from the guilt of sin, and restored to the favor of God; by sanctification we are saved from the power and root of sin, and restored to the image of God."[100] Here we are presented with what is perhaps the very heart of Wesley's theology.[101] This is expressed in the idea of the grace of God as *both* unmerited favor saving us from the guilt of sin and restoring us legally before God,[102] and the (also unmerited) power of God in our lives by the Holy Spirit's presence which enables us to root out sin and transform us into Christlikeness.[103] This being the case, witness can also proceed by acknowledging the legal as well as moral fall of humankind, while seeing the work of mission ultimately not only in re-setting the juridical ledger, but in the ongoing spiritual restoration of humankind into the likeness for which they were actually created. Moreover, Snyder observes that,

> One missiological implication of preceding [prevenient] grace is that God's Spirit is the missionary. God is already active in all persons, cultures, societies, and to a degree in many (not all) religions. God works for good, limiting the effects of evil, and seeking to bring people to himself. . .The work of Christian mission is so to cooperate with God's preceding grace that people may experience God's convicting, justifying and sanctifying grace.[104]

PREVENIENT GRACE AND THE MEANS OF GRACE

We have already discussed a key element of Wesley's theology was the synergistic interaction between God's empowering, prevenient grace, and grace-enabled human response back toward God. Part of Wesley's understanding of how people are meant to be empowered by, and met

---

100. John Wesley, "On Working Out Our Own Salvation," 2.1 (Sermon dated to 1785).

101. Outler notes that the similar terminology was used earlier by Thomas Manton and William Tilly in referring to the various operations of the grace of God. See Outler, "Introduction, Commentary and Notes," 3:203 n. 24.

102. Cf. Eph 2:8; Col 2:14. This is historically the primary focus on the understanding of grace in the West, especially following the Reformation.

103. Cf. 2 Cor 3:17–18

104. Snyder, "Missional Flavor," 65.

by, God's gracious power is by way of what he called (reflecting earlier Anglican terminology) the *means of grace*.[105] Wesley uses the traditional Anglican definition of the means of grace as well, that of an "outward sign of inward *grace*, and a *means* whereby we receive the same;"[106] Kenneth J. Collins notes that in this we can observe that grace "emerges in the context of words, signs and actions, and other media that communicate the substance of both divine favor and empowerment."[107] In Wesley's view, the "chief of these means" are individual or congregational prayer (and it seems to me that, broadly speaking, he would include worship in this), the reading, hearing and meditation on the Scriptures, and partaking of the Eucharist.[108] Importantly, Wesley emphasizes here that these *means* are necessarily meant to lead toward the *end* of drawing the believer into the knowledge and love of God—devotion and ritual are important means by which God's people encounter and are empowered by God's Spirit.[109] At the same time, Wesley warns against these being turned into ends in themselves, of being turned into a folk religion in which people are relating to the rituals of Christian faith without living faith.[110]

Like that of Macarius-Symeon before him, Wesley's focus in his understanding of grace emphasizes both God's gracious empowering, without which no approach to God would even be possible, as well as the "ordinary" means by which the grace of God may be accessed. Wesley marshals a number of passages in the New Testament in which the emphasis is on human persistence in approaching God, such as the "ask, seek, knock" passage in Matt 7:7–11, thus in noting that those who would approach God and access the "pearl of great price" of God's grace are exhorted to continue asking, seeking and knocking.[111] The emphasis here is on God-empowered human response to God's grace.

---

105. Outler, "Introduction, Commentary and Notes," 1.377; Outler believes the first use of this is in "The General Thanksgiving" in the 1661–1662 edition of the *Book of Common Prayer*.

106. John Wesley, "The Means of Grace," 2.1. (Sermon dated either 1739 or 1746).

107. Collins, *Shape of Grace*, 257.

108. John Wesley, "The Means of Grace," 2.1.

109. Ibid., 2.6.

110. Ibid., 2.2–3. We use the modern term "folk religion" to concisely describe Wesley's explanation of a substandard understanding of the elements of a means of grace.

111. Ibid., 3.1–2.

Finally, Wesley concludes that care should be taken to recognize that God cannot be limited by these means in conveying his grace, and that God can do whatever he wants, whenever he wants, "either in or out of any of the means which he hath appointed."[112] God may, indeed, utilize in Christ other means as the message of the reality of Jesus moves among new cultures and peoples.

This optimistic understanding of prevenient grace needs, of course, to be held in balance "so that the distinction between preceding and justifying grace" doesn't get somehow lost. As Ben Witherington explains, while the benefit of the atoning death of Christ was indeed made *available* to all people,

> Nevertheless, Wesley did not believe that one derived *saving* benefit from that death *unless* one appropriated those benefits through faith in Christ. Sermons like "The Great Assize" make abundantly evident that at the end of the day Wesley did not believe that all in fact *would* be saved. Thus the task of evangelism was of paramount importance. There was a lost world out there that could be saved, for God had not decreed in advance that any were unredeemable. Whether they would be saved depended on the proclamation of the Gospel and the response to that proclamation.[113]

CHRISTIAN PERFECTING, OR SANCTIFICATION

In John Wesley's classic *A Plain Account of Christian Perfection*, he quotes two of his brother Charles' hymns which touch on the subject of union with God. Both of these use language which sounds quite reminiscent of the kind of theological and devotional expression found earlier in the ancient Christian East. This kind of expression had entered post-Reformation expression through the work of those such as Arndt on the Continent, and others in Britain who had been influenced by the revived interest in the writings of the early Church. Thus in Charles Wesley's first quoted hymn, we see what can be understood as an expression of the language of *theosis*:

> Heavenly Adam, Life divine,
> Change my nature into thine;
> Move and spread throughout my soul,

---

112. Ibid., 5.4.
113. Witherington, "*Preparatio Evangelii*, 71.

> Actuate and fill the whole;
> Be it I no longer now,
> Living in the flesh, but thou.[114]

The second hymn quoted is that much more fascinating, because here Charles Wesley (and hence his brother John, quoting him) seems to be using language apparently drawn[115] from the Macarian homilies; here is the relevant part of the Macarian *Homily* 18.10. In Wesley's revision of this passage, it reads,

> As a stone in the bottom of the sea is every way surrounded with water; so are these every way drenched with the Holy Spirit, and made like to CHRIST himself, possessing unalterably within themselves the virtues of the power of the Spirit, being blameless within and without, and spotless, and pure.[116]

Compare this with the third verse of another hymn, which he also quotes in his *Plain Account of Christian Perfection*:

> Eager for thee I ask and pant,
> So strong the principle divine
> Carries me out with sweet constraint,
> Till all my hallowed soul is thine;
> Plunged in the Godhead's deepest sea,
> And lost in thy immensity.[117]

---

114. Charles Wesley, "Since the Son Hath Made Me Free," fourth verse; quoted in John Wesley, *A Plain Account of Christian Perfection*, 9. See also Christensen, "Christian Perfection," 224–25.

115. Of course, the question may legitimately be raised as to whether Wesley is truly quoting if his source is his *own* revision of the Macarian *Homilies*; Kenneth J. Collins suggests that Wesley was likely introduced to the Macarian *Homilies* in a German edition through his Moravian friends (Collins, *Theological Journey*, 198). Even if that were the case, however, Wesley is using an English edition which was found in Anglican circles. In the passage from Wesley's revision of Macarian *Homily* 18:10 (10:9 in Wesley's revised edition), it is clear that Wesley's edition is quoting almost verbatim from Thomas Haywood's 1721 translation. See "Macarius the Egyptian" (Haywood trans.), 282.

116. *Homily* 10.9; "Macarius the Egyptian," equivalent to *Homily* 18.10; Pseudo-Macarius, 145.

117. Charles Wesley, "Come Holy Ghost, All Quick'ning Fire," third verse; quoted in John Wesley, *Plain Account of Christian Perfection*, 9. Christensen quotes the final two lines of this in connection with the idea of *theosis* in Wesley's hymns, though he misses the possible Macarian connection (Christensen, "Christian Perfection," 224).

The Macarian connection with this hymn continues with the verse following the one quoted above. Consider the conclusion of the same *Homily*:

> The Lord has promised to all that believe in him, and ask in truth, that he will, give to them the mysteries of the ineffable communion of the Spirit; and therefore let us, having entirely devoted ourselves to the Lord, make haste to attain the good things we have before-mentioned, being consecrated both in soul and body, and nailed to the cross of CHRIST, and giving glory to the Father, and the Son, and the Holy Spirit, unto ages.[118]

And Charles Wesley:

> My peace, my life, my comfort thou,
> My treasure and my all thou art!
> True witness of my sonship, now
> Engraving pardon on my heart,
> Seal of my sins in Christ forgiven,
> Earnest of love and pledge of heaven.[119]

It would seem that the idea of sanctification, as expressed above by Charles Wesley, may have been influenced by his reading of Macarius-Symeon; yet Wesley has also folded in the element of forgiveness in connection with faith in Christ and the crucifixion, this being applied to the life of the worshiper both in purification (Macarius-Symeon's emphasis here) and in recognition of the atonement and forgiveness (included by Wesley).

What is meant here by "sanctification"? Expanding, perhaps, on the brief definition offered from Wesley's *Plain Account*, Howard Snyder describes the basic idea of sanctification, or Christian perfecting, as the

> Spirit-given ability to love God with all our heart, soul, strength and mind and our neighbors as ourselves. The central issue is the work of the Spirit in transforming us (personally and communally, as the church) into the image of Christ; of forming in us the character of Christ, which is the equivalent to the fruit of the Spirit. Christian perfection is having and living out "the fullness of Christ" or "the fullness of the Spirit."[120]

---

118. *Homily* 10.10; "Macarius the Egyptian." (equivalent to *Homily* 18.11; Macarius, *Homilies*, 156).

119. Charles Wesley, "Come Holy Ghost, All Quick'ning Fire," fourth verse.

120. Snyder, "Missional Flavor," 68.

As was the case with the Wesleyan concepts of salvation as healing as well as on the Wesleyan concept of prevenient grace, this idea of sanctification and perfecting also involves a Wesleyan synthesis between Western and Eastern theology. Randy Maddox thus notes that

> Wesley's theology presents a creative integration of the juridical and therapeutic emphases that have historically tended to diverge in Eastern and Western Christianity. Wesley was deeply sympathetic with the characteristic Eastern concern for *divinizing grace*. Precisely for this reason, his integral connection of justification to this divinization bears promise for helping to recover a theological wholeness that can contribute to the healing of the long-suffering divide between Eastern and Western Christianity.[121]

We can observe in the above summary of Wesley's theology of grace in conversation with historical Eastern and Western theology elements of the four themes of Wesleyan missional theology pointed out earlier by Snyder[122]: The theme of divine empowerment by prevenient grace, enabling the process of salvation as healing, including growth in the restored image of God. Ultimately, believers are meant to experience being empowered by grace to walk daily in a process of union with God in sanctification.

As we have observed, this theme of Spirit-empowered Christian life is one of the primary themes in Wesley's writing and thought, and it was directly connected with his understanding of mission. For Wesley, the question of whether God's people were living lives identifiably Christian in character had evangelistic and missiological implications. More than this, however, is what that meant in what we earlier expressed as a *centripetal* focus on union with God resulting in personal holiness and a more *centrifugal* focus in which this theme of union is understood to necessarily lead to action.

One of the most lucid expressions of this is in Wesley's sermon on "Scriptural Christianity." Significantly, Wesley's text for this sermon was Acts 4:31, "And they were all filled with the Holy Ghost." He thus begins with a discussion about the power of the Holy Spirit, and a description of the Spirit filled life of personal holiness.[123] From there he continues,

---

121. Maddox, *Responsible*, 256.
122. See above, 118–19.
123. John Wesley, "Scriptural Christianity," Introduction, 1–5.

however, more than once noting the example of Christians "in ancient days,"[124] and going on to note that, "the Christians of old. . .labored, having opportunity, to 'do good unto all men,' warning them to 'flee from the wrath to come.'"[125]

In Wesley's "The General Spread of the Gospel," we saw that a Holy-Spirit empowered personal and communal holiness, fueled by those who follow Jesus living in internal union with God in Christ, and living lives reflecting that transformation, would eventually lead to the evangelization of the world.[126] In "Scriptural Christianity," we see that the Spirit-filled, transformed life will *necessarily* spill over into a life of both service and proclamation, of *witness*, an inward reality which is expressed in outward action.

CONCLUSION

As we observed in the previous chapter, Macarius-Symeon's theology of union with God emerged as he interacted critically, yet contextually, with the Jewish and Hellenic mysticism in his fourth-century milieu. How does Wesley expand this "Macarian" interaction? Wesley takes the contextual and transformational elements of this model, both in terms of an *indigenous* understanding of interaction with culture and a prophetic *pilgrim* model which challenges the culture. Wesley emphasizes that a Spirit-empowered life will not only have an impact upon those around us, and outwardly to the very ends of the earth, but those thus filled and empowered will be *intentional* in their proclamation and service in the midst of those in the wider world.

Randy Maddox described a paradox of sorts regarding the grace of God. "Without God's grace," Maddox wrote, "we *cannot* be saved; while without our (grace-empowered, but uncoerced) participation, God's grace *will not* save;"[127] Maddox referred to this idea as "responsible grace."[128] While there has been a fair amount of discussion of synergy in the way Wesley developed his theology, this synergy can thus also be understood in the context of our role in witness. We are called to a confidence borne of a trust in the Lord's providence, and yet a consciousness

---

124. Ibid., 1.10
125. Ibid., 2.3.
126. See above, 119–21.
127. Maddox, *Responsible*, 19.
128. Ibid.

that this means not a passive quietism, but a calling to be "energetic collaborators with God in the greatest adventure of world history."[129] God's Spirit is at work, and we must go into the fields and allow him to work in and through us. This remains something of an undergirding ethos, a contrast to the rebuke received by the young William Carey, that "When God pleases to convert the heathen, He will do it without your help or mine."[130] Moreover, engaging a worldview in the context of union with God necessarily goes beyond even proclamation and works of service, but moves toward building a community of faith of those from various backgrounds to learn to be part of a body of people who are seeking to move toward ever-deepening union with God in Christ together. The idea that the deepening of one's union with and relationship with the Lord was meant to lead into a deeper engagement with mission and service is very Wesleyan, and continues to be instructive to us today.

David Hempton provides an interesting historical example of how this played out. In his history of American Methodism, David Hempton recalled the remarkable career of nineteenth-century Methodist missionary William Taylor. Hempton described Taylor's approach to missions as "distinctively Methodist" in a number of ways. The one highlighted here, however, is the connection Taylor drew between *sanctification* and *mission*: "As an old-fashioned believer in entire sanctification, he believed that such experience was the foundation of world mission. Sanctification existed not for personal benefit alone, but to send people out to win souls."[131]

For Wesley and his colleagues, mission was connected with union with God, and this, in turn, has a Trinitarian expression to it in its more fully developed sense. The incarnation itself, including the death and resurrection of Jesus as the Word and Son of God, brings us into the life of the Trinity as we are brought to faith, and God fills us with the life of the Holy Spirit. Thus empowered, we are free to be united to one another, empowered to go out into the world, and to enter truly into an incarnational *missio Dei* in which the incarnation is not only our empowering and unifying life, but also our model.

We will conclude this chapter with the quote with which we opened the introduction of this project. It bears repeating as a means to lead us

---

129. Hempton, *Methodism*, 162.
130. Tucker, *Jerusalem*, 123.
131. Hempton, *Methodism*, 175.

into the chapters ahead. In the final year of his life, the remarkable missionary and translator Henry Martyn was in Persia. There he met with a number of Sūfīs, people engaged in Islamic mysticism. In his journal, Martyn wrote,

> These Soofies are quite the methodists of the East. They delight in every thing Christian, except in being exclusive. From these . . . you will perceive the first Persian church will be formed, judging after the manner of men.[132]

It is to the context of historic Sufism that we will turn next. What lessons can we learn from our application of Walls' *indigenous* and *pilgrim* principles, as we interact with a religious worldview which has its own form of the classic mystical paradigm of ascension, vision and transformation? Can we discover that the grace of God is already active in this context? How might this interaction challenge and encourage us in our quest to walk in ever closer union with our Lord, and to proclaim the Gospel of Jesus the Messiah throughout the world?

---

132. Martyn, *Journal and Letters*, 2.383. See also above, 1.

5

Sufism

A Brief Overview

> Such men of Christ's pure Spirit have received,
> Who was Himself of Holy Ghost conceived.
> Thou also hast from God the soul inmost,
> Which is the sign in thee of Holy Ghost.
>
> Persian Poet Mahmoud Shabastiary (1288–1340),
> *Gulshan-l-Raz*[1]

INTRODUCTION—THE JOURNEY THUS FAR

WE BEGAN THIS STUDY with an examination of early Jewish and Hellenic ascension and vision mysticism, which we'd noted James Davila refers to as shamanism. Using Ezekiel's vision of the glory of God on his throne-chariot, or Merkavah, early Jewish mystics such as the writer of 1 Enoch sought to understand how they, too, might ascend and experience a transforming vision of God on his throne. We observed this taken up to a degree by Philo of Alexandria, even as he sought to remain rooted in Torah. We also observed how this language and apparently practice was used in some of the writings from Qumran, particularly the Songs of the Sabbath Sacrifice (4Q 405), and the manner in which this appears to have been developed in the following centuries. We also noted how emerging rabbinic Judaism developed this shamanistic means of ascent to God's

---

1. Dehqani-Tafti, *Christ and Christianity in Persian Poetry*.

throne, even as it wrestled with the potential implications of what it saw as an understanding of "two powers in heaven" which would lead to a bi-theistic idea of God's essence.

Over the following two chapters, we observed how the early community of Jesus followers interacted in a manner which contextually used the language and thought forms of this kind of mysticism, yet sought to center it on the person of Christ in the empowerment of God's grace in the Holy Spirit. We observed this in the manner in which many of the New Testament writings spoke into this context, though we also recognized that some elements within the Christian community seemed to merge belief in Jesus with this kind of anthropocentric schema. On the other hand, writings such as the fourth-century Homilies of Macarius-Symeon exemplify an ethos similar to that which was observed in the New Testament writings, interacting with and utilizing the language of ascension and vision mysticism even as they seek to ground their response in the reality of transformation in Jesus.

Finally, we looked to the eighteenth-century writings of John and Charles Wesley and their colleague John Fletcher, who incorporated elements of the kind of language of union with God found in the earlier Macarian writings into their understanding of sanctifying and transforming union with God in Christ. Expressing this with intertwined themes of the prevenient grace of God, the restoration of the image of God in humankind, salvation as healing and sanctification, they sought to take this centripetal response of the early church to the ascension and vision mysticism of its day and recognize that lives and communities thus transformed will express that transformation centrifugally in proclamation, service and the development of community life which is empowered by the presence of the Holy Spirit.

In this chapter, we will review the early history of Sufism, including some elements of interaction with Christian faith. We will begin with an examination of how the Muslim community sought to apply a version of Andrew Walls' principle: How was an indigenous principle applied within Sūfī theology and practice, and how was the pilgrim principle applied vis-à-vis a frequently skeptical (and occasionally dangerous) Muslim leadership? We will observe how Sūfī tradition interacted with and sought to ground as well as legitimate itself within the orthodox Islamic tradition. A key element of this was Sūfī exegesis of the received Islamic text, the Qur'ān, using mystical and allegorical methodology similar to that which had also been in use in the Jewish and Christian communities.

As we observe some themes of ascension, vision and transformation, including themes of death and resurrection, within the Sūfī context, we will seek to grasp how this was understood. Was the idea in these themes focused on a self-generated, more shamanistic empowerment, or was it rather one in which God's grace and blessing were seen as central? In our examination of the Christian tradition, we observed themes of the uncreated and prevenient grace of God, salvation as healing, creation of humankind in God's image and perfecting union with God through his Messiah. What might parallel, or indeed, contrast, with these themes within the Sūfī idea of ascension and vision mysticism? Moreover, as we observed in the previous chapter, there was a theme of utilizing what Wesley referred to as the "means of grace" in connecting with God both individually and as a community of faith. What "means of grace" will we find operative in the Sūfī tradition?

HISTORY OF EARLY ISLAM AND THE EMERGENCE OF SUFISM

Writing prior to the rise of Islam, the fifth century historian Sozomen (Salminius Hermias Sozomenus) was himself from Arab background, with family roots in Gaza. His grandfather and their family came to embrace the Christian faith in response to the successful exorcism of the member of a neighboring family by Hilarion, who J. Spencer Trimingham reports had served as an observer at the Council of Nicaea.[2] Born into a family following the indigenous faith of the region, Hilarion himself came to faith in Jesus when he was engaged in study in Alexandria.[3] Hilarion engaged in a ministry of evangelism, prayer, and laying hands on the sick among the desert dwellers of southern Palestine, Gaza and elsewhere. He was a respected and beloved figure, following the example of St. Anthony, under whose tutelage Hilarion had earlier served.[4] It was under the ministry of Hilarion, too, that Alapion, a relative of Sozomen's grandfather, was healed, and the entire family brought to faith in Christ. Sozomen himself was both raised and educated in Palestine among the monks.[5] Interestingly, Sozomen describes these "Saracens" (that is,

---

2. Trimingham, *Christianity Among the Arabs*, 105.
3. Sanneh, *Disciples*, 62.
4. Ibid.
5. Sozomen, *Ecclesiastical History*, 233.

Arabs) as being descended from Ishmael, and following a number of Jewish customs, including circumcision and the avoidance of eating pork.[6]

The monks of the desert can thus be said to have had a decisive effect on whatever amount of Christianization actually took place in Northern Arabia. Their simplicity was admired, and later reflected in the way the early Arab Muslim leadership was portrayed in their interaction with the luxurious and corrupt Byzantines.[7] A rather direct comparison is quoted from both Kūfī and Ṭabarī by El Cheikh, asserting, "Yes indeed, they (the Muslims) are monks during the night and abstainers during the day."[8] While this is certainly something of an idealized account of the later Muslim community, it is clear that the lifestyle of simplicity and self-denial exemplified by the monks was one which was held in admiration.

In Southwest Arabia, in what is now Yemen, there was another center of Christian faith, in Najran and Himyar. As was the case with the Arabian North, traditional sources (both Christian and Muslim) attribute the entry of the Christian faith to miracle-performing, fearless holy men. Interestingly, it is Muslim historian Ibn Hisham, quoting Christian sources, who describes the work of one Phemion in bringing the gospel to Najran, although at the end of both versions of the account translated and presented by Arthur Jeffery, there is a line regarding how the religion of the people later became corrupted.[9] Another Christian document (identified as such by its beginning: "In the name of the Father, and of the Son, and of the Holy Spirit, one sole God.") describes the ministry and martyrdom of one Azqir, who is said to have performed miracles before he was killed for his faith.[10]

In connection with the rise of Islam vis-à-vis the Christian community in the Middle East, one important element which has been noted by several scholars was the apparent absence of any translation of the Scriptures or even liturgy into the Arabic language, and the degree to which this may have contributed to Christianity's failure to truly penetrate Arab

---

6. Sozomen, *Ecclesiastical History*, 375. Ignaz Goldziher, on the other hand, suggests that the idea of Ishmael as a common ancestor of quarreling northern and southern Arabs was developed as a device to promote unity. See Goldziher, *Muslim Studies*, 96.

7. El Cheikh, *Byzantium*, 34–39.

8. al-Kūfī, *Kitāb al-futūḥ*, 1:15; al-Ṭabarī, *Tārīkh al-rusul wa al-mulūk*, 4.2126; quoted in El Cheikh, *Byzantium*, 36.

9. Jeffery, "Christianity in South Arabia," 188–92.

10. Ibid., 192–95.

society. Neal Robinson, for example, has noted that it is "unlikely that the canonical Christian scriptures or other Christian writings were translated into Arabic before the rise of Islam."[11] It is certainly frustrating that while Epiphanius can be quoted as having recorded that the "pagan Arabs of Petra celebrated the epiphany of Venus in the Arabic language,"[12] there doesn't seem to be solid evidence for the celebration of a Christian liturgy among even some of the Arabs who had been Christianized for centuries. While acknowledging the unsubstantiated possibility of an early translation of the Scriptures into Arabic,[13] Lamin Sanneh points out the loss, not only for the Arabs, but for the broader Christian community, in the failure to have translated the Scriptures into their language:

> One can only imagine the Arab cultural possibilities for a Hellenized Christianity, and for the world, had the Scriptures from the start been available to the Arabs in their own tongue, for then, imbibing from the genealogy of the Prince of Peace and inspired by his example, their freewheeling nomadic zeal might have taken a wholly different religious direction.... The Scripture of the Arab Christians was foreign to the Arabs, and that deficit Islam supplied with decisive authority with its exclusive Arabic Qur'ān.[14]

Islam emerged in the Middle East in the seventh century, and rapidly spread from its Arabian cradle throughout the region. Although there was more of a Jewish than Christian presence in central Arabia in the period in which Muhammad began preaching,[15] it has been noted that there was some interaction between Muhammad and members of the Christian community. When they were under persecution in Mecca, Muhammad had sent some of his followers to the Christian kingdom of Abyssinia (Ethiopia) for refuge.[16] They remained there for a time under the protection of the ruler, in spite of reported attempts by the Meccan

---

11. Robinson, *Christ in Islam and Christianity*, 17.

12. Shahîd, *Byzantium and the Arabs*, 437.

13. Sanneh, *Disciples*, 60.

14. Ibid., 61, 63–64. It is ironic that it was fairly soon after the Muslim conquest that there was such an effort to translate the Gospels (or perhaps the Diatessaron) into Arabic; see on this Newman, *Early Christian-Muslim Dialogue*, 7, 16–17.

15. See Goldziher, *Muslim Studies*, 21.

16. See Ibn Ishāq, *Life of Muhammad*, 150–53; see also Newman, *Christian-Muslim Dialogue*, 2. Ibn Ishāq's was the earliest full biography of Muhammad.

authorities to have them extradited.[17] Worth noting in this connection is the fact that the word used in the Qur'ān for the Apostles of Jesus (and only for them) is *hawāriyūn*, which A. H. Mathias Zahniser has noted is cognate with *hawārya*, the word for the Apostles in the Ethiopic New Testament.[18]

It was from among the Christian community in Najrān that Muhammad had his most well-known interaction with the Christians, following his conquest of Mecca, when a delegation from this area came to make a treaty with him. They came expecting a warm reception, and on one level Muhammad was hospitable, even allowing them to pray in the mosque.[19] Initially, he challenged them to an ordeal involving calling God's curse upon whoever was in error, as recorded in Q 3.61:

> But whoever disputes with you in this matter after what has come to you of knowledge, then say: Come let us call our sons and your sons and our women and your women and our near people and your near people, then let us be earnest in prayer, and pray for the curse of Allah on the liars.

Their having declined this, he made an agreement with them allowing them religious freedom in Najrān in exchange for a regular tribute of clothing and/or money.[20] It was written for them that,

> The people of Najrān and their dependants enjoy the protection of God and Muhammad, for their life, their religion, their land, and property, for their churches and the practice of their religion—no bishop or monk or wāqif will be forced to give up his position—and for all that is in their hand, little or much, provided it be not the product of usury or blood-money from heathen times.[21]

It is possible that later, it was at least partly as a consequence of interaction with Christians of Najrān that Muhammad had some of the familiarity he seems to have had with at least some elements of the Christian faith, with one recorded instance of one priest from Najrān having

---

17. Ibn Ishāq, *Life of Muhammad*, 152–153. One of those who fled, 'Ubaydullah b. Jahsh, became a Christian while in Ethiopia; see Ibn Ishaq, *Life of Muhammad*, 527–28.
18. Zahniser, *Mission*, 9.
19. Balci, "An Islamic Approach," 118.
20. Margoliouth, *Mohammed and the Rise of Islam*, 434.
21. Bell, *Origin*, 178–79.

preached in the marketplace in Muhammad's hearing a message not unlike that in the earlier chapters of the Qur'ān.[22]

Interestingly, two of the early Muslim disciples who seemed to have the most extensive knowledge of the biblical tradition hailed from Southeast Arabia. Ka'b al-Ahbār was an early follower of Islam from Himyar who was a companion of Muhammad, and died during the caliphate of 'Uthmān. Ka'b recounted many biblical stories, including some from the gospels, but seems to be repeating them from oral sources.[23] A generation later, a Jewish convert to Islam from Yemen, Wahb ibn Munabhih wrote two works with many biblical quotations as well as stories about desert monks.[24] The *Kitāb al-Mubtada'* and many of the *Isrā'īliyyāt* traditions said to have been collected by Wahb have since been lost, but a subsequent compiler, Tha'labī, preserved much of this biblical and traditional Jewish and Christian material in his *Qisas al-Anbiya'*.[25]

Within a century, Muslims were ruling a vast swath of territory from Spain in the West, across North Africa the Levant, and east into parts of South Asia. A significant portion of those now under Muslim hegemony were in fact Christians; and there was a varied reaction to the incursion of the new rulers. On the one hand, we read the words of Maximus the Confessor, an orthodox Christian who would have seen the Byzantine Empire as essentially Christian. We can get a feel for his shock as he writes in response to early reports of the rapid military conquests of Islamic forces in the mid-seventh century:

> For indeed, what is more dire than the evils which today afflict the world? What is more terrible for the discerning than the unfolding events? What is more pitiable and frightening for

---

22. Margoliouth, *Mohammed and the Rise of Islam*, 43. Please note that Margoliouth is not suggesting that Muhammad was influenced by his much later interaction with the delegation of Christians from Najrān, but from possible earlier encounters.

23. Andrae, *Garden*, 20–21.

24. Ibid., 22–26.

25. See Ibid., 23. Andrae names the work of Tha'labī as the *'Arā'is al-bayān*, though this title is of a work by a different author. It is likely that Andrae meant to refer to the *Qisas al-Anbiya'*. See also Wasserstrom, "Jewish Pseudepigrapha," 87–114; Riddell, "Islamic Variations," 65–66. Annemarie Schimmel also notes that members of some Sūfī orders wore *halqa be-gūsh*, earrings, as a sign of servitude (perhaps to the shaykh); see Schimmel, *Deciphering*, 39. One could perhaps speculate if this could be something of a reflection of Exod 21:5–6, in which a bondservant wishing to belong to his master in perpetuity has his ear pierced with an awl, and wears an earring to display his decision for the remainder of his life.

those who endure them? To see a barbarous people of the desert overrunning another's lands as though they were their own; to see civilization itself being ravaged by wild and untamed beasts whose form alone is human.[26]

On the other hand, those who had suffered under Byzantine persecution in some ways felt themselves to have been relieved of relatively oppressive rule.[27] Pressure to adopt the faith of their new rulers would be progressively applied over the ensuing decades, though this tended to be economic, political and social rather than by military force. Such attempts to coerce conversion to Islam increased especially after the fall of the Umayyad Caliphate and the beginning of the Abbasid Caliphate in AD 750.[28]

Islam itself had been influenced by both Jewish and Christian traditions, and it would seem that it was especially the humility and simplicity of the desert monks which attracted the admiration of Muhammad. We can observe this in the Qur'ān itself. We noted in the introduction[29] that it is written in Q 5:82b: "thou wilt surely find that, of all people, they who say, 'Behold! We are Christians,' come closest to feeling affection for those who believe [in this divine writ]: this is so because there are priests and monks among them, and because these are not given to arrogance." We also noted the apparent connections noticed by Richard Bell in regard to the setting for the famous "light verse" of Q 24:35–37. There are connections of both history and, perhaps more importantly, of parallel themes here which are worth exploring, and which will be examined in the pages ahead.

CHRISTIAN MYSTICISM AND THE EMERGENCE OF SUFISM

It has long been recognized that at least some elements of early Christian mysticism, particularly that of the monks of the Egyptian and Syrian wilderness, played a role in the emergence of Sufism in the early centuries of Islam. Fred Donner, writing on the topic of early Islamic piety, considers the best discussion on this topic to be in Tor Andrae's above-quoted classic, *In the Garden of Myrtles: Studies in Early Islamic Mysticism*, although

26. Hoyland, *Seeing Islam as Others Saw it*, 77–78.
27. Swanson, "Arabic as a Christian Language?" 2–3;
28. Griffith, "The Monks of Palestine," 2–4.
29. See above, 2–3.

Donner cautions that he finds Andrae "overemphasizing the influence of Christianity."[30] Andrae indeed seems to give a strong role to Christian spirituality, though he is hardly alone in this. This having been noted, when we observe the very positive manner in which the monks were held by the pre-Islamic Arabs, and the apparent respect with which pious simplicity was held by the early Muslims, it is particularly important for us to explore this briefly.[31]

The well-known pre-Islamic Arab poet Imru' al-Qais (sixth century), as was the case with other Arab poets, often used the image of the desert monks as an image of light shining from a distance. Thus Imru' al-Qais, the poet of the desert, writes in his Muʿallaqāt, "in the evening she brightens the darkness, as if she were the lamp of the cell of a monk devoted to God."[32] This seems to have been echoed in the twenty-fourth Sūrah of the Qurʾān noted earlier.

More boldly, Andrae wrote concerning the influence of this tradition on both Muhammad and the Muslim community afterwards, in asserting, "One might quote numerous examples to show how at least a certain body of knowledge related to the life and sayings of the famous monastic saints must have been a living part of the oral tradition transmitted to Muslim ascetics from Christian sources,"[33] including part of the traditions transmitted by Wahb ibn Munabhih.[34] Andrae believed and taught that Christian and Muslim seekers after God often met and shared their experiences with one another, in a true spiritual dialogue,[35] though it became increasingly clear that this was not regarded by the Sūfī writers as a dialogue of equals.[36]

Another area in which the Sūfī tradition displays some of the influence of Christian as well as other monastic traditions is in the development of the Sūfī "monastic" tradition and the establishment of the khānqāh, or Sūfī monastery. Toby Mayer attributes the emergence of this

---

30. Donner, *Narratives of Islamic Beginnings*, 73 n. 37.

31. It is important to note, however, that Sūfism is not merely an amalgam of outside Christian or Neoplatonic influences. See Karamustafa, *Sufism*, 9–12; A. J. Arberry's quotation from correspondence with Reynold Nicholson, in *History of Sufism*, 41; Trimingham, *Sufi Orders*, 138; and Ernst, *The Shambhala Guide*, 8–18.

32. Bell, *Origin of Islam*, 45.

33. Andrae, *Garden*, 30.

34. Ibid., 24.

35. Ibid., 31.

36. Ibid., 32.

to Ibn Karrām (d. 870), who worked "at the then eastern extremity of the Muslim world," where Mayer sees the influence of "the remnants of Manichean or Buddhist religious institutions."[37] This location and period could also indicate the presence and influence of the Syrian Christian monastic tradition. Margaret Smith has pointed out the wide usage of loan words from Syriac religious vocabulary in the Ṣūfī tradition, including dhikr, or "remembrance," usually expressed in quiet or audible chanting and cognate to the Syriac dukrānā.[38] Böwering has also noted that the practice of dhikr itself "includes aspects resembling the repetition of the name of God and hesychastic prayer of eastern Christianity," although he adds the caveat that "patterns of historical influence have not been conclusively demonstrated."[39] Trimingham recognizes this connection as well (noting the use of precisely the same words), but also that it is solidly grounded in the Qur'ānic tradition. The practice of dhikr is sometimes based upon a Ṣūfī interpretation of a number of verses concerning "remembering," including those such as Q 3:191, referring to those "who remember God when they stand, and when they sit, and when they lie down to sleep."[40] Twentieth-century missionary-scholar W. Temple Gairdner, in his *The Rebuke of Islam*, describes dhikr as being the "mode whereby the soul could capture ecstacy and with it a period of union with the divine All"[41]—a topic to which we shall shortly return. Importantly, and in common with the Eastern Syrian monastic tradition, these *khānqāhs* were not only centers for *i'tikāf*, or spiritual retreat, but also bases from which the distinctive spiritual ethos of the Ṣūfī schools in question could propagate their views in the surrounding area.[42] Smith goes on from here to suggest that this Christian influence came into Sufism through means which might be regarded as "underground": that there were Christians who outwardly embraced Islam, but inwardly remained in the Christian faith, particularly among the Syrians.[43]

One finds, too, a number of stories about and connected with Jesus within Ṣūfī writings: Some of these may very well have a Christian source,

37. Mayer, "Theology and Sufism," 264.

38. Smith, *Studies in Early Mysticism*, 136–37. There is also a likely connection with the Hebrew root *zkr*; see Seevers, "Remembrance," 643–47.

39. Böwering, "Ḏekr," 229.

40. Trimingham, *Sufi Orders*, 194.

41. Gairdner, *Rebuke of Islam*, 128.

42. Mayer, "Theology and Sufism," 264.

43. See Smith, *Studies in Early Mysticism*, 124.

occasionally canonical. Thus there is a hadīth recorded in Ibn al-Husayn al-Sulamī's *Kitāb al-Futuwwah* ("The Book of Chivalry") which states,

> It is most rewarding to love the lonely and poor ones and care for them. Through 'Abdullah ibn Muhammad ibn 'Ali ibn Ziyad we learn that 'Abdullah ibn 'Amr heard the Prophet say, "The servants whom Allah loves best are his poor and lonely servants." Somebody asked, "What is their state, O Messenger of Allah?" He answered, "They are the ones who have nobody and nothing but their religion. On the Day of Last Judgment they will be brought to Jesus, the son of Mary."[44]

The importance in this emphasis, it seems to me, stems from that which was expressed by Mahmoud Ayoub in the quotation in the introduction,[45] as well as the historical observation of Lamin Sanneh: Two men, one an educated Muslim, another an educated follower of Jesus of Muslim background, both exhorting God's people to embody the life of Jesus in this manner before the house of Islam.

GROUNDING AND LEGITIMATING SUFISM IN ISLAMIC ORTHODOXY

One of the issues in the early emergence of Sufism was, in effect, how a kind of internal, "Islamic" version of Walls' indigenous and pilgrim principles could be applied to Sūfī belief and practice. There was a certain degree of urgency in this, too, as there were circumstances in which Sūfī figures were actually executed for what was perceived, at least, to be heretical theology vis-à-vis orthodox, usually Sunni Islam. Eleventh-century Sūfī writer Qushayrī wrote his famous *Risāla*, his essay on *Principles of Sufism*, in part to undergird the legitimacy of Sūfī practice vis-à-vis Islamic orthodoxy, as well as to ensure that the Sūfī communities were not engaging in practices or speculation which would lead to their becoming unmoored from the broader Muslim community.[46] This was one of several important works of the period with a similar emphasis, beginning with Abū Tālib al-Makkī's (d. 966) *Qūt al-Qulūb* ("Food of Hearts"),[47]

---

44. al-Sulami, *Sufi Chivalry*, 41.

45. See above, 3.

46. Of course, this does not necessarily mean that Qushayrī and others were completely successful in this. Indeed, as Trimingham notes, the orthodox remained skeptical even of the writings of Qushayrī specifically (Trimingham, *Sufi Orders*, 143).

47. Mayer, "Theology and Sufism," 268, and Arberry, *Doctrine of the Sūfīs (Kitāb*

and culminating with Abū Hamīd al-Ghazālī's (d. 1111) magnum opus, *Ihya' 'Ulūm ad-Dīn* ("Revitalization of the Religious Disciplines") which sought to defend Sufism as legitimately grounded in Islamic orthodoxy. Sufism had come under fire, in part because of the radical antinomianism of some Sūfī sects.[48] Part of this more orthodox Sufism's self-legitimization also involved joining in the censure of other groups which were considered to be beyond the pale and involved in bid'a, or unacceptable innovation in theology.

For example, Ghazālī wrote a strong condemnation of a group to whom he refers as the *Bātinīyya* (literally "esoteric" or even "insider;" though the interpretation of the Qur'ān often followed by Sūfīs is also of the "esoteric" rather than "exoteric" sort); in this case, it was against those who overly allegorized and thus denied the reality of "Paradise and Hell . . . the Hūrīs and the [celestial] palaces."[49] Karamustafa refers as well to another work of Ghazālī, the Persian *Hamā qat-i ahl-i ibāhat* ("Idiocy of Antinomians"), in which Ghazālī attacks those who have completely eschewed ritual observances and indulged in gross sexual immorality.[50] In both these cases, it seems clear that a key component Ghazālī's purpose is to ensure that such aberrant groups aren't able to damage the image of Sufism in general in the broader Muslim community

Qushayrī includes in his *Risāla* a chapter on the inner meaning of Sufism itself. In a theme of death and resurrection which we will engage later in this chapter, Abu'l-Qāsim al-Junayd (d. 910)[51] is quoted as saying that "Sufism means that God causes you to die to yourself and gives

---

al-Ta'arruf li-madhab ahl al-tasawwuf), xv. The other key works usually cited in this theme include al-Kalābādhī's *Kitāb al-Ta'arruf li-Madhab Ahl al-Tasawwuf* ("The Doctrine of the Sūfīs"), al-Sarrāj's *Kitāb al-Luma'* ("Book of Flashes"), al-Sulamī's *Tabaqāt al-* ("Generations of Sufis") (all in Arabic), and 'Alī al-Hujwīrī's *Kashf al-Mahjūb* ("Revelation of the Mystery," or "Unveiling the Veiled") (in Persian). Translated extractions of all of the above, as well as some others, are available in Renard, trans., *Knowledge of God in Classical Sufism*. Mayer notes that one effect of the circulation of multiple texts on this theme was a degree of "imposition of homogeneity" in terms of the doctrinal norms in the general Sūfī community (Mayer, "Theology and Sufism," 269), and indeed, that this led to the spread of Sūfī thought throughout a significant proportion of the Muslim community by the time of the twelfth century emergence of the Sūfī orders (Mayer, "Theology and Sufism," 271).

48. See Goldziher, *Islamic Theology*, 157.
49. al-Ghazālī, "Esoteric Sects," 262.
50. Karamustafa, *Sufism*, 160.
51. Ibid., 15–18, for a brief outline of Junayd's life and teachings.

you life in Him."⁵² Junayd similarly refers to both Sūfī asceticism and their willingness to suffer persecution and misunderstanding, saying, "The Sūfī is like the earth—every kind of abomination is thrown upon it, but naught but every kind of goodness grows from it."⁵³ Qushayrī also quotes Abū Bakr al-Shiblī (d. 946), among whose definitions of Sufism are included the beautiful understanding that, "The Sūfīs are children in the lap of God."⁵⁴

Of course, most scholars agree that the term itself, *tasawwuf*, is derived from the Arabic word *sūf*, or wool, referring to the woolen clothing worn in ascetic simplicity by the earliest generation of Sūfīs.⁵⁵ Although this terminology was originally centered on those who were focused on *zuhd*, ascetic renunciation, by the mid-ninth century the meaning of the term had focused upon the growing movement centered in Baghdad centered on mystical piety.⁵⁶

Another crucial element integrated into the manner in which the Sūfī movement sought to legitimate itself theologically was by demonstrating that the Sūfī path was not merely a genuinely Islamic way according to the received text of the Qur'ān and traditions, but was in fact the best way to understand these. It is crucial to grasp how important this point was to the Sūfī community, connected as it was to the very legitimacy of Sufism as an expression of Islam. The interpretation of the Qur'ān was one of the key means by which the broader Muslim community would seek to demonstrate whether Sufism was to be understood in reference to their own internal indigenous principle, or censured within their pilgrim principle as representing *bid'a*, or "innovation" in theology beyond acceptable bounds. Thus Abū Nasr as-Sarrāj (d. 988), in his *Kitāb al-Luma'* ("The Book of Flashes"), seeks to describe a Sūfī approach to the Qur'ān as follows:

> Allāh, glorified and exalted, said, "Do they not seek to interiorize the Qur'ān? Had it come from any but God they would have

52. al-Qushayrī, *Principles of Sufism*, 302.
53. Ibid., 304.
54. Ibid., 305.
55. Schimmel, *Mystical Dimensions*, 14; see also Karamustafa, *Sufism*, 6; Kalābādhī, *Doctrine*, 5; and the more extensive discussion of the meaning and breadth of terminology for Sūfīs in Ernst, *Shambhala Guide*, 18–27; among other things, Ernst points out that the term tasawwuf refers to the "process of becoming a Sūfī" (Ernst, *Shambhala Guide*, 21).
56. Karamustafa, *Sufism*, 6–7.

found in it copious contradictions" (Q 4:82). God is indicating that, in their interiorizing of the Qur'an, they arrive at deep interpretations. But had the Qur'an come from other than God, they would discover numerous conflicting statements.[57]

The Qur'ān, the scripture of Islam, is regarded as being more than merely a sacred text as such by orthodox Muslims. It is regarded as the precise word of God, his very speech, sent down via the angel Gabriel to Prophet Muhammad.[58] It is considered by Sunni Muslims, at least, to be eternal and uncreated, inscribed on the *lawh al-mahfūz* (or "well-preserved tablet") from which it "descended" initially to the lowest heaven and finally bit-by-bit to humankind.[59] In the Sūfi context, it has also been regarded as "the work around which all speculation, teaching and experience revolve,"[60] though as we shall see, at times the connection with the apparent meaning of the verses in their actual context could become rather tenuous.

The Qur'ān is not considered an easy book to understand; indeed, full translatability of the Qur'ān to non-Arabic languages is understood to be impossible.[61] Even for those whose primary tongue is Arabic, there are a great many schools of interpretative thought concerning its text. Jane Dammen McAuliffe[62] provides an overview of some of the key figures in the history of Qur'ānic commentary, each representing a genre of interpretive literature: the classical commentary of Tabarī (838–923),[63] the Sūfi commentary of Tustarī (d. 896),[64] the legal commentary of 'Arabī

---

57. as-Sarrāj, *Kitāb al-Luma'* (*The Book of Flashes*), ch. 51, in Renard, *Knowledge of God*, 92–93.

58. Von Denffer, *'Ulūm al-Qur'ān*, 17.

59. Ibid., 24. Kalābādhī states that it is agreed that the "Qur'ān is the real word of God, and that it is neither created, nor originated in time, nor an innovation" (Kalābādhī, *Doctrine*, 21).

60. Katz, "Mysticism," 10.

61. Robinson, *Discovering the Qur'ān*, 9.

62. Jane Dammen McAuliffe is an internationally recognized scholar of Islam, and a former president of the Amercan Academy of Religion.

63. McAuliffe, "Medieval Interpretation," 191–93.

64. Ibid., 193–94. See also al-Tustarī, *Tafsīr al-Tustarī*.

(d. 1148),⁶⁵ and the more fundamentalist commentary of Ibn Taymiyya's disciple Ibn Kathīr (1301–1373).⁶⁶

Here we will, of course, focus on the Ṣūfī commentary, such as was represented in McAuliffe's list by Sahl al-Tustarī. It should be noted, however, that Tustarī is neither the earliest Ṣūfī commentator on the Qur'ān of whom we have record, nor does his style of interpretation represent the only kind used by Ṣūfīs. Michael A. Sells⁶⁷ has offered translations and analyses of several of the passages of Qur'ānic commentary written much earlier by Ja'far as-Ṣādiq (702–765). Although Ja'far was the sixth Shī'ī Imam, his exegetical writings had an influence across the Islamic world. The influence of Ja'far's commentary reached beyond the Shī'ī world to touch the broader community of Ṣūfīs, though Sells suggests that later redactors may have edited out some of the Shī'ī particulars of Ja'far's commentary.⁶⁸ Ja'far's work presents some of the earliest example of the use of *ta'wīl*, or symbolic commentary,⁶⁹ which came to occupy a fairly central place in much Ṣūfī interpretation of the Qur'ān.⁷⁰ Paul Nwyia, in describing Ja'far's exegetical ethos, suggests that he is reading the Qur'ān in the light of his experience.⁷¹ Interestingly, David Pinault states that "*Ta'wīl* is a particularly Shiite form of exegesis, one which arose in part because of dissatisfaction with the mere zahir of the sacred text."⁷² Of course, Pinault also recognizes that, while verses excerpted from a source text (in this case, of course, the Qur'ān) may be "grouped by the exegete in such a way as to reveal previously unsuspected meanings," he also notes that "in their new context the verses bear a freight of significance that has little

---

65. Ibid., 194–96. Not to be confused with the well-known Ṣūfī figure by the same name, who was also from Spain.

66. McAuliffe, "Medieval Interpretation," 196–98. McAuliffe rounds out her list with the modern figures of the Shī'ī commentator Ṭabāṭabā'ī and the modern Islamist ideologue Sayyid Qutb.

67. Michael Sells is an internationally recognized scholar and translator of works of Arabic poetry and Islamic mysticism.

68. Sells, *Early Islamic Mysticism*, 77.

69. Ibid.

70. As Sells notes, the story of Yusuf is understood by Ṣūfīs to present Yusuf as a master of *ta'wīl* of sorts, able to interpret dreams and symbols. (See Sells, *Early Islamic Mysticism*, 42–43).

71. Nwyia, *Exégèse Coranique*, 160–161; see also Awn, "Classical Sufi Approaches," 140.

72. Pinault, *The Shiites*, 31.

to do with their literal meaning."⁷³ Of course, as Katz notes, though such allegorical exegesis is "necessarily contextual,"⁷⁴ "these imaginative forms of mystical interpretation enrich the signification of the literal sources, but they can never cancel or alter them."⁷⁵ Surprisingly, Trimingham suggests that the use of *ta'wīl* was not normative among ordinary Sūfīs or "certainly not that of the orders."⁷⁶ As we will soon observe here and in the following chapter, however, use of *ta'wīl*-based exegesis is not at all uncommon, even in some of the most influential writings in South and Central Asian Sufism. That having been noted, we will find that Sūfī Qur'ān exegesis did not follow simply one, uniform path, but often included elements found in some of the other schools of thought.

The Jewish and Christian communities developed a multilayered, four-fold system of the interpretation of their respective scriptures, that of literal, allegorical, moral or homiletical, and mystical. The Islamic tradition tends as well to follow the Jewish and Christian ideas of a four-fold sense of the interpretation of the Qur'ān, though what these senses or elements are can vary more than was the case with the preceding two systems. Thus the more fundamentalist Ibn Taymiyya is focused on relational as well as chronological proximity to the revelation of the Qur'ān, with the Qur'ān first properly being interpreted by comparison with other passages from the Qur'ān, then by the Sunna or traditions of Muhammad, then by the statements of the Companions of Muhammad, and finally by the statements of the Successors, those of the generation following Muhammad.

In Medieval Jewish thought, this came to be described under the acronym PaRDeS, with the consonants representing the initial letters for the four modes of interpretation in the Jewish schema (*p'shat, remez, derash*, and *sōd*). The schema, if not the acronym, is found considerably earlier in Jewish exegetical thought. Similarly, it has been illustrated that a similar system was in use among Medieval Christian scholars. In the latter case, the devotional as well as intellectual element of interpretation received an emphasis; James Ginther observes the viewpoint that the "ultimate key to the exposition of scripture is found not in the dynamic

---

73. Ibid., 37–38.
74. Katz, "Mysticism," 28.
75. Ibid., 20.
76. Trimingham, *Sufi Orders*, 140 n. 1.

relationship between reader and text, but rather in that between reader and Creator."⁷⁷

Kristin Zahra Sands begins a discussion on Sūfī exegesis with the Hadīth of Ibn Masʿūd which had a tremendous influence on the direction of Qurʾānic interpretation generally and particularly that of the Sūfīs, though she points out that non-Sūfīs such as Tabarī also used this tradition in their own interpretation. The Hadīth is translated,

> The messenger of God said, "The Qurʾān was sent down in seven ahruf. Each harf has a back (zahr) and a belly (batn). Each harf has a border (hadd) and each border has a lookout point (muttalaʾ)."⁷⁸

For Tabarī, the "back" (*zahr*) refers to what becomes "apparent" (*zāhir*) when the verse is recited, and its "belly" (*batn*) is its "hidden" (*batana*) interpretation (*taʾwīl*).⁷⁹ The "lookout point" (*muttalaʾ*) past the "borders" (*harf*) refers to the delineation between that which is acceptable and that which attracts the judgment of God.⁸⁰ This is a decidedly orthodox understanding of this Hadīth, especially when one adds in Sands' observation that in Tabarī's understanding, the "inner" meaning "is not given to man until the Day of Resurrection."⁸¹

How does a Sūfī exegete look at this same Hadīth? The view of the aforementioned Sahl al-Tustarī, while certainly similar in many respects to that of Tabarī, has a very different take particularly with regard to the final point, the *muttalaʾ* For Tustarī, the sense of the *zāhir*, the *bātin*, and the *hadd* are more or less analogous to their meanings for Tabarī. The distinction in the understanding of Tustarī (and others after him, such as Abū Tālib al-Makkī) came with that of the *muttalaʾ*, in which it is recognized as an Islamic analog to the mystical Jewish sense of sod. Tustarī sees the "lookout point" not so much in the sense of judgment as does Tabarī, but rather as "a vantage point of the heart" (*qalb*)⁸² from which

---

77. Ginther, "Robert Grosseteste," 245. See also Walfish, "Medieval Jewish Biblical Interpretation," 4–7. On this topic, see also Synan, "The Four "Senses and Four Exegetes," 225; Hall, *Reading Scripture*, 132–76; Böwering, "Scriptural 'Senses,'" 353, Katz, "Mysticism," 18, and McAuliffe, "Medieval Interpretation," 315.

78. Sands, *Sūfī Commentaries*, 8.

79. Sands goes on to note that *taʾwīl* as used by al-Tabarī is used "in its sense of the unfolding of events, not interpretation" (Sands, *Sūfī Commentaries*, 9).

80. Sands, *Sūfī Commentaries*, 8–9.

81. Ibid., 9.

82. Ibid.

someone who is perhaps more spiritually on a higher level can perceive understandings of the Qur'ān.[83]

Although he doesn't cite the same Hadīth as a part of his interpretive schema, the earlier Ja'far as-Sādiq has his own four levels of Sūfī interpretation:

> The book of God has four things: literal expression (*'ibārah*), allusion (*ishārah*), subtleties (*latā'if*) and the deepest realities (*haqā'iq*). The literal expression is for the commonality (*'awāmm*), the allusion is for the elite (*khawāss*), the subtleties are for the friends [of God] (*awliyā'*) and the deepest realities are for the prophets (*anbiyā'*).[84]

It is interesting that the editor and translator of the volume in which the above quote appears, Michael A. Sells, remarks in passing about the similarities between Ja'far's hierarchy of interpretation and those of medieval Jewish and Christian commentaries from the same period. Even the terminology can be the same, although sometimes used differently: Another commentator, Rūzbihān al-Baqlī, even refers to the hidden symbolic treasures in the Qur'ān as *rumūz*, similar to the Hebrew *remez*, and carrying related meaning.[85]

As would have been expected, there were serious arguments back and forth about the validity of the more esoteric styles of interpretation, with the attack coming especially from the strictly orthodox, Hanbalī theologian Ibn Taymiyya. The response to that attack was varied and often subtle; it is only Ghazālī that we find directly firing back arguments not merely defending esoteric *ta'wīl*, but attacking those whose exegesis he sees as "restricted."[86] He presses in, suggesting that, "the one who claims the Qur'ān has no other meaning than what exoteric exegesis has explained, should know that he has acknowledged his own limitations and therefore is right with regard to himself, but is wrong in an opinion which brings everyone else down to his level."[87]

One final important element of Sūfī exegesis which is very central in understanding how they see the Qur'ān and its interpretation relates

---

83. Ibid., 10.

84. Ja'far al-Sādiq, *Spiritual Gems*, 1. By restricting the "deepest realities" to the "prophets," perhaps Ja'far was indicating that they are not for those in the present age.

85. Sands, *Sūfī Commentaries*, 10.

86. Ibid.

87. Ibid.

to the issues of what constitutes "clear" meaning (*mukhamāt*) and what constitutes "ambiguous" (*mutashābihāt*) in what the Qur'ān actually says. The relevant verse here is Q 3:7,

> He it is who has bestowed upon thee from on high this divine writ, containing messages that are clear in and by themselves (*mukhamāt*),- and these are the essence of the divine writ—as well as others that are allegorical (*mutashābihāt*). Now those whose hearts are given to swerving from the truth go after that part of the divine writ which has been expressed in allegory (*mutashābih*), seeking out [what is bound to create] confusion, and seeking [to arrive at] its final meaning (*ta'wīl*) [in an arbitrary manner];[88] but none save God knows its final meaning. Hence, those who are deeply rooted in knowledge say: "We believe in it; the whole [of the divine writ] is from our Sustainer—albeit none takes this to heart save those who are endowed with insight.

Of course, the importance of this passage is hardly limited to Sūfīs alone: Tabarī, for example, considers the verses to be *mutashābihāt* if they clearly cannot be explained by anyone other than God; examples given include the isolated letters with which some of the chapters of the Qur'ān begin.[89]

Thus we observe that in classical Sūfī commentary, it is not so much that the Sūfī community is attempting to allegorize away the *sharī'a*, so much as they seek to remain grounded in the *sharī'a* (which could be understood, from the Sūfī perspective, as maintaining their grounding in a "pilgrim" stance), while moving upwards from the principles of the law and required practices to a deeper life of union with God (into a kind of "indigenous" application of these principles of orthodox Islam and interpretation of the Qur'ān).

ASCENSION, VISION, AND TRANSFORMATION IN SUFISM

The Sūfī idea of salvation was in some ways understood as a reflection and imitation of Muhammad's overnight journey from Mecca to Jerusalem (*isrā'*) and from there in ascent through the heavens (*mi'rāj*)—with some not-insignificant parallels with the earlier examined ideas of ascension, vision and transformation in early Jewish mysticism. Michael

---

88. Of course, by adding the interpretive phrase "in an arbitrary manner," Asad is here making clear his own fairly negative viewpoint of interpretation involving *ta'wīl*.

89. Sands, *Sūfī Commentaries*, 14–15.

Sells describes the influence and importance of the ascension tradition in Sufism as "a continual subtext, evoked by subtle allusions to inspiration, vision of the divine, and the gaze of the contemplator."[90]

The ascension tradition in Islam takes as its key text the first verse of Q 17:1:

> Limitless in His glory is He who transported His servant by night from the Inviolable House of Worship [at Mecca] to the Remote House of Worship [at Jerusalem]-the environs of which We had blessed-so that We might show him some of Our symbols: for, verily, He alone is all-hearing, all-seeing.[91]

The above is focused on the *isrā'*, usually understood as the miraculous journey from Mecca to Jerusalem (hence translator Asad's additions), but it is generally expounded in combination with Q 53:1–18, which is often understood as a description of Muhammad's mystical experience in ascent to the heavens:

> Consider this unfolding [of God's message], as it comes down from on high! This fellow-man of yours has not gone astray, nor is he deluded, and neither does he speak out of his own desire: that [which he conveys to you] is but [a divine] inspiration with which he is being inspired—something that a very mighty one has imparted to him: [an angel] endowed with surpassing power, who in time manifested himself in his true shape and nature, appearing in the horizon's loftiest part, and then drew near, and came close, until he was but two bow-lengths away, or even nearer. And thus did [God] reveal unto His servant whatever He deemed right to reveal, The [servant's] heart did not give the lie to what he saw: will you, then, contend with him as to what he saw? And, indeed, he saw him a second time by the lote-tree of the farthest limit, near unto the garden of promise, with the lote-tree veiled in a veil of nameless splendour..." [And withal] the eye did not waver, nor yet did it stray: truly did he see some of the most profound of his Sustainer's symbols.

The combination of these passages into an often detailed narrative took place over time, via both Ḥadīth and other ever more elaborated narratives. There are some interesting connections between the idea of Muhammad's ascent as *miʿrāj* and the element in Jewish ascension mysticism

---

90. Sells, *Early Islamic Mysticism*, 47.

91. Note that the bracketed place names in this verse are Asad's interpretive glosses, these are, of course, not in the Arabic of the Qur'ān itself.

which touched on the "ladder" in Jacob's dream in Gen 28:12. In Hebrew, the "ladder" is *sullām*, but in the Ethiopic *Book of Jubilees*, the word used to translate this is *maʿāreg*, and although this word doesn't actually appear in either of the qurʾānic passages quoted above, it is used in the unrelated *Surāh al-Maʿārij* (The Ways of Ascent; literally "the ladders").[92] Horovitz goes further, suggesting direct influence of the apocalyptic and *Hekhalōt* literature upon Muhammad himself;[93] while this may be too speculative, it certainly seems that there was an influence upon the manner in which these passages from the Qurʾān were interpreted.

While these two passages describe the *isrāʾ* and the *miʿrāj*, respectively, there is one more passage relating a "transformational" event which took place in the context of the "opening" of Muhammad's breast. A key importance of Q 94:1–6 lies in its appearance in many of the traditional accounts of Muhammad's journey and ascension.

> Have we not opened up thy heart, and lifted from thee the burden that had weighed so heavily on thy back? And [have We not] raised thee high in dignity? And, behold, with every hardship comes ease: verily, with every hardship comes ease! Hence, when thou art freed [from distress], remain steadfast, and unto thy Sustainer turn with love.

These accounts are elaborated significantly in the *Sahīh Muslim Hadīth* as well as in Ibn Ishāq's eighth-century *Life of Muhammad*. There are various features of the story which frequently appear in these *miʿrāj* accounts, with varying levels of elaboration. These include a test of choosing the right drink (milk, representing *fitra*, or innate character, rather than wine, honey or water),[94] with the result being that he is told

---

92. Horovitz, "Muhammeds Himmelfahrt," 174–76; see also Altmann, "'The Ladder of Ascension,'" 1–2; and Vuckovic, *Heavenly Journeys*, 2, 45–47, and 137 n. 1. Bousset also cites what he sees as connections between not only the Jewish, but also the Zoroastrian context on the *miʿrāj*; see Bousset, "Die Himmelsreise der Seele," 249, 249–50 n. 1.

93. Horovitz, "Muhammeds Himmelfahrt," 165. Caveats aside, however, Michael Sells has also noticed a number of similarities between the ascension accounts in the *Hekhalōt* literature and that of the developed accounts of the miʿrāj. See Sells, "Bewildered Tongue," 102–7.

94. Found, for example, in Imam Muslim, *Sahīh Muslim* Hadīth (Hadīth 309), in Sells, *Early Islamic Mysticism*, 49, as well as Ibn Ishāq, 182. Vuckovic also notes that honey was considered potentially dangerous, as it could be used to produce an alcoholic beverage (Vuckovic, *Heavenly Journeys*, 144 n. 35). It may be worth noting in this context that in the classic Jewish *Pardes* account of the four rabbis ascending to

(in the Ibn Isḥāq version of the story) that he "has been rightly guided, and so will your people be."[95] Muhammad is depicted as meeting the various prophets either at the Temple in Jerusalem,[96] or rising through the various heavens and meeting prophets at each one.[97] Muhammad sees and describes the "lote tree of the boundary" mentioned in Q 53:14–16, in one account describing four rivers coming from beneath its trunk, the Nile, the Euphrates and the two rivers of Paradise.[98] The *Sahīh Muslim* accounts also contain an elaboration of *Sūrah* 94, in which Muhammad states explicitly that his breast was opened and washed with water from the well of *zamzam*.[99] One account in the *Muwatta'* of Imam Malik involves authority over the spiritual world: Muhammad encounters an *'ifrīt*, a particularly strong kind of *jinn*,[100] and is instructed by Gabriel in the words to say in prayer to repel it.[101] Finally, in both *Sahīh Muslim* and in Ibn Isḥāq, Muhammad is portrayed as "bargaining" with God (on the

---

Paradise, the description of Ben Azzai becoming "smitten" is followed by Prov 25:16: "If you have found honey, eat only enough for you, lest you have your fill of it and vomit it."

95. Ibn Isḥāq, *Life of Muhammad*, 182. Sells notes that in some Hadīth accounts, this account of drinks comes after the *mi'rāj* rather than before it; see excerpts from *Sahīh Muslim* Hadīth (Hadīth 314) as well as Sells' own remarks in Sells, *Early Islamic Mysticism*, 52–53.

96. Ibn Isḥāq, *Life of Muhammad*, 182–84.

97. Imam Muslim, *Sahīh Muslim* Hadīth, in Sells, *Early Islamic Mysticism*, 50–53; Ibn Isḥāq, 186–87 also includes this apparently alternate account.

98. *Sahīh Muslim* Hadīth (Hadīth 314), in Sells, *Early Islamic Mysticism*, 53.

99. Ibid., 52 (Hadīth 314 in Sells, this point also in *Sahīh Muslim* Hadīth 313 and 315). Zamzam is a well found within Al-Masjid al-Harām, the great mosque of Mecca, and which Muslim tradition identifies with the well which sprung up in accordance with the pleas of Hagar. *Sahīh Muslim* Hadīth 75:311 contains a variant of this in which this cleansing of Muhammad's heart took place in his childhood. In this version of the story, Gabriel removes a blood clot from Muhammad's heart, telling him, "That was the part of Satan in thee" (Siddiqi, trans., *Sahīh Muslim*, 1.124). See also Vuckovic, *Heavenly Journeys*, 21.

100. Sachiko Murata and William Chittick define *jinn* as creatures "of ambiguous and somewhat mysterious nature who were created out of fire, which combines the qualities of light and clay" (Murata and Chittick, *Vision of Islam*, 340). Iblīs (Satan) is considered a jinn, and as generally understood in Islam, jinn can be believers or unbelievers, as is the case with humans.

101. Rahimuddin, *Muwatta' Imām Mālik*, 401. See also Vuckovic, *Heavenly Journeys*, 35–36.

advice of Moses) to bring the number of daily required prayers for his community from fifty down to five.[102]

A question which has been discussed at length in Islamic sources has been with regard to whether the *isrā'* and the *mi'rāj* happened *physically*, or whether it was a *spiritual* journey in perhaps a vision or a dream. Although the majority view among modern Sunnis would favor a literal interpretation involving Muhammad's having been miraculously transported physically,[103] Ibn Ishāq makes a case for a spiritual journey. He asserts that it was following the questioning of Muhammad's vision that Q 13:62 was revealed, speaking of a vision given as a test, and that according to Muhammad's wife 'Ā'isha, his "body remained where it was but God removed his spirit by night;"[104] she also argued against the idea of Muhammad's having claimed to have seen the Almighty, citing Q 6:103, "No human vision can encompass Him, whereas He encompasses all human vision."[105]

This then leads into the rather relevant question of whether Muhammad can be understood to have actually seen God enthroned at the climax of his ascension. The account in Abū 'Abd al-Rahmān al-Sulamī's (d. 1021) *The Subtleties of the Ascension* (*Latā'if al-Mi'rāj*) gives little detail regarding the possibility of Muhammad's actual *visio Dei* (in contrast, Colby observes, to the ascension accounts in much of the early Jewish and Christian literature).[106] Some of the discussion on this revolves around the comparison between Moses and Muhammad. In Q 7:143, Moses requests to see God; in contrast with the biblical account,[107] God's presence shatters the mountain and Moses is struck unconscious.

---

102. *Sahīh Muslim* Hadīth (Hadīth 309), in Sells *Early Islamic Mysticism*, 51–53; Ibn Ishāq, 186–87.

103. Muhammad Asad, in the fourth appendix of explanatory notes to his translation of the Qur'ān, recognizes the ambiguity of Muhammad's account, and the multiplicity of interpretations, even among Muhammad's own companions. Nonetheless, he asserts that "the great majority of the Companions believed that the Night Journey and the Ascension were *physical* occurances" (Asad, Notes and Appendices to *The Message of the Qur'ān*, Appendix IV, paragraph 2 (3.1137).

104. Ibn Ishāq, *Life of Muhammad*, 183. See also Kalābādhī, *Doctrine*, 26–27, where he similarly sees Muhammad's journey and especially his vision of God as having been with "spiritual eyes" or with his "heart" rather than with his physical eyes. See also Awn, *Classical Sufi Approaches*, 151 n. 18.

105. Colby, "Introduction, Notes and Commentary," 230 n. 57.

106. Ibid., 17.

107. In Exod 33:18–22; 34:4–8.

In Sulamī's *Subtleties*, there is a comparison of sorts which can be taken as implying at least that Muhammad saw *more* than Moses. Saying 15 of the *Subtleties* reads,

> Junayd was asked about the saying of God (be he powerful and lofty), "*You were not next to Mount Sinai when we called.*"[108] He called to Musa because he was behind the veil, and he whispered to Muhammad because he had torn through the veils. The one who is behind the veil is called to, and the one who crosses the veil is whispered to. As for the one who passes away from these stations, he shelters him and honors him above the realms of being.[109]

Consider in this context as well part of saying in the *Subtleties*, which reads in part concerning the vision of God that, "God (be he exalted) manifested [*tajallī*] himself to our Prophet, Muhammad, through the attributes [*sifāt*] of bounty [*kārīm*] and beauty [*jamāl*]."[110] Note that here God is depicted as manifesting Godself to Muhammad, though the latter's interaction with God is via God's attributes (*sifāt*) rather than God's essence (*dhāt*), and, significantly, the remainder of this saying indicates that the attributes through which God's self-disclosure to Muhammad took place had a corresponding effect upon Muhammad's character: "[God] welcomed him with reverence and kindness, so he increased his kindness, reverence, compassion and intercession with people."[111]

Ja'far as-Sādiq, interpreting the same passage concerning Moses in the sense of *fanā'* and *baqā'* in one of the earliest such uses of these terms.

> The mountain ceased to be at the [very] mention of beholding its Lord, and Moses fainted at seeing the flattened mountain. Then how could he have [sustained] seeing his Lord with his eyes, eye to eye? The slave's beholding of God [entails that] the slave is effaced [*fanā'*]; and the Lord's seeing of the slave [entails] the eternal subsistence [*baqā'*] of the slave in/through his Lord.

(Ja'far) [also] said: Three things are impossible for the slaves unto their Lord: the divine Self-disclosure [*tajallī*], means for attachment

---

108. Q 28:46.

109. Sulamī, *Subtleties*, 61. Notice the imagery of God's presence as "veiled," and of the veil's removal.

110. Sulamī, *Subtleties*, 81, 184.

111. Ibid., 81. Worth bearing in mind in the midst of this discussion is Kalābādhī's brief discussion whether, on the one hand, the "names of God are neither God, nor other than God," or whether "the names of God are God" (Kalābādhī, *Doctrine*, 20).

[*wusla*] and gnosis [*maʿrifa*]. For no eye sees Him, no heart attains to Him, no intelligence knows Him—because the basis in gnosis lies in being apart; the basis for connection lies in distance, and the basis for witnessing [*mushāhada*] lies in separation.[112]

Jaʿfar is here making a segue from the idea of the vision of God in a direct sense (e.g., with regard to Moses' abortive vision) into a statement about the very journey toward the spiritual vision of God (often described with the term *mushāhada*, witnessing[113]) which is central to Sūfī practice, and of the impossibility of even such inward "witnessing" apart from God's initiative. The indication later on in Jaʿfar's commentary on 25:20 and 26:62 is that God's prophets are always *inwardly* engaged in *mushāhada*, always beholding God within themselves.[114] Part of the discussion on this in Sūfī contexts thus included the question of the degree to which the "witnessing" of God by Muhammad could then serve as a model for Sūfīs, as well as the degree to which such gazing by Muhammad could be considered unique to him.[115]

Sūfī tradition received these narratives, and whether the journey itself was understood to have been physical or entirely spiritual, the narrative comes to also be understood as a metaphor for the journey of the mystic into union with the Almighty. The *miʿrāj* then becomes "a type of allegory, each stage of his journey symbolically representing a stage along the Sūfī's path."[116] The interplay between a literal and mystical understanding of the *miʿrāj* accounts is particularly on display in the early account in Abū ʿAbd al-Rahmān al-Sulamī's *The Subtleties of the Ascension* (*Latāʾif al-Miʿrāj*), with the author's preface noting that he sought to present ". . . what the sages of the community said about the journey of the Prophet on the night of the ascension, from the subtleties of meanings to the reality of states."[117]

---

112. Sādiq, *Spiritual Gems*, 39–40; 266–67.

113. Please note that the feminine Arabic *mushāhada* (with or without a final "h" in transliteration) and the Persian form, *mushāhadat*, are the same word in terms of meaning, and are used interchangeably here, especially since we have quotations translated from both Arabic and Persian sources.

114. Mayer, Introduction and Notes to Jaʿfar al-Sādiq, *Spiritual Gems*, lx. See also Sādiq, *Spiritual Gems*, 101–2; 105–6.

115. Colby, "Introduction, Notes and Commentary," 17–18.

116. Ibid., 13.

117. Sulamī, *Subtleties*, 31; see also Colby, "Introduction, Notes and Commentary," 15.

Using the term *mi'rāj* in connection with a developed scheme of the spiritual ascent of the mystic is seen in works on the subject such as a small book attributed to 'Abd al-Qādir al-Jīlānī (d. 1166) entitled *Ghawthiyya*, but alternately titled *Mi'rājiyya*.[118] They developed a path of illumination which scholar Annemarie Schimmel describes as an ascending path of *sharī'a*, or the law of Islam, *tarīqa*, or the path, through *ma'rifa*, or enlightenment, and finally then *haqīqa*, or realization of the truth into *fanā'* and *baqā'*.[119] In connection with these, Jīlānī assigned corresponding *maqāmāt* (sing. *maqām*), or stations, levels of attainment. Thus one begins at the level of *nāsūt*, the "natural human state" focused on the outward obedience of following the commands, *malakūt*, as the name implies, "the nature of angels" in the path of purification (*tarīqa*), and *jabarūt* is the "nature of power," following the way of enlightenment (*ma'rifa*).[120]

Another description of a similar, but different idea which is characterized by an inner descent rather than ascent is quoted by Schimmel from the writings of Abū al-Husayn al-Nūrī (d. 907) as well as of noted collector of Hadīth traditions al-Hakīm al-Tirmidhī (824–892). They posit a movement of concentric "circles," each referencing a verse from the Qur'ān. It begins from the external *sadr*, or breast, connected with the external regulations of Islām, with reference to Q 39:22. From there it moves in one level to the *qalb*, or heart, and connects this with *īmān*, or faith, referencing Q 49:7, in which these external religious forms become internalized. It is at the next level that we once again encounter familiar Sūfī terminology, for the journey moves next to the *fu'ād*, or inner heart, regarded here as the place where *ma'rifa* can be absorbed (citing Q 53:11) and "knowledge from God" can be received (cf. Q 18:65). Finally, the *lubb*, or innermost heart is reached, wherein is realization of *tawhīd*, the absolute unity of God.[121]

An additional understanding of the path to salvation in Sufism involves devotion to a *pīr*, a kind of high-level spiritual director/saint,

---

118. Trimingham, *Sufi Orders*, 160.

119. Schimmel, *Mystical Dimensions*, 98–99.

120. Trimingham, *Sufi Orders*, 160–61.

121. Schimmel, *Deciphering*, xiv–xv. She compares this idea of inner journey with that described by Heiler in his *Ersheinungsformen und Wesen der Religion*, 18–21. Ernst translates the related Q 3:190 as "In the creation of the heavens and earth, in the alternation of night and day, there are signs for those who possess the inner heart" (Ernst, *Shambhala Guide*, 38).

devotion to whom is meant to be an aid towards the eventual goal of union with God. The "guided path" of Sufism (which is generally a complement to the descriptions above, rather than an alternative) is conceptualized as a system of ascending into union with God through progressive union with one's own pīr (*fanā' fī' al-shaykh*), through this into union with the Prophet Muhammad (*fanā' fī'r-rasūl*) and finally through these stages somehow reaching for union with God (*fanā' fī Allāh*).[122]

FANĀ' WA-BAQĀ': AN OVERVIEW

'Alī ibn 'Uthmān al-Jullābī al-Hujwīrī is an eleventh century Sūfī figure whose most well-known writing is the Persian compendium and apologetic for Sufism, the aforementioned *Kashf al-Mahjūb*, remains one of the most important writings on Sufism available.[123] He attributed the initial use of the terms *fanā'* and *baqā'* (often translated as "annihilation" and "abiding," respectively) to ninth-century Sūfī writer Abū Sa'īd Ahmad ibn 'Īsā al-Kharrāz.[124] In spite of Hujwīrī's usually insightful pen, Kharrāz appears to have been preceded by others in regard to *fanā'* and *baqā'*. It is clear, however, that the writing of Kharrāz on this topic was an influence on one of the most important Sūfī figures, Abū l-Qāsim al-Junayd, and in particular on his *Kitāb al-Fanā'*.[125] As Michael A. Sells has noted in his edited collection of early Sūfī writings, it would appear that these had been used perhaps a century earlier by the Shī'ī commentator and Sūfī scholar Ja'far as-Sādiq in order to express what he understood to be a concept of union with God.[126] Some Sūfīs seek to explain it in conjunction with Q 55:26–27 (Arberry) in the Qur'ān, which reads,

> All that dwells upon the earth is perishing,
> yet still abides the Face of thy Lord, majestic, splendid.

In spite of the loose etymological connection with *fanā'* and *baqā'* in vocabulary (*fānin* for "perishing" and *yabqā* for abiding), it has been noted that this represents more an example of Sūfī eisegesis than of an

---

122. Schimmel, *Mystical Dimensions*, 216.

123. Although Hujwīrī and his *Kashf al-Mahjūb* will be a central focus in the following chapter, we quote him here as he was a key source seeking to address the earliest use of *fanā'* and *baqā'*.

124. Hujwiri, *Revelation*, 143.

125. Böwering, "Baqā' wa Fanā," 722.

126. Sells, *Early Islamic Mysticism*, 77.

idea which grew out of an "organic reading" of the text.[127] That notwithstanding, Ja'far as-Sādiq utilizes another passage with which he connects *fanā'* and *baqā'*. In Q 7:143, Moses is depicted as asking God to reveal himself to him (c.f. Exod 33:18). In the Qur'ānic version of the story, God instructs Moses to look at a mountain, and when the mountain crumbles at God's presence, Moses swoons. Ja'far interpreted this in terms of *fanā'* and *baqā'*:

> "He replied: "You will not see me," that is, you are not able to see me because you pass away. How can that which passes away (*fānin*) find a way to that which abides (*bāqin*).[128]

What is the meaning of these terms in Sufism? As has been noted earlier, this varies between those in a state of "intoxication" (*sukr*) and "sobriety" (*sahw*),[129] though there is a significant degree of overlap. Perhaps a more general definition which would touch on both streams of thought might be that offered by Gerhard Böwering: "As a correlative pair of notions, in which *fanā'* logically precedes *baqā'*, it is applied to two levels of meaning, the passing away of human consciousness in the divine and the obliteration of imperfect qualities in the soul by substitution of new, divinely bestowed attributes."[130] This definition encompasses both a metaphysical (and/or psychological) as well as a moral definition of union.

Another way of understanding a more general idea of *fanā'* and *baqā'* and the process by which these can be attained from one South Asian perspective is found in the following explanation, based on the insights of the late Muhammad Enamul Haq. The importance in Sūfī contexts of the process of "dying before one's death"[131] is highlighted by Haq as a four-step process: Beginning with meditations on the attributes of God (*athbāt-i-sifāt*[132]), the next stage involves the turning away from this focus on the attributes in order to attempt to focus on the essence of God,

---

127. Böwering, "Baqā' wa Fanā'," 722.
128. Ja'far as-Sādiq, "Qur'ānic Commentary," 80.
129. Schimmel, *Mystical Dimensions*, 58.
130. Böwering, "Baqā' wa Fanā'," 722.
131. Haq, *Sufi-ism in Bengal*, 80.
132. As an aside, note the etymological similarity with the Hebrew cognate sephirot in the Kabbalah tradition, both of which refer to revealed attributes, in the latter case sometimes uncreated and within God's essence. See also Hames, *Art of Conversion*, 124–25.

negating the affirmations of God's attributes which had been the focus of the previous stage.[133] The state of *fanā'* is then approached, understood in part as an ecstatic experience of union with the Beloved, that is, God,[134] and meant to lead ultimately to *baqā'*, the abiding in God continuously, but in this conception without pleasure or pain,[135] in a manner which seems more akin to the ideas of Indian religions rather than of *baqā'* in the sense in which it is more frequently understood in more classical Sufism.

This brings in the question of the influence of South Asian religions on the very idea of *fanā'* and *baqā'*. Haq compares the Indian Sūfī conception of union with God and that of the concepts of mysticism found in Upanishadic Hinduism and Buddhism. In the former case, he compares the idea of *fanā'* and *baqā'* as often understood in the Indian context with that of *mōksa*, emancipation, in Hinduism,[136] and the "pessimistic attitude" found in Indian Sufism he suggests betrays the influence of the Vendantic doctrine of *māyā*.[137] Haq also briefly discusses the connections which he sees between *fanā'* and *baqā'* and the Buddhist idea of *Nibbāna*; that just as *fanā'* can often be understood as a state of ecstasy in which all desire apart from that for God is annihilated, with *baqā'* is understood as a state of blissful tranquility following *fanā'*.[138] Correspondingly, Haq says that "the state of 'Nibbāna' exactly resembles the state of the extinction of a flame and at the same time it is 'blissful.'"[139] In a similar vein, Trimingham also writes, "None of the orders in India could escape being influenced by their religious environment. Many branches became very syncretistic, adopting varieties of pantheistic thought and antinomian tendencies."[140]

The "Intoxicated" Tradition

Particularly for the more intoxicated Sūfis, *fanā'* refers to the kind of idea characterized most vividly in the literature by the stories of Abū Yazīd

---

133. Haq, *Sufi-ism in Bengal*, 82.
134. Ibid., 83.
135. Ibid., 84.
136. Ibid., 129.
137. Ibid., 130.
138. Ibid., 132–133.
139. Ibid., 133.
140. Trimingham, *Sufi Orders*, 98.

Bistāmī (804–878) and Husayn ibn Mansūr al-Hallāj (d. 922). This idea of *fanā'* is a more radical idea, leaning towards a language of pantheism. In this stream of thought, *fanā'* is seen as a state which "obliterates the human attributes and annihilates man completely in the object of adoration, taking him out of himself."[141]

Fairly early on in Sūfī thought, a stream of thought emerged which was centered upon the *alastu* passage, Q 7:172. This passage reads,

> And when thy Lord took from the Children of Adam,
> from their loins, their seed, and made them testify
> touching themselves, "Am I not your Lord?"
> They said, "Yes, we testify"—lest you should say
> on the Day of Resurrection, "As for us, we were heedless of this,"
> or lest you say, "Our fathers were idolaters
> aforetime, and we were seed after them.
> What, wilt Thou then destroy us for the deeds of the
> vain-doers?"[142]

This was understood, in some ways fairly directly, as an event taking place involving the pre-existing spirits of humanity. God asked them, "Am I not your Lord?" (*alastu bi-rabbikum?*), and the response is "Yes, we witness it" (*balā shahidnā*). While this can be (and often is) referred to as the *mīthāq*, or "primordial covenant" between God and humankind, one finds it more often alluded to in the literature of the period as the "Day of *Alastu*" (that is, the "day of 'Am I not?'").[143] Schimmel writes,

> The goal of the mystic is to return to the experience of the "Day of *Alastu*," when only God existed, before He led future creatures out of the abyss of not-being and endowed them with life, love and understanding so that they might face him again at the end of time.[144]

The general understanding of this passage, of course, was mainly the idea that God will hold each human being accountable to an acknowledgement of the truth regarding God's unity and reality. No one can claim an excuse for veering off into idolatry. As noted above, many Sūfīs took this in a more mystical direction, seeing a return to the reality of only God's existence is a goal of the mystical path. This union was

---

141. Schimmel, *Mystical Dimensions*, 58.
142. Arberry translation.
143. Schimmel, *Mystical Dimensions*, 24.
144. Ibid.

understood by some Sūfīs in a manner which went beyond just a cognitive acknowledgement of the basic truth about God, but rather in a more intoxicated sense, in which the moment of covenant was understood as

> a spiritual banquet in which the wine of Love was distributed to humanity so that everyone received the share which he or she will have in this life. Here, the imagery of wine is used not for the final goal of the mystic's unification with God and his being filled with Him, but rather as the starting point of the flow of Divine grace at the beginning of time.[145]

Perhaps the most famous of the "intoxicated" Sūfīs was Husayn ibn Mansūr al-Hallāj. Hallāj was the Sūfī who in a state of spiritual ecstasy exclaimed, "If you do not know Him, then at least know His signs, I am that sign (*tajallī*) and I am the Truth [*ana' al-Haqq*]!"[146]—in other words, "I am the ground of Reality." On the outset, it sounds like someone with an ego gone wild, and on one level, it is not difficult to understand why Muslim authorities executed him with unusual cruelty. One of those in the same city was Junayd, one of the more "sober" of the Sūfīs and who understood union with God in *fanā'*, but that this is "only realizable if we distinguish between what the Law commands and what the Law forbids."[147] Farīd al-Dīn 'Attār (1145–1220) notes that when Junayd heard Hallāj utter these words, he exclaimed, "What gibbet will you stain with your blood!" accurately predicting Hallāj's execution.[148]

Historically, Muslims have regarded any suspected of belief in *hulūl*[149] with deep hostility, as it seems like a form of *shirk*.[150] This is something of a foreshadowing of one of the very accusations for which Hallāj is

---

145. Schimmel, *Deciphering*, 109.

146. al-Hallāj, *The Tawasin*, 46. See also Mayer, "Theology and Sufism," 267. Note the close connection with John 10:38, although in the broader context, Hallāj seems to be speaking in the sense of wahdat al-wujūd, what Mayer refers to as "objective theonomism" (Mayer, "Theology and Sufism," 275).

147. Massignon, *Passion of al-Hallāj*, 1.77.

148. Ibid., 1.127.

149. Ordinarily understood to refer to "incarnation," and often used as such in Arabic by Christians. As will be noted here, it is frequently misunderstood by Muslim readers to refer to something like a Hellenic apotheosis rather than something more akin to a biblical understanding of incarnation as uniquely applied to the person of Jesus the Messiah.

150. Literally "association," referring to the sin of "associating" any created being with the essence of God; that is, idolatry.

traditionally said to have been executed,[151] and of which he would be cleared among a part of the Muslim community only in a future generation.[152] Massignon later observes, importantly, that while Hallāj used the term *hulūl*, he nonetheless "makes use of this word as a poetic approximation, but explicitly rejects it among his definitions (regarding Q 57:3, etc)."[153]

Of course, *hulūl* referred as well to the idea of the infusion of the Spirit of God into the material creation (*hulūl al-Rūh*); Massignon writes of the potentially Christian origin of the idea,[154] although the later critique within Islam of a union which Hallāj describes as *'ayn al-jam'* (union of essence with essence) was later attacked by others as being excessive.[155] This critique that union with the divine essence is not possible, but only with divine names or attributes,[156] sounds much like the idea expressed later in a Christian context by Gregory Palamas (1296–1359) and others of the importance of recognizing the distinction between the goal of union with God's energies and yet the impossibility of union with his essence.[157]

Louis Massignon (1883–1962) startlingly describes Hallāj in death with rather highly-charged Christological terminology as

> manifesting to all on the gibbet, that particular night, in a prolonged ecstasy of the body triumphant over death, the immortal personality of the Qur'ānic Christ, the soulful effigy of the Spirit

---

151. Massignon, *Passion of al-Hallāj*, 1.470. The account given by Carl Ernst indicates, however, that Hallāj was actually convicted in the case for a suggestion found in his writings that those unable to go on hajj could perform it locally around a replica, though the account makes it clear that those in power were already predisposed to find an excuse to get rid of him (see Ernst, *Words of Ecstasy*, 102–10, esp. 106–7). Karamustafa argues against the idea that Hallāj was executed for his Sūfism, though the account seems to make it clear that part of the reason for which the Baghdad Islamic leadership went after him included what could certainly sound like extreme language; Karamustafa's point in addressing this is to affirm that the Sūfis were not generally in a precarious position vis-à-vis the Islamic hierarchy. See Karamustafa, *Sufism*, 26.

152. Massignon, *Passion of al-Hallāj*,1.40.

153. Ibid., 3.48, n. 167.

154. Ibid., 1.525–26; 526 n. 72.

155. Ibid., 2.35. As it was usually confronted in Sūfi literature, it seems to me that the idea of *hulūl* carried with it the idea of apotheosis, that is, of a human who attains to godhood or merger into the essence of God, rather than the idea of the Incarnation as generally understood in the Christian sense.

156. Ibid.

157. See Zizoulas, *Being as Communion*, 91 n. 75.

of God, "The one whom they have not killed, whom they have not crucified. . ." (Q 4:157).¹⁵⁸

There is here a sense that Hallāj saw himself as, or was seen by others later as, somehow embodying the Spirit of God. Thus the verse concerning Jesus, understood by the majority of Muslims as a denial of the actual physical crucifixion of Jesus,¹⁵⁹ is here understood as a denial that the true essence of Jesus (and, by comparison, Hallāj) could be killed. It is in this context that Massignon asserts that, "Prior to his death . . . Hallāj became the Divine Spirit: like Jesus. It is not a question of a reincarnation of Christ in Hallāj, but of a sanctifying assimilation with the Spirit by Whom Christ was conceived."¹⁶⁰ While Sells may very well have a point in his critique of Massignon's fairly Christocentric perspective, it is nonetheless curious that Hallāj seems to be connecting himself with Christ-related themes.

A striking illustration from a relatively more modern Sūfī writer, Inayat Khan (1882–1927), directly uses the crucifixion of Christ in connection with *fanā'* and *baqā'*, though he almost seems to allude to the manner in which the earlier discussion on Hallāj did:

> Fanā' is not necessarily a destruction in God. Fanā' results in what may be called a resurrection in God, which is symbolized by the picture of Christ. The Christ on the cross is narrative of Fanā'; it means, "I am not." And the idea of resurrection explains the next stage, which is baqā', and which means, "Thou art," and this means rising towards All-might. The divine spirit is to be recognized in that rising towards All-might.¹⁶¹

---

158. Massignon, *Passion of al-Hallāj*, 1.36. Of course, in something of a parallel to Donner's critique of Andrae, it is worth noting here Sells' caveat regarding what he considers "apologetic distortions caused by Massignon's overtly Christological perspective on Hallāj" (Sells, "Bewildered Tongue," 363 n. 4).

159. Massignon, *Passion of al-Hallāj*, 4.156.

160. Ibid., 1.595. Fascinatingly, in an attached footnote (Massignon, *Passion of al-Hallāj*, 1.595 n. 28), Massignon recognizes several key Islamic figures who accepted the crucifixion and resurrection of Christ, including Ghazāli, Hamadhānī, Suhrawardī, and Fakhr Rāzī. See in connection with this Lawson, *The Crucifixion and the Qur'ān*..

161. Khan, *The Way of Illumination*, 205.

Reynold A. Nicholson[162] wrote a short book, *The Idea of Personality in Sufism*,[163] in which he addressed in particular how this unfolds in the life and writings of Hallāj. Like his contemporary Louis Massignon, he recognizes that there are Christian elements found in Hallāj's passion narrative, including prayers such as "forgive the people and do not forgive me,"[164] which he sees as implying an idea of "vicarious sacrifice."[165] His use even of what we have already demonstrated as the rather theologically charged term *hulūl* to describe Jesus is particularly startling. He quotes Hallāj's seemingly radical statement, "Glory to God who revealed in His humanity the secret of His radiant divinity, and then appeared to his creatures visibly in the shape of one who eats and drinks."[166]

Of course, as Ori Z. Soltes[167] points out, this may simply be pointing to the idea that Hallāj "taught that any mystic can achieve that sort of godhood—and most interestingly, he focused not on Muhammad as his model but on Jesus. That is, he recognized in Jesus not the unique God-Man of Christian thought but an outstanding model of self-perishing (*fanā'*) for the mystic to emulate."[168] Nonetheless, the point of including Hallāj in this discussion is to illustrate that there are already some perceived connections between the idea of *fanā'* and that of identification with the crucifixion of Christ.

Discussion on the meaning of Hallāj's life and legacy continued for hundreds of years, indeed, in many ways continues even today. The famed Persian poet Jalāl al-Din Rūmī (1207–1273), writing several hundred years after Hallāj's death, explained what it was he thought was actually meant by Hallāj's most famously radical statement:

> Take the famous utterance "I am the Divine Truth." Some people consider it a great pretension. But "Ana'l haqq" is in fact great humility. . . . He has annihilated himself and given himself to the

---

162. Reynold A. Nicholson (1868–1945) was one of the most important scholars and translators of Islamic material, from both Arabic and Persian, in the first half of the twentieth century. Many of his translations are still considered standard.

163. Nicholson, *Idea of Personality in Sufism*.

164. Ibid., 36.

165. Ibid., 37.

166. Ibid., 30.

167. Ori Z. Soltes is a scholar of ancient Jewish, Christian and Muslim mysticism. He currently teaches at Georgetown University in Washington, DC.

168. Soltes, *Searching for Oneness*, 82.

winds. He says, "I am the Divine Truth," that is, "I am not, He is all, nothing exists but God, I am pure not-being, I am nothing."[169]

Rather than a kind of pantheism, Rūmī understood Hallāj to be expressing the most profound level of humility imaginable. Nicholson comes to much the same conclusion, and expands on it, providing some Christological interpretation of his own in the process. Nicholson observes, for example, that while Hallāj famously stated, "Ana l-Haqq," he also expressed the transcendence and otherness of God and the reality that the Creator must be other than the creature.[170] Without denying that Sūfī mysticism has, in fact, at times gone off into pantheism, Nicholson sought to illustrate how the ultimate goal of Sufism was positive rather than negative, *baqā'* rather than *fanā'*, and once past *sukr* ("intoxication"), seeks in *sahw* ("sobriety") to continue in following the *sharī'a*, or religious law. Ultimately, the idea is to thus avoid the trap of an antinomianism which considers itself above religious obligation.[171]

Significantly, Nicholson notes that even as is the case in Christian mysticism, fulfillment is found "not in denying its own existence, but in affirming that it lives, moves, and has its being in the eternally active Will of Allāh, and which, as a rule, expresses itself in language drawn from the closest form of personal relationship that we can imagine, namely, love."[172]

Nicholson sees that in much of Sūfī thought, God is understood here to be the "only real agent in existence,"[173] and that what sounds so radical is in reality not meant as an expression of ontology, but rather of psychology, that is, Sūfīs such as Hallāj are simply expressing what they see as their experience of God's transcendence.[174] Bearing in mind that there are some potentially positive connections between the "intoxicated" Sūfī tradition in regard to *fanā'* and *baqā'*, we move now from there into an examination of the "sober" view of this understanding of union with God.

---

169. Schimmel, *Deciphering*, 134.
170. Nicholson, *Idea of Personality in Sufism*, 14.
171. Ibid.
172. Ibid., 14–15.
173. Ibid., 21.
174. Ibid., 22.

The "Sober" Tradition

In contrast to the more radical statements such as those of Hallāj, many of the early Sūfī writers sought to ensure that they were expressing their Sufism within the context of orthodox Islamic practice. Aside from a genuine commitment to Islam and a desire to avoid antinomianism, there was likely also the need to demonstrate to the wider Islamic world that Sufism was an advancement and deepening of orthodox Islam, rather than a deviation from it; this could be understood as an internal Islamic application of Walls' pilgrim principle, to ensure that the indigenous element of Sūfī mysticism didn't slip outside of the acceptable boundaries of Islam.

Qushayrī's *Risāla* can be quite useful in its discussion of these issues: while the passages which Qushayrī quotes cover a number of different concepts, mainly in opposing pairs, underlying all of them seems to be the tension between *sharī'a* and *ma'rifa* (law and mystical knowledge), between mystical union (*jam'*) on the one hand, and the degree of distinction or separation from the Creator (*farq*) which enables worship to be meaningful.[175] Thus we find written, "Without separation there is no worship. Without union there can be no true knowing."[176] He expands on this in a brief poetic interlude,

> Divine law is an order through the requiring of worship.
> Reality is the witnessing of lordship.
>
> No divine law unsupported by haqiqa is acceptable.
> No reality unbound by divine law is acceptable.
>
> Divine law is performed through the efforts of creatures.
> Reality is a report from the disposition of the real.
>
> Divine law is that you worship it.
> Reality is that you witness it.
>
> Divine law is the performance of what is commanded.
> Reality is the witness of what has been decreed and preordained, hidden and made manifest.
>
> I heard the master Abu 'Alī ad-Daqqāq, God's mercy upon him, say:

---

175. Sells, *Early Islamic Mysticism*, 116–17.
176. al-Qushayrī, "Interpreting Mystical Expressions from the Treatise," 117.

> His saying (1:5) "You we worship" shows a mindfulness of divine law, and (1:5) "In you we seek refuge" is an affirmation of reality.[177]

Qushayrī goes on to note that, "Separation is the witnessing of 'others-than-God' . . . union is witnessing the others through God. Union of union is the utter perishing and passing away of all perception of any 'other-than-God.'"[178] It is this very Sūfī focus on *fanā'* and *baqā'* that is deepened and further clarified in Qushayrī's discussion of "separation" and "union."[179] Qushayrī also describes how the one (*fanā'*) leads to the other (*baqā'*) not merely in the metaphysical, but also in the moral sense: *fanā'* is thus understood as "shedding of blameworthy characteristics" and *baqā'* as the "maintenance of praiseworthy characteristics."[180]

Practically, what this implies is that there is an emphasis here on the moral as well as the metaphysical aspect of *fanā'* and *baqā'*, with mystical experience remaining rooted in devotional and moral life. While this also is meant to include a very deep level of experience of God's presence, it is meant to transform one's earthly life to a higher level. This is expressed quite beautifully by Junayd, who simply says that, "Sufism means that God makes you die to yourself and makes you alive in Him,"[181] and goes on, with imagery bearing a striking resemblance to that of Christian baptism,

> The saint who desires to attain to the unification of the human will with the Divine Will . . . should be as a dead body in the hands of God, acquiescing in all the vicissitudes which come to pass through His decree and all that is brought about by the might of His power, for the saint is submerged in the ocean of Unity.[182]

In the writings of many of these Sūfī writers, these concepts of death and life seem to emerge repeatedly, and often in ways which seem very close to the kinds of ideas which are found in the Scriptures, and as well are found in the Christian mystical tradition. Indeed, some of the very illustrations used in the Sūfī writers on *fanā'* and *baqā'* are found almost

177. Ibid., 141–42.
178. Ibid., 118.
179. Sells, *Early Islamic Mysticism*, 86.
180. Qushayrī, "Interpreting Mystical Expressions from the Treatise," 119–20.
181. Smith, *Readings from the Mystics of Islam*, 20.
182. Ibid., 21.

directly within the Christian tradition. Thus, for example, ʿAttār uses as a metaphor the story of the phoenix in order to point to the life given over to annihilation and renewed;[183] this metaphor, in a slightly different form, was used by Clement of Rome (d. c. 99) in his late first-century "Epistle to the Corinthians."[184] While it is highly unlikely that ʿAttār borrowed this specifically from the writings of Clement of Rome, the use of this expression may be an indication that a metaphor which was apparently in use in Christian circles in an earlier period had later also come into use within Sūfī discourse.

Another example of this kind of parallel in language about union with God is found in the form of a recurring metaphor in the Syrian Christian mystical writing of the period, that of the pearl diver, who strips off all of his outer garments, enabling him to dive into the sea and risk death in order to retrieve the most precious pearls. We noted earlier the use of this metaphor in the Macarian *Homilies*[185] in chapter 3; this was also used by, among others, Ephrem the Syrian (d. 373) and Isaac of Nineveh (d. 700),[186] sometimes with virtually the same wording. This imagery was later taken up by Sūfī writers such as Hujwīrī[187] and Ibn al-Fārid (1181–1235),[188] for the same purpose and used in a nearly identical manner: Shedding the encumbrances of the "worldly" life in pursuit of the higher life of the Spirit.

We will close this section with the words of Jalāl al-Dīn Rūmī, who wrote with great beauty on the theme of annihilation and abiding. In this case, the verse seems to echo a theme familiar from the Gospels:

> Can bread give strength or feed,
> Unless it first be broken for the need?
> Or shall the vine,
> With grapes uncrushed, for others yield its wine?[189]

In another passage, Rūmī quotes a Jesus statement from the Gospels, relating it to the death-and-resurrection symbolism of the *samāʿ*.[190]

183. Ibid., 55–60.
184. Clement of Rome, "Epistle to the Corinthians," Ch. 25, 12.
185. Homily 15:51; Macarius, *Homilies*, 132.
186. Smith, *Studies in Early Mysticism*, 88, 98–99.
187. Hujwiri, *Revelation*, 372.
188. Nicholson, *Studies in Islamic Mysticism*, 262.
189. Smith, *Readings from the Mystics of Islam*, 70.
190. For an explanation of the *samāʿ*, including the meaning of the distinctive

"If you sow a seed without its shell it will not sprout, but when you plant it into the ground with its shell it will sprout into a great tree."[191] In both cases, it is the symbolism of the necessity of the death of self (the *nafs* or carnal nature).

MEANS OF GRACE: ACCESS TO DIVINE POWER IN SUFISM

In previous chapters, we have examined how Jewish and then Christian believers sought to understand a process of ascension, vision and transformation. Some traditions approached this in a manner which James Davila described as "shamanism," that is, with a focus upon the human effort made with an innate power which enables the human adept to ascend the heights toward the presence of the Almighty. Others saw such ascension and/or vision (whether physical or spiritual) as taking place at God's initiative, and with the empowerment of God's gracious presence.

In the classic Sūfī tradition, we have observed that for the most part, there is an understanding similar to that which we have observed in Christian writings: an emphasis on the centrality of God's empowering in approaching God, whether this has been understood (at least sometimes) as a physical reality, as in the many views of the *mi'rāj*, or the spiritual realities of ascent toward transforming union with God. It's important to recognize that some of the "intoxicated" figures seem to occasionally veer off into what can on some levels appear to be more shamanistic, even when one recognizes that in their perception, at least, it is expressed in the context of annihilation of the self in radical union with the Real. It is also important to bear in mind that there was, as Trimingham notes, from the twelfth century onwards, a formalization of Sūfī ritual into a "mechanization...of mystical experience; the realization that this experience can be induced for the ordinary man in a relatively short space of time by rhythmical exercises involving posture, control of breath, co-ordinated movements, and oral repetitions;"[192] or where the concept of *fanā'* has become reduced to "a vague pantheism,"[193] all of which (and more, including the use of power words, invocation of angels and use

---

version of the *samā'* as practiced by in the Mawlawīyya Sūfī order founded by Rūmī, see below, chap. 5.

191. This sounds close to John 12:24. Quoted in Friedlander, *Whirling Dervishes*, 87.

192. Trimingham, *Sūfī Orders*, 199.

193. Ibid., 165.

of drugs) feed into the idea of shamanism. While these were (and often remain) part of the larger picture of Sufism in practice, the emphasis which we're examining is on a God-empowered movement into a union with God which reflects more of a "unity of witness" (*wahdat al-shuhūd*) than of "unity of existence" (*wahdat al-wujūd*). In the more orthodox sense, then, it can be acknowledged that Sufism "affirms nonetheless the role of the divine initiative, the gratuity of the gift of visions and graces, and the passive receptivity of the nafs (soul) that, as it empties itself of the contingent, receives."[194] At the same time, Sufism includes within its ambit the concept of *mujāhada*, spiritual "*jihād*" in striving against the influence and temptations of the sin nature, though in a synergistic rather than shamanistic sense.[195] Of course, there is another side to ritual here, too: Ghazālī refers to ritual acts of obedient worship, even without a full intellectual apprehension of their purpose, serves as a "remedy" for the "poison" and "malady" of ignorance and disobedience. Ritual may also be understood as an "aid" to the practice of *dhikr*.[196]

As was the case with the earlier themes of union which we observed in early Christian circles, God's empowerment comes as believers respond to him, what Wesley referred to as "means of grace." In Sufism, this includes both the practices of Muslims generally, as well as some practices which are particularly Sūfī.[197] Most commonly, this is expressed in the form of *dhikr*,[198] or "recollection," often ritualized prayer in the form of chanting; *hadra*,[199] or "presence;" this is sometimes interchangeable with *samā*,' literally "hearing," and involves a gathering of Sūfīs which may include various forms of dhikr performed in a group, music, and or dance, depending upon the *tarīqa*; and *fikr*, the focus on cognitive apprehension of spiritual truths, which can be expressed corporately in a *halaqa*,[200] the Sūfī "circle" of discussion of sacred writings. Of course, in practice, these frequently spill over into one another, rather than being completely distinct rituals.

194. Trimingham, *Sufi Orders*, 151.

195. Ibid., 149.

196. See al-Ghazālī, *Deliverance from Error*, 87–88, and Awn, *Classical Sufi Approaches*, 150.

197. Subhan, *Saints and Shrines*, 90–101.

198. Generally pronounced *zikr* in most of the Persian-influenced Muslim world, including South Asia.

199. As above, pronounced *hazra* in South Asia.

200. Or frequently *halqa*.

Dhikr is the most common or foundational of these, and some suggest that this is the practice which distinguishes Sūfī Muslims from Muslims who are not involved with Sufism.[201] The exhortation to gratefully "remember" God continuously is present in a number of places in the Qur'ān ; in Q 2:152 ("so remember Me, and I shall remember you; and be grateful unto Me"), Q 33:41 ("Remember God with unceasing remembrance"); additionally, Böwering lists Q 5:91, Q 7:205, Q 13:28, Q 18:24 and Q 33:55 as frequently-cited supporting passages from the Qur'ān regarding *dhikr*.[202] Böwering also makes reference to a *Hadīth qudsī*[203] which has God saying, "I am the Companion of the one who remembers Me."[204]

Moreover, the Sūfī tradition connects the practice of *dhikr* with the "Day of *Alastu*." The words attributed to God's reminder to humanity of God's ultimate Lordship, "Am I not your Lord?" (*alastu bi-rabbikum*) thus came to be regarded as the original *dhikr*. It is the "remembrance" of this original *dhikr* in the spirit of the Sūfī which can send the Sūfī into a state of ecstatic union.[205]

In practice, *dhikr* usually involves the repetition of the names or attributes of God, or sometimes short devotional phrases,[206] resembling, as was noted earlier, the hesychastic prayers of the Christian desert monks.[207] This is indeed described in terms which sound reminiscent of the manner in which the "prayer of the heart" in eastern Christianity is described.[208]

201. Chittick, *Beginner's Guide*, 64.

202. Böwering, Ḍekr, 229.

203. *Hādīth* are described as recording the words and actions of Muhammad, often recorded as "Muhammad said" or "Muhammad did." *Hādīth qudsī* ("holy sayings") are a special category of *hadīth* which can be characterized as beginning with "Muhammad says that God says," and in which Muhammad directly quotes God's word. See Murata and Chittick, *Vision of Islam*, xxiii, 339.

204. Böwering "Ḍekr," 229.

205. Kalābādhī, *Doctrine*, 166; see also Schimmel, *Mystical Dimensions*, 172.

206. Ernst, *Shambhala Guide*, 92.

207. Böwering, "Ḍekr," 229.

208. See Maloney, "Introduction and Notes," xvi; and Gardet, "Ḍhikr, 223–225. Gardet makes continual comparisons between dhikr and the "prayer of the heart" as described in *The Way of a Pilgrim* (see French, trans., *The Way of a Pilgrim*. Ware, *Orthodox Church*, 73–75, and 75 n. 2, notes parallels between hesychist prayer and *dhikr*, though he also recognizes that "points of similarity must not be pressed too far." Thomas F. Michel also makes note of what he sees as similarities between *dhikr* and "the théomnémie of the Christian Byzantine tradition and the Russian 'Jesus Prayer'" (Michel, *Christian View of Islam*, 188).

Ibn 'Ata' Allāh al-Iskandarī, who wrote in the thirteenth century what is recognized as the first Sūfī manual of *dhikr*, broadly defines *dhikr* as follows:

> Remembrance of God is liberation from ignorance and forgetfulness through the permanent presence of the heart with the Truth. It has been said that it is the repetition of the Name Invoked by the heart and the tongue. It is alike whether it is God who is remembered, or one of His attributes, or one of His commandments, or one of His deeds, or whether one draws a conclusion based on any one of these. Remembering God may take the form of a supplication to Him, or the remembrance of his Messengers, Prophets, saints, or anyone related to Him or close to Him in some way, or because of some deed, such as reciting the Qur'ān, mentioning God's Name, poetry, singing, a conversation or a story.[209]

A definition this broad actually includes all of the elements in this final overview under the "umbrella" of *dhikr*; we can emphasize again that the distinctions between these elements blend and blur into one another, and even the terms here have flexible definitions.

There are two main types of *dhikr*, performed both individually as well as corporately. There is *dhikr jalī*, audible *dhikr*, which is referred to as "recollection with the tongue,"[210] and *dhikr khafī* (quiet *dhikr*) or *dhikr qalbī* (*dhikr* of the heart), regarded as "recollection with the heart."[211] *Dhikr* is meant to be a means of transforming the Sūfī believer by "polishing the mirror of his heart so that it becomes pure enough to reflect God's beauty."[212] It is considered the "spiritual food of the mystic,"[213] and Abū Nasr al-Sarrāj is quoted as having compared the heart to the infant

---

209. al-Iskandarī, *Key to Salvation*, 45. See also Ernst, *Shambhala Guide*, 92–93. Consider the similarity of this description of *dhikr* with the concept of continual prayer in John Cassian's fifth-century Conferences: "This formula then shall be proposed to you of this system, which you want, and of prayer which every monk in his progress towards continual recollection of God, is accustomed to ponder, ceaselessly revolving it in his heart, having got rid of all kinds of other thoughts" (John Cassian, *Conferences*, Part I, 405). William Chittick makes a point to distinguish *dhikr* from *du'ā*, or supplicatory prayer (Chittick, *Beginner's Guide*, 64), so there is clearly some variation in definitions.

210. Gardet observes the centrality of *niyya*, or intention of the heart, in the performance of either *dhikr jalī* or *dhikr khafī* (Gardet, "Dhikr," 225).

211. Schimmel, *Mystical Dimensions*, 171; see also Böwering, "Dekr," 231.

212. Ibid.

213. Ibid., 168.

Jesus, and the practice of *dhikr* to his mother's milk.[214] The metaphor of a well-nourished believer in constant connection and remembrance of God being compared with a green tree[215] is found in a number of Sūfī writings in connection with the constant presence of inward recollection of God spiritually nourishing the Sūfī.[216] Indeed, the practice of *dhikr* as remembrance is meant to facilitate the dwelling of God's presence in the heart of the Sūfī believer, at least metaphorically. Qushayrī says that it "is recorded in a certain book that Moses (peace be upon him) asked, 'O my Lord, where do you dwell?' God Most High revealed to him, 'In the heart of my believing servant;" Qushayrī goes on to explain that this is in regard to "the dwelling of the remembrance of God in the heart."[217]

Dhikr is also the basis for *mushāhada*, which refers to contemplation, but also alludes to the idea of the beatific vision.[218] It is often combined with the idea of *murāqaba*, focused contemplation (or vigilant awareness),[219] but this combination is meant to move the Sūfī toward a place of "participation in the being of that which is being contemplated—God, Muhammad, or one's director, living or dead."[220] On the one hand, the idea of *murāqaba* is meant to be focused upon God, and is related to the Hadīth in which Muhammad replies to Gabriel's question as to the meaning of *ihsān*[221]: "Ihsān is that you worship God as if you see Him, for if you do not see Him, yet He sees you."[222] The initial idea of *murāqaba* is really focused not only on a meditative practice, but on a moral dimension of recognizing God's omniscience and omnipresence, and that God sees everything we say and do. The idea is thus that belief, ritual and way of life are brought into harmony with one another, by a God-empowered moving toward God.[223] This moral dimension as the fruit of

---

214. Sarrāj, *Kitāb al-luma'*, 116, quoted in Schimmel, *Mystical Dimensions*, 168.
215. E.g., Ps 1:3, Ps 52:8, Jer 17:8
216. See Schimmel, *Mystical Dimensions*, 168–69.
217. Qushayrī, *Principles*, 210–11.
218. Trimingham, *Sufi Orders*, 139; Schimmel, *Mystical Dimensions*, 141.
219. Schimmel, *Mystical Dimensions*, 141.
220. Trimingham, *Sufi Orders*, 146.
221. *Ihsān* can be defined as doing things well, or beautifully (see Schimmel, *Mystical Dimensions*, 29, and Murata and Chittick, *Vision*, 340).
222. This Hadīth is found in a number of places, e.g., *Sahīh Muslim* 1, 4, 6; we quote it here from Qushayrī, *Principles*, 157–58.
223. Trimingham, *Sufi Orders*, 147.

remembrance of God in *dhikr* (and by implication, in related *murāqaba* practice) comes out in an unusual passage in Qushayrī:

> It is written in the Christian Scriptures, "Remember Me when you are provoked to anger, and I will remember you when I am provoked to anger. Be content with my help for you, for it is better than your help for yourself.[224]

In addition to the strictly moral aspect of *dhikr* and *murāqaba*, there are also some passages concerning spiritual power for the one who is thusly focused without distraction upon God. In the earlier section on the *miʿrāj*, there was a brief interlude on Muhammad's frightening confrontation with an *ʿifrit*, a kind of *jinn* (or broadly speaking, demon) en route in his ascension. Qushayrī mentions briefly something about authority over the demonic:

> It is said, "When His remembrance takes possession of the heart and a demon approaches, the demon will writhe on the ground just as a man does when demons approach him. When this happens, all the demons gather around this demon and ask, 'What happened to him?' One of them says, 'A human being has afflicted him.'"[225]

This idea of *murāqaba* involving focused concentration upon (and even participation in) one's spiritual director (*pīr, murshid, walī*).[226] A related practice is that of *tawajjuh*, concentration upon the mental image of one's *shaikh* (alluded to earlier in discussing *fanāʾ fī al-shaikh* as a prelude to *fanā fī Allāh*). A number of Sūfi sources make statements such as "Make thy shaikh thy *qibla*."[227] Again, the purpose is noted to be polishing the heart as a mirror so as to reflect the face of the Beloved;[228] one should recognize the presence of God through and beyond the mental image of the *shaikh*.[229] This may be understood reciprocally as well; the shaikh may also "watch over" the *murīd* (disciple) in a similar manner.[230]

Concerning *dhikr* as practiced in a group setting, sometimes referred to as *dhikr al-hadra* ("*dhikr* of the presence," at least sometimes with

---

224. Qushayrī, *Principles*, 212.
225. Ibid., 212–13.
226. Trimingham, *Sufi Orders*, 146.
227. Ibid., 213. *Qibla* is the direction in which one should face for prayers.
228. Trimingham, *Sufi Orders*, 213–14.
229. Böwering, "Ḏekr," 231.
230. Schimmel, *Mystical Dimensions*, 237.

reference to the "presence" of Muhammad, rather than the omnipresent God),[231] this is sometimes to be preferred over solitary *dhikr*, which is considered in some Sūfī orders to be more spiritually "dangerous."[232] Moreover, in his treatise on dhikr, Iskandarī compares solitary to communal *dhikr* more in terms of "amplification" of sorts, as follows:

> The likeness between the invocation of one person alone and that of a group is as the likeness between one *muezzin*[233] and a group of *muezzins*. Just as the voices of a group of *muezzins* cut through the mass of air more than one voice does, so too does the invocation of a group of people of one heart make a deeper impression and have a stronger impact in lifting the veils from the heart than does the invocation of one invoker by himself.[234]

A *hadra* gathering takes place on Friday (Thursday evening in Western usage) or special occasions, and involves some set prayers, *dhikr*, and often some music as well; hence the overlap with the terminology of *samāʿ*.[235] In regard to these circles of communal *dhikr*, Qushayrī quotes a Hadīth in which Muhammad says, "'Pause and graze in the meadows of Paradise when you pass them.' Someone asked, 'What are the meadows of Paradise?' He answered, 'The circles of men making remembrance of God.'"[236] Iskandarī wraps this around the idea of the *sakīna*. The *sakīna* is often defined as the presence of the Divine,[237] though here Iskandarī instead defines *sakīna* as "peace." He thus writes, "A people do not sit invoking God without the angels surrounding them, mercy enveloping them, peace (*sakīna*) descending upon them, and God remembering them amongst those with Him."[238] Iskandarī subsequently continues with a short excursus of grammatical/etymological analysis of *sakīna*, looking at root meanings of tranquility, repose, and "that which makes man be or

---

231. Trimingham, *Sufi Orders*, 201, 204.

232. Gardet, "Dhikr," 224. Gardet refers, for example, to the *Rahmāniyya tarīka*, who thus believe that a Sūfī adept should have considerable experience with *dhikr* within the context of a *hadra* before engaging in solitary *dhikr*.

233. A *muezzin* is the person who gives the call to prayer from a mosque.

234. Iskandarī, *Key to Salvation*, 62.

235. Trimingham, *Sufi Orders*, 204–5.

236. Qushayrī, *Principles*, 208.

237. See, for example, Schimmel, *Mystical Dimensions*, 209.

238. Iskandarī, *Key to Salvation*, 55. See also Böwering, "Dekr," 229; Böwering translates *sakīna* as "divine Presence" in the same passage.

become calm," especially in connection with the reading of the Qur'ān.[239] Considering the clear connections between the Arabic *sakīna* and the Aramaic *shekīnah* in terms of both meaning and etymology, the parallels in this passage following this in Iskandarī is that much more remarkable:

> It is said that peace [again, *sakīna*] is a mystery like the wind, or was created with a face like a human being, or that it is a spirit from God that speaks to men and guides them when they differ on a matter, and so on. From what we have already mentioned, peace [*sakīna*] is probably something similar to that which descends on whoever recites the Qur'ān or gathers to invoke, because it belongs to the Spirit and the angels. God knows best![240]

While related to *hadra* in the sense that it is part of collective Sūfī gatherings, *samāʿ* (literally "hearing") more specifically refers to devotional rituals frequently involving music or dance. *Samāʿ* is always a corporate activity (hence the connection with *hadra*), and can take a number of forms. The element of music and dance in Sūfī ritual has been a source of controversy within the Sūfī community for centuries; indeed, one of the key *tarīqas*, the *Nakshbandhīyya*, forbid both music and dance entirely.[241] Sūfī practitioners of *samāʿ* will cite in defense of dance passages such as Q 39:75a: "the angels surrounding the throne of [God's] almightiness, extolling their Sustainer's glory and praise."[242] In defense of the use of music, they will also cite Hadīth in which Muhammad seems to be encouraging the beauty in chanting the Qur'ān, particularly one quoted in Ghazālī's *Ihya' 'Ulūm ad-Dīn*: "Enhance [or 'ornament'] the Qur'ān with your voice."[243]

The theme of death to self and resurrection to life is enacted metaphorically in the type of *samāʿ*[244] made famous by the Mawlawīyya order of Anatolia inspired by Rūmī. The clothing worn includes a *sikke*, the high, honey-colored felt hat which is symbolic of a tombstone.[245] The *semazens*, dancers, come out wearing a *khirqa*, a long, black cloak, symbol-

---

239. Iskandarī, *Key to Salvation*, 55.
240. Ibid.
241. Ernst, *Shambhala Guide*, 179.
242. Ibid., 131.
243. al-Ghazālī, *Ihya' 'Ulūm ad-Dīn*, 1.173; see also Friedlander, *Whirling Dervishes*, 131.
244. Sometimes written as *sema*.
245. Friedlander, *Whirling Dervishes*, 86.

izing the tomb. Underneath this, they wear a *tennūre*, a long, white skirt representing one's death shroud, and a *dasta gul*, the short white jacket worn on top, the name of which literally means "bouquet of roses."[246] In the *samāʿ*, the dancers begin in their black cloaks, but then dramatically drop them, symbolically emerging from their tombs, dropping their "worldly attachments," and spinning in what is meant to be an imitation of the angels which the Qurʾān describes in Q 39:75 cited above.[247]

Fikr is sometimes regarded as the opposite side of the spiritual coin from *dhikr*, in which particular spiritual truths are the subject of contemplation;[248] although it can clearly still come within the boundaries of *dhikr* itself, considering Iskandarī's broad definition above. Gardet describes *fikr* thus, "concentrating upon a religious subject, [the adept] meditates according to a certain progression of ideas or a series of evocations which he assimilates and experiences."[249] This also is the idea reflected by Kalābādhī, when in the closing chapter of his *Kitāb al-Taʿarruf* he quotes Abu'l-Qāsim of Baghdad, who describes the two kinds of "audition," which sound like *fikr* and *samāʿ*. Of the first he says, "one man listens to a discourse, and derives therefrom an admonition: such a man only listens discriminately and with his heart present."[250]

As with all of the other "means of grace" thus described, *fikr* is done both in solitary study and meditation, as well as in group discussion and listening. The word *halaqa*, or sometimes *halqa*, refers to a "study circle" and is used both within and outside of Sūfī gatherings. There have been *halaqas* focused upon exegesis of the Qurʾān, Hadīth and *fiqh*.[251] Depending upon who was leading and who was involved with a particular *halaqa*, it might be held in a variety of locations, including mosques, homes, in places of business, or even outside, and were a key part of how a master (Sūfī or otherwise) would teach and prepare disciples,[252] which could sometimes include women.[253] In rural Bengal in the sixteenth to eighteenth centuries, the establishment of a *halqa yi-jumʿa* (Friday as-

---

246. Ibid., 86–87.
247. See above, 190.
248. Gardet, "Dhikr," 223.
249. Gardet, "Fikr," 891.
250. Kalābādhī, *Doctrine*, 167.
251. Hallaq, "Islamic Law," 154–55, 170. Fiqh is Islamic jurisprudence.
252. Robinson, "Education," 505–6.
253. Ibid., 527.

semblies) was an important factor in solidifying the roots of Islamic (including presumably Ṣūfī) practices.[254] Such study circles comprised of disciples of a Ṣūfī leader listening to and interacting with the leader's discourses, or studying important texts together, brings to mind the kind of groups which must have formed around leaders such as Junayd in Baghdad. Moreover, as we shall examine in greater detail in the following chapter, gatherings for the 'urs celebrations sometimes involve the full scope of such activities, including halaqa discussions, and this is all considered integral to the spiritual activities of the celebration. A notable example of this is at the 'urs of 'Alī ibn 'Uthmān al-Jullābī al-Hujwīrī, commonly known as "Dātā Ganj Baksh" ("bestower of gifts") in Lahore, Pakistan.[255]

Thus these elements of *dhikr*, *hadra/samā'*, and *fikr/halaqa* become the means by which the Ṣūfī follower ritually integrates her faith with the rest of her life. Trimingham notes,

> In practice, the three main spheres of religious apprehension—belief, the ritual through which, and the way of life in which, it is expressed—are brought into harmoniously balanced relationship. Faith is not intellectual apprehension as such. Belief retains its hold because it is a system of life. Ritual is the medium which conveys, re-enacts, teaches intuitively, and binds.[256]

Given the integration of *fikr* and *halaqa* into Ṣūfī devotions and ritual, one might more accurately suggest that "faith is not merely intellectual apprehension," but rather than engaging the teachings as well as spiritual power of the saints was properly understood to be "of a piece" and part of spiritual growth toward ascending into union with and spiritual "vision" of God. Moreover, these expressions of faith are neither shamanistic, nor completely passive, but rather synergistic, understood as a human response to the enabling and empowering prevenient grace of God that is seen in the early Christian movement, in Wesley, and in classical Sufism, too.[257] Of the four-fold themes we have explored until now, in this chapter we have seen much on sanctification and transforming union with God, with the idea that this is into the image of God. There is

---

254. Eaton, *Bengal Frontier*, 231.

255. See Huda, "Dātā Ganj Baksh's 'Urs," 377–94, as well as the fuller discussion of Hujwīrī in the following chapter.

256. Trimingham, *Sufi Orders*, 147.

257. See Zahniser, "Wesleyan Synergism," 227–34.

also the significant presence of an understanding of grace rather parallel to that of a biblically grounded understanding of prevenient grace. The motif of healing, however, while not absent, doesn't seem to be quite as prominent in our exploration thus far.

We will further explore the above themes in the following chapter in the writings of two of these saints with connections with South Asia: the aforementioned ʿAlī ibn ʿUthmān al-Jullābī al-Hujwīrī, who was born in Afghanistan, and lived many years in Lahore in what is now Pakistan, and Sharaf al-Dīn Manerī of Bihar on the eastern side of the Indian Subcontinent.

6

'Alī Ibn 'Uthmān Al-Hujwīrī and Sharaf Al-Dīn Manerī

> Similarly, the power of fire transmutes to its own quality anything that falls into it, and surely the power of God's will is greater than that of fire; but fire affects only the quality of the iron without changing its substance, for iron can never become fire.
>
> 'Alī ibn 'Uthmān al-Hujwīrī, *Kashf al-Mahjūb*[1]

INTRODUCTION: BIOGRAPHICAL AND HISTORICAL OVERVIEW

'Alī ibn 'Uthmān al-Hujwīrī and Sharaf al-Dīn Manerī are two of the more important figures in South Asian Sufism. Their most influential writings are *Kashf al-Mahjūb* ("Removing of the Veils") and *Maktūbāt-i Sadī* ("The Hundred Letters"), respectively. Written hundreds of years ago in Persian, they are still widely read throughout South Asia, mainly in Urdu and English translation.

Thus far, we have examined the interaction of early Christian and Wesleyan thought with the themes of ascension, vision and transformation in ancient Jewish and Hellenic mysticism, with an emphasis culminating in union with God in the person of the Incarnate Messiah. In this chapter we will seek to trace these very themes in the writings of the two towering figures of South Asian Sūfī thought. In the previous chapter, we examined the manner in which some of these themes were reflected

---

1. Hujwiri, *Revelation*, 245.

in the history and practice of early classical Sufism, and sought as well to understand how some of the key writers in the early Sūfī tradition applied versions of Walls' *indigenous* and *pilgrim* principles within their own milieu: How did these figures use their sacred text, the Qur'ān, as well as Muslim tradition and consensus to underline the legitimacy of their distinct approach to spiritual life within the broader Muslim community? Finally, even as we considered the manner in which Wesley and his colleagues integrated the idea of the means of grace into their communal spirituality, we also sought to find elements in which this synergistic idea of interaction with God's presence is expressed in the Sūfī milieu represented by these classical writings and accounts. In this chapter, we examine the same themes in the writings of these two figures in South Asia. We will proceed thematically, examining varying elements in turn, and the interaction with these in both Hujwīrī and Manerī. We will begin with a brief overview of the biographies of both of these men, as well as a basic introduction to their writings.

Alī ibn 'Uthmān al-Hujwīrī

Shaikh 'Alī ibn 'Uthmān al-Hujwīrī is one of the most influential figures in the history of Sufism.[2] Writing in the eleventh century CE, Hujwīrī, as his name implies, was born and raised in the Hujwer area of Ghazna in Afghanistan.[3] He traveled widely, meeting and interacting with many central Sūfī figures of his day.[4] Having been initiated into Sufism by Abū 'l-Fadl Muhammad ibn al-Hasan al Khuttalī (d. late tenth century) thus connected with Junayd of Baghdad, of whose spiritual lineage Khuttalī descended),[5] Hujwīrī's travels took him as far west as Damascus, as well as Baghdad, into Central Asia, and finally to the Punjabi city of Lahore in South Asia.[6] Nicholson infers from Hujwīrī's narrative of his own brush with lust and exhortation to celibacy that Hujwīrī was married briefly but

---

2. Ernst, "Foreword to *Revelation*," vii–viii.
3. Rabbani, "Preface, Notes and Commentary," xiv.
4. Karamustafa, *Sufism*, 99.
5. Rabbani, "Translator's Preface," xv; Nicholson, "Preface," xiii–xiv; Karamustafa, *Sufism*, 101; Hujwiri, *Revelation*, 166–67. V. A. Zhukovsky and Anna Suvorova trace Hujwīrī's spiritual lineage as going back through Khuttalī to Abū'l Hasan al Husrī, to Abū Bakr al-Shiblī, to Junayd. See Zhukovsky, "Persian Sufism," 476, and Suvorova, *Muslim*, 207 n. 6.
6. Nicholson, "Preface," xiv.

unhappily.[7] He died in 1073 and was buried in his adopted hometown of Lahore, where his tomb became (and remains) an object of veneration as well as a place of prayer, of spiritual inquiry and of reputed spiritual power.[8] In the Indian Subcontinent, he is often known as Data Ganj Baksh, or the "Bestower of Treasures," a title which was given to him in the years following his death.[9] Subsequent Sūfī figures were reported to have made *ziyāra'*, pilgrimage, to Hujwīrī's tomb, in some versions to seek "permission" to enter India;[10] the most famous of these was the Chishtī saint who is arguably the best-known and most widely-venerated Sūfī saint in South Asia. Moʿīnuddīn Chishtī (1141–1230), often referred to as *Gharīb Nawāz* ("Benefactor of the poor"), commenced his work in India with a vigil at Hujwīrī's tomb before moving on to his eventual home in Ajmer.[11] Muhammad Iqbal (1877–1938) included a section on Hujwīrī in the eleventh section of his poem, "The Secrets of the Self" as an exemplar of Sufism who is faithful to orthodox Islam.[12]

The *Kashf al-Mahjūb*, Hujwīrī's best-known and most important text, is one of the earliest writings on Sufism to be written in Persian rather than in Arabic.[13] The *Kashf al-Mahjūb* is Hujwīrī's only extant text;

---

7. Ibid.; Hujwiri, *Revelation*, 360–66, in which Hujwīrī provides both his own difficult testimony and seeks to uphold the ideal of the celibate life as at least a valid option for Sūfīs. Subhan suggests concerning this "testimony" (Hujwiri, *Revelation*, 364) that "the words in question may be taken to refer to his experience of 'falling in love' without going to the length of entering the matrimonial state" (Subhan, *Saints and Shrines*,.126).

8. Ernst, *Shambhala Guide*, vii–viii.

9. Karamustafa, *Sufism*, 99.

10. Subhan says that some Sūfīs believe that Hujwīrī holds "supreme authority over the saints of India, and that no new saint entered the country without first obtaining permission from his spirit. Thus it was that the saints who subsequently came to India from outside first paid a visit to his shrine" (Subhan, *Saints and Shrines*,128).

11. Subhan, *Saints and Shrines*, 128–29.

12. Iqbal, *Secrets*, 95–99. Iqbal was a key twentieth century South Asian Muslim poet and philosopher. See Glassé, *Concise Encyclopedia*, 218. Masoodul Hasan wrote that Iqbal told him personally that "the idea for a separate homeland for the Muslims" occurred to him as he was praying at Hujwīrī's tomb. See Hasan, *Hazrat Data Ganj Bakhsh*, 7; see also Schimmel, *Indian Subcontinent*, 8, and Böwering, "Hojviri," 430.

13. Reynold A. Nicholson's original published translation of the *Kashf al-Mahjūb* included a subtitle that it was the "oldest Persian Treatise on Sūfīsm," and a more recent translation and commentary by Wahid Baksh Rabbani also is subtitled "The Earliest Persian Treatise on Sūfīsm" (Rabbani, *Kashful Mahjub*, cover, ix). Although this has been challenged by Böwering, "Hojviri," 429, who rather believes that Ismāʿīl ibn Mohammad Mostamlī's (d. 1042/3) earlier *Sharh-i-Taʿāruf* has that honor, and

if not for what appears to have been a series of misfortunes, his oeuvre would have been more extensive.[14] In the beginning of the *Kashf*, he explains that two of these works were lost essentially through theft and attempts by others to claim the writings as their own, and uses these accounts to explain why he periodically inserts his name into the discussion throughout his text.[15] He notes that he is writing this work at the request of a disciple, possibly Abū Sa'īd al-Hujwīrī, who is recorded as having asked a series of basic questions on the nature of Sufism.[16] The purpose of the *Kashf* is set forth as follows:

> I have composed this book for the polishers of hearts which are infected by the veil of "clouding" but in which the substance of the light of the Truth is existent, in order that the veil may be lifted from them by the blessing of reading it, and that they may find their way to spiritual reality.[17]

Hujwīrī's *Kashf al-Mahjūb* builds upon the Arabic writings of predecessors such as Sarrāj, Kalābādhī and especially Qushayrī's *Risāla*, from which the *Kashf* quotes liberally;[18] Hujwīrī refers to both Sulamī and "the Master" Qushayrī as sources for the *Kashf al-Mahjūb*,[19] though there are subtle differences, too. For example, Qushayrī's *Risāla* includes the following two anecdotes:

Ahmet Karamustafa, who asserts that this distinction actually belongs to 'Abd Allāh Abū Ansārī's (1006–1088) *Sad Maydān* ("The Hundred Fields")(Karamustafa, *Sufism*, 95). Mojaddedi suggests that Böwering is correct in terms of actual dates, though he still would suggest that the Kashf is the oldest independent treatise (Mojaddedi, "Kaŝf," 664), as the Sharh is a commentary on an Kalābādhī's earlier, Arabic work, the *Kitāb al-Ta'āruf*.

14. Karamustafa, *Sufism*, 101; Nicholson, "Preface," xv–xvi.

15. Hujwiri, *Revelation*, 2.

16. Ibid., 3–4, 6–7. Abū Sa'īd al-Hujwīrī was reportedly a member of the same *silsila*, or Sūfī lineage, as 'Alī ibn 'Uthmān al-Hujwīrī. See Rabbani, "Translator's Preface," 6 n. 1.

17. Hujwiri, *Revelation*, 5. This theme of the "polishing" of the heart as a "mirror" is recurrent in the writings of both Hujwīrī and Manerī.

18. Nicholson, "Preface," xvi, xix. Zhukovsky notes that the *Kashf* and the *Risāla* not only covered much of the same material, but were written at nearly the same time. See Zhukovsky, "Persian Sufism,"13.

19. Hujwiri, *Revelation*, 114. Both Qushayrī and Hujwīrī begin their respective treatises with biographical sketches, with Qushayrī beginning with Sūfī figures from the eighth and ninth centuries, and Hujwīrī going all the way back to the Muhammad's companions. See Renard, *Friends of God*, 243.

> Someone saw Habib al-'Ajami in a dream and asked: "Are you dead, Habib al-'Ajami?" He said: "Far from it! My Persianhood (*'ujma*) has left me and I reside in a bliss (*ni'ma*)." It is related that al-Hasan al-Basri entered the mosque in order to pray the sunset prayer. He found Habib al-'Ajami there serving as the prayer leader and he did not pray behind him, because he was afraid that Habib would mispronounce the [words of] the prayer due to the foreignness of his tongue. On that night in a dream he saw someone who said: "Why didn't you pray behind him? Had you prayed behind him, all your prior sins would have been forgiven!"[20]

We see here that Qushayrī refers to Habīb al-'Ajamī (that is, Habib the non-Arab or the Persian), though the initial anecdote concerning him implies that his "Persian-ness" will finally be done away with in glory[21]—almost as though it is a liability to be overcome. The story following that one presents one of the key figures of the early Sūfī tradition, Hasan al-Basrī (d.728), who is rebuked in a dream for his refusal to pray behind Habīb as a non-Arab.[22] Significantly, though mentioned here and a couple of other places in the *Risāla*, Habīb is not included in the biographies of important Sūfī figures in the first part of the book. Conversely, in the *Kashf al-Mahjūb*, Habīb al-'Ajamī is the *first* biography presented in Hujwīrī's lengthy section on "Eminent Sūfīs of Later Times," and it begins with a somewhat different version of Hasan's refusal to pray behind Habīb. The one who appears to Hasan in Hujwīrī's version of the events is *God*! Hasan asks the Almighty what his good pleasure would be, and God replies that if he had allowed himself to be led in prayer by Habīb, restrained by his intention toward God from taking offense at any pronunciation errors Habīb made, it would have pleased him. Hujwīrī's short biography of Habīb continues with a story of Hasan's miraculous escape from persecuting authorities due to Habīb's integrity and holiness; the account seems to imply that Habīb is at least Hasan's equal in spiritual stature.[23] Hujwīrī's subtle shift, illustrated with this figure, indicates that he had a concern to speak to his Persian (and perhaps more broadly, implied Indo-Persian) context.

---

20. Qushayri, *Epistle on Sufism* 396–97.
21. And even this being described with an Arabic play on words.
22. See Glassé, *Concise Encyclopedia*, 173.
23. Hujwiri, *Revelation*, 88–89. For more on the dynamic between Arab and 'Ajam, see Goldziher, *Muslim Studies*, 98–136.

The *Kashf al-Mahjūb* was, in turn, influential[24] on the subsequent writings of 'Attār, Nur ad-Dīn 'Abd ar-Rahmān Jāmī (1414–1492)[25] and Dara Shikoh (1615–1659).[26] 'Attār in particular, in his *Tadhkirat al-Awliyā'* recounts some of the same biographical anecdotes from the *Kashf*, sometimes with more detail, or embellishment, in the stories of Sūfī saints.[27]

Indeed, writing on Hujwīrī's impact on the area of Punjab, where the saint settled at Lahore, Mohammad Idris and Mugheel Ahmed state,

> Ali Hujwiri built the ideological structure of Indo-Muslim mysticism during the early medieval period. An analysis of the development of Muslim mystical thought in India shows that the Punjab acted not merely as a repository of the Muslim mystical traditions but a focal point in the process of its diffusion.[28]

Thus Hujwīrī's writings both built upon the foundations laid by earlier figures, but also served as the predecessor of subsequent Sūfī thought in the Indian Subcontinent. In addition to the influence Hujwīrī's *Kashf al-Mahjūb* was to bear upon subsequent writers in the Persian-speaking world, such as 'Attār, we find the "ideological structure" at work in the writings of others on the Indian Subcontinent. An example of this influence is found in the life and writings of Sharaf-al-Dīn Manerī of Bihar, author of the *Maktūbāt-i Sadī*.

Sharaf al-Dīn Manerī

Sharaf al-Dīn was the son of another Sūfī figure, Shaikh Yahya Manerī, and his mother Razia Bibi, from Maner in what is now the state of Bihar in India.[29] Although many other accounts of Manerī's life place his birth in the early 1260s (and hence dying in 1381 at around 120 years of age),[30] Paul Jackson's more recent research examining Manerī's writings

---

24. Suvorova, *Muslim Saints*, 40.
25. Noted Persian Sūfī poet and thinker.
26. Son of Mughal Emperor Shah Jahan and his favorite wife Mumtaz, and noted Sūfī poet, Dara Shikoh lost a power struggle with Muhiuddin (later crowned Emperor Aurangzeb) to succeed his father.
27. See Renard, *Friends of God*, 46; 253–55; see also 'Attār, *Tadhkirat al-Awliyā'*
28. Ahmed, "Role of Mysticism," 12.
29. Jackson, "Traditions of Spiritual Guidance," 146.
30. E.g., Jackson, "Introduction and Notes," 1; Askari, *Medieval Bihar*, 32.

as well as the *malfūzāt*[31] recording of his discourses led him to conclude that Manerī was actually born about 1290.[32] Engaging in his early studies in his hometown, as a teenager he was taken by Maulana Sharaf al-Dīn Tau'ama of Bukhara to the Bengal city of Sonargaon, as the latter was passing through on his way from Delhi to Bengal.[33] In Sonargaon Manerī completed his initial education in various branches of Islamic studies.[34] He fell ill and was told by physicians that he needed to engage in sexual activity; he thus either married,[35] or possibly obtained a slave girl for the purpose, and the union produced one son, Zaki al-Dīn.[36] When he returned to Bihar in 1323, he left his son in the care of his own mother, and decided to travel to Delhi in search of a spiritual guide.[37]

Manerī's time in Delhi was initially discouraging: he met Bū Alī Qalandar (d. 1324),[38] but the latter was perhaps too much of an "intoxicated" Sūfī to be appropriate guide for Manerī; he also met the celebrated Nizām al-Dīn Awliyā' (d. 1325), but the great Shaikh of Delhi told him that he wasn't meant to be Manerī's guide.[39] Significantly, he was aware of controversies surrounding some Sūfī practices, and had met not only Nizām al-Dīn, but also listened to a *tadhkīr* (religious discourse) by Zia al-Dīn Simnanī, who bitterly opposed the Sūfī practice of *samā'*[40] practiced by Nizām al-Dīn and his followers.[41] Just as Manerī was about to give up and depart, he was introduced to Shaikh Najīb al-Dīn Firdausī, founder

---

31. *Malfūzāt* refers to the recorded discourses of a Muslim saint (Renard, *Friends of God*, 7).

32. Jackson, "Introduction to *In Quest of God*," xvi; and Jackson, "Use of the Quran," 33.

33. Askari, *Medieval Bihar*, 32.

34. Ibid.

35. Ibid.

36. Jackson, "Spiritual Guidance," 147, suggests that it was a slave girl, as she is never mentioned by him in any writing or recorded discourse, but goes on to note that this arrangement was certainly done in accordance with Islamic law. The son thus produced, Zaki al-Dīn, "had the full rights of a legitimate son."

37. Jackson, "Spiritual Guidance," 147.

38. Also known as Sharāf al-Dīn Panipatī.

39. Jackson, "Introduction to *In Quest of God*," xvi. Of course, as both of these men were dead within eighteen months of Manerī's arrival in Delhi, he would likely have needed to search for another spiritual guide anyway (see Jackson, "Spiritual Guidance," 147).

40. *Samā'* could include both elements of music or of dance.

41. Askari, *Medieval Bihar*, 33.

of the *Firdausīyya silsila*,⁴² who took Manerī on as his disciple: When Manerī met Firdausī for the first time, the Shaikh greeted his would-be disciple, saying, "O dervish, for years I have been sitting in wait for you. I have a sacred trust which is to be conferred on you."⁴³ Manerī was to remain with him for the next eight years until Firdausī's death, following which he made his way back to Bihar.⁴⁴ It was en route through Bihar that Manerī was overcome with a desire for the life of a God-seeking hermit, and thus he turned to stay in the jungle of Bihia in Bihar, after a year of which he moved to a cave in Rajgir, an area famous for Hindu, Buddhist and Jain ascetics.⁴⁵ Manerī remained in Rajgir for many years, living an ascetic life of meditation in a cave. Schimmel suggests that this was perhaps in imitation of Muhammad's practice of meditating in the caves above Mecca.⁴⁶

Knowledge of Manerī's presence permeated the area, however, and visitors seeking spiritual and well as political aid and advice began coming to him regularly. This resulted in Manerī's decision to begin coming to the town of Bihar for Friday prayers, so as to provide an opportunity for others to meet with him, though he would then return to his narrow cave at Rajgir. Eventually, perhaps inevitably, a shelter was constructed for him; his son and now elderly mother were brought to the town of Bihar from Maner.⁴⁷ Finally, about 1337, on the orders of no less than Muhammad bin Tughlaq (d. 1351), Sultan of Delhi, a *khānqāh*⁴⁸ was

42. That is, the Sūfī lineage of the *Firdausīyya*, which takes Najib al-Dīn Firdausī as their founding figure. The *Firdausīyya* branched off from another lineage, the Central Asian-originated *Kubrawīyya* order (Lawrence, *Notes*, 72).

43. Lawrence, *Notes*, 72.

44. Jackson, "Spiritual Guidance," 147.

45. Jackson, "Introduction to *In Quest of God*," xvi–xvii.

46. Schimmel, *Deciphering*, 48. Of course, such austerities were not uncommon among mystics of indigenous Hindu, Jain and Buddhist traditions which were also well-represented at Rajgir, so there could have conceivably been influence from there as well. Manerī's interaction with the Hindu population with whom he was familiar included a significant degree of respect. Although he was quite diligent in the orthodoxy of his views regarding the nature of God, he was "impressed by the discipline undertaken by Hindus to pursue religious studies as fruitfully as possible" and was "appreciative of the profound religious experience of great sages." See Jackson, "The Mystical Dimension," 278.

47. Askari, *Medieval Bihar*, 33–34.

48. A *khānqāh* (also known as a *ribāt*, *zāwiya*, and *tekke*, depending upon where and among whom it is located), is a Sūfī residential facility, rather like a monastery, and often built around the tomb of a well-known Sūfī sheikh. See Renard, *Friends of God*, 200.

constructed for Manerī's use.⁴⁹ Here he was to eventually establish the *tarīqa* and *silsila* of the Firdausīyya in Bihar.⁵⁰ He spent the rest of his days at the *khānqāh*, "devoted to prayer; study; teaching; meeting many visitors; conducting assemblies; and writing letters to disciples who could not come to him."⁵¹ Even before he died, he had become known by the honorific titles *Makhdūm al-Jahān* ("Master of the World")⁵² and the related *Makhdūm al-Mulk* ("Master of the Kingdom").⁵³ Remaining at the *khānqāh* until his death on January 2, 1381, he was buried next to his mother.⁵⁴

Manerī's tomb in Bihar Sharif⁵⁵ remains a popular place of pilgrimage for Muslims across South Asia. His intercession is sought throughout the year, and many thousands come to his *'urs* celebration every year.⁵⁶ The cave in which he lived in Rajgir is likewise a pilgrimage center, and the warm spring therein has also acquired the name *Makhdūm Kund*.⁵⁷ Among some South Asian Muslim people, his name is even used, along

---

49. Jackson, "Introduction to *In Quest of God*," xvii. Tughlaq also asked Manerī to produce a guidebook on mysticism for him. See Schimmel, *Indian Subcontinent*, 19. Schimmel also mentions that Manerī produced not only guidebooks (which she does not name), but also a commentary on Abū Najīb Suhrawardī's Ādāb al-Murīdīn (On Proper Conduct of the Disciples), written shortly after his permanent move to Bihar town from his cave in Rajgir. Significantly for this study, Bruce Lawrence sees this commentary as the "basis for all his subsequent writings and speculations. It expands the pithy directives of Abū Najīb by relating them to his own interior quest for truth" (Lawrence, *Notes*, 76); see also Schimmel, *Indian Subcontinent*, 33. This practical application of the more systematic treatise of Suhrawardī into the interior as well as practical life found in Manerī is precisely the type of relationship we can observe between the *Kashf* of Hujwīrī and the Maktūbāt-i Sadī and other correspondence and writings of and in relation to Manerī

50. Lawrence, *Notes*, 72.

51. Jackson, "Introduction to In Quest of God," xvii.

52. Jackson, "Use of the Quran," 37.

53. Lawrence, *Notes*, 72.

54. Jackson, "Spiritual Guidance," 148.

55. The "Sharif," honorific, meaning "noble" is added to the name of the town of Bihar in which Manerī is buried as a way of noting that the town is a particularly honorable place because of the presence of Manerī's tomb.

56. Jackson, "Spiritual Guidance," 148. The 'urs refers to the "marriage" of the soul of the saint at death with the saint's Lord.

57. Jackson, "Introduction to *In Quest of God*," xvii.

with the names of several other celebrated Muslim saints, in a thanksgiving ritual for safe travel.[58]

The *Maktūbāt-i Sadī* was compiled in about 1346 by his chief disciple and aide, Zain al-Dīn Badr-i-Arabī from his correspondence with Qazi[59] Shams al-Dīn, an official; the same disciple also compiled the subsequent *Maktūbāt-i Do Sadī*.[60] It has been compared with the *Kashf al-Mahjūb* in terms of its scope and importance in the subsequent history of Sūfī teaching in South Asia,[61] and was, reportedly, consulted regularly by Mughal emperor Aurangzeb.[62] Nonetheless, both works were considered essential in the process of Islamic learning in Medieval South Asia, with the emphasis of the one something of a complement to that of the other;[63] Syed Hasan Askari thus writes in his preface to Paul Jackson's 1980 English translation of the *Maktūbāt-i Sadī* that "the *Kashf al-Mahjūb* is more a work *about* Sufism, while *The Hundred Letters* is a work *of* Sufism."[64] Bruce B. Lawrence, writing in the forward to the same volume, described this work as displaying an "artful balance—between reflection and conduct . . . between attachment to the Law and pursuit of the Way, between sobriety and ecstasy. . . . The Hundred Letters . . . are unrivaled—and cannot be surpassed—as an invitation to experience the Sufi Way as a Sufi master experienced it and described it."[65] An important element which one observes in the writings of Manerī, even more than is the case with Hujwīrī, is that he is consciously seeking to contextualize his letters for the Indo-Persian context. Thus while Manerī liberally quotes from the Qurʾān and the traditions, as well as from earlier classical Sūfī figures, we can also observe his use of illustrations from classical

---

58. Jaʿfar Sharif, *Qānūn-i-Islām*, 137. This was written in the nineteenth century by an Indian Muslim from the southern part of the Indian Subcontinent. It is thus particularly interesting to note that Manerī's name was being used in folk ritual among Muslims in the Deccan, an area considerably distant from the location of Manerī's ministry or burial site.

59. "Judge"; from the Arabic *qāḍī*.

60. Askari, *Medieval Bihar*, 34–35.

61. Lawrence, "Foreword to *The Hundred Letters*," xviii–xix.

62. Askari, *Medieval Bihar*, 34. Reynold A. Nicholson, who translated Hujwīrī's volume into English, turned down a request to translate the *Maktūbāt-i Sadī*; on this, see Askari, "Preface to *The Hundred Letters*."

63. Askari, "Preface," xii.

64. Ibid.

65. Lawrence, "Foreword," xix.

Persian writings, and will also come across quotations sourced from the Indian, Hindu milieu in which he lived and taught.[66]

For example, Manerī presents a discussion on how God gives special light of revelation concerning God's attributes to certain great people in particular. He quotes from part of Q 58:22 and Q 42:52, in both cases focused (perhaps with a bit of *ta'wīl* in his interpretation) on God's having given special light to certain people, "so that by means of that light they might find a Way to the world of divine attributes" [*sifāt*].[67] From there, however, Manerī goes on to further illustrate his point with a picture from the classical Persian *Shāhnāmeh*, or "Book of Kings," saying that "'only a second Rustam could master Rakhsh', the horse of Rustam."[68]

Importantly, both of these volumes demonstrate a concern observed in earlier works in Arabic, to demonstrate that Sufism represented a balance already described by Qushayrī between *sharī'a* and *ḥaqīqa*. Hujwīrī and Manerī both sought to present the Ṣūfī path as not merely faithful to the orthodox Islamic tradition, but as the *best* way of understanding the Muslim faith. In doing this, their writings are replete with the kind of exegesis of the Qur'ān referred to as *ta'wīl*, focused on spiritual, often symbolic or allegorical explanations of the meaning of the sacred text. One theme found in the writing of both authors, in common with a number of their predecessors writing in Arabic, involves explanations of both the intoxicated (*sukr*) and sober (*sahw*) understandings of Ṣūfī thought and practice.[69] The writings of both these men are briefly connected in another manner as well: Even as Hujwīrī is found quoting the writings predecessors and contemporaries such as Qushayrī, we find Manerī quoting from Hujwīrī as an authoritative source on topics such

---

66. Ironically, Hujwīrī's *Kashf*, although written in Persian, contains a couple of allusions not from Persian, but rather from the same classical Arabic love poems of the "Majnūn-Laila" genre, even observing in one place that these were written by "Qays of the Banū 'Āmir." See Hujwiri, *Revelation*, 258, 353.

67. Maneri, *Hundred Letters*, 60.

68. Ibid. Compare this use of Persian literature with Qushayrī's use of Arabic literature, particularly the Majnūn-Laila love poems of pre-Islamic Arabia. See Qushayri, *Epistle*, 329, including n. 605 on the same page.

69. An interesting essay on this which includes a discussion of this theme in Hujwīrī's *Kashf al-Mahjūb* is Mojaddedi, "Creation of a Popular Typology," 1–13. Mojaddedi notes (1) that while a number of Ṣūfī writers had explored the themes of spiritual intoxication and sobriety, Hujwīrī was the first to express these using Abū Yazīd al-Bisṭāmī and Junayd, respectively, as representatives of this typology.

as fasting,⁷⁰ the need to continually seek God,⁷¹ and the permissibility and utility of listening to music as a form of devotion.⁷² In each of these cases, it is interesting that Manerī cites Hujwīrī specifically as a Sūfī authority whose orthodoxy is widely recognized.

SŪFĪ SOUTH ASIA: INDIGENOUS AND PILGRIM IN HUJWĪRĪ⁷³ AND MANERĪ

In the previous chapter, we discussed the manner in which a number of writers produced systematic works in Arabic in which a Sūfī stance was understood as not merely a legitimate means of understanding the Islamic tradition and interpretation of the Qur'ān (an internal "pilgrim" principle), but was also presented as the best way to enter into the life of Islam (the corresponding internal "indigenous" principle). Writing at a time when Sufism was clearly under attack by some of the more orthodox elements in the Muslim community, Hujwīrī, like many of his predecessors writing in Arabic, sought to demonstrate the legitimate orthodoxy of Sufism, and could be as straightforward as Ghazālī in both his defense of Sūfī orthodoxy and even the superiority of the Sūfī approach to the Qur'ān.

Following an introductory prayer and some comments, Hujwīrī begins with some decidedly orthodox usage of the Qur'ān, citing Q 16:98, asking God's blessing in reading the Qur'ān should include seeking refuge in God from "the stoned Devil" as well as purging the self of lust and selfishness, according to Q 79:40–41.⁷⁴ His orthodox stance continues as Hujwīrī differentiates between the kind of veil which can be removed (*hijāb-i-ghaynī*, or "veil of clouding"), and that which is unremoveable (*hijāb-i raynī*, or "veil of essence").⁷⁵ These he ties into his *Ash'arite* theological stance,⁷⁶ citing a tradition which recorded Muhammad as having said, "Everyone finds easy that for which he was created," and tying in

70. Maneri, *Hundred Letters*, 129.

71. Ibid., 196.

72. Ibid., 388.

73. Nicholson gives the verse references to the Qur'ān in the older Flügel numbering; we have changed these to the standard Egyptian verse numbering, which the Rabbani translation uses.

74. Hujwiri, *Revelation*, 3.

75. Ibid., 4–5.

76. Ernst, *Shambhala Guide*, ix–x. Ernst notes that his *Ash'arite* stance was something which he held in common with Qushayrī.

Q 83:14 and Q 2:6, which for Hujwīrī strengthens the element of God's eschatalogical sovereignty.[77] "Ash'arite" refers to adherents to the theological position of Abū al-Hasan 'Alī ibn Ismā' īl al-Ash'arī (d. 936), who sought to safeguard *tawḥīd* in emphasizing the uncreated nature of the Qur'ān and the eternal attributes (*ṣifāt*) of God, asserting that these are "neither He nor other than He" vis-à-vis God's self.[78] This became the majority position within Sunni Muslim theology.[79] Hujwīrī also entered into what was an ongoing discussion among *Ash'arite*, concerning the relationship between God and his attributes (*ṣifāt*); in this case, he observes that the attributes of God (such as knowledge, power and life) "are not He nor a part of Him, but exist in Him and subsist by Him."[80] In so saying, Hujwīrī seeks to strengthen what he sees as a potentially endangered idea of *tawḥīd* by removing the attributes of God completely from the discussion regarding the degree to which these may be understood as being within his being.

Hujwīrī has his own way of expressing the idea of spiritual ascent in the Sūfī context. Early on, he examines several passages of the Qur'ān, noting how the relationship of individuals with their soul is transformed as one progresses more deeply into the path. Thus, in observing that the "animal soul," the *nafs al-ammāra* of Q 12:53, is the "greatest of all veils between God and Man,"[81] he alludes to the Sūfī progression from the *nafs al-ammāra*, to the *nafs al-lawwāma*, the "self-accusing soul" of Q 75:2, culminating in the *nafs al-mutmu'inna*, the "soul at peace" of Q 85:27–30.[82] The "self-accusing soul" comes up again a bit later with regard to God's allowing accusation and persecution to test the believers.[83] Thus we see that Hujwīrī seeks to join classical orthodox and Sūfī approaches in his own exegesis of the text of the Qur'ān. The idea is to demonstrate that a Sūfī approach to spiritual life and interpretation is acceptable from the perspective of orthodox Islam. Hujwīrī moves from there, however,

---

77. Hujwiri, *Revelation*, 4.

78. Mayer, "Theology and Sufism," 269.

79. Murata and Chittick, *Vision of Islam*, 245–46. See also Joseph L. Cumming's recently published essay on parallels between this understanding of the *ṣifāt* and the *dhāt*, or essence of God: "Sifāt al-Dhāt," 111–45.

80. Hujwiri, *Revelation*, 14.

81. Ibid., 9.

82. Sands, *Sūfī Commentaries*, 166 n. 61.

83. Hujwirī, *Revelation*, 62.

to underline the superiority of a Sūfī understanding which, in his view, integrates spiritual experience with textual knowledge.

The first chapter of the *Kashf*, "On Knowledge," has Hujwīrī quoting positive passages from the Qurʾān regarding knowledge (Q 35:28), yet at the same time warning against acquiring "useless knowledge" (Q 2:96).[84] He expands on what is meant by "knowledge," however, into "Divine" knowledge and "Human" knowledge, corresponding to *haqīqa* ("truth") and *sharīʿa* ("law").[85] While we can see that Hujwīrī is thus exerting himself to maintain the grounding in the law, he asserts that both sides are necessary, that the

> outward and inward aspects cannot be divorced. The exoteric aspect of Truth without the esoteric is hypocrisy, and the esoteric without the exoteric is heresy. So, with regard to the Law, mere formality is defective, while mere spirituality is vain.[86]

As was the case with his forebears and contemporaries writing in Arabic, Hujwīrī sought to present a balanced, reasonably sober understanding of Sufism, and in doing so he often wrote with incisive thought, and sometimes a sharpened pen, with some decidedly dry wit mixed in. Thus, in debate with an orthodox Muslim who was opposed to the Sūfīs, Hujwīrī's interlocutor asserted that, "There are twelve heretical sects, and one of them flourishes amongst those who profess Sufism." Hujwīrī replied, "If one sect belongs to us, eleven belong to you; and the Sūfīs can protect themselves from one better than you can from eleven"[87]

On the other hand, seeking to integrate a "pilgrim" principle into the mix, Hujwīrī could also be equally impatient with some of the more "intoxicated" of the Sūfīs, and in particular those who made claims of "total annihilation" into God's essence (*fanāʾ yi kulliat*); he refers to this as "manifest error" and those who hold it he calls "ignorant and mistaken men."[88] Interestingly, and perhaps ironically, Hujwīrī derides those holding to belief in this kind of "annihilation," because it is similar to that of what he understands to be the view of the Christians:

> The Nestorians of Rūm and the Christians hold that Mary annihilated by self-mortification all the attributes of humanity

---

84. Ibid., 11.
85. Ibid., 14.
86. Ibid.
87. Hujwiri, *Revelation*, 16.
88. Ibid., 243.

and that the Divine subsistence became attached to her, so that she was made subsistent through the subsistence of God, and that Jesus was the result thereof, and that he was not originally composed of the stuff of humanity, because his subsistence is produced by realization of the subsistence of God; and that, consequent to this, he and his mother and God are all subsistent through one subsistence, which is eternal and an attribute of God.[89]

The concern which Hujwīrī expresses here concerning *fanā' yi kulliat* echoes concerns of others about the use, particularly by Hallāj, of the term *hulūl*. It may be recalled from the previous chapter that *hulūl* is the term often used for *incarnation*. This train of thought in effect reproduces what Kenneth Cragg has pointed out may be a confusion from within the text of the Qur'ān itself. The idea in the incarnation is not that of the Qur'ānic *ittikhadh* (loosely, "adoption"), which would be something like the above, not some sort of *apotheosis* which historic Christian faith rightly repudiated, but rather the very idea of *tanzīl* itself in terms of a divine descent and condescension.[90]

Importantly, however, Hujwīrī was quite torn as to whether to apply the above condemnation to Hallāj himself, although he did roundly condemn others who he says claimed to be Hallāj's followers, and to whom Hujwīrī refers, tellingly, not only as "*Hallājīs*," but as "*Hulūlīs*." Regarding Hallāj himself, however, he lists various figures who accepted him, including Qushayrī, who said concerning Hallāj that, "if he was genuinely spiritual he is not to be banned on the ground of popular condemnation, and if he was banned by Sufism and rejected by the Truth (*al-Haqq*), he is not to be approved on the ground of popular approval."[91] Hujwīrī concludes by saying,

> you must know that the sayings of al-Hallāj should not be taken as a model, inasmuch as he was an ecstatic, not firmly settled, and a man needs to be firmly settled before his sayings can be considered authoritative. Therefore, he is dear to my heart, yet his "path" is not soundly established on any principle, and his state is not fixed in any position, and his experiences are largely mingled with error.[92]

---

89. Ibid., 244.
90. See Cragg, "Incarnatus non est," 26.
91. Hujwiri, *Revelation*, 150.
92. Ibid., 152.

Thus, Hujwīrī here manages to maintain his condemnation of his perception of the error of *hulūl*, while avoiding condemning Hallāj.

It is interesting to see how this idea plays out in various ways as Hujwīrī continues through his treatise, particularly parsing between the exoteric and esoteric, and finding a few surprising parallels with biblical understandings in some areas. Thus the discussion on Sufism begins with an exhortation to humility from Q 25:63, adding that those who walk in meekness "shall be rewarded with the highest place in Paradise."[93] From there the focus moves to a contrast between *safā* and *kadar* (purity and impurity).[94] This interaction focuses on the story of Yūsuf, and brings this into a further discussion on *fanā'* and *baqā'*.[95]

As Hujwīrī sees it, in the Yūsuf story the women of Egypt are initially portrayed as being entranced by his beauty in the sense of *kadar* (that is, impurity), but later they exclaim, "This is no [mere] human being" (Q 12:31) in a state of "annihilation."[96] For Hujwīrī, purity and *fanā' wa-baqā'* are intrinsically linked, in a manner very reminiscent of Christian language, "because purity is the attribute of those who love, and the lover is he that is dead (fānī) in his own attributes and living (bāqī) in the attributes of the Beloved."[97] Here one is once again reminded of Paul's words in Gal 2:20. Paul's point of being reckoned dead, yet sustained in life by God, seems to be further amplified in the more allegorical exegesis which Hujwīrī provides concerning Q 2:154, "Do not call dead those who are slain in the way of God. Nay, they are living."[98] Without denying the meaning in its context (where it referred to those literally killed in battle), Hujwīrī uses this passage in conjunction with the principle of giving sacrificially noted in Q 3:92, "sacrificing" one's spirit by renouncing self-interest. Thus, those whose desires are thus "slain," who "put to death the deeds of the body" (Rom 8:13), are truly living.

The importance of purity on multiple levels is emphasized in an anecdote from Shiblī, who here Hujwīrī quotes as citing Q 24:30, "Tell the believers to restrain their eyes," referring to both restraining one's

---

93. Ibid., 30, in an interesting (though conceivably coincidental) parallel with Matt 5:5.

94. This contrast to that between clear and murky water; this observation was brought to our attention by Dr. A. H. Mathias Zahniser.

95. Hujwiri, *Revelation*, 143.

96. Ibid., 32.

97. Ibid.

98. Ibid., 194.

physical eyes from what is forbidden, and that one's spiritual eyes ought to be focused on God alone. Continuing with Q 17:72, Shiblī emphasizes that, "In truth, until God clears the desire of lust out of a man's heart the bodily eye is not safe from its hidden dangers, and until God establishes himself in a man's heart the spiritual eye is not safe from looking at other than him."[99]

Another, perhaps apologetic element in Hujwīrī's thought here is the comparison between Muhammad and Moses and David from the Hebrew Scriptures, in which inevitably Muhammad is demonstrated to be superior. Usually this is in regard to Muhammad having deeper, esoteric knowledge of God as compared with one of these earlier figures. For example, he quotes Q 20:25–26, which has Moses asking God to "enlarge" his breast, and make his task easy for him; in his "existence," there is no "non-existence," as he took initiative to request this from God. Conversely, God is depicted as having reminded Muhammad that he had taken the initiative to enlarge Muhammad's breast (Q 95:1–3). Thus Muhammad had non-existence without existence.[100]

We see a similar comparison, this time with David, and similarly the comparison is here brought into connection with the idea of annihilation and abiding. This time it relates to the comparison between the state of "sobriety" and the state of "intoxication." Quoting Q 2:251, Hujwīrī notes that David killed Goliath in a state of sobriety, in control of himself. Muhammad, on the other hand, killed in battle in the midst of ecstasy—and the killing was attributed to God (Q 8:17). Thus Muhammad is assumed to be superior as it was God who did something directly through him.[101] Another prophet who comes up, though not in this comparative sense, is Ibrahim, and the passage in Q 6:76–78. Although in its context, the passage seems to point to a rejection of created things as deities, here, and in a number of other places, this anecdote comes up repeatedly as pointing to Ibrahim's ability to recognize God's presence in all things.[102] Finally, there is a comparison between those in relationship with Adam, and those who are in relationship with God. This is based on Q 33:72 and Q 28:16 concerning those in relationship with Adam, and Q 25:63 and Q 43:68, regarding the relationship between humankind and God.

99. Ibid., 156.
100. Ibid., 41.
101. Ibid., 185.
102. Ibid., 91.

"Relationship to Adam," it reads, "ends at the Resurrection, whereas the relationship of the servant of God always subsists and is unalterable."[103]

Thus, we see Hujwīrī seeking to balance between what he sees in the Qur'ān as *sharī'a* and *haqīqa*, initially laying a foundation of more classical exegesis, but then subsequently bringing in some more esoteric Qur'ānic exegesis, particularly in expounding on Sūfī principles which aren't as clear in the literal meaning of the text.

The *Maktūbāt-i Sadī* of Sharaf al-Dīn Manerī, in spite of a number of similarities, is rather different in nature from Hujwīrī's *Kashf al-Mahjūb*. Reproduced and distributed within Manerī's lifetime,[104] the tone of the *Maktūbāt-i Sadī* is often very personal and reflects their origin as correspondence between the pīr and one of his main disciples, Shams al-Dīn. This is the basis of the exegesis which is found in these letters, too. Manerī shares with Hujwīrī a concern for remaining rooted in the orthodox, textual tradition of Islam, and we see examples of both classical as well as more esoteric exegesis. What we see emphasized more, though, is the pastoral nature of this exegesis, applying these texts thus explained to life situations which his disciple would have been encountering.

Since the *Maktūbāt-i Sadī* is not a systematic work as was the case with the *Kashf*, the classical and more esoteric exegesis is more mixed; one doesn't see from the order in which these are presented a more classical foundation being laid as a basis from which to venture into more Sūfī-style exegesis. Some of the more esoteric exegesis one finds in Manerī sounds like it may be part of a wider, earlier tradition.

Sometimes the exegesis is very homiletical, and seems only very tangentially related to the text. Thus we find Manerī quoting Q 47:19, "There is no god but God!" but moving from this into describing four stages of faith in God in terms of practical response. In other words, if one believes that "there is no god but God," what is one's inner response to that particular truth? Thus there is the hypocritical confessing without faith, and then the speaking with what he calls "conventional" belief, perhaps with "rational proofs;" this he nonetheless derides as being "fit for old women;" orthodox, but perhaps rather dry and dead. He continues to describe the third view, of realizing that every action flows "from the same source." This is more than merely having one's information correct; it is moving into relationship with the Almighty. The fourth stage

---

103. Ibid., 159–60. This particular excursus rather brings to mind the second-Adam Christology of 1 Cor 15:45–49.

104. Jackson, "Introduction and Notes," 3.

is where all that is perceived is light, everything is understood as being infused with God's presence. While referencing the experience of Mansūr al-Ḥallāj of losing oneself in contemplation of God, he is quick to clarify that this does not imply that the person in this stage becomes God, or has actually ceased to exist. He moves from this into quoting two more verses (Q 55:26 and Q 28:88) to underline the fact that ultimately it is only God who is eternal.

Manerī's exposition on repentance is more conventional, but no less pastoral in execution. He begins not only quoting Q 24:31, but with a fairly conventional exposition of it, that this verse was "revealed to the companions of the Prophet and all repented and became models of abjuring infidelity and embracing faith in the one true God," and attractively describing repentance as a "beautiful carpet on which you perform your devotions."[105] He does not, perhaps cannot, leave it just at this level; indeed, in view of his own interpretation of Q 47:19 above, it would almost be wrong for him to do so. He moves from there to Q 7:143, which quotes Moses as expressing repentance, but which Manerī interprets as, "I turned from myself to You because of my passionate desire to see your face," focusing on the meaning of repentance as "turning back."[106]

Here and elsewhere, Manerī also injects a very human element which underlines the pastoral nature of his letter, and his concern that his readers not become discouraged because of their own lack of perfection. He emphasizes the gradual nature of repentance, and of the need for its repetition,[107] and quotes Tustarī (d. 896) on the need to continually recall the sins of one's past as a guard against pride, similar, perhaps to Paul's words in 1 Tim 1:15, describing himself as "chief" of sinners.[108]

We find, then, a certain element of compassion in Manerī 's exposition. He notes that the complete extinction of anger and sexual desire is neither possible nor even desirable; he observes that the Qur'ān commends "those who swallow their anger" (Q 3:134), not the annihilation of anger.[109] He goes on to describe the proper place of each of these, concluding that the

> sexual appetite and anger are like dogs and horses. Without these two, one cannot go hunting for eternal bliss. The precondition

---

105. Maneri, *Hundred Letters*, 12–15.
106. Ibid., 16.
107. Ibid., 16–17.
108. Ibid., 17.
109. Ibid., 75.

is to bring both to heel. If they gain the upper hand, then they can wreak a man's destruction. The whole purpose of austerities is to break the dominance of these two qualities and place them firmly under control. It is possible to do this.[110]

In the same vein, Manerī later quotes 2:286, "God does not impose on any soul more than it can bear;" seeking to encourage his disciple with a message of God's mercy and generosity.[111] This brings to mind a similar passage in 1 Cor 10:12–13, in which it is noted that while the believers need to be watchful, at the same time there is mercy in the fact that God will "not let you be tempted beyond your ability." While God desires purity and devotion in our lives, there is also a deep sense of mercy expressed here, all with the overall goal of encouragement.

Of course, not everything dovetails with the biblical witness, and occasionally the Sūfī path veers from the soaring exposition of union with God, plunging into the depths of folk religion. Manerī is by no means immune to this. We find him exhorting his disciple to the mantra-like use of the final two chapters of the Qur'ān (and other passages, too), which admittedly are generally used as charms. He thus writes that,

> God will preserve from all sadness, adversity and misfortune until the following Friday, anyone who, after the Friday prayer, and before commencing any work, recites seven times the opening chapter of the Quran and the one hundred and twelfth chapter on Unity, as well as the last two chapters (113 and 114) of the Quran. For the removal of what is irksome, let the sixty-second chapter of the Quran on Congregational Prayer be recited every evening. . .let a person retire somewhere and, holding his hands aloft, say one hundred times: "O Master, O Master!" and he will receive whatever he desires from the Lord. If he says this one thousand times, all his needs will certainly be met.[112]

A strong emphasis in Manerī's exegesis and his writing generally is in the exhortation for the believers to have a spiritual director, a guide. Thus Q 9:119, regarding association with the righteous, and Q 42:52,

---

110. Ibid.
111. Ibid., 100.
112. Ibid., 141. Of course, we have modern Christian preachers who make similar exhortations (and perhaps also be said to represent a stream of Evangelical folk religion), and it can be noted that in this passage, at least, Manerī doesn't seem to go to the point of making folk objects such as amulets from these verses, as Nizām al-Dīn describes doing. See Nizam ad-Din Awliya, *Morals for the Heart*, 304.

noting that "God guides whomsoever he wishes," which seem on the surface to be more individualistic in nature, are shaped into a case for spiritual guidance from a shaikh, saying that one needs a guide along the "road to the Kaaba": it is not enough to be able to see the road with one's eyes and have enough strength in one's legs. Imagine what it must be like on that Road along which 124,000 prophets have traveled, yet no trace of their journey remains!"[113]

Manerī also emphasizes the importance of seeking to imitate Muhammad's life, quoting Q 3:31 as "Imitate me (Muhammad) and God will befriend you,"[114] as well as the repeated saying "Fear God and obey me," attributed by Manerī to Muhammad.[115] While this is at one level a simple exhortation to a lifestyle of purity, as is the case elsewhere, Manerī seeks to take this to a deeper level. Particularly in the case of the latter quotation, there is an element of connection in his further exegesis with the classic Sūfī theme of the tension between *sharīʿa* and *haqīqa*. Here he offers an understanding of the *sharīʿa* and *haqīqa* which explains their being symbiotically related to one another. "The Way[116] is a path that stems from the Law," he writes, with the law (*sharīʿa*) understood as being focused on the various religious practices which are considered obligatory, whereas "the Way seeks the reality behind all these prescribed things. . .in general, the observance of all that pertains to the senses comes under the ambit of the Law, while the observance of all that is concealed in the inner purity of the body has to do with the Way."[117] There is a rather Platonic sense about all of this, of the visible being a sign and a pointer to a deeper reality, but in a way in which Manerī very proactively affirms the reality of the material world against any antinomian tendencies.

Here Manerī describes union with God, sometimes soaring into terms which seems to actually combine something of the idea of "sober" and "intoxicated" Sūfī ideas. Thus,

---

113. Manerī, *Hundred Letters*, 26.

114. Ibid., 107.

115. Ibid., 101. Jackson inserts a reference here to Q 3:50 in which the saying is actually that of Jesus. The refrain is repeated in relation to Jesus in Q 43:63, as well as in the mouths of other prophets (in overall analogous support to Muhammad's mission) throughout Q 26:108, 110 (Noah), 126, 131 (Hūd), 144, 150 (Salīh), 163 (Lūt), and 179 (Shuʿaib). This observation was pointed out to me by Dr. Dale Walker.

116. "Way" in the text I have is *tarīqa* rather than *haqīqa* in this passage, though there are likely variants in the primary sources. See Manerī, *Maktubate Sadi*, 138.

117. Manerī, *Hundred Letters*, 102.

> What does it mean to be joined to the Lord? It means that, for the sake of God, one is cut off from what is in any way base. Being closely united would mean becoming lost in the very depths of God! To this corresponds a great freedom from preoccupation with things other than God. On the other hand, to the extent that a person becomes free from preoccupation with God, to the same extent he becomes separated from Him.[118]

Here, then, it would seem that we find both soaring and sobriety, all within a few lines.

Continuing in Letter 15, focused upon the theme of union with God, Manerī has a brief section in which he muses on the "Day of *Alastu*"[119] referred to in the previous chapter, in which Q 7:172 recounts the primordial covenant between God and humankind. As we noted in the previous chapter, this has often been interpreted by Sūfīs as a spiritual goal to which the disciple longs to return, and a spiritual "memory" which can be triggered by the practice of *dhikr* in the Sūfī's communal and individual practice. Manerī considers the moment of *alastu* to be a foundation which is meant to influence the entire life of the Sūfī. He exclaims that

> One gulp from the cup of "Am I not" gives so much pleasure that throughout his entire lifetime it can never be erased from his soul. Indeed, his life consists of that delight and the desire of that Light is like the center and treasure of his own being. He is not inclined toward this world and is unable, even for a moment, to abandon that wine!
>
> Your lovers have become intoxicated from eternity.
> They have come, their heads swaying with "Am I not?"
> Imbibing this wine and savoring its fragrance,
> They become spiritual sots due to "Am I not?"[120]

The goal of Sufism is often articulated in terms of *fanā' wa-baqā'* (as discussed above), and Manerī discusses this in connection with Q 13:39, "God effaces or establishes whatever He pleases."[121] From this Manerī extrapolates a brief explanation of the meaning of annihilation and abiding

---

118. Ibid., 65.
119. See on this in the previous chapter.
120. Maneri, *Hundred Letters*, 66.
121. Ibid., 67.

in God, rather startlingly alluding to becoming as 'Īsā is described in Q 4:171:

> At every moment a Sufi dies, only to obtain a new form of existence, coming further under the control of the desire of self-effacement and absorption in God.... At every step absorption and affirmation are obtained, so that the Sufi celebrates two feasts there: one that of absorption, and the other a feast of affirmation. At this stage, it is fitting that he should be called "the Spirit of God" or "the Word of God;" such a title will become like a robe that fits him perfectly.[122]

Thus here we see Manerī seeking to explain this passage in a manner which gets at what he sees as its inner meaning, yet at the same time with an eye to pastoral application. That he does so using Jesus as his exemplar in this situation (even if he doesn't name him) makes it that much more interesting.

Indeed, one of the more surprising references concerning Jesus in Manerī is a close quote from John's Gospel 3:3. In this passage, Jesus is speaking to an elder in the Jewish community who approaches him secretly by night, Jesus speaks to him, saying "Truly, truly I tell you, unless one is born again [or "born from above"], he cannot see the kingdom of God." Manerī quotes this passage, in Arabic, in two separate places, in both cases attributing the statements to Jesus.

The first of these is in Letter 6 from *Maktūbāt-i Sadī*, on the qualifications of a spiritual director (*shaikh*). Manerī quotes Jesus as saying, "A man cannot be reckoned among the host of angels in heaven and on earth, that is, those who have attained divine illumination, unless he be born again!"[123] Manerī follows this by an explanation in which he sees this idea of being "born again" in terms of "emerging from bondage to...human inclinations" and being enabled to "see the other world. Both this world and the world to come are evident—that is what it means to be born again."[124] This quotation is repeated in the *Maktūbāt-i Do Sadī*, the subsequent, and more eclectic collection of letters, Letter 13, addressed to "Shaikh Omar."[125] In the connected passage in the *Maktūbāt-i Do Sadī*, the Arabic quotation of Jesus' words are identical to that of the quotation

---

122. Ibid.
123. Maneri, *Hundred Letters*, 31.
124. Ibid.
125. Maneri, *Quest*, 38–41; and Manerī, *Maktubate Do Sadī*, 107–13.

in the *Maktūbāt-i Sadī*,[126] though the explanation offered by Manerī is somewhat richer, and is worth quoting at length. He writes,

> It is related that Jesus said: "Whoever is not born again in the heavenly and earthly realms does not enter." In other words, just as through his birth by appearance [first birth] he comes into this realm and he sees the world of this realm, in a similar fashion, by the coming to birth of qualities [second birth] he enters into both the heavenly and earthly realms. Whatever divine secrets and treasures are in the heavenly realm are seen by him. This is called "manifestation" [*kashf*].[127]

It is particularly interesting that Manerī is suggesting that a "second birth" will enable the disciple to grasp the spiritual realm "unveiled," that is, God will grant *kashf*, removal of the veil, and be thus enabled to perceive the light of God in the heavens and the earth (*as-samawāti wa al-ʿardi*).

ASCENSION, VISION AND TRANSFORMATION IN SŪFĪ SOUTH ASIA

In our earlier examination of the theme of ascension, vision and transformation in the mysticism of various traditions, a common issue was whether the initiative and power for the journey was primarily (or entirely) an anthropocentric, shamanistic schema of theurgically generated power, or whether the initiative and power was that of the grace and

---

126. In both cases, the Arabic reads: *lan yalija malakūta as-samawāti wa al-ʿardi man lam yūlad marratayni*. We find it interesting that the vocabulary of this passage (*as-samwāti -ʿardi*), the precise wording for "the heavens and the earth" in the beginning of Q 24:35, a frequently-cited text in Sūfī thought. See Manerī, *Quest*, 40; and Manerī, *Maktubate Do Sadī*, 110.

127. Manerī, *Quest*, 40; and Manerī *Maktubate Do Sadī*, 110. Manerī is not the first Sūfī figure to quote this passage. More than two hundred and fifty years earlier, the Persian Sūfī ʿAyn al-Qudāt al-Hamadhānī quoted the same passage, again in Arabic, in his *Tamhīdāt*. Hamadhānī's quote is worded in a slightly different manner; he has Jesus saying, "He who was not born twice will not enter the Kingdom of Heaven." He goes on to explain this as well in a manner which is similar to, though not completely the same as, that of Manerī, saying that "the wayfarer must be born twice. He must be born once through his mother, so that he can see himself and this perishing world. And he should once be born of himself, so that he can see God and that everlasting world." See Papan-Matin, *Beyond Death*, 81. It's also worth noting that in a more recent translation of a Manerī's *malfuz* (record of Manerī's oral teaching), Manerī quotes from the *Tamhīdāt*, so he certainly is familiar with it. See Manerī, *Mine of Meaning*, 136, 140, 193.

blessing of God, and into which the participation of the "traveler" was invited.

Both Hujwīrī and Manerī address the issues surrounding the *miʿrāj*, the emphasis in the discussion being upon the spiritual application of ascent toward the Almighty in much the same manner as was described in the previous chapter, though again, with some unique insights.

For Hujwīrī, part of his interaction with the *miʿrāj* tradition involved its usage in demonstrating the superiority of Muhammad over other prophets, particularly Moses. For example, in Q 7:143, a reflection of Exod 33:18, Moses asks God to show God's own self to him; God's presence destroys the mountain and Moses faints. Hujwīrī interprets this as *sukr*, that Moses is fainting in spiritual ecstasy, and cannot bear the nearness of God. He contrasts this with Muhammad's sobriety (*sahw*) in coming at the *miʿrāj* a mere "two bow lengths" from God's presence. Hujwīrī uses this as well to demonstrate what he sees as the superiority of the abiding state of sobriety (*baqāʾ bi-Allāh*) as opposed to the state of annihilation and intoxication (*fanāʾ fi-Allāh*).[128] Later on, a similar comparison is made again between Muhammad and Moses with regard to the topics of *musāmarat*, or conversation, and *muhādathat*, which is something like intimate conversation at night between lovers. Moses is described as failing in his attempt to see God in spite of conversing with God in the day time, whereas Muhammad is said to be as "dumb before the revelation of God's majesty" as he approaches within "two bowlengths of God" *at night*, when lovers converse.[129]

Hujwīrī regards the *miʿrāj* as having happened to Muhammad physically, rather than just a purely spiritual journey. He compares the *miʿrāj* of Muhammad with that of Bistāmī, in which the saint describes a spiritual journey which mirrors that of the account of Muhammad, and in which he identifies increasingly closely with divinity.[130] Hujwīrī ultimately asserts that the "ascension of the prophets takes place outwardly and in the body, whereas that of saints takes place inwardly and in the

---

128. Hujwīrī, *Revelation*, 186. Of course, in this same section of the *Kashf*, Hujwīrī also describes those (such as Abū Yazīd al-Bistāmī), who see *sukr* as being superior to *sahw*, and there cites David's sober killing of Goliath (in Q 2:251), in which the killing is attributed to David, vs. Muhammad's intoxicated killing of the Quraysh in battle (in Q 8:17), in which the killing is attributed to God (Hujwiri, *Revelation*, 185).

129. Hujwiri, *Revelation*, 380–81. See also Awn, *Classical Sufi Approaches*, 151 n. 19.

130. However, see also Renard, *Friends of God*, 266, where the author describes Bistāmī's ascension as "a rather loose analogy."

spirit."¹³¹ Elsewhere, Hujwīrī claims that when Muhammad was in God's presence, he wished to be dissolved into God, though God chose to keep Muhammad with his companions as "proof of God" in his obedience to the religious ordinances.¹³²

This is clarified later on. While not denying the physical nature of the *miʿrāj* itself, Hujwīrī nonetheless does not claim that Muhammad viewed God with his physical eyes, but rather asserted that it was with "spiritual eyes" that Muhammad received the vision of God. Thus Hujwīrī suggests that Muhammad told ʿĀʾisha that he did not see, as she was focused on externals and would have understood this as physical vision, but told Ibn ʿAbbās that he *did* see God, since, Hujwīrī says, Ibn ʿAbbās understood the spiritual nature of his vision.¹³³

Like Hujwīrī, Manerī also sought to emphasize an understanding of the *miʿrāj* in such a way as to uphold the importance of following the requirements of *sharīʿa*, even as these requirements were often significantly reinterpreted. In Manerī's 32nd letter, on the prayer ritual, he emphasizes that Muhammad brought back the prayer liturgy "from the pure realm of 'two bowlengths from God.'"¹³⁴ Elsewhere, Manerī's take on Muhammad's vision in Q 53:9 involved Muhammad being raised to the heavens so that angels could learn from the reverence of his prayers, he was returned to earth to serve as an example to humankind.¹³⁵ He doesn't understand the *salāt* liturgy to be merely a matter of "rule-keeping" as popularly under-

---

131. Hujwīrī, *Revelation*, 238. Rabbani, whose commentary on the *Kashf* is interspersed with his translation, emphasizes that, in his view, the *miʿrāj* was "not of a spiritual nature like the experience of *fana-fi-Allah* commonly enjoyed by the Friends of God (*auliya-Allah*), but it was of a physical nature experienced in the state of physical sobriety" (Rabbani, 194).

132. Hujwiri, *Revelation*, 283. See also Awn, *Classical Sufi Approaches*, 145.

133. Hujwiri, *Revelation*, 331. Kalābādhī, *Doctrine*, 26–27, also leans toward a spiritual interpretation, though he notes that there were others who understood the Muhammad's ascent as physical. In expressing his own support for a "spiritual" *miʿrāj*, Kalābādhī presents a much stronger quote from ʿĀʾisha, saying "Whoever asserts that Muhammad saw his Lord, lies" (Kalābādhī, *Doctrine*, 26). Mayer notes how this apophatic Ashʿarite theological stance also helped in explaining the idea of the "vision of God," with the use of the common Ashʿarite phrase *bi-lā kayf* (lit., "without how") in explaining (or perhaps, deciding not to attempt an explanation of) the vision of God. See Mayer, "Theology and Sufism," 272. This idea of explaining the "vision of God" in terms of the *bi-lā kayf* appears in Hujwīrī's discussion of *mushāhadat*, literally "witnessing" or "contemplation," but frequently containing the idea of spiritual vision.

134. Maneri, Hundred Letters, 124.

135. Ibid., 21–22.

stood, but Manerī integrates this into his overall understanding of the spiritual growth and progression of the disciple. Thus we find Manerī exhorting his disciple Shams al-Dīn,

> You have not yet reached the stage of ascent. You do not possess such magnificence that they bring you Muhammad's mount, Buraq, to your door. What should you do? You should don the garb of lustrous purity and run into the glorious heavenly mosque, among the faithful who are clothed with angelic virtues. First enter and then go to the back row of servants. Stand there on the step of petition. At length you will come out in the front row of the friends who have been seated on the carpet of the secret of the Master. It is He who has combined in prayer, according to his own good pleasure, all the pillars of the Law.[136]

The ascension metaphor gets pushed further a little later in this same letter, and the themes displayed begin increasingly to resemble some of what we encounter in Christian contexts. Later in this same letter, Manerī begins to describe prayer not only as an entering into the throne room of God, but of the heart becoming the very throne itself; there comes to mind the picture which Macarius-Symeon gives in his first homily concerning the heart or soul of the believer as the very *Merkavah*, or chariot-throne of God which serves and bears the presence of the believer's Lord.[137] Manerī writes:

> It has been said that when prayer and supplication become united for a disciple, he advances from the stage of dissipation to the light of the prayer of union. Then his body can be compared to the Kaaba, his heart to the divine throne, while his head is caught up in the Lord! In the *Sharh-i-Taʿaruf*,[138] those who have gained the divine Presence have been described in these terms: "Their lights have torn the curtains, while their secrets have spun around the divine throne; and their ability will be brought to light in the presence of the Master of the throne."

---

136. Ibid., 124.

137. See, for example, chapter 3. It bears repeating here, of course, that the significance of asserting the parallels between Macarius-Symeon and Manerī on this point is in no way to suggest that Manerī is mainly displaying this influence, but rather that parallels such as this may help to facilitate dialogue, witness and as we shall see, discipleship.

138. This quote is actually from the Arabic *Kitab al-Taʿaruf* (Kalābādhī, *Doctrine*, 2), though Manerī is quoting it here from the *Sharh-i-Taʿaruf*, the Persian commentary on Kalābādhī's treatise.

When the light of the faith of a disciple, in the abundance of his zeal, begins to rotate around the divine throne, every mirror reflecting his worth becomes exalted, since those constantly engaged in the prayer of union and holiness attain such a stage as is unattainable except with the help of purity.[139]

Manerī often sets allusions to the *miʿrāj* in the context of discussions about pastorally framed topics. For example, in Letter 51 in the main collection of correspondence, Manerī is writing on the topic of how God conveys a greeting of peace (*salām*) to those who are his, in what are mainly contexts which will come after death. Quoting an unnamed poet, Manerī notes that,

> He who is greeted by the Beloved,
> And receives news from His presence,
> Shines like the sun in the circle of His servants:
> What can I relate? It is but a tale of slavery!

It is from here that Manerī moved into a connected allusion to the *miʿrāj*, relating, "On the night of nearness and bounty, God Almighty said to the Prophet: 'O Prophet, peace be upon you!'"[140] There is an element of providing both hope and an exemplar. Without denying that there was something unique about Muhammad's *miʿrāj*, his ascent, there is a push toward seeing the *miʿrāj*, or at least aspects of the narrative, as providing something spiritually ascendant to which the Sūfī may aspire. In another allusion in which the *miʿrāj* is folded into the theme of ascending into union with God, Manerī uses the metaphor of the hunting bird:

> Here is needed a falcon, which, after escaping the snares laid by Satan in this world, can set out toward the world of purity, just as a bird would fly when released from the snare, its heart in tune with its flight, its flight with its thinking, its thinking with the divine secret, and the divine secret will attune it to God Himself. This happened to the Chosen One, who in a single stride was in the mosque of Aksa, and in another traversed all the heavenly stations, arriving at the highest degree of nearness to God. The wine of union was bestowed upon him. He obtained marvelous

---

139 Manerī, *Hundred Letters*, 125. We will return to this particular letter later on in this chapter, as we consider the understanding we find in the writings of Hujwīrī and Manerī on the "means of grace;" for Manerī, we find that these clearly correspond to a grace-empowered entering into transforming relationship.

140. Ibid., 207.

relations, passing beyond the pale of both worlds, he found repose with his Friend.[141]

Here it would seem that Manerī has moved from the concern which was emphasized in Hujwīrī to use the *mi'rāj* to demonstrate Muhammad's superiority over other prophets as well as saints. Manerī's concern is a pastoral invitation to his disciple to likewise join the spiritual "flight" into the presence of the Beloved. There is also a hint of spiritual ascent being an element in overcoming the powers of darkness.

Hujwīrī and Mushāhadat as Vision

Hujwīrī recognized the validity of the vision of God in the midst of spiritual contemplation, or *mushāhadat*, emphasizing the Ash'arite idea of *bilā kayf*, "without how," in his understanding of what it means to visually contemplate the Almighty. Hujwīrī also makes the connection between *mushāhadat* and *fanā'* in his own comments on a quote from Abū Sa'īd Fadlallāh ibn Muhammad al-Mayhanī. Mayhanī said that Sufism itself is "the name of direct vision of God;"[142] Hujwīrī muses on this, explaining that this "alludes to *mushāhadat* (contemplation) which is violence of love, and absorption of human attributes in realizing the vision of God, and their annihilation (*fanā'*) by the everlastingness of God."[143]

Mushāhadat is frequently described by Hujwīrī in connection with its companion term, *mujāhadat*, or ascetic self-mortification.[144] He considers the two principles to be inseparable, and that without proactive ascetic practice, the *mushāhadat* is unobtainable. For Hujwīrī, as for many Sūfī figures, ascetic practices are an essential part of the kind of life which can enable the adept to enter into *mushāhadat*.[145] It is in connection with the centrality of action that Hujwīrī cites Abū Hanifa, who exhorted the

---

141. Ibid., 293.

142. Hujwiri, *Kashful Mahjub*, 169. We are quoting Rabbani's translation for this line. Rabbani also includes a relevant comment of his own in regard to this topic: "In Urdu literature the word mushahadah connotes actual seeing with the eyes. But according to Sufi terminology the word mushahadah means seeing with the *inner* eyes. It is almost the same as the spiritual experience of fana-fi-Allah" (Rabbani, "Translator's Preface and Notes," 169) (emphasis in the original).

143. Hujwiri, *Revelation*, 165.

144. Ibid., 85.

145. Ibid., 95.

learned authority Dāwud Tā' ī, saying, "Practice what you have learned, for theory without practice is like a body without a spirit."[146]

How does Hujwīrī understand this *action*, this *mujāhadat*? Is it a kind of shamanistic idea of producing the power to see the Almighty, or is it a synergistic idea of human response to the drawing of God (or, for that matter, a monergistic idea in which God alone is actually acting)? Hujwīrī explores the various viewpoints before offering his own position. On the one hand, he thus quotes Sahl al-Tustarī, who saw *mujāhadat* as the "direct cause (*'illat*)"[147] of *mushāhadat*, quoting Q 29:69 in favor of his position: "But as for those who strive hard in Our cause—We shall most certainly guide them onto paths that lead unto Us."[148] On the other hand, Hujwīrī also quotes a Hadīth in which Muhammad says that even he will not be saved by his works, but is also dependent upon God's mercy, as well as passages from the Qur'ān such as Q 6:125a: "And whomsoever God wills to guide, his bosom He opens wide with willingness towards self-surrender [unto Him]; and whomsoever He wills to let go astray, his bosom He causes to be tight and constricted."[149] Having presented a brief account of both positions, Hujwīrī then offers his own understanding, as usual seeking a balance between these two. He avers,

> As a matter of fact, effort (*mujahidah*) is possible only by God's grace (*taufiq*). Allah's grace is as much a prerequisite of man's ability to worship as the ability to worship is a prerequisite for God's grace. Similarly *mushahidah* (contemplation) depends upon *mujahidah* as much as *mujahidah* on *mushahidah*. It is the flash of Divine Bounty which guides man to make an effort. That being the case, grace can easily be regarded as a prerequisite of effort.[150]

Part of the idea is that, for Hujwīrī, *mushāhadat* involves a singular focus on and contemplation of the Almighty, to the point at which one sees God *everywhere*, his "every look becomes an act of contemplation [*mushāhadat*]."[151]

146. Ibid., compare Jas 2:26.
147. Hujwiri, *Revelation*, 201.
148. Ibid., 202.
149. Ibid., 202–3.
150. Hujwiri, *Kashful Mahjub*, 214–15.
151. Hujwiri, *Revelation*, 275.

We can see here that Hujwīrī, while strongly advocating moving toward an idea of union with God which includes the element of at least *inward* vision, he is also seeking to ground this understanding in a recognition of God's abiding gracious presence which enables such seeking to begin with. In so doing, it would seem that Hujwīrī's words and position here are not far from the synergistic ideas advocated by Macarius-Symeon and Wesley.

Manerī and Tajallī as the Manifestation of God

Manerī also includes some discussion of *mushāhadat*, but we also find in his letters a particular focus on the related theme of *tajallī*, "sign" or the grace-empowered manifestation of God to the believer.[152] This is the primary theme of Letter 14 of the main collection. Toward the beginning of this letter, Manerī writes that *tajallī* is "a revelation of the divine essence [*dhāt*] and attributes [*sifāt*]."[153] Manerī's assertion that God reveals here his *essence* as well as his *attributes* is somewhat unusual, though it is a theme which is repeated in a number of places, including this same letter. Using another Persian literary metaphor, he notes that the transformed soul of the believer "becomes like the rising sun of the divine beauty, and like Jamshed's cup it reveals the essence of the Lord, as well as his attributes."[154] In the same letter, however, Manerī seems to scale back to the more traditional understanding of the revelation of God's attributes vs. God's essence, asserting that a revelation, as such, of God's essence is impossible due to God's immutability.[155]

Two themes which are observed in Manerī's understanding of *tajallī* are both integrated into this letter. One is a discussion on what Manerī sees as *tajallī ruhānī*, *tajallī* which finds its origin in the power of the human soul, and *tajallī rabbānī*, *tajallī* which originates with the empowering grace of God. He explains the importance of discerning between the two, because in *tajallī ruhānī*, the soul is "illuminated with the beauty of its own attributes," yet "does not have the power to do away with unruly

---

152. It may be recalled from the previous chapter that the famous exclamation of Hallāj was "If you do not know Him, then at least know His signs, I am that sign (*tajallī*) and I am the Truth [*ana'l-Haqq*]!" (Hallāj, *Tawasin*, 46).

153. Manerī, *Hundred Letters*, 61; see also Manerī, *Maktubate Sadī*, 94.

154. Manerī, *Hundred Letters*, 62.

155. Ibid., 63.

tendencies completely."[156] Manerī insists, moreover, that this type of "self-empowered" *tajallī* "does not bring peace to the heart, neither does it cleanse the heart of impurities or liberate it from doubt and suspicion, nor is the bliss of complete understanding bestowed upon it."[157] In short, Manerī is warning his reader of the dangers of a shamanistic, anthropocentric pursuit of the experience of God—in effect, trying to apply something like Walls' *pilgrim* principle within his own Islamic context.

The other theme here is not only the contrasting understanding of *tajallī rabbānī*, but the repeated theme of the purified soul as a mirror which is capable of reflecting the glory of the Almighty, and that "a person genuinely experiences himself as a mirror of the essence and attributes of the Exalted Friend! When the mirror becomes clean, it can reflect whatever the Lord wishes to manifest in it."[158] He then goes on to describe the various types of gracious manifestations which the Lord can thus grant: the grace of immortality, such as that of Khidr[159] and Elijah,[160] that of hearing God, as did Moses,[161] the grace of miraculous provision, as was granted to Mary,[162] and importantly, the grace of creative power, as was given to Jesus (citing Q 5:110, where Jesus creates living birds out of clay).[163] The idea, clearly, is that once one's spirit is free from the "veils" which block God's complete manifestation in the believer, God can empower the adept in any manner in which God chooses.

There are some parallels here with some of the biblical material we have examined in earlier chapters. The language is strikingly close to that of 2 Cor 3:18, which was at the center of the theme of union with God in Macarius-Symeon's writings, and the idea of the spirit as a mirror of God's gracious presence, as well as the idea of this kind of gracious

156. Ibid., 62.

157. Ibid., 63.

158. Ibid.

159. Khidr (sometimes the more Persianized Khizr) is identified with the unnamed figure who Moses follows in search of wisdom. Moses is ultimately confused by the figure's seemingly wrong actions, but as Khidr dismisses Moses, he explains each action. Khidr appears frequently in Sūfī narratives, as well as in folk religious traditions across the Muslim world.

160. Manerī, *Maktubate Sadī*, 95; not in Manerī, *Hundred Letters*.

161. Manerī, *Hundred Letters*, 63.

162. Manerī, *Maktubate Sadī*, 95–96; not in Manerī, *Hundred Letters*.

163. Manerī, *Hundred Letters*, 63. He also refers to the "gracious" manifestation of death, and being able to kill with a glance; this particular example, is not found in Manerī, *Hundred Letters*. See Manerī *Maktubate Sadī*, 96.

manifestation (*tajallī*) leading to transformation which enables God to display God's own self in the life of those so graciously transformed.

For Manerī, much of the danger of moving into an anthropocentric idea of manifestation and union rather than one centered on and empowered by God is connected with the need for the disciple to be instructed by working under the authority of a "perfect" *shaikh*, one who is "experienced in mystical matters." The idea is that the disciple can thus "benefit from the blessing conferred on him by the spiritual wealth" of the *shaikh*.[164] Stressing the importance then of the disciple's seeking the proper kind of *tajallī* through a proper intermediary, he quotes Q 2:189, noting that one should "Enter a house through the door!"[165] Manerī closes this point with a bit of Persian poetry:

> If you travel the way without benefit of any intermediary,
> You will fall headlong from the Way into a pit!
> Follow a spiritual guide that, by his bounty,
> Sooner or later you may reach the realm of the King.[166]

Of course, this brings the question of who might qualify as a "perfect" *shaikh* or spiritual director. Certainly this is an issue which Manerī believes is central to a disciple's spiritual well-being. It is a topic which also arises in Manerī's discussion of his understanding of the equivalent to the "means of grace" (though he doesn't use that term directly).

We have observed the idea of union with God from various angles—*fanā' wa-baqā'*, *mushāhada*, and *tajallī*. The three of the fourfold elements of union which we have discussed in previous chapters are present here: sanctification and perfecting transformation, this transformation bringing the believer more into line with the human ideal of the image of God, and the reality of the necessary empowerment for this being in the prevenient grace of God. All these are present in the writings of Hujwīrī and Manerī. As was the case in the previous chapter, however, there seems to be less emphasis on the idea of a healing motif in the classical Sūfī writings.

---

164. Maneri, *Hundred Letters*, 63.

165. Ibid. In context, the verse reads, "However, piety does not consist in your entering houses from the rear, [as it were,] but truly pious is he who is conscious of God. Hence, enter houses through their doors, and remain conscious of God, so that you might attain to a happy state."

166. Maneri, *Hundred Letters*, 64. It's not clear who Manerī is quoting in this passage.

THE MEANS OF GRACE IN HUJWĪRĪ AND MANERĪ

The idea of God's approaching his servants in the midst of their God-empowered obedience, that is, via the means of grace, is found in the writings of both Hujwīrī and Manerī. Hujwīrī provides fewer details on this than Manerī, but there are still principles relating to the synergy of grace-enabled faith and action found in Hujwīrī.

For example, in a later section of the *Kashf*, Hujwīrī discusses *īmān*, or faith. Here he describes his understanding from the perspective of orthodox Islam of how faith and action are meant to integrate with one another. Hujwīrī discusses the relationship between faith, works, "gnosis" (*ma'rifa*), and salvation or security (*najāt*). He notes that there are some who understand that salvation rests on both faith and obedience, whereas others understand salvation to rest on *ma'rifa*. Hujwīrī understands these to work together, although he places more of an emphasis on the more Sūfī-oriented principle of *ma'rifa*.

> You must know that the orthodox Muslims and the Sufis are agreed that faith has a principle (*asl*) and a derivative principle (*far'*), the principle being the verification in the heart, and the derivative being observance of the (Divine) command. Now the Arabs commonly and customarily transfer the name of a principle to a derivative by way of metaphor, e.g., they call the light of the sun "the sun." In this sense the former of the two parties mentioned above apply the name of faith to that obedience (*tā'at*) by which alone a man is made secure from future punishment.... The other party, however, asserted that gnosis, not obedience, is the cause of security. Obedience, they said, is of no avail without gnosis, whereas one who has gnosis but lacks obedience will be saved at the last ...[167]

> The Apostle has said, "None of you shall be saved by his works." When he was asked, "Not even you?" He replied, "Yes, not even me, unless God's bounty (*Rahmat*) comes to my help." Therefore, according to the consensus of Muslim divines, *īmān* is really *ma'rifa*, of course, with inner belief (*tasdiq-bil-qalb*) and outer action (*aml*).[168]

Hujwīrī seems to clearly uphold a principle of salvation by the grace (in this case, *fadl*) and mercy (*rahma*) of God, and works of obedience must emerge from that grace. Moreover, Hujwīrī also emphasizes that

---

167. Hujwiri, *Revelation*, 287, slightly modified.
168. Hujwiri, *Kashful Mahjub*, 300–1, slightly modified.

both *īmān* and *maʿrifa*, rightly understood, are empowered by and even identified with love. Hujwīrī describes this by insisting that "what we call obedience (*tāʿat*) is actually the outward expression of love, because the acts of worship are as much functions of the body as vision is the function of the soul (*qalb*), observation of the eye and repentance of the heart. In case the body abstains from obedience, the heart cannot, as it is the seat of love."[169] Although Hujwīrī does not present practical elements of an understanding of worship or obedience as "means of grace," he offers a framework in which it may be understood, from a perspective which is both faithful to Sunni orthodoxy as well as reflective of the Sūfī tradition. Hujwīrī is, it would seem, seeking to apply an Islamic version of Walls' *indigenous* and *pilgrim* principles.

In a subsequent passage in a section on *tahārat*, or purification, we can observe some degree of integration between both the principles outlined above and some of the practical elements of spiritual life and worship. Describing spiritual applications for each step in the process of *wudū*, or ritual washing prior to liturgical prayer, Hujwīrī briefly discusses how "outward and inward purification must go together; e.g., when a man washes his hands he must wash his heart clean of worldliness . . . In all religious ordinances the external is combined with the internal; e.g., in faith, the tongue's profession with the heart's belief."[170] Of course, in yet another section on *namāz*,[171] Hujwīrī cautions those who would see the performance of the commanded rituals (in this case, of liturgical prayer) as a means to the end of inducing some spiritual state; he says that "prayer is a Divine command and is not a means of obtaining either 'presence' (*hudūr*) or 'absence' (*ghaybat*), because a Divine command is not a means to anything."[172] At the same time, there is a parallel here to what Hujwīrī had earlier written concerning the spiritual understanding of *wudū*; here each element of the *namāz* liturgy is connected spiritually with an element of inward spiritual life, the outward actions both reflecting and facilitating the inner life of relationship with the Beloved.[173]

Perhaps more controversially, Hujwīrī considers whether poetry and music (*samāʿ*) is lawful, and, included with this, whether these may

---

169. Ibid., 301.

170. Hujwiri, *Revelation*, 292.

171. *Namāz* is Persian for the Arabic *salāh*, Muslim liturgical prayers.

172. Ibid., 301.

173. Ibid.

be considered a means of grace or a hindrance to those who believe. He seems quite positive about poetry, observing that one Ummaya had "come close to Islam by his poetry."[174] Even here, however, Hujwīrī does not provide unequivocal approval for poetry, but rather cautions the believers against poetry which "consists of what is unlawful, such as backbiting, calumny and abuses."[175]

On music, Hujwīrī is careful, but at the same time seeks to parse between those whose love of music is genuinely spiritual, and those whose musical inclinations may be harmful. He also cautions those who would be dogmatically self-righteous on this issue, asserting that anyone "who says that he finds no pleasure in sounds and melodies and music is either a liar and a hypocrite or he is not in his right senses, and is outside the category of men and beasts."[176]

Manerī describes his own understanding of spiritual exercises in a manner which is analogous to the idea of "means of grace" in several places in his letters; perhaps the most lucid and direct discussion of this topic is in Letters 32–35 of his *Maktūbāt-i Sadī*, which are focused on Manerī's spiritual interpretation of the "pillars," the required practices of Islam.[177] For example, in Letter 32, "On *Namāz*,"[178] Manerī begins by describing those activities which he sees as leading to greater "purification and sanctification" and maintaining a 'saintly heart.'"[179] In this instance, Manerī names ritual prayer, recitation of the Qur'ān, and *dhikr*. Manerī quickly follows this up, however, with a disclaimer noting that only if there is no *shaikh* or *pīr* available should this be followed without a guide. Recall from just above, that Manerī places great importance on the guidance of a spiritual director, and when one is present, the directives of the *shaikh* for the disciple concerned should be followed.

Manerī's emphasis, however, is here really on *namāz*, ritual or liturgical prayer. He explains that, properly understood and with the proper spiritual intention, *namāz* fulfills all of the required commands of Islam; Manerī writes that God "has combined in prayer, according to His own

174. Hujwiri, *Kashful Mahjub*, 407.
175. Ibid.
176. Hujwiri, *Revelation*, 401.
177. See Jackson, "Introduction and Notes," 430 n. 55.
178. Like Hujwīrī, Manerī uses the Persian *namāz*, as is common practice even today throughout most of South Asia, rather than the Arabic *salāh* to refer to ritual prayer.
179. Maneri, *Hundred Letters*, 123. See also Manerī, *Maktubate Sadī*, 164.

good pleasure, all of the pillars of the Law."[180] He describes the manner in which the prayer ritual fulfills the other commands toward fasting, giving alms, and pilgrimage. One of the surprising and fascinating turns here is the manner in which Manerī speaks of *namāz* as *jihād*, in the sense of entering into a spiritual "holy war." He writes,

> In prayer a person can also discover the meaning of the holy war.[181] Ablutions can be compared to donning armor. The prayer leader is like a general, while the people resemble the army. The leader stands in the front line of the sanctuary, where the battle will be joined. The people are drawn up in ranks behind him. United, they come to his aid. When they are victorious in their holy war, they share the booty among themselves. When the leader gives the final blessing of peace, he distributes the grace of the Lord of Glory.[182]

That Manerī is actually describing this as "means of grace" (referring to the closing blessing of the liturgical prayer) is particularly significant.

This comes just prior to the above-quoted passage in which Manerī describes prayer as a means of entering spiritually into the very throne room of God. Having described much of this within the context of orthodox, Sunnī, liturgical prayer, Manerī then moves beyond this; indeed, moving beyond merely the community of Muslim disciples in the classical sense. First, he moves beyond liturgical prayer to an idea of internal prayer flowing out of Desire for God, named here as the Friend. He says that, due "to the ardor of their desire, those who are longing to see the Friend pray much, even without inclination or prostration."[183] Manerī quotes another unnamed poet in Persian, describing a spiritual view of prayer in which he sees a fading of sectarian distinctions,

> The prayer of lovers is not a matter of inclinations and prostrations;
> The very same pain afflicts Muslim, Christian and Jew.
> When the only direction for prayer is the beauty of the Beloved,
> Love comes and abolishes all other loci of prayer.[184]

---

180. Manerī, *Hundred Letters*, 124.

181. In the original text, the term translated here as "holy war" is *jihad*, which has a wider use than military conflict, though the imagery of Manerī's metaphor here is clearly military. See Manerī, *Maktubate Sadī*, 165.

182. Manerī, *Hundred Letters*, 124.

183. Ibid., 126.

184. Ibid..

Maneri goes on concerning his view not only of prayer, but of the proper direction (*qibla*) toward which prayer is meant to be performed, and in this he continues from the poem which he just quoted. Maneri writes that,

> One beloved of God has said that before the Rock of Jerusalem or the Kaaba came into existence, the direction for the prayer of lovers was the One without beginning! In place of sacred enclosures and places established by men,[185] the direction of those who long for the Friend has become what it was in the beginning. In this tavern of self-forgetfulness and abode of affliction, the Rock of Jerusalem or the Kaaba has been demarcated to console the hearts of seekers and travelers.[186]

Maneri sees the depth of the spiritual life to move beyond even the direction for prayer in Mecca or Jerusalem, but insists that the true, indeed, *original qibla* is in the direction of God. All of this is meant to present the place of prayer as the means which, properly understood, fulfill all of the requirements of orthodox Islam, but ultimately bring one into a depth of relationship with the Almighty. Indeed, Maneri insists that neither the sufferings of hell nor the pleasures of Paradise exceed the depth of relationship with the Beloved into which prayer is understood as the door. Maneri finally exclaims to the disciple to whom he is writing,

> Behold! The door of generosity is open. The table is laid with good things. Make haste! Discover your true self![187]

The next letter, Maneri's 33rd to his disciple, is on fasting. As was the case with prayer, this letter likewise presents fasting as a means by which God meets and reveals himself to his disciples, often expressed in terminology which reflects the idea of ascension and vision. Maneri quotes a Hadith found as well in Muslim's well-known collection of *Sahih* traditions, saying that the "man who fasts experiences a twofold joy: the breaking of the fast and seeing God."[188] Although in its original context, this Hadith seems to be referring to a future happy meeting with the Almighty following death, Maneri clearly interprets it as an experience of divine vision, and thus sees fasting as a means by which the power of God

185. Dr. Dale Walker has compared this with Acts 7:48.
186. Maneri, *Hundred Letters*, 126.
187. Ibid., 127.
188. From *Sahih Muslim*, Book 6, "On Fasting," Hadith 2566; Maneri, *Hundred Letters*, 126.

is manifest to the believer. As in the previous letter, Manerī combines this with an emphasis on, in this case, chanted prayer. Thus he relates a story concerning Khwaja Ma'rūf Karkhī (d. c. 815), a Sūfī figure, who was observed

> engrossed in contemplation.[189] He was standing beneath the divine throne, singing God's praise in the abundance of his gratitude. A query came from the Lord of the angels: "Who is this?" though He knew him very well. One of the angels said: "O Lord, this is Your distinguished servant!" God said: "My servant Ma'ruf Karkhi is intoxicated with the wine of my love. No one can recuperate from love of Me except by seeing Me!"[190]

Manerī follows up this story by quoting another Hadīth, again emphasizing the idea that fasting and prayer will bring the believer into God's presence. He quotes, "Make your bellies hungry, your livers thirsty and your bodies hungry, that perhaps you might see Allah in this world."[191] Manerī doesn't end there, however, but continues, quoting an unnamed source, "'He who has seen, has arrived.' And whoever has arrived at God Himself has passed beyond the stage of transience of things and even beyond that of permanence. He has been consumed in adoration of the divine face."[192] On the one hand, there is an emphasis on prayer, contemplative chanting and fasting as a means through which God draws the disciple into his presence, but on the other hand, there is still this element that there are *means* by which *God* works in the disciple's life. It is interesting that Manerī speaks of fasting, in this case, with language almost Eucharistic in terms of recognition of the divine presence: "O brother, when you are filled with His bounty and a table is laid out with His grace, then abstention from eating is not to prolong the pleasure of His grace, but to find Him in His treasury, as the Beloved."[193]

The connection in this regard with the pillar of *zakat*, or almsgiving, is somewhat more subdued in its description as a means of grace,

---

189. The word in the original text here is *takbīr*, which refers to the recitation of the phrase "Allāhu Akbar," "God is great." The implication is that Karkhi was doing so as *dhikr*. See Manerī, *Maktubate Sadī*, 170.

190. Manerī, *Hundred Letters*, 128.

191. This Hadīth appears as well in Hujwīrī's *Kashf al-Mahjūb* (Hujwiri, *Revelation*, 324), though we have not encountered it in either the collection of Bukhari or of Muslim.

192. Manerī, *Hundred Letters*, 128.

193. Ibid., 130.

perhaps because Manerī writes as a Sūfī, and a kind of monastic poverty is assumed for such adherents. Still, there is a comparison with the idea of a lover and the "genuineness" of a claim to love: love necessarily involves an offering of the lover's heart, body and goods to the Beloved, corresponding (in Manerī's view) to faith as expressed in the *shahāda*, prayer as expressed in *namāz*, and alms as expressed in *zakāt*.[194]

In the following Letter, on *hajj*, the Pilgrimage to Mecca, Manerī continues to utilize Lover-Beloved language, including references to the Arabic *Majnūn-Laila* poetry. Like Majnūn, he writes of seeking the beauty of the Beloved in the signs and dust of the Beloved's dwelling. "Everyone who is prohibited from seeing the beauty of the Friend consoles himself with a sign of the Beloved."[195] Manerī even asserts that approaching either Moses or Messiah will not avail, since these also receive their life from the Almighty.[196]

In any case, Manerī certainly seems to understand sincere entry into the *hajj* as a means of grace. Referring to the account of Bistāmī, he relates how Bistāmī's perception escalated from merely seeing the *Kaaba* to spiritually perceiving the "Lord of the house."[197] Manerī quotes Bistāmī as saying that

> When I reached the Holy Place, the divine favor swept me into its embrace; the curtain of whatever is not God was removed from my power of discernment; my heart was illumined with the flame of mystical knowledge; my being was inflamed by the lights of divine illumination; and this saying filled my head: "You have come to visit Me with an honest heart, and the One who is visited has the right to bless the one who visits Him!"[198]

Thus it would seem that Manerī takes the *hajj* very seriously, and regards it as a means by which God meets the believer, and in the midst of which the sincere believer can experience the manifestation of God. But Manerī doesn't end there; he moves on to effectively spiritualize the

---

194. Ibid., 132–33.

195. Ibid., 134.

196. Ibid., 135, obviously at variance with the biblical understanding of Messiah as being within God's Essence; see for example, John 1:14–18, and the remarks on this passage in chapter 2, as well as Bauckham, *Jesus and the God of Israel*, 51.

197. Manerī, *Hundred Letters*, 134.

198. Ibid.

hajj to an *inward* pilgrimage. Here he quotes Muhammad ibn Fazl (d. 931),[199] who says,

> I am astonished at those who seek His house in the world. Why do they not seek His manifestation in their hearts? He might be found in His house, or He might not, but His manifestation they can always enjoy. If it is a divine ordinance to visit a stone once a year and cast one's glance upon it, how much more obligatory is it to visit the heart where He can be seen 360 times a day through one's inward glances! A visit to the heart should take precedence over the canonical pilgrimage!"[200]

Not only, then does Manerī seem to regard the pilgrimage to Mecca as a means of grace in the midst of which God may be apprehended, but he goes beyond this. The idea of meeting God within the heart is a means of grace of the same measure as, and perhaps superior to, the pilgrimage itself. This also hearkens back to Manerī's earlier-quoted idea that God is himself the true *qibla*.[201]

In a subsequent Letter, on "The Effective Formula," on the first part of the *shahāda* and meditation on the unity of God,[202] Manerī speaks of the absolute necessity of recognizing the absolute unity of God, to the point of denying the existence of anything else, even the self. He then moves on to speak of how moving into this realm of grace actually transforms the believer into union with God:

> They have said that an animal, when it falls on a pile of salt, becomes salt. When one creature can have this effect on another, the former altering the latter through its own properties, then why should not the King of Truth be able to achieve this effect? The servant immersed in a mystic state, by witnessing Him, would be changed from his human condition and conducted to the world of possession,[203] and then he would be taken beyond this stage and made a mere nothing, so that only God Himself

---

199. A very short biography is included in Hujwīrī's *Kashf al-Mahjub*, in which his full name is given as Abū Muhammad 'Abdallāh Muhammad ibn al-Fadl al-Balkhī. See Hujwiri, *Revelation*, 140–41, from which Manerī is likely quoting.

200. Maneri, *Hundred Letters*, 136.

201. Ibid., 126.

202. The title of this letter implies both the cognitive understanding of God's unity as well as the use of this phrase in dhikr.

203. That is, *malakūt*, or the angelic world. See Manerī *Maktubate Sadī*, 200, and Schimmel, *Mystical Dimensions*, 270.

would remain[204]—He alone would speak and He alone would hear. The man would simply be a sign in the middle.[205]

For Manerī, then, there is a strong element of God's gracious working in bringing the believer, or the "traveler" (*sālik*), as it is often expressed, into God's unity and into transforming union with God.

In the previous chapter, we briefly examined the elements of *dhikr* and the related *murāqaba* ("remembrance" of God, usually through silent or audible chanting, and contemplative meditation), *hadra/samāʿ* (Ṣūfī gatherings and engagement in devotional ritual, as noted above often with poetry, music or even dance), and *fikr/halaqa* (cognitive engagement with Ṣūfī texts and teachings), as possible Ṣūfī parallels to the "means of grace." We also briefly mentioned the manner in which these come together at the *ʿurs* celebration of Hujwīrī, commonly known as "Dātā Ganj Baksh" ("bestower of gifts") in Lahore, Pakistan.[206] A brief examination of this enables us to observe how some of the elements of Ṣūfī practices in the classical sources play out in a modern milieu.

Qamar-ul Huda,[207] the author of a brief essay describing these practices, discusses the central place of the text of the *Kashf al-Mahjūb* itself. Huda notes that not only is the *Kashf* "a significant text in Ṣūfī historiography" and "the most important work to be read by modern-day Ṣūfīs in Pakistan," but also that even now "there is an intriguing connection between this text and modern Ṣūfī practices of worship, spiritual guidance, and the process of unveiling the veils,"[208] touching on all of the aforementioned elements of a Ṣūfī means of grace.

In the case of each of these elements, the account at Hujwīrī's tomb indicates that there is an effort to ensure that the elements of Ṣūfī ritual remain assiduously within the bounds of Sunni Muslim orthodoxy. Among other things, this is an indication that continued evaluation of the orthodoxy and propriety of such practices seems to be part of a dynamic process of interpretation. In Huda's account, for example, a local

---

204. This line may also be translated, "as his human nature is dissolved, then the essence of God's manifestation will be continually poured out upon him." See Manerī, *Maktubate Sadī*, 200.

205. Manerī, *Hundred Letters*, 154.

206. Huda, "Dātā Ganj Bakhsh's *ʿUrs*," 377–94.

207. Huda is a scholar of Islam, with expertise in Islamic mysticism. He is currently a Senior Program Officer in the Religion and Peacemaking Center of the United States Institute of Peace.

208. Huda, "Dātā Ganj Bakhsh's *ʿUrs*," 377; 383.

Sūfī leader, Hakīm Muhammad Mūsā, emphasizes *dhikr al-Qur'ān*, contemplative chanting of the Arabic text of the Qur'ān,[209] as a beginning point.[210] From there, however, Mūsā explains the three modes of *dhikr*: Of seeking blessing with verbal *dhikr*, then that of purifying the heart to make space for God,"[211] and finally that which is described as having been "built upon love (*muhabbat*); it draws upon God's self-disclosure (*sirr*)[212] to the spiritual seeker."[213] There is a sense here of the common Sūfī theme of beginning with a strong "anchor" into orthodoxy, and moving from there into more "inner" modes of devotion. In dramatically explaining this final mode of *dhikr*, Mūsā exclaims that this is "where the Spirit of God provides a vision, a direct vision of light and eternal love! *Dhikr* is the only path to Allah!"[214] Mūsā then leads his disciples in chanting what Manerī had described as the "effective formula," the first part of the *shahāda*, "*Lā ilāha illā Allāh*." The Sūfī at the shrine of Hujwīrī seems to tie the group practice of *dhikr* not only with Hujwīrī's life and writings, but these become intertwined with other elements of Sūfī thought, such as seeking union with God through contemplative meditation on God's oneness.

The second key element which Huda describes in the rites connected with the celebrations at Hujwīrī's tomb complex is that of *samā'*, recitation of poetry and music. In Huda's description, this includes sung poetry in praise of Muhammad (*na'tiyyā*) and in veneration of Hujwīrī, as well as praises to God (*hamd*). Much of this is in the form of *qawwālī*, the distinctive music associated with Sūfī musicians throughout South Asia. Huda describes *qawwālī* as being, in a manner similar to *dhikr*, "repetitive both poetically and rhythmically, which reinforces the importance of establishing an inner habitual devotion."[215] *Samā'* is here regarded primarily as a vehicle which can aid devotees in entering into a state of

---

209. And as Huda points out in a footnote, listening to the dedicated reciters of the Qur'ān. See Huda, Dātā Ganj Bakhsh's *'Urs*," 392 n. 15.

210 Huda, "Dātā Ganj Bakhsh's *'Urs*," 381.

211. Ibid.

212. Sirr can also be translated "secret" or "mystery."

213. Huda, "Dātā Ganj Bakhsh's *'Urs*," 381. Huda also notices that these three types of *dhikr* are found as well in Kalābādhī's *Kitāb al-Ta'arruf*, Sarrāj's *Kitāb al-Luma'* and Qushayrī's *Risāla*. See Huda, "Dātā Ganj Bakhsh's *'Urs*" 393 n. 19.

214. Huda, "Dātā Ganj Bakhsh's *'Urs*," 381.

215. Ibid., 382.

wajd, ecstasy, with the possibility of experiencing a vision of, or spiritual experience of, the divine.

It is interesting that Hujwīrī himself expressed some degree of ambivalence regarding *samāʿ*. He considered poetry and music to be a possible means of entering into an ecstatic state of union with the Almighty, though he also cautioned against the potential for the misuse of these into other directions. Certainly in the use of *samāʿ* in this manner, it would seem that there is the possibility of this as a means of grace, but we should also acknowledge the possibility of *samāʿ* being used *shamanistically* as a means of ascension and vision. Within this context, however, it does seem to me that there is an emphasis on a synergy which would rely on God's empowering and enabling to enter on some level into the divine presence.

The final practice described in Huda's account is that of the study circle, the *halaqa*. Huda describes this part of the activities as follows:

> Aside from being available in numerous editions, the *Kashf al-Mahjūb* is used publicly during the *ʿurs* in circles of discussion (*halaqa*) on the shrine's grounds, where Sūfī shaikhs or their prominent *murīds* read short passages out loud to pilgrims. Unlike Qurʾānic recitation, Sūfī shaikhs use this time of reading of the text as an opportunity for pilgrims to question the inner meanings of the passages. Pilgrims then take the opportunity to raise questions with the shaikh about his interpretation. This joint intellectual and spiritual engagement with the text among Sūfī shaikhs, *murīds*, and pilgrims is a process of mutual discovery of Data Ganj Bakhsh's *tasawwuf*.[216]

In Huda's view, this practice of group discussions of passages in the *Kashf al-Mahjūb* is understood to be part of the process of entering into pilgrim life during the *ʿurs* celebration. This practice is done in a manner which seeks to "filter" even the *Kashf* itself, in a manner which is meant to help those involved develop expressions of Sufism which remain grounded in the Islamic tradition. For example, passages read should be those which find support in the Qurʾān and Hadīth passages; surprisingly, it is not merely assumed that this will be the case in every passage in the *Kashf al-Mahjūb*.[217] Again, we can observe how these communities seek to imply an in-house Sūfī Muslim view of Walls' indigenous and pilgrim principles, both seeking to indigenize, for example, in terms of the use of

216. Ibid., 383.
217. Ibid., 384.

music, but also to be sure that their practices reflect a genuinely Muslim ethos. Importantly, however, it is also recognized that this process of discussion and discovery must be integrated both in terms of community and in terms of spiritual experience. Huda notes that shaikhs and *murīds* seeking to guide this discussion face a complex task in discerning the best manner in which to do this for the pilgrims who have come. Huda explains that experienced "shaikhs and *murīds* know that the elements of *tasawwuf* cannot be communicated merely through a cerebral discussion. Rather, the group at the *halaqa* must be transformed by the experiential nature of the talk and text."[218]

This speaks of an integration of cognitive and spiritual of the 'urs celebration, and seems to indicate that elements of a Sūfī means of grace are found not only in the writings of figures such as Hujwīrī and Manerī, but also in living communities which continue to utilize these insights and practices in their own spiritual life.

CONCLUSION

In chapter 5, we moved on from the examination of themes of ascension, vision and transformation, as well as the idea of the means of grace in the writings and lives of some of the figures of early Sufism, writing mainly in Arabic. We sought to see how their response to these spiritual issues involved their implementing a kind of Sūfī and Muslim understanding of Andrew Walls' indigenous and pilgrim principles. In this chapter, we have examined these same themes in the lives and writings of two early Sūfī figures connected with South Asia, Hujwīrī and Manerī, examining how they indigenized their understanding of Sufism, even as they sought to ensure that it remained within the bounds of Islamic orthodoxy.

In the concluding chapter, we will examine what we have observed in early Sufism in these areas, and determine how these beliefs and practices may aid in an understanding of developing Christian witness and community in Sūfī contexts. We will especially be considering how this may be done in a manner which can be indigenously relevant as well as prophetically faithful

---

218. Ibid., 387.

7

Conclusion

> Only a path that comes from God can lead to Him and only such a path can guarantee the soul final beatitude and union with the One. Only traditional authority can protect the soul from the great dangers that lurk upon the path of him who wishes to climb mountains without a guide and without following an existing trail. The end of the one path is the absorption of the soul in its divine prototype; the end of the other is the dissolution and decomposition of the very substance of the soul. The soul of man was made by God and only He has the right to re-mould it. He has given man the urge for the mystical life and the desire for the perfection which lies at the end of the path. He has also provided for man the genuine means to reach this end.
>
> Seyyed Hossein Nasr[1]

A REVIEW OF THE GROUND COVERED THUS FAR

IN THIS CONCLUDING CHAPTER, we will again seek to understand how we might apply Andrew Walls' *indigenous* principle and *pilgrim* principles in the context of Sūfī communities. We will pay attention especially to interaction with practices of seeking union with God which the late Alan Segal described as *ascension, vision* and *transformation* mysticism. In earlier chapters, we sought to critically examine how Christian leaders of earlier generations, such as Macarius-Symeon and John Wesley, sought to ensure that such seeking for union took place in a manner in which the

---

1. Nasr, "Mystical Quest," 32.

means and the goal were understood to be the grace of God in Jesus. This is in contrast to the more *shamanistic* kinds of ascension mysticism which was found in some early Jewish, Hellenic, Sūfī and even Christian circles. We also described how the element of *transformation* was expressed in the intertwined Wesleyan elements of the image of God in humankind, a therapeutic view of salvation as inclusive of the healing of the soul, the drawing and empowering of God's prevenient grace, and the Holy Spirit empowered process of Christian perfecting, also referred to as sanctification. Wesley also recognized that worship and teaching, interaction with the Scriptures and fellowship, and partaking of the Eucharist can be understood as means of grace in the midst of which God meets his people. Finally, we examined the classical Sūfī tradition itself, first in a broader, historical overview, and then with a special focus on two of the more important figures for South Asian Sufism, 'Alī ibn 'Uthmān al-Hujwīrī and Sharaf al-Dīn Manerī.

In each of these cases, we considered how *Christian* figures such as Macarius-Symeon and John Wesley parsed between what was acceptable in practice (using Walls' *indigenous* principle) and what needed to rather be filtered out from continuing practice (considering Walls' *pilgrim* principle). We went beyond simply *Christian* application of these ideas, and sought to understand how these principles may have been utilized, for example, by Philo of Alexandria in his Jewish/Hellenic context, and how Sūfī figures sought to ensure that their practices of Sufism remained credibly within the boundaries of the overall Sunni Islamic tradition, including how classical Sufism viewed and utilized some of their practices within the rubric of their understanding of means of grace.

To summarize, in the preceding chapters, we

1. Analyzed the elements of ascension, vision and transformation mysticism in early Jewish and Hellenic mysticism. We observed that this reflected, to a significant degree, what James Davila described as *shamanistic* practices—they were designed to empower the devotee through correctly performed rituals, though with no genuine element of relationship with the Deity.

2. We then examined the manner in which the early Christian community interacted contextually in this milieu, utilizing Andrew Walls' *indigenous* and *pilgrim* principles, and focused mainly on the New Testament Scriptures and the *Homilies* of Macarius-Symeon. We discovered that these early Christian writings seemed to hold well

to a balance of speaking *indigenously* in the language of ascension and vision mysticism, yet often turning it upon its head in a *pilgrim* focus on the *descended* Messiah. We also observed that the four elements of Wesleyan spirituality connected with union with God all were present in both the Scriptures and in the Macarian *Homilies*.

3. Next, we examined the critical appropriation of this early Christian understanding of union with God by John Wesley and his colleagues. Crucially, we observed that Wesley didn't just uncritically pass on or absorb these teachings received both from early Christian writings as well as through more recent Anglican and Pietist sources, but he sought to ensure the language in which it was expressed was rather more reflective of the ethos of the Reformation. Importantly, Wesley took an understanding of union with God which was more *centripetal*, drawing in and more focused on the individual, and expressed it in such a manner as to ensure it became *centrifugal*, that the idea of union with God was understood to flow into a life of virtue, outreach, service and mission.

4. In the final two chapters, we examined first the general classical Sūfī writings, particularly elements which were related to the theme of union with God, and observed a significant number of parallels with both early Christian and Wesleyan understandings of *theosis* and/or *sanctification*. Of the four elements of Snyder's "Wesleyan Theology of Mission," three were clearly expressed: The idea of humankind in God's image, that of God's presence as empowering and prevenient grace, and that of sanctification and *theosis*, as noted above. The one element which wasn't really expressed in the writings examined was that of salvation as healing. Nonetheless, this is a Scriptural concept and we feel that it would be useful to express this in the context of discipling relationships.

In this brief conclusion we wish to examine as well as illustrate what might be gleaned from this research which may be useful in encouraging communities of faith in Jesus the Messiah in Sūfī contexts. What might be helpful in moving individuals, families and communities toward deeper union with God in Christ, and perhaps serve as building materials for a theology of mission and community for the Sūfī context.

SŪFĪ TARĪQA MODEL FOR JESUS-CENTERED COMMUNITY

The question remains, then, regarding how to apply these understandings of ongoing discipleship within a faith community empowered by the gracious, uncreated presence of God's Spirit. How can we apply this broadened understanding of salvation involving *theosis* and ongoing life in Christ in a grace-filled community of believers within the Sūfī context? As important as initial evangelism is to mission in such circumstances, we need to take care that we avoid falling into the trap of being so focused on evangelistic presentations that we miss the bigger picture of how discipleship can move forward among those who are coming to faith in Jesus, and how this can be viewed in a long-term sense, in the context of *community*. While we have noted above some of the exploration of how an understanding of *theosis* might be an aid in an evangelistic presentation, we believe that a Macarian-Wesleyan model would embrace that aspect of interface, but envelope it into a broader framework of ongoing life.

In brief, a Macarian-Wesleyan *tarīqa* would have an emphasis on transforming union with God in Christ, rooted in the Hebrew Scriptures and the New Testament, with an emphasis on the themes of the prevenient grace of God, the restoration of the image of God in humankind, salvation as healing and sanctification. Expressed in the language of the context in which a community of faith in Christ is emerging (in the sense of Walls' *indigenous* principle), this transformation then seeks to influence the surrounding society both *centripetally* in drawing people into the community by means of the reality and drawing of God's Spirit as well as *centrifugally* sent out in proclamation, service and the development of community life which is empowered by the presence of the Holy Spirit. A key part of this community life would center on the means of grace of individual and congregational prayer and worship, interaction with the Scriptures, and regularly partaking of the Eucharist.

Rooted in the Scriptures

One of the principles observed in each part of this study has been an emphasis on validating the approach to mysticism by ensuring a foundation in the received text of the scriptures, although the scriptures concerned are not the same in each case.[2] This is crucial for applying Walls' in-

---

2. In the context of this dissertation, it is assumed that as people from within Sūfī communities are coming to faith in Jesus, the principle of grounding their mysticism in the scriptures would be transferred for them from a focus on the Qur'ān to a

digenous principle in such a manner that it is balanced by the pilgrim principle, and isn't thus completely absorbed by the context.

Thus, for all of his engagement with Platonic thought, Philo of Alexandria remains concerned to ground his writings in principles of exegesis of the Torah. In the New Testament writings, particularly the Johannine passages in which we observed engagement with the context of Jewish ascension mysticism, we see both *indigenous* and *pilgrim* principles at play. Recalling that much of the *Merkavah* mysticism sought to base itself on an understanding of the vision of the enthroned glory of God in the opening chapter of Ezekiel, we see both an *indigenous* use of the language of ascension mysticism in passages such as John 14, but also a *pilgrim* correction of the more shamanistic *Merkavah* tendencies by centering the focus on the Messiah who has descended to earth. This continues as well in the Macarian *Homilies*, grounding the idea of ascension, vision and transformation in a proper understanding of Ezekiel's *Merkavah* vision, interpreted Christologically through the lens of 2 Cor 3:7—4:6. The scriptural undergirding is quite clear as well in Wesley's emphasis on transforming union with God.

What, then, of the classical Sūfī context which we examined? Central to the purpose of both Hujwīrī and Manerī is the theme that Sūfī thought is faithful to the received scriptural tradition of the Qur'ān. Part of the means by which these Sūfī writers engaged in this was with the use of ta'wīl in their exegesis of the Qur'ān, seeking to demonstrate the "inner" meaning of the text. How can an emerging community of Jesus followers in a Sūfī context engage this in terms of both the *indigenous* and the *pilgrim* principles?

The obvious, though partial, answer is that the allegiance which these believers have previously demonstrated toward the Qur'ān may carry over into their viewing the Hebrew Scriptures and the New Testament in an equally foundational manner. Indeed, as a community of faith engages in parsing between what the gospel can retain as *indigenous* and what should be challenged with regard to the *pilgrim* principle, it is primarily in using the Bible as a touchstone that these can be differentiated.

What of the Qur'ān itself? Must it be discarded entirely? A. H. Mathias Zahniser has helpfully suggested that, while the Qur'ān may not be recognized by such believers as scripture, it may still be viable for them to "benefit from models and meanings in the Qur'ān compatible with the

focus on the Bible.

New Testament witness."[3] That is to suggest that communities of faith in Jesus could very well choose to utilize the Qur'ān in their ongoing life and witness—with the proviso that this would necessarily be subject to comparison with the foundational biblical text, and no longer regarded as being on the same level as the biblical witness in terms of revelation. One element which may enable this to be more plausible is the very method of *ta'wīl* utilized by the Sūfī exegetes.[4]

Ascension, Vision, Transformation? Union with God as Fanā' wa-Baqā'

A central theme of Sūfī thought and practice is that of union with God, which has connections with the Sūfī idea of *mushāhada*, literally "with one's own eyes,"[5] generally understood to refer to a kind of inner "vision" of God. As was noted in the previous chapter, Hujwīrī saw a connection between this idea of vision and that of *mujāhada*, "striving," often in the sense of ascetic exercises.[6] This is important to us here, not least because *mushāhada* can be considered a parallel to the whole enterprise of union with God, but also because it raises the question of whether this vision (and hence this idea of union) is understood in a shamanistic manner, or in a manner which would be consistent with the biblical idea of union. Hujwīrī cites the earlier-quoted Abū Hanifa statement ("theory without practice is like a body without a spirit"),[7] and then goes on to affirm that the effort for God as well as the vision of God are possible only by the

---

3. Zahniser, "Doctrine of the Incarnation," 35.

4. Concerning *ta'wīl* as a means of interpretation, one may be reminded of the words of Albert C. Outler in a rather different context. He noticed that as Wesley read the words of Clement of Alexandria's *Stromata*, and the Gnostic-like path Clement seemingly offered therein, "It was almost as if Wesley had read *agape* in the place of the Clementine *gnosis*, and then had turned the Eastern notion of a vertical scale of perfection into a genetic scale of development within historical existence" (Outler, "Introduction to *John Wesley*," 31). Outler suggests that Wesley is, in a sense, bringing out the "inner" meaning of Clement's understanding, and perhaps provides something of an example of how, in our rather different Sūfī context, *ta'wīl* might be fruitfully applied.

5. See Lane, *Arabic-English Lexicon*, 1610a. This translation and resource was pointed out to me by Dr. A. H. Mathias Zahniser. The word "witnessing" is also frequently used in English translations of the term.

6. Hujwiri, *Revelation*, 95.

7. Ibid.

grace of God (*taufīq*).⁸ This seems to place the idea of the inner vision of God in line with a more synergistic Macarian-Wesleyan understanding, and can be potentially useful for the community of faith.

While *mushāhada* may be understood as a goal of Sufism here, the means which are meant to move the believer toward the inward vision are *murāqaba*, "vigilant awareness and contemplation,"⁹ as well as *dhikr*, remembering." One key element of this, and in the entire idea of transforming union, is that such contemplation is meant to move the Sūfī into "participation in that which is being contemplated."¹⁰

Manerī similarly has an emphasis on *tajallī*, "splendor," which can be understood as a gracious manifestation or sign of God to the believer.¹¹ Manerī makes a point of distinguishing between the more shamanistic *tajallī ruhānī*, originating within the human soul, and *tajallī rabbānī*, which originates in and is empowered by the grace of God.¹² Having differentiated between these two, Manerī then moves into describing how, in connection with *tajallī rabbānī*, the soul must be purified of all that veils it from reflecting the reality of God as a mirror.

From there, Manerī warns his reader that the only way the believer may enter into *tajallī rabbānī*, rather than inadvertently into the anthropocentric *tajallī ruhānī*, is in relationship and union with a "perfect *sheikh*" as a proper intermediary for the believer. He may thus experience the overflow of the blessing of the "spiritual wealth" of the *sheikh*.¹³ We earlier observed that Manerī loosely quoted part of Q 2:189, "Enter a house through the door!"¹⁴ In this case, emphasizing that the "door" would be the "perfect *sheikh*" who Manerī considers so essential. This is especially fascinating in view of Jesus' words in John 10:1–11, in which he describes himself as the door or gate of the sheepfold, and to salvation itself.

Consider in this context the Macarian interaction with 2 Cor 3:7—4:6, described in chapter 3, with such a rich depth of understanding of

8. Ibid., 214.
9. Schimmel, *Mystical Dimensions*, 141.
10. Trimingham, *Sufi Orders*, 146.
11. Manerī, *Hundred Letters*, 60–63.
12. Ibid., 62–63.
13. Ibid., 63.
14. See previous chapter, 246.

what it means to enter progressively more deeply into Christ, who is the gracious manifestation of God. Macarius-Symeon tells us

> The face of the soul is unveiled, and it gazes upon the heavenly Bridegroom face to face in a spiritual light that cannot be described, mingling with Him in all fulness of assurance, being conformed to His death, ever looking with great desire to die for Christ, and trusting with assurance to receive by the Spirit a perfect deliverance from sin and from the darkness of the passions; in order that having been cleansed by the Spirit, sanctified in soul and body, it may be permitted to become a clean vessel to receive the heavenly unction and to entertain the true King, even Christ; and then it is made meet for eternal life, being henceforward a clean dwelling-place of the Holy Spirit.[15]

This grace-empowered union and communion with God seem to speak to the very themes of *mushāhada* and *tajallī rabbānī*, with the inner vision of spiritual reality empowered by the gracious manifestation of God in Messiah.

We can be reminded of Reynold Nicholson's insights on this topic. Nicholson recognized that the Sūfī understanding of *fanā'* and *baqā'* could, especially among the "intoxicated" (*sukr*), potentially veer off into a more pantheistic, *wahdat al-wajūd* understanding of Sufism rather than the more orthodox *wahdat al-shuhūd* understanding which is more compatible with a biblical understanding of faith. Nicholson illustrates how the ultimate goal of Sufism is *baqā'* rather than *fanā'*, and once past *sukr* ("intoxication"), seeks in *sahw* ("sobriety") to continue in following the *sharī'a*, or religious law. Ultimately, the idea is to thus avoid the trap of an antinomianism which considers itself above religious obligation. Nicholson compares this with his understanding of Christian mysticism, noting that therein as well the goal is "not in denying its own existence, but in affirming that it lives, moves, and has its being in the eternally active Will of Allah, and which, as a rule, expresses itself in language drawn from the closest form of personal relationship that we can imagine, namely, love."[16] We can be reminded as well of Tor Andrae's observations in this context that, "To the Sufi, the disappearance of the self has a meaning no different, in principle, than it has to the Apostle Paul, when he says: '. . . it is no longer I who live, but Christ who lives in me' (Gal 2:20). Sufi

---

15. *Homily* 10.4, Macarius, *Homilies*, 78.
16. Nicholson, *Idea of Personality in Sufism*, 14–15.

mysticism uses the term *baqā*, 'abiding.' 'Disappearance' is to disappear in God through God. 'Abiding' is to live with God."[17]

Both of these scholars see a direct parallel here, comparing the Sūfī idea of union with that expressed by Paul. Moreover, as Qushayrī had recognized, there is a moral dimension to this idea of *fanā'* and *baqā*, too: "fanā' is thus understood as 'shedding of blameworthy characteristics' and baqā' as the 'maintenance of praiseworthy characteristics.'"[18] Certainly in such a context, the goal of being empowered by the Spirit of God to be more Christ-like in character and transformed inwardly is one which is not merely within the ambit of biblical Christian thought, but rather is essential to it. Yet that will need to be understood in the context of the ontological reality of Jesus' divine nature.

For Hujwīrī, purity and *fanā' wa-baqā'* are intrinsically linked, in a manner very reminiscent of Christian language, "because purity is the attribute of those who love, and the lover is he that is dead (*fānī*) in his own attributes and living (*bāqī*) in the attributes of the Beloved."[19] This again reminds one of Paul's words in Gal 2:20 quoted above by Tor Andrae. Paul's point of being reckoned dead, yet sustained in life by God, seems to be further amplified in the more allegorical exegesis which Hujwīrī provides concerning Q 2:154, "Do not call dead those who are slain in the way of God. Nay, they are living."[20] Without denying the meaning in its context (where it referred to those literally killed in battle), Hujwīrī uses this passage in conjunction with the principle of giving sacrificially noted in Q 3:92, "sacrificing" one's spirit by renouncing self-interest. Thus, those whose desires are thus "slain," who "put to death the deeds of the body" (Rom 8:13), are truly living! While Hujwīrī isn't quoting Paul here, there is a potential bridge here worth exploring further.

This theme of moving from death into life is a recurrent one in both Christian and Sūfī contexts. Even some of the same illustrations for this are shared: The metaphor, for example, of the pearl diver, who sheds his clothes so as to be able to plumb the depths in search of pearl-bearing

---

17. Andrae, *Garden of Myrtles*, 123–24.
18. Qushayrī, "Interpreting," 119–20.
19. Hujwiri, *Revelation*, 32.
20. Ibid., 194.

oysters, is one which is shared by early Christian writers, including Macarius-Symeon,[21] and Sūfī writers, including Hujwīrī.[22]

As we have seen, Wesley as well as Macarius-Symeon understood this desire to ascend into relationship with God, and also finding it by grace—both in terms of pardon as well as in terms of God's enabling presence. The answer, then to the Sūfī's question of union with God is that it is found in and through union with Christ the Word. Jesus is the *insān kāmil*, the perfect or ideal human; he is our *eternal murshid* or *pīr*, our *perfect* spiritual guide and director. As we approach him, we unite ourselves with him in faith and ultimately through the grace-filled initiation of death and resurrection baptism, understood here as a means of grace in which God meets the new believer. Properly understood according to the Sūfī idea of "dying before our death," we are united to Jesus in *fanā' fī'l-shaykh*; or dissolution into the very "perfect *sheikh*" envisioned by Manerī. This could be understood as a reflection on Rom 6:3–11, using Sūfī terminology. Since 'Īsā, Jesus, is *ghair al-makhlūq*, the Uncreated, within the very identity of God himself, *fanā' fī'l-shaykh* and *fanā' fī Allah*, union with God, collapse into one another and are part of an organic whole—empowered and enabled by the gracious presence of God's Spirit to move from the crescendo of *fanā'* into the abiding relationship of *baqā'*.

The Means of Grace in the Community of Sūfī Believers in Messiah

How is this relationship with God in his Messiah to be sustained, both for individuals as well as for the broader community of faith? This is another area in which a proper understanding of the "means of grace" can be given importance. We can recall that John Wesley continued with the Anglican view of the means of grace, defined as "outward sign of inward *grace*, and a *means* whereby we receive the same."[23] In the previous two chapters, we have noted that a Sūfī understanding of the required practices of Islam can be understood in a manner analogous to the idea of the "means of grace" (rather than just accrual of merit). Manerī in particular reinterprets all of the pillars of Muslim practice by means of *ta'wīl*: Thus liturgical prayer is seen as a source of "spiritual

---

21. Homily 15:51; Macarius, *Homlies*, 131–32.
22. Hujwiri, *Revelation*, 372.
23. John Wesley, "The Means of Grace," 2.1.

cleansing and sanctification," though here also Manerī repeats the caveat that this should be understood thusly in connection with one's *sheikh* or spiritual director. Moreover, he describes the congregational prayer as spiritual *jihād*, comparing the prayers to the actions of an army heading into battle, concluding that when the "leader gives the final blessing of peace, he distributes the grace of the Lord of Glory" as though it were the spoils of war.[24] For Manerī, the specific liturgical rules (e.g., concerning the *qibla*, or direction for prayer) are less important than the intention of the heart.[25] Certainly the emphasis on the spiritual aspects of prayer, as opposed to the mechanics of prayer, dovetails well with a New Testament understanding of "means of grace."

Manerī goes on to describe the other pillars of faith in similarly spiritualized terms. While he affirms the importance of the *hajj* pilgrimage, he also affirms the primacy of perceiving the *Lord* of the house in a visit to the *Kaaba*; he culminates this with an observation that while one *may* experience the manifestation of God on *hajj*, one can actually encounter God in the heart every day.[26] *Zakāt* implies offering one's heart, body and goods to the Beloved,[27] and the meditation on the *shahāda* (in particular, the first clause, reminiscent of the Hebrew *shemaʿ*)[28] brings the reader once again full circle to the reality of being transformed into the likeness of that upon which one contemplates.[29] Fasting during the month of Ramadan is likewise described as a means by which *God* works in the life of the believer.[30] Manerī's very Eucharistic-sounding statement concerning fasting is worth repeating here, in part because there is a potential connection which goes beyond fasting for our purposes in community-building in the context of Sūfī community: "O brother, when you are filled with His bounty and a table is laid out with His grace, then abstention from eating is not to prolong the pleasure of His grace, but to find Him in His treasury, as the Beloved."[31]

---

24. Manerī, *Hundred Letters*, 123.
25. Ibid., 126.
26. Ibid., 136.
27. Ibid., 132.
28. See Woodberry, "Reusing Common Pillars," 174.
29. Manerī, *Hundred Letters*, 154.
30. Ibid.
31. Ibid., 130.

As J. Dudley Woodberry pointed out a number of years ago, each of these pillars come from Jewish and Christian sources;[32] nonetheless, we can observe here an "in-house" Sūfī figure who demonstrates how such elements can not only be reinterpreted in a manner which would make their continuing use plausible in a context of a faithful community of Jesus-followers. Not only this, but they may even serve as reinterpreted elements of means of grace for communities which choose to continue to utilize them. These can potentially be reinterpreted in such a way as to enable these practices to be part of congregational life. At the same time, such reinterpretation allows these practices to be part of the life of faithful Jesus-followers as part of their life in Christ (thus retaining their *indigenous* function), yet reinterpreted in such a manner as to ensure *pilgrim* faithfulness to the centrality of Jesus.

We recall chapter 4, where we observed that John Wesley considered three broad areas as "means of grace": individual or congregational prayer (and it seems to me that, broadly speaking, he would include worship in this), the reading, hearing and meditation on the Scriptures, and partaking of the Eucharist.[33] As noted in chapters 5 and 6, there are three distinctly Sūfī areas which serve a similar purpose. These are *dhikr*, "recollection," often ritualized prayer in the form of chanting; *hadra*, "presence;" this is sometimes interchangeable with *samāʿ*, literally "hearing," and involves a gathering of Sūfīs which may include various forms of *dhikr*, as well as music or dance performed *in a group*; and *fikr*, theological teaching and interaction, which can be expressed corporately in a *halaqa*,[34] the Sūfī "circle" for discussion of sacred writings. Of course, in practice, these rituals frequently spill over into one another, rather than being completely distinct.

With regard to *dhikr*, there is promise as well as potential pitfalls against which we must be aware. Certainly this form need not be discarded outright, as chant is a form of meditation and worship the Christian community of faith has used for many centuries; the very structure of Psalm 136 seems to indicate this clearly. At the same time, some elements of *dhikr* perhaps preclude its being absorbed uncritically into the believing community.[35] Indeed, the fact that some Sūfīs may use *dhikr* as a

32. Woodberry, "Reusing Common Pillars," 171–86.
33. John Wesley, "The Means of Grace," 2.1.
34. Or frequently *halqa*.
35. I. Lilias Trotter (1853–1928; pioneering missionary in Algeria) was also quite negative about the potential for the use of *dhikr* in the life of the believer or

means of working themselves into a frenzy or autohypnosis should give us pause about how to integrate this form into communal devotional life. Once again, it would seem that *dhikr* is a form which will require some amount of transformation for its incorporation into the life of the community of Jesus-followers.

How might this be accomplished? In at least one context in work among Muslims in South Asia, *dhikr* has been utilized in a discipleship context, as a means for oral learners to memorize the Scriptures through repetitive recitation.[36] In addition to traditional subjects for *dhikr* (such as the *Fātiha* prayer, which opens the Qur'ān) or, in the context of a celebration of a festival such as Ramadan, or in a celebration focused on the Incarnation, a real focus can be made upon recitation, singing and chanting of particularly the passages which are focused on the Incarnation. These would be such as the birth narratives of the Gospels, the prologue of John's Gospel, and the *kenosis* passage of Phil 2:5-11, both in *dhikr jalī*, chanting and singing aloud in praise and worship (but focused truly on God, rather than on getting oneself into a particular emotional/spiritual state) and quietly in silent meditation as a group, perhaps with time included for each one to share spiritual impressions in the midst of meditation on a given passage. This can become a kind of "group study" of a more spiritual, and perhaps less didactic nature.

The study circle, or *halaqa*, should also be a central part of such community life. Ideally, this can involve not just one gifted teacher expounding on the text of the New Testament or the Hebrew Scriptures, but

---

fellowship, focusing rather strongly on the hypnotic rather than the devotional side of *dhikr* (see Trotter, *Sevenfold Secret*, 5). While care certainly does need to be taken that *dhikr* be focused in a healthy manner, there are some, at least, who have seen the usefulness of this ritual for devotion and worship, and even evangelism. James L. Barton (1855-1936; missionary and human rights activist in the Ottoman Empire), in his earlier *The Christian Approach to Islam*, 205), cites the positive view of Duncan Black Macdonald (1863-1943, scholar of Islam) as in favor of exploring the use of *dhikr*, as well as a "Dr. Wilson" as considering *dhikr* as having "little or no value for the Christian." Phil Parshall (now retired; scholar and pioneering missionary among Muslims) also advocates both *dhikr* and indigenous-style music (Parshall, *Bridges to Islam*, 133). In his more recent work, Don McCurry (now retired; scholar and missionary in Pakistan) expresses doubt about the use of *dhikr*, though as noted earlier, he was more positive regarding other elements of Sūfī understandings (McCurry, *Broken Family*, 200).

36. Personal observation in several fellowships of Muslim Jesus followers, some of whom had Sūfī roots. Given that *dhikr* actually means "remembrance," it seems particularly appropriate that it would be used, in part, for this purpose.

can include discussion designed to bring out the insights of various others in the group. Each one may have spiritual insights, life experiences, stories. This could also include parallel knowledge of passages from the Qur'ān or Sūfī stories which will not only illuminate the meaning of the text for everyone, but also provide spiritual nourishment as they discuss and pray concerning how the scriptures can and should be applied in their lives.

The area of the *samā'* or *hadra* as a means of grace in a community of Sūfī Jesus followers could perhaps include the kind of presentation and performance which was described in the introduction to this project—an account of a young man presenting his song at the *'urs* meeting.[37] We had the opportunity to witness something similar to this in the annual meeting of a cluster of fellowships of believers in South Asia several years ago. Following both sessions of *dhikr* and singing of praise songs using Muslim-style tunes, the meeting was opened for presentations by other members of the congregation. One young man, twenty-five years old, rose and stood before the congregation, visibly nervous, as he pulled a tattered sheet of paper from his pocket, unfolded it, and began to sing a beautiful *ghazal* of his own composition, a hymn of several verses in praise of his Messiah. Many in the congregation were brought to tears.

It is crucial, however, to recall that people in a Sūfī context are often involved in folk religious practices. How can the needs which some seek to meet through such practices be met as people learn to walk with God in Christ? We can observe how these needs are met in the spiritual life of the community of Jesus-followers. The relational power of prayer, worship, interaction with the scriptures, are a crucial part of how relationship with Christ is sustained. Ideally, the spiritual life of the community can be integrated with an understanding of how God, in his Messiah and by the Holy Spirit's power, desires to meet the very day-to-day needs which Muslims (Sūfīs and non-Sūfīs alike) perceive and seek to meet through folk practices.[38]

---

37. See above, 20–21.

38. A significant example of the importance of understanding the implications of folk practices is found in Brooks, "May Puritix," 31–41, also cited in Musk, *Kissing Cousins?*, 183–84. The *may puratrix* ritual used by women of a Central Asian Muslim people group involves praying over smoking cooking oil "toward the spirits of the dead, particularly dead relatives" (Brooks, "May Puritix," 131). In the event, Brooks mostly concludes that this ritual would likely need to be discarded, but acknowledges that this is still a "fluid process" (see Brooks, "May Puritix," 41, and Musk, *Kissing Cousins?* 184). This is instructive in our context as well, although we are dealing here

It is bearing this in mind that we can suggest integrating the Eucharist as a means of grace into the life of the congregation as a part of (perhaps the culmination of) the *samāʿ*. An understanding of the Lord's Supper would have to be done in such a manner that it was genuinely indigenous. It can be crucial to discuss the whole context of the Passover event which led up to the Crucifixion. The entire narrative of Passover, Covenant and the final meal in the upper room can enter into this: Discussing the deliverance from Egypt, the elders of Israel eating together in God's presence on the mountain, bound together in unity by God's uncreated presence by his Spirit as the community partakes of the bread and the fruit of the vine together. It would be appropriate to include passages from other contexts which would connect spiritually with the Sūfī milieu. Selections, for example, from Macarius-Symeon's *Homily* 47, about deliverance from Egypt and of the Messiah as the Passover Lamb, might very well be read for the occasion:

> The children of Israel march away, when they have kept the Passover. The soul moves onwards, when it has received the life of the Holy Passover, and has tasted of the Lamb, and been anointed with His blood, and has eaten the true bread, the living Word. A pillar of fire and a pillar of cloud went before the Israelites, protecting them : the Holy Spirit strengthens these, warming and guiding the soul in a way that can be felt.[39]

Perhaps these insights can contribute toward seeing people who are part of Sūfī communities to truly become "Methodists of the East," walking in the love of Jesus, and filled with the holy power and uncreated grace of His sanctifying Spirit.

A good way to conclude would be to present a picture of what a fellowship of Sūfī-background believers might look like. It might be especially instructive to place this example during the most festive season of the Muslim calendar, Ramadan. The month of Ramadan is of great importance to Muslims because it is believed that during this month that the holy Qur'ān began to be revealed to the Prophet Muhammad. This is most famously commemorated in Q 97:

> Behold, from on high have We bestowed this [divine writ] on the Night of Destiny.

---

with broader, more generally acceptable elements of indigenous culture.

39. *Homiliy* 47.11; Macarius, *Homilies*, 295.

> And what could make thee conceive what it is, that Night of Destiny?
>
> The Night of Destiny is better than a thousand months:
>
> In hosts descend in it the angels, bearing divine inspiration by their Sustainer's leave; from all [evil] that may happen—
>
> Does it make secure, until the rise of dawn.[40]

Significantly, Ramadan is also seen by especially many Sūfī Muslims as a form of spiritual *jihād*, or struggle, to overcome one's flesh; this is considered part of *jihād akbar*, or the "greater struggle" against the flesh and sin nature,[41] and fasting as a means to subdue the flesh and draw closer to God,[42] and even to be granted a vision of God and to "hear the word of God in their hearts."[43]

On the one hand, we don't believe that any of the rituals or elements described above need to be discarded in their entirety, as, properly understood, they would be useful and retain great depth of meaning for the believing community. At the same time, neither do we believe they can merely be accepted as they are without syncretism taking place. For example, central to the celebration of Ramadan is the celebration of the Qur'ān as the final revelation of God, something which a faithful, believing community, cannot work into their life as a community of faith in Messiah. Another element which could not be absorbed into the community is that of the emphasis on the legal aspect of the life of the individual, very much often focused on the minutiae of legal practice; if such practices were absorbed, they would need to be infused with new meaning.

We do believe, however, that there is much potential scope for the integration of the celebration of Ramadan into the life of the believing community, and we believe that this has much potential for enhancing the life of the community of faith, for deepening the spiritual lives of the individual members of the faith community, and for bearing fruitful witness to the life of Messiah in the context of the larger Muslim community. As noted above, Ramadan is a celebration of the coming among humankind of what Sunni Muslims, at least, consider the eternal,

---

40. It may be worth noting in this context that Richard Bell and others have suggested that the wording of this passage may indicate a connection with the nativity of Jesus. See Bell, *The Qur'ān: Translated*, 2.669 n. 2.

41. Hujwiri, *Revelation*, 200–1.

42. Ibid., 324–25.

43. Maneri, *Hundred Letters*, 129.

uncreated word of God in the Qur'ān. It carries an idea parallel to the statement found in John 1:14, "And the Word became flesh and took up residence among us, and we saw his glory, glory as of the one and only from the Father, full of grace and truth."[44] But in Islam, the word became "book," to be recited. Ramadan is thus theologically parallel to *Christmas* on this level, indeed, in the Muslim community, the closest thing to the celebration of Christmas is the fast-ending festival of *'Idu'l Fitr*. It is the most joyous celebration, and the annual celebration on which gifts are given to children and greetings are exchanged. Certainly it seems that a celebration so central to Muslim community life may potentially be of great value to the believing community, as women and men seek to live out their lives in love for God and one another, and as witnesses to the surrounding community. This seems particularly so in the case of a celebration and cycle of rituals such as Ramadan, which have such liminal value for the believing community, taking them out of the flow of ordinary life, with more of a ritual and chronological focus on the spiritual.

The community of believers in Jesus could *transform* the celebration of Ramadan particularly in the two problem areas described above. What about the issue of the focus of the celebration itself? How can this be addressed? Ramadan is already a celebration of the descent of the Word of God among humankind. Rather than this being a celebration of the Qur'ān as eternal book, it could become a celebration focused on the Incarnation of the living Word, who entered humankind in a unique way and took our reality upon himself, entering time and space on our behalf. He joined himself with us that we might be brought into relationship and union with God. In this sense, as implied above, it could functionally become the celebration of Christmas in the community of 'Īsā followers among the Muslims, celebrating Ramadan as are their neighbors, yet with a different focus. Outwardly, they would thus avoid being perceived by the broader Muslim community of having become *irreligious*. At the same time, the celebration can be a source of strength and faith as a community in Messiah as they fast and celebrate the Word made flesh.

The second area regarding motivation for Ramadan observance must also be considered carefully. A potential solution may be one which was already noted above as found among some of the Sūfīs: Seeing the fast of Ramadan as part of personal *jihād*, the struggle to overcome the flesh. Doing this not merely as an individual, but as part of a community

---

44. Lexham English Bible translation.

of faith, and as a joyous sacrifice to God as revealed in Christ may provide just the kind of transformation that would inhibit a resurgence of Islamic legalism in the context of the believing fellowship.

NARRATIVE EPILOGUE: WHAT MIGHT THIS LOOK LIKE?

Perhaps the best way to conclude this chapter, and this project, would be to turn our minds back to the narrative of the *'urs* celebration described in the introduction. What might a community of faith in Jesus look like for them? Considering the excitement of that festal evening, as they move into faith in the possibility of experiencing something like the *fanā' wa-baqā'* of which their *pīr* spoke, what would a community of faith look like? How would it be similar, and how would it be different, from what they have experienced at the *'urs*? Many of the forms are familiar, yet some things will express a *pilgrim* shift—perhaps a greater openness to the teaching and leadership role of women in the congregation, the temptation to revert to folk practices, and above all, the centrality of Jesus. Bear in mind that what is described here is a kind of "general" model; how it would play out on the ground would vary according to the situation as well as the decisions of the elders of the emerging community. It is hoped that this project will provide a model which can be fruitfully adapted in specific cultural situations in various parts of the world.

We will seek now to imagine how such a community might respond during Ramadan.

Hasan's Contribution

Hasan was feeling quite buoyant, really, on this fine autumn afternoon as he made his way through the crowded bazaar set up during Ramadan. It was getting close to *iftār*,[45] the fast breaking time in the evening, and he needed to hurry or he wouldn't make it in time to the *jamā'at*[46] at Mustafa Bhai's house. He was cutting the time close, but he really wanted to give everyone a treat today, and come with a big pot full of *halīm*—the incomparable South Asian stew, made especially during Ramadan, of meat, lentils, wheat and other grains. While Ramadan was special *every* year, this one was more special than any time before it: seven months ago, after many months of thinking through both the increasingly un-

---

45. The fast-breaking ritual at sundown during *Ramadan*.
46. Arabic for "assembly," equivalent to the Greek *ekklesia*.

avoidable "truth" and the frightening potential "consequences," Hasan had done as Mustafa had been urging and prayed that God would reveal the truth about how one could truly enter into union with him. It was only two weeks later that *he* appeared in Hasan's dream, dressed in white: Unmistakably, it was 'Īsā al-Masīh, pleading with him, holding out his hands to Hasan in love and hope, and saying only three words: "Come to me!" Now this Ramadān, he was celebrating with the small but growing number of *murīds* meeting at Mustafa's apartment nearly every day to break the fast together, pray, worship, do *dhikr* together, and celebrate what Mustafa referred to as *mā'idah*.⁴⁷

Hasan reached the *halīm* stall at last and asked them to give him ten servings to take out in a large clay pot. What a blessing to be in such close fellowship, and to walk with other believing Muslim sisters and brothers in ever-deeper union with Almighty Allāh!

Winding his way back through the bazaar, carrying his large pot of delicious *halīm*, Hasan found his way to the door of Mustafa's building, and then struggled up the two flights of stairs to the now-familiar door, and rang the bell. He was glad to have made it; he really wouldn't have wanted to miss taking *iftār* with everyone. Yusūf answered the door with a big smile and took the clay pot from Hasan, his face beaming that much more widely as he smelled its contents. He greeted Hasan with a vigorous, "*As-salām 'alaīkum*," receiving back a hearty "*Wa'alaīkum as-salaam, wa rahmatullāhi wa barkātuh!*"⁴⁸ Yusūf was, like Hasan, a fairly new member of the *jamā'at*, and he was also here for his first Ramadān as a follower of 'Īsā. Hasan entered and saw through the crack in the kitchen door that Mustafa's wife was making last-minute preparation for the *iftār*. Yusūf quickly handed the *halīm* pot to Mustafa, who carried it into the kitchen.

The other eight members of the *jamā'at* were already seated in a circle and ready as Mustafa invited Hasan to go wash in preparation for the meal and prayers which would follow. He quickly washed, placed his prayer cap on his head, and took his seat with the others. By now the food was coming out, and each one showed the day's weariness and anticipation of the fast-breaking to come. Finally, they could hear the *adhān*, or call to prayer, from the mosque just a block away, and each one took a date and then a long, cool drink of lemonade. They then quickly polished

---

47. Arabic for "table," as well as the title of the fifth *Sūrah* of the Qur'ān. In some South Asian contexts, *mezbani*, an "invitation to a ceremony" is used for this in the context of the community of those who have come to faith in Jesus.

48. Traditional Muslim greetings of peace and blessing.

off the fried vegetables, fruit and other snacks, and when the *halīm* was brought out, Hasan beamed with pride as Mustafa announced that he had brought it for everyone.

The food finished, they each filed into the bathrooms and washed their mouths and hands, and then lined up to pray as they had always done, ever since they were children. "*Allāhu Akbar!*"[49] Mustafa chanted as they went through their paces of the traditional liturgy the *salāh*. With the second round, however, instead of verses from the Qur'ān in Arabic, Mustafa's wife, Salīma, chanted the first three verses of *Yūhānna* in their native language,

> In the beginning was the Word,
> And the Word was with God
> And the Word was God
> He was with God in the beginning.
> Through him all things were made;
> without him nothing was made that has been made.

"*Allāhu Akbar!*" came the chant again, and they all bowed, foreheads pressed to the ground.

After the *salāh* was finished, they rearranged themselves into a circle, and this time 'Alī, who had been a follower of 'Īsā for more than seven years, was asked if he had something which he wanted to share. He smiled and told again a story that they had all heard at least once, of how 'Īsā had appeared to him in a dream, and how not long afterwards he had met another believer in him in the bazaar. Over three weeks of conversations with Bilāl, the urgency of their discussion fueled by the vision, Ali had put his faith in 'Īsā. He had struggled afterwards with some ostracism from his family, and had almost lost his wife Hafsa in the process, but now she sat contentedly across from him, now his sister in faith as well as his wife and the mother of their four boys who were playing in the other room.

The praises began again, with Hafsa herself contributing a *qawwālī*[50] she had composed about 'Īsā's love for his people, and more *dhikr* based on various verses in the *Injīl*.[51] These were becoming more and more familiar to Hasan as they met daily. Finally, after nearly an hour of songs, prayer for one another, and *dhikr*, Mustafa's wife brought out a chapati,

---

49. "God is great!"
50. Devotional style of music rooted in Islamic South Asia.
51. New Testament.

unleavened flat bread, and a cup of grape juice. Salīma described first how Prophet Mūsa had spilled the sacrificial blood on the people of Israel, saying, "this is the blood of the covenant," before taking the elders of the people up to the mountain, where they "saw God, and ate and drank."[52] She then connected this with the words of ʿĪsā to his disciples as they remembered both the sacrificial rescue from Pharaoh and this same event—"this cup is the New Covenant in my blood"[53]—making explicit the connection between the one seen on the mountain and the one who presented the cup to the disciples. The message ended, and with Mustafa leading, they chanted one final *dhikr* about their ʿĪsā, who died and rose from the dead, as they dipped pieces of chapati into the juice.

As he said his final salaams and walked home, Hasan marveled at how spiritually "full" he felt in this month of fasting, and how excited he was even for the next day's fasting, for it would be capped by fellowship as wonderful as this had been. The meal had brought them together as brothers and sisters, and as they prayed, chanted, worshiped, and ate together, they were becoming a family in the mercy of al Masīh.

52. Exodus 24:8–11.
53. 1 Corinthians 11:25.

Bibliography

Abusch, Tzvi. "Ascent to the Stars in a Mesopotamian Ritual: Social Metaphor and Religious Experience." In *Death, Ecstasy and Other Worldly Journeys*, edited by John J. Collins and Michael Fishbane, 15–39. Albany, NY: SUNY Press, 1995.

Afzal, Cameron. "Wheels of Time: *Merkavah* Exegesis in Revelation 4." In *Society of Biblical Literature 1998 Seminar Papers*. 2 Vols., 1.465–82. Atlanta: Scholars, 1998.

Alexander, P. S. "Comparing Merkavah Mysticism and Gnosticism: An Essay in Method." *Journal of Jewish Studies* 35 (1984) 1–18.

Altmann, Alexander. "The Ladder of Ascension." In *Studies in Mysticism and Religion Presented to Gershom G. Scholem on His Seventieth Birthday by Pupils, Colleagues and Friends*, edited by E. E. Urbach, R. J. Zwi Werblowsky, and Ch. Wirszubski, 1–32. Jerusalem: Magnes, 1967.

Anderson, Neil D. *A Definitive Study of Evidence Concerning John Wesley's Appropriation of the Thought of Clement of Alexandria*. Lewiston, NY: Edwin Mellon, 2004.

Andrae, Tor. *In the Garden of Myrtles: Studies in Early Islamic Mysticism*. Translated by Birgitta Sharpe. Albany: State University of New York Press, 1987.

Andrewes, Lancelot. *Ninety-Six Sermons*. Oxford: John Henry Parker, 1850.

Arberry, Arthur John. Introduction to *The Doctrine of the Sūfīs (Kitāb al-Taʿarruf li-madhab ahl al tasawwuf)*. Cambridge: Cambridge University Press, 1977.

——— *An Introduction to the History of Sufism*. New York: Longmans, Green & Co., 1942.

———, trans. *The Koran Interpreted*. New York: Touchstone, 1955.

Arndt, Johann. *An Extract from Johann Arndt's True Christianity (Books 1–4)*, in *A Christian Library: Consisting of Extracts from and Abridgements of the Choicest Pieces of Practical Divinity which have been Published in the English Tongue*, Vol. 1. Edited by John Wesley. London: T. Cordeux, 1819.

———. *True Christianity*. Translated by Peter Erb. New York: Paulist, 1979.

Arnold, Clinton E. *The Colossian Syncretism: The Interface Between Christianity and Folk Belief at Colossae*. Grand Rapids: Baker, 1996.

Asad, Muhammad. *The Message of the Qurʾān: The Full Account of the Revealed Arabic Text Accompanied by Parallel Transliteration.Translated and Explained*. 3 Vols. Bristol, England: Book Foundation, 2003.

Askari, Syed Hasan. *Islam and Muslims in Medieval Bihar*. 2nd edition. Patna, Bihar, India: Khuda Bakhsh Oriental Public Library, 1998.

———. Preface to *The Hundred Letters*, by Sharafuddin Maneri. New York: Paulist, 1980.

Athanasius. *On the Incarnation of the Word of God*. Translated by Penelope Lawson. Crestwood, NY: St. Vladamir's Seminary Press, 1993.

'Attār, Farid al-Dīn. *Muslim Saints and Mystics: Episodes from the Tadhkirat al-Awliyā' (Memorials of the Saints)*. Translated by A. J. Arberry. London: Routledge, 1966.

Augustine. *Confessions and Enchiridion*. Edited and Translated by Albert C. Outler. Philadelphia: Westminster, 1955.

———. *The Works of Aurelius Augustine: A New Translation*. 15 vols. Edinburgh: T. & T. Clark, 1871–1876.

Aulén, Gustaf. *Christus Victor: An Historical Study of the Three Main Types of the Idea of Atonement*. Translated by A. G. Hebert. New York: Macmillan, 1969.

Aune, David. *Revelation*. Word Biblical Commentary 52a–c. 3 vols. Dallas: Word, 1997.

Awn, Peter. "Classical Sufi Approaches to Scripture." In *Mysticism and Sacred Scripture*, edited by Steven T. Katz, 138–52. New York: St. Martin's, 2000.

Ayoub, Mahmud. *A Muslim View of Christianity: Essays on Dialogue*. Edited by Irfan A. Omar. Maryknoll, NY: Orbis, 2007.

Bacher, Wilhelm, et al. "Tannaim and Amoraim." In *The Jewish Encyclopedia*, vol. 12, edited by Isadore Singer, 49–54. New York: Funk and Wagnalls, 1906.

Baker, Dom Aelred. "Pseudo Macarius and the Gospel of Thomas." *Vigiliae Christianae* 18 (1964) 215–25.

Balci, Israfil. "An Islamic Approach Toward International Peace." In *Muslim & Christian Reflections on Peace*, edited by J. Dudley Woodberry, Osman Zamrut, and Mustafa Koylu, 116–22. Lanham, MD: University Press of America, 2005.

Barrett, C. K. *The Gospel According to St. John: An Introduction with Commentary and Notes on the Greek Text*. London: SPCK, 1978.

Barthélemy, D., and J. T. Milik, eds. *Discoveries in the Judean Desert I: Cave 1*. Oxford: Oxford University Press, 1955.

Barthélemy, Dominique. "Est-ce Hoshaya Rabba qui cesura le 'Commentaire Allegorique'? A partir des retouches faites aux citations bibliques, etude sur la tradition textualle de Commentaire Allegorique du Philon." In *Études D'Histoire du Texte de l'Ancien Testament*, 140–73. Fribourg and Göttinngen: Editions Universitaires and VandenHoeck and Ruprecht, 1978.

Barton, James L. *The Christian Approach to Islam*. College of Missions Lectureship, Fifth Series. Boston: Pilgrim, 1918.

Bauckham, Richard J. *The Climax of Prophecy: Studies on the Book of Revelation*. Edinburgh: T. & T. Clark, 1993.

———. *Jesus and the Eyewitnesses: The Gospels as Eyewitness Testimony*. Grand Rapids: Eerdmans, 2006.

———. *Jesus and the God of Israel: God Crucified and Other Studies on the New Testament's Christology of Divine Identity*. Grand Rapids: Eerdmans, 2008.

———. *Jude, 2 Peter*. Word Biblical Commentary 50. Waco, TX: Word, 1983.

———. *The Theology of the Book of Revelation*. New Testament Theology. Cambridge, UK: Cambridge University Press, 1993.

Bauenfiend, O. "Nikaō Ktl." In *Theological Dictionary of the New Testament*, edited by Gerhard Kittel and Geoffrey W. Bromily, 4.943. Grand Rapids: Eerdmans, 1964.

Beale, Gregory K. *The Book of Revelation: A Commentary on the Greek Text*. The New International Greek Testament Commentary. Grand Rapids: Eerdmans, 1999.

Becker, John, and Erik Simuyu. "The Watering of Discipling." In *From Seed to Fruit: Global Trends, Fruitful Practices, and Emerging Issues among Muslims.* J. Dudley Woodberry, ed., 125–39. Pasadena, CA: William Carey, 2008.

Bell, Richard. *The Origin of Islam in its Christian Environment.* London: Macmillan, 1926.

———. *The Qur'an: Translated, with a Critical Rearrangement of the Surahs.* 2 vols. Edinburgh: Edinburgh University Press, 1937, 1939.

Bennett, Clinton. "In Dialogue with Truth: A Critical Biography of Henry Martyn." In *Approaches, Foundations, Issues and Models of Interfaith Relations*, edited by David Emmanuel Singh and Robert Edwin Schick, 195–239. Delhi and Hyderabad, India: ISPCK/HMI, 2001.

Berthold, Heinz, ed. 1973. *Makarios/Symeon: Reden und Briefen: Die Sammlung I des Vaticanus Graecus 694 (B).* 2 vols. Berlin: Akademie-Verlag, 1973.

Blumenthal, David R, trans. and notes. *Understanding Jewish Mysticism: A Source Reader. The Merkabah Tradition and the Zoharic Tradition.* New York: Ktav, 1978.

Bodi, Daniel. *The Book of Ezekiel and the Poem of Erra.* Freiburg, Switzerland: Universitätsverlag & Göttingen: Vandenhoeck and Ruprecht, 1991.

Borgen, Peder. *Early Christianity and Hellenistic Judaism.* Edinburgh: T. & T. Clark, 1996.

Bousset, D. W. "Die Himmelsreise der Seele." *Archiv fur Religionswissenschaft* 4 (1901) 136–69, 229–73.

Böwering, Gerhard. 1989. "Baqā' wa Fanā." In *Encyclopedia Iranica*, vol. III., edited by Ehsan Yashater, 722–24. New York: Bibliotheca Persica, 1989.

———. "Ḏekr." In *Encyclopedia Iranica*, vol. VII, edited by Ehsan Yashater, 229–33. New York: Bibliotheca Persica, 1996.

———. "Hojviri, Abu'l-Hasan 'Ali." In *Encyclopedia Iranica*, vol. XII, edited by Ehsan Yashater, 429–30. New York: Bibliotheca Persica, 2004.

———. "The Scriptural 'Senses' in Medieval Sūfī Qur'ān Exegesis." In *With Reverence for the Word: Medieval Scriptural Exegesis in Judaism, Christianity, and Islam*, edited by Jane Dammen McAuliffe, Barry D. Walfish, and Joseph W. Goering, 346–65. New York: Oxford University Press, 2003.

Box, G. H. "The Idea of Intermediation in Jewish Theology: A Note on Memra and Shekinah." *Jewish Quarterly Review* 23 (1932–1933) 103–19.

Boyarin, Daniel."The Gospel of the *Memra*: Jewish Binitarianism and the Prologue to John." *Harvard Theological Review* 94.3 (2001) 243–84.

Boyd, Gregory A. *God at War: The Bible & Spiritual Conflict.* Downers Grove, IL: InterVarsity, 1997.

Braude, William G., trans. *Pesikta Rabbati: Discourses for Feasts, Fasts and Special Sabbaths.* 2 vols. New Haven, CT: Yale University Press, 1968.

Brightman, Robert S. "Gregory of Nyssa and John Wesley in Theological Dialogue of the Christian Life." PhD diss., Boston University, 1969.

Brock, Sebastian P. *The Bible in the Syriac Tradition (Revised Edition).* Piscataway, NJ: Gorgias, 2006.

Brodie, Thomas L. *The Gospel According to John: A Literary and Theological Commentary.* New York: Oxford University Press, 1997.

Brooks, Elisabeth. "May Puritix: Praying into Smoking Oil." *International Journal of Frontier Missions* 17.4 (2000) 31–41.

Brown, Raymond E. *The Gospel According to John.* The Anchor Bible. 2 vols. Garden City, NY: Doubleday, 1966–1970.
Brownlee, William H. *Ezekiel 1–19.* Word Biblical Commentary 28. Waco, TX: Word, 1986.
Bruce, F. F. *The Epistles to the Colossians, to Philemon, and to the Ephesians.* The New International Commentary on the New Testament. Grand Rapids: Eerdmans, 1984.
Bultmann, Rudolf. *The Gospel of John: A Commentary.* Translated by G. R. Beasley-Murray. Edited by R. W. A. Hoare and J. K. Riches. Oxford: Basil Blackwell, 1971.
Burgoyne, S. R. *The Christian Church and the Convert from Islam.* Lucknow, India: Lucknow, n.d.
Burns, Stuart Keith. "Charisma and Spirituality in the Early Church: A Study of Messalianism and Pseudo-Macarius." PhD diss., University of Leeds, 1999.
———. "Divine Ecstasy in Gregory of Nyssa and Pseudo-Macarius: Flight and Intoxication." *Greek Orthodox Theological Review* 44.1–4 (1999) 309–27.
Caird, G. B. *A Commentary on the Revelation of St. John the Divine.* New York: Harper & Row, 1966.
Campbell, Ted A. "Back to the Future: Wesleyan Quest for Ancient Roots: the 1980s." *Wesleyan Theological Journal* 32.1 (1997) 5–16.
———. *John Wesley and Christian Antiquity.* Nashville: Kingswood, 1991.
Carey, William. *An Enquiry of the Obligations of Christians, to Use Means for the Conversion of the Heathens.* Leicester: Ann Ireland, 1792.
Carmichael, Calum M. *The Story of Creation: Its Origin and Its Interpretation in Philo and the Fourth Gospel.* Ithaca, NY: Cornell University Press, 1996.
Cassian, John. *Conferences.* In *Nicene and Post-Nicene Fathers, Second Series.* Edited by Philip Schaff and Henry Wace. Translated by Edgar C. S. Gibson. New York: Christian Literature, 1894.
Charette, Blaine."'Tongues as of Fire': Judgment as a Function of Glossolalia in Luke's Thought." *Journal of Pentecostal Theology* 13.2 (2005) 173–86.
Charles, R. H. *Critical and Exegetical Commentary on the Revelation of St. John.* The International Critical Commentary. 2 vols. New York: Charles Scribner's Sons, 1920.
Charlesworth, James H. *Critical Reflections on the Odes of Solomon. Volume 1: Literary Setting, Textual Studies, Gnosticism, the Dead Sea Scrolls, and the Gospel of John (Journal for the Study of the Pseudopigrapha Studies Series 22).* Sheffield: Sheffield University Press, 1998.
———, trans. 2009. *The Earliest Christian Hymnbook: The Odes of Solomon.* Eugene, OR: Cascade.
Chilton, Bruce D., trans. *The Isaiah Targum.* The Aramaic Bible 11. Wilmington, DE: Michael Glazier, 1987.
Chittick, William C. "Ibn Arabi." *The Stanford Encyclopedia of Philosophy.* (Fall 2008 Edition). Edward N. Zalta, ed. 2008. Online: http://plato.stanford.edu/archives/fall2008/entries/ibn-arabi/.
———. *Sufism: A Beginner's Guide.* Oxford: OneWorld, 2000.
———. "Worship." In *The Cambridge Companion to Classical Islamic Theology*, edited by Tim Winter, 218–36. Cambridge: Cambridge University Press, 2008.
Christensen, Michael J. "John Wesley: Christian Perfection as Faith Filled with the Energy of Love." In *Partakers of the Divine Nature: The History and Development*

of *Deification in the Christian Traditions*, edited by Michael J. Christensen and Jeffrey A. Wittung, 219–29. Grand Rapids: Baker Academic, 2007.

Cicero. *The Republic and the Laws (Oxford World's Classics)*. Edited by Jonathan Powell, Translated by Niall Rudd. Oxford: Oxford University Press, 2009. (Orig. Pub. 1998)

Clement of Rome. "Epistle to the Corinthians." In *The Ante-Nicene Fathers*, vol. 1, edited and translated by A. Cleveland Coxe, 1–22. Buffalo: Christian Literature, 1885.

Clendenin, Daniel B. "Partakers of Divinity: The Orthodox Doctrine of Theosis." *Journal of the Evangelical Theological Society* 37.3 (1994) 365–79.

Coke, Thomas. *The Journals of Dr. Thomas Coke*. Edited by John Vickers. Nashville: Kingswood Books, 2005.

Colby, Frederick S. *Introduction, Notes and Commentary on the Subtleties of the Ascension: Early Sayings on Muhammad's Heavenly Journey*. Louisville, KY: Fons Vitae, 2006.

Colless, Brian E., trans. *The Wisdom of the Pearlers: An Anthology of Syriac Christian Mysticism*. Kalamazoo, MI: Cistercian, 2008.

Collins, John J. "Genre, Ideology and Social Movements in Jewish Apocalypticism." In *Mysteries and Revelations: Apocalyptic Studies since the Uppsala Colloquium* (Journal for the Study of the Pseudopigrapha Supplement Series 9), edited by John J. Collins and James H. Charlesworth, 11–32. Sheffield: Sheffield Academic Press, 1991.

———. "The Place of Apocalypticism in the Religion of Israel." In *Ancient Israelite Religion: Essays in Honor of Frank Moore Cross*, edited by Patrick D. Miller, Jr., Paul D. Hanson and S. Dean McBride, 539–58. Philadelphia: Fortress Press, 1987.

———. "A Throne in the Heavens: Apotheosis in pre-Christian Judaism." In *Death, Ecstasy and Other Worldly Journeys*, edited by John J. Collins and Michael Fishbane, 15–39. Albany, NY: SUNY Press, 1995.

Collins, Kenneth J. *John Wesley: A Theological Journey*. Nashville: Abingdon, 2003.

———. "The Influence of Early German Pietism on John Wesley." *The Covenant Quarterly* 48 (1990) 23–42.

———. "John Wesley's Critical Appropriation of Tradition in His Practical Theology." *Wesleyan Theological Journal* 35.2 (2000) 69–90.

———. *The Theology of John Wesley: Holy Love and the Shape of Grace*. Nashville: Abingdon, 2007.

Copenhaver, Brian P., ed. and trans. *Hermetica: The Greek Corpus Hermeticum and the Latin Asclepius in a New English Translation, with Notes and Introduction*. Cambridge: Cambridge University Press, 1992.

Cragg, Kenneth. "Incarnatus non est: The Qur'an and Christology." In *Jesus and the Incarnation: Relfections of Christians from Islamic Contexts*, edited by David Emmanuel Singh, 21–29. Oxford: Regnum, 2011.

Cumming, Joseph L. "Sifāt al-Dhāt in al-Ash'arī's Doctrine of God and Possible Christian Parallels." In *Toward Respectful Understanding & Witness Among Muslim: Essays in Honor of J. Dudley Woodberry*, edited by Evelyne A. Reisacher, 111–45. Pasadena, CA: William Carey, 2012.

Dalman, Gustaf. *Aramäisch-neuhebräisches Handwörterbuch zu Targum, Tal und Midrasch* Göttingen: E. Pfeiffer, 1938.

Davila, James R. *Descenders to the Chariot: The People Behind the Hekhalot Literature (Supplements to the Journal for the Study of Judaism)*. Leiden: Brill Academic, 2001.

———. "The He khalot Literature and Shamanism." In *Society of Biblical Literature, 1994 Seminar Papers*, edited by Eugine H. Lovering, Jr., 767–89. Atlanta: Scholars, 1994.

DeConick, April D. *The Original Gospel of Thomas in Translation, with Commentary and New English Translation of the Complete Gospel*. London: T. & T. Clark, 2006.

———. *Recovering the Original Gospel of Thomas: A History of the Gospel and Its Growth*. London: T. & T. Clark International, 2005.

———. *Seek to See Him: Ascent & Vision Mysticism in the Gospel of Thomas*. Leiden: E. J. Brill, 1996.

———. *Voices of the Mystics: Early Christian Discourse in the Gospels of John Thomas and Other Ancient Christian Literature*. Sheffield: Sheffield Academic, 2001.

———. "What is Early Jewish and Christian Mysticism?" In *Paradise Now: Essays on Early Jewish and Christian Mysticism*, edited by April D. DeConick, 1–24. Atlanta: Society of Biblical Literature, 2006.

DeConick, April D. and Jarle Fossum. "Stripped Before God: A New Interpretation of Logion 37 in the Gospel of Thomas." *Vigiliae Christianae* 45 (1991) 123–50.

Dehqani-Tafti, Hassan. *Christ and Christianity in Persian Poetry*. London: Sohrab Books, 1986. Online: http://www.farsinet.com/ChristInPersianPoetry/.

DeMaris, Richard E. *The Colossian Controversy: Wisdom in Dispute at Colossae*. Journal for the Study of the New Testament, Supplementary Series 96. Sheffield, UK: Sheffield Academic, 1994.

De Souza, Luís Wesley. "'The Wisdom of God in Creation': Mission and the Wesleyan Pentalateral." In *Global Good News: Mission in a New Context*, edited by Howard A. Snyder, 138–52. Nashville: Abingdon, 2001.

Donner, Fred M. *Narratives of Islamic Beginnings: The Beginnings of Islamic Historical Writing*. Princeton: Darwin, 1998.

Dörries, Hermann. *Symeon von Mesopotamien: Die Überlieferung des messalianischen Makarios-Schriften*. Leipzig: J.C. Hinrichs Verlag, 1941.

Dörries, Hermann, Erich Klostermann, and Matthias Kroeger, eds. *Die 50 Geistlichen Homilien des Makarios*. Berlin: Walter de Gruyter & Co., 1964.

Drijvers, Henrik Jan Willem. "Facts and Problems in Early Syriac Christianity." *The Second Century* 2.3 (1982) 157–75.

Dunn, James D. G. "Jesus, Table-Fellowship and Qumran." In *Jesus and the Dead Sea Scrolls*, edited by James H. Charlesworth, 254–72. The Anchor Bible Reference Library. New York: Doubleday, 1992.

Durkheim, Emile. *The Elementary Forms of Religious Life*. Translated by Karen E. Fields. New York: Free Press, 1995.

Eaton, Richard M. *The Rise of Islam and the Bengal Frontier 1204–1760*. Delhi: Oxford University Press, 1997.

Eliade, Mircea. *The Sacred and the Profane: The Nature of Religion*. Translated by Willard R. Trask. San Diego: Harvest/HBJ Book, 1959.

———. *Shamanism: Archaic Techniques of Ecstasy* (Bollingen Series). Translated by Willard R. Trask. Priceton: Princeton University Press, 1964.

Elior, Rachel. "The Emergence of the Mystical Traditions of the *Merkabah*." In *Paradise Now: Essays on Early Jewish and Christian Mysticism*, edited by April D. DeConick, 83–103. Atlanta: Society of Biblical Literature, 2006.

El Cheikh, Nadia Maria. *Byzantium Viewed by the Arabs*. Cambridge, MA: Harvard Center for Middle Eastern Studies, 2004.

Erb, Peter. Introduction to *True Christianity*. New York: Paulist, 1979.
Ernst, Carl W. Foreword to *Revealing the Mystery (Kashf al-Mahjub)* by 'Alī ibn 'Uthmān al-Hujwīrī. Accord, NY: Pīr, 1999.
———. *The Shambhala Guide to Sufism*. Boston & London: Shambhala, 1997.
———. *Words of Ecstasy in Sufism*. Albany, NY: SUNY Press, 1985.
Eskola, Timo. *Messiah and the Throne*. Tübingen: Mohr Siebeck, 2001.
Evans, Craig A. "The Colossian Mystics." *Biblica* 62 (1982) 188–205.
Evelyn-White, Hugh G. *The Sayings of Jesus from Oxyrhynchus*. Cambridge: Cambridge University Press, 1920.
Finlan, Stephen. "Can We Speak of Theosis in Paul?" In *Partakers of the Divine Nature: The History and Development of Deification in the Christian Traditions*, edited by Michael J. Christensen and Jeffery A. Wittung, 68–80. Grand Rapids: Baker Academic, 2007.
———. "Second Peter's Notion of Divine Participation." In *Theōsis: Deification in Christian Theology*, edited by Stephen Finlan and Vladimir Kharlamov, 32–50. Eugene, OR: Pickwick, 2006.
Fisch, S. *Ezekiel: Hebrew Text & English Translation with an Introduction and a Commentary*. London & Bournemouth: Socino, 1950.
Fischel, Henry A. "The Uses of Sorites (Climax, Graditio) in the Tannaitic Period." *Hebrew Union College Annual* 44 (1973) 119–51.
Fletcher, John. "An Essay on the Doctrine of the New Birth." *The Asbury Theological Journal* 53.1 (1998) 35–56.
———. *The Works of the Rev. John Fletcher*, 4 vols. New York: T. Mason and G. Lane, 1836.
Fletcher-Louis, Crispin H. T. "Heavenly Ascent or Incarnational Presence? A Revisionist Reading of the *Songs of the Sabbath Sacrifice*." In *Society of Biblical Literature 1998 Seminar Papers*. 2 vols. 1.367–99. Atlanta: Scholars, 1998.
Flint, Peter. "Jesus and the Dead Sea Scrolls." In *The Historical Jesus in Context*, edited by Amy-Jill Levine, Dale C. Allison, Jr., and John Dominic Crossan, 110–31. Princeton: Princeton University Press, 2006.
Flusser, David. "The Parable of the Unjust Steward: Jesus' Criticism of the Essenes." In *Jesus and the Dead Sea Scrolls*. The Anchor Bible Reference Library. Edited by James H. Charlesworth, 176–97. New York: Doubleday, 1992.
Ford, J. Massyngberde. *Revelation: A New Translation with Introduction and Commentary*. The Anchor Bible 38. Garden City, NY: Doubleday, 1975.
Fossum, Jarl E. *The Image of the Invisible God: Essays on the influence of Jewish Mysticism on Early Christology*. Göttingen: Vandenhoeck & Ruprecht, 1995.
Francis, Fred O. "Humility and Angelic Worship in Col 2:18." In *Conflict at Colossae: A Problem in the Interpretation Early Christianity, Illustrated by Selected Modern Studies*, edited by Fred O. Francis and Wayne A. Meeks, 163–95. Cambridge, MA: Society of Biblical Literature, 1974.
French, R. M., trans. *The Way of a Pilgrim and the Pilgrim Continues His Way*. San Francisco: HarperOne, 1991.
Friedlander, Shems. *Rumi and the Whirling Dervishes*. New York: Parabola, 2003.
Furnish, Victor Paul. *II Corinthians*. The Anchor Bible 32A. Garden City, NY: Doubleday, 1984.
Gairdner, W. H. T. "First Study." In *The Vital Forces of Christianity and Islam*, edited by J. H. Oldham, 11–43. London: Oxford University Press, 1915.

Bibliography

———. *The Rebuke of Islam*. London: United Council for Missionary Education, 1920.
García Martínez, Florentino, and Wilfred G. E. Watson, trans. *The Dead Sea Scrolls Translated: The Qumran Texts in English*. Grand Rapids: Eerdmans, 1996.
Gardet, Louis. "Dhikr." In *The Encyclopedia of Islam, New Edition*, Vol. 2. Edited by B. Lewis, Ch. Pellat and J. Schacht, 223–27. Leiden, Netherlands: E. J. Brill, 1965.
———. "Fikr." In *The Encyclopedia of Islam, New Edition*, vol. 2, edited by B. Lewis, Ch. Pellat and J. Schacht, 891–92. Leiden, Netherlands: E. J. Brill, 1965.
Ghazālī, Abū Hāmid al- ("Al-Ghazzali"). *Deliverance from Error: Five Key Texts Including His Spiritual Autobiography, al-Munqidh min al-Dalal* (2nd ed). Translated by R. J. McCarthy. Louisville: Fons Vitae, 2004.
———. *Fadā'ih al-Bātiniyya wa Fadā'il al-Mustazhiriyya*. Edited by A. Badawi. Cairo: al-Dār al-Qawmiyya, 1964.
———. *Fadā'ih al-Bātiniyya wa Fadā'il al-Mustazhiriyya*. Edited by A. Badawi. Cairo: al-Dār al-Qawmiyya, 1964.
———. "A *Fatwā* of al-Ghazzālī against the Esoteric Sects." In *A Reader on Islam: Passages from Standard Arabic Writings Illustrative of the Beliefs and Practices of Muslims*, edited and translated by Arthur Jeffery, 254–79. The Hague, Netherlands: Mouton, 1962.
———. *Ghazālī: The Ninety-NineBeautiful Names of God*. Translated by David B. Burrell and Nazih Daher. Cambridge, UK: The Islamic Texts Society, 1995.
———. *Al-Ghazālī's Ihya' 'Ulūm ad-Dīn: Revitalisation of the Sciences of Religion* (Abridged by Abd el Salam Haroun). 2 vols. Revised and Translated by Ahmad A. Zidan. Cairo: Islamic, 1997.
———. *Mishkât Al-Anwar ("The Niche for Lights")*. Translated by W. H. T. Gairdner. London: Royal Asiatic Society, 1924.
Gieschen, Charles A. *Angelomorphic Christology: Antecedents and Early Evidence*. Leiden: Brill, 1998.
———. "The Lamb (Not the Man) on the Divine Throne." In *Israel's God and Rebecca's Children: Christology and Community in Early Judaism and Christianity*, edited by David B. Capes, April D. DeConick, Helen K. Bond, and Troy Miller, 227–43. Waco, TX: Baylor University Press, 2007.
Gilbert, Gary. "Acts of the Apostles: Introduction and Annotations." In *The Jewish Annotated New Testament*, edited by Amy-Jill Levine and Marc Zvi Brettler, 197–252. New York: Oxford University Press, 2011.
Gine, Pratap Chandra. Νόμος *In Context: Philo, Galatians and the Bengali Bible*. Delhi: ISPCK, 2001.
Ginther, James R. "Laudat Sensum et Significationem: Robert Grosseteste on the Four Senses of Scripture." In *With Reverence for the Word: Medieval Scriptural Exegesis in Judaism, Christianity, and Islam*, edited by Jane Dammen McAuliffe, Barry D. Walfish, and Joseph W. Goering, 237–55. New York: Oxford University Press, 2003.
Glassé, Cyril. *The Concise Encyclopedia of Islam* (rev. ed.). London: Stacey International, 2002.
Glasson, T. Francis. *Greek Influence in Jewish Eschatology*. London: SPCK, 1961.
Goldziher, Ignaz. *Introduction to Islamic Theology and Law*. Translated by Andras and Ruth Hamori. Princeton: Princeton University Press, 1981.
———. *Muslim Studies*. Translated by C. R. Barber and S. M. Stern. Chicago: Aldine, 1966.

Golitzin, Alexander. "Recovering the 'Glory of Adam': 'Divine Light' Traditions in the Dead Sea Scrolls and the Christian Ascetical Literature of Fourth-Century Syro Mesopotamia." Paper given at the International Conference on the Dead Sea Scrolls, St. Andrews, Scotland, on June 28, 2001.

———. Review of *Holiness: Rabbinic Judaism and the Greco-Roman World*, by Hannah K. Harrington. *St. Vladamir's Theological Quarterly* 43 (2003) 461–68.

———. "A Testimony to Christianity as Transfiguration: The Macarian Homilies and Orthodox Spirituality." In *Orthodox and Wesleyan Spirituality*, edited by S. T. Kimbrough, Jr., 129–56. Crestwood, NY: St. Vladimir's Seminary Press, 2002.

Gregory the Great. *Forty Gospel Homilies*. Cistercian Studies 123. Translated by Dom David Hurst. Kalamazoo, MI: Cistercian, 1990.

Grelot, Pierre. "La Géographie Mythique d'Hénoch et ses Sources Orientales." *Revue Biblique* 65 (1958) 33–69.

Griffith, Sidney H. "The Monks of Palestine and the Growth of Christian Literature in Arabic." *The Muslim World* 78.1 (1988) 1–28.

Grillmeier, Aloys. *Christ in Christian Tradition. Volume 1: From the Apostolic Age to Chalcedon*. Translated by John Bowden. Atlanta: John Knox, 1975.

Gruenwald, Ithamar. *The Apocalyptic and Merkavah Mysticism*. Leiden: E. J. Brill, 1980.

———. *From Apocalypticism to Gnosticism*. Frankfurt am Main: Verlag Peter Lang, 1988.

——— "Reflections on the Nature and Origins of Jewish Mysticism." In *Gershom Scholem's Major Trends in Jewish Mysticism: 50 Years After*, edited by Peter Schäfer and Joseph Dan, 25–48. Tübingen: J. C. B. Mohr, 1993.

Hall, Christopher A. *Reading Scripture with the Church Fathers*. Downers Grove, IL: IVP Academic, 1998.

Hallāj, Mansūr al-. *The Tawasin*. Translated by Aisha al-Tarjumana. Berkeley: Diwan, 1974.

Hallaq, Wael B. "Islamic Law: History and Transformation." In *The New Cambridge History of Islam*, edited by Robert Irwin, 142–83. Cambridge: Cambridge University Press, 2010.

Halperin, David J. *The Faces of the Chariot*. Tübingen: J. C. B. Mohr, 1988.

Hames, Harvey J. *The Art of Conversion: Christianity & Kabbalah in the Thirteenth Century*. Leiden: Brill, 2000.

Hanson, Paul D. "Jewish Apocalyptic against its Near Eastern Environment." *Revue Biblique* 78 (1971) 31–58.

Haq, Muhammad Enamul. *A History of Sufi-ism in Bengal*. Dhaka: Asiatic Society of Bangladesh, 1975.

Harrak, Amir. Introduction to *The Acts of Mār Mārī the Apostle*. Atlanta: Society for Biblical Literature, 2005.

Harris, J. Rendel. *The Doctrine of Immortality in the Odes of Solomon*. London: Hodder & Stoughton, 1909.

Harris, Rendel, and Alphonse Mingana. *The Odes and Psalms of Solomon, 2 Vols.* Manchester, UK: The University Press, 1920.

Hasan, Masoodul. *Hazrat Data Ganj Bakhsh: A Spiritual Biography*. Lahore: Hazrat Data Ganj Bakhsh Academy, 1971.

Haywood, Thomas. Preface to *Primitive Morality, or the Spiritual Homilies of St. Macarius the Egyptian*. London: W. Taylor, 1721.

Hiebert, Paul G. "Conversion, Culture and Cognitive Categories." *Gospel in Context* 1.4 (1978) 24–29.
Heiler, Friedrich. *Ersheinungsformen und Wesen der Religion.* Stuttgart: W. Kohlhammer, 1961.
Heitzenrater, Richard P. "John Wesley's Reading of, and References to, the Early Church Fathers." In *Orthodox and Wesleyan Spirituality*, edited by S. T. Kimbrough, Jr., 25–32. Crestwood, NY: St. Vladamir's Seminary Press, 2002.
Hempton, David. *Methodism: Empire of the Spirit.* New Haven: Yale University Press, 2005.
Herrin, Nicholas. *Thomas: The Other Gospel.* Louisville: Westminster John Knox, 2007.
Heschel, Abraham Joshua. *Heavenly Torah as Refracted Through the Generations.* Edited and translated by Gordon Tucker. New York: Continuum, 2006.
Hiebert, Paul G. "Critical Contextualization." *Missiology: An International Review* 12.3 (1984) 287–96.
Himmelfarb, Martha. "The Parting of the Ways Reconsidered: Diversity in Judaism and Jewish-Christian Relations in the Roman Empire: 'A Jewish Perspective'." In *Interwoven Destinies: Jews and Christians Through the Ages*, edited by Eugene J. Fisher, 47–61. New York: Paulist, 1993.
———. "The Practice of Ascent in the Ancient Mediterranean World." In *Death, Ecstasy and Other Worldly Journeys*, edited by John J. Collins and Michael Fishbane, 123–37. Albany, NY: SUNY Press, 1995.
Horovitz, Josef. "Muhammeds Himmelfahrt." *Der Islam* 9 (1919) 159–83.
Horovitz, Haym S., and Israel A. Rabin, ed. *Mechiltā de-Rabbi Ishmael cum Variis Lectionibus et Adnotationibus.* Jerusalem: Wahrmann, 1970.
Howe, Mary Blye. *Sitting with Sufis: A Christian Experience of Learning Sufism.* Brewster, MA: Paraclete, 2005.
Hoyland, Robert G., ed. *Seeing Islam as Others Saw It: A Survey and Evaluation of Christian, Jewish and Zoroastrian Writings on Early Islam.* Princeton: Darwin, 1997.
Huda, Qamar-ul. "Celebrating Death and Engaging in Texts at Dātā Ganj Bakhsh's ', Urs." *The Muslim World* 90.3–4 (2000) 377–94.
Hughes, Thomas Patrick. *A Dictionary of Islam.* London: W. H. Allyn, 1895.
Hujwīrī, 'Alī ibn 'Uthmān al-Jullabi al-. *Kashf al-Mahjūb.* Edited by V. A. Zhukovsky. Tehran: Amīr Kabīr, 1957.
———. *The Kashful Mahjub. "Unveiling the Veiled": The Earliest Persian Treatise on Sufism.* Translated by Wahid Baksh Rabbani. Kuala Lumpur, Malaysia: A. S. Noordeen, 2000.
———. *Revelation of the Mystery (Kashf al-Mahjub).* Translated by Reynold A. Nicholson. Accord, NY: Pīr, 1999.
———. "The Revelation of Realities Veiled (*Kashf al-Mahjūb*) [Excerpt]." Translated by John Renard. In *Knowledge of God in Classical Sufism: Foundations of Islamic Mystical Theology.* New York: Paulist, 2004.
Ibn Ishaq. *The Life of Muhammad: A Translation of Ibn Ishaq's Sirat Rasul Allah.* Translated by Alfred Guillaume. Karachi: Oxford University Press, 1982.
Idel, Moshe. *Ascensions on High in Jewish Mysticism: Pillars, Lines, Ladders.* Budapest: Central European University Press, 2005.
———. *Kabbalah: New Perspectives.* New Haven: Yale University Press, 1988.
———. *Messianic Mystics.* New Haven: Yale University Press, 1998.

Idris, Mohammad, and Mughees Ahmed. "Role of Mysticism in Socio-Political Change in Sub-Continent: A Case Study of Ali Hujwiri's Impact on History of the Punjab." *Berkeley Journal of Social Sciences* 1.9 (2011) 1–13. Online: http://www.berkeleyjournalofsocialsciences.com/Sep-Oct%201.pdf.

Iqbal, Muhammad. *The Secrets of the Self (Asrār-I Khudī)*. Translated by Reynold A. Nicholson. London: Macmillan, 1920.

Isaac, E., trans. "1 (Ethiopic Apocalypse of) Enoch, A New Translation and Introduction." In *The Old Testament Pseudopigrapha, Vol. 1: Apocalyptic Literature and Testaments*, edited by James H. Charlesworth, 5–90. New York: Doubleday, 1983.

Iskandarī, Ibn 'Ātā ' Allāh al-. *The Key to Salvation: A Sufi Manual of Invocation*. Translated by Mary Ann Khory Danner. Cambridge, UK: Islamic Texts Society, 1996.

Jackson, Paul. Introduction and Notes to *The Hundred Letters*, by Sharafuddin Maneri. New York: Paulist, 1980.

———. Introduction to *In Quest of God: Maneri's Second Collection of 150 Letters*, by Sharafuddin Maneri. Anand, Gujarat. India: Gujarat Sahitya Prakash, 2004.

———. "The Mystical Dimension." In *The Muslims of India: Beliefs and Practices*, edited by Paul Jackson, 254–84. Bangalore: Theological Publications in India, 1988.

———. "Sheikh Sharafuddin Maneri's Use of the Quran in his Maktubat-i Sadi." In *Islam in India: Studies and Commentaries. Volume 1: The Akbar Mission and Miscellaneous Studies*, edited by Christian W. Troll, 33–42. New Delhi: Vikas, 1987.

———. "Traditions of Spiritual Guidance. Spiritual Guidance in Islam, a Case Study: Sharafuddin Maneri." *The Way* 27.2 (1987) 144–52.

Jaeger, Werner. *Two Rediscovered Works of Ancient Christian Literature: Gregory of Nyssa and Macarius*. Leiden: E. J. Brill, 1954.

James, William. *The Varieties of Religious Experience*. New York: Longmans, Green, 1902.

Jeffery, Arthur. "Christianity in South Arabia." *Anglican Theological Review* 28.3 (1945) 185–205.

———. Introduction and Notes to *A Reader on Islam: Passages from Standard Arabic Writings Illustrative of the Beliefs and Practices of Muslims*. Edited and Translated by Arthur Jeffery. 'S-Gravenhage, Netherlands: Mouton, 1962.

Jenkins, Philip. "Sufi Rising." *Boston Globe*, January 25, 2009.

Jerome. "The Life of St. Paul the First Hermit." In *The Desert Fathers*. The Fontana Library. Translated by Helen Waddell, 43–51. London: Collins, 1965.

Johnson, Luke Timothy. *Religious Experience in Early Christianity*. Minneapolis: Fortress, 1998.

Kalābādhi, Abū Bakr al-. *The Doctrine of the Sūfīs (Kitāb al-Ta'arruf li-madhhab ahl al-tasawwuf)*. Translated by A. J. Arberry. Cambridge: Cambridge University Press, 1977.

Kanagaraj, Jey J. *"Mysticism" in the Gospel of John: An Inquiry into its Background*. Sheffield: Sheffield Academic, 1998.

Karamustafa, Ahmet T. *Sufism: The Formative Period*. Berkeley, CA: University of California Press, 2007.

Käsemann, Ernst. "Eine Apologie der urchristlichen Eschatologie." *Zeitschrift für Theologie und Kirche* 49 (1952) 272–96.

———. "An Apologia for Primitive Christian Eschatology." In *Essays on New Testament Themes*, translated by W. J. Montague, 169–95. London: SCM, 1964.

Kateregga, Badru D., and David W. Shenk. *A Muslim and a Christian in Dialogue*. Harrisonburg, VA: Herald, 1980.

Katz, Steven T. "Mysticism and the Interpretation of Sacred Scripture." In *Mysticism and Sacred Scripture*, edited by Steven T. Katz, 7–67. Oxford: Oxford University Press, 2000.

Kee, H. C., trans. "Testaments of the Twelve Patriarchs." In *The Old Testament Pseudopigrapha, Vol. 1: Apocalyptic Literature and Testaments* (The Anchor Bible Reference Library), edited by James H. Charlesworth, 775–828. New York: Doubleday, 1985.

Keener, Craig S. *1–2 Corinthians*. The New Cambridge Bible Commentary. New York: Cambridge University Press. 2005.

———. *The Gospel of John: A Commentary* (2 vols). Peabody, MA: Hendrickson, 2003.

———. *The Spirit in the Gospels and Acts: Divine Purity and Power*. Peabody, MA: Hendrickson, 1997.

———. "The Tabernacle and Contextual Worship." *The Asbury Journal* 67.1 (2012) 127–38.

Kelly, J. N. D. *Early Christian Doctrines*. New York: Harper & Row, 1978.

Khan, Inayat. *The Way of Illumination. The Sufi Message*, Vol. 1. Delhi: Motilal Banarsidass, 1988.

Kittel, Gerhard, ed. *Theological Dictionary of the New Testament*. Translated by Geoffrey W. Bromiley. 10 vols. Grand Rapids: Eerdmans, 1964.

Klostermann, Erich, and Heinz Berthold, ed. *Neue Homilien eds Makarios/Symeon: Aus Typus III*. Berlin: Akademie-Verlag, 1961.

Knibb, M. A., trans. "Martyrdom and Ascension of Isaiah." In *The Old Testament Pseudopigrapha, Vol. 1: Apocalyptic Literature and Testaments* (The Anchor Bible Reference Library), edited by James H. Charlesworth, 143–76. New York: Doubleday, 1985.

Knight, Michael Muhammad. *Journey to the End of Islam*. Berkeley, CA: Soft Skull, 2009.

Kohler, Kaufmann. "Memra." *The Jewish Encyclopedia*, Vol. 8. Edited by I. Singer, 464–65. New York: Funk and Wagnalls, 1904.

———. "Merkabah." *The Jewish Encyclopedia*, Vol. 8. Edited by I. Singer, 498–500 New York: Funk and Wagnalls, 1904.

Kurowski, Mark T. "The First Step toward Grace: John Wesley's Use of the Spiritual Homilies of Macarius the Great." *Methodist History* 36.2 (1998) 113–24.

Kūfi, Ibn A'tham al-. *Kitāb al-futūh*. Haydarābād al-Dakan (Hyderabad, India): Matbaʻat Majlis Dāi'rat al-Maʻārif al-ʻUthmānīyah, 1968. Quoted in Nadia Maria El Cheikh, *Byzantium Viewed by the Arabs*. Cambridge, MA: Harvard Center for Middle Eastern Studies, 2004.

Kvanvig, Helge. *Roots of Apocalyptic: The Mesopotamian Background of the Enoch Figure and of the Son of Man*. WMANT 61; Neukirchen-Vluyn, Germany: Neukirchener Verlag, 1988.

Lambdin, Thomas O., trans. *The Gospel of Thomas*. In *The Nag Hammadi Library*, edited by James M. Robinson, 124–38. Leiden: Brill, 1996.

Lane, Edward William. *Arabic-English Lexicon*. 8 vols. London: Willams & Norgate, 1863.

Lawrence, Bruce B. Foreword to *The Hundred Letters*, by Sharafuddin Maneri. New York: Paulist. 1980.

———. *Notes from a Distant Flute: The Extant Literature of pre-Mughal Indian Sufism*. Tehran: Imperial Iranian Academy of Philosophy, 1978.

Laws, Sophie. *In the Light of the Lamb: Imagery, Parody and Theology in the Apocalypse of John*. Good News Studies 31. Wilmington, DE: Michael Glazier, 1988.

Lawson, Todd. *The Crucifixion and the Qur'ān: A Study in the History of Muslim Thought*. Oxford: Oneworld, 2009.

Lee, Hoo-Jung. "The Doctrine of New Creation in the Theology of John Wesley." PhD diss., Emory University, 1991.

———. "Wesley and Macarius on the Life of Prayer." Presentation, the 12th Oxford Institute of Methodist Theological Studies, Christ Church College, Oxford University, August 12–21, 2007.

Lenz, John R. "Deification of the Philosopher in Classical Greece." In *Partakers of the Divine Nature: The History and Development of Deification in the Christian Traditions*, edited by Michael J. Christensen and Jeffrey A. Wittung, 47–67. Grand Rapids, MI: Baker Academic, 2007.

Levertoff, Paul Phillip. *Meal of the Holy King*. London: Hebrew-Christian Church, 1925.

Levey, Samson H. "Akiba: Sage in Search of the Messiah: A Closer Look." *Judaism* 41 (1992) 334–45.

———, trans. *The Targum of Ezekiel: Translated, with a Critical Introduction, Apparatus and Notes*. The Aramaic Bible 13. Wilmington, DE: Michael Glazier, 1987.

Levine, Amy-Jill. *The Misunderstood Jew: The Church and the Scandal of the Jewish Jesus*. New York: HarperOne, 2006.

Levy, Jacob. *Wörterbuch über die Talmudim und Midraschim: nebst Beiträgen*. 2 vols. Darmstadt, Wissenschaftliche Buchgesellschaft, 1963.

Lieb, Michael. *The Visionary Mode: Biblical Prophecy, Hermeneutics, and Cultural Change*. Ithaca, NY: Cornell University Press, 1991.

Lightfoot, J. B. *St. Paul's Epistles to the Colossians and to Philemon: A Revised Text*. London: Macmillan, 1875.

Lincoln, Andrew T. *Ephesians*. The Word Biblical Commentary 42. Dallas: Word, 1990.

Litwa, M. David. "2 Corinthians 3:18 and its Implications for Theosis." *Journal of Theological Interpretation* 2.1 (2008) 117–33.

Lossky, Vladamir. *Mystical Theology of the Eastern Church*. London: James Clarke, 1957.

"Macarius of Egypt." *The Homilies of Macarius*. A Christian Library 1, edited by John Wesley. London: T. Cordeux, 1819. Online: http://wesley.nnu.edu/john_wesley/christian_library/vol1/CL1Part2.htm.

"Macarius the Egyptian." *Primitive Morality, or the Spiritual Homilies of St. Macarius the Egyptian*. Translated by Thomas Haywood. London: W. Taylor, 1721.

"Macarius the Egyptian." *The Fifty Spiritual Homilies of St. Macarius the Egyptian*. Translated by Arthur J. Mason. Translations of Christian Literature. London: SPCK, 1921.

Macdonald, Duncan Black. *Aspects of Islam*. New York: Macmillan, 1911.

Maddox, Randy. *Responsible Grace: John Wesley's Practical Theology*. Nashville: Kingswood, 1994.

———. "The Wondrous Love of God: Wesleyan Emphases on the Atonement." Theta Phi Lecture, Asbury Theological Seminary, Wilmore, KY. March 12, 2009.

Mallouhi, Christine A. *Waging Peace on Islam*. Downers Grove, IL: InterVarsity, 2000.

Maloney, George A. Introduction and Notes to *The Fifty Spiritual Homilies and the Great Letter*, by Pseudo-Macarius. Mahwah, NJ: Paulist, 1992.

Maneri, Sharafuddin. *The Hundred Letters*. Translated by Paul Jackson. New York: Paulist, 1980.

———. *Letters from a Sufi Teacher*. Translated by Bhaijnath Singh. Benaras and London: Theosophical Publishing Society, 2009.

———. *Maktubate Do Sadī* [Another Hundred Letters]. Translated by A. K. M. Fajlur Rahman Munshi. Dhaka: Bangladesh Taj, 2011.

———. *Maktubate Sadī* [One Hundred Letters]. Translated by A. K. M. Fajlur Rahman Munshi. Dhaka: Bangladesh Taj, 2007.

———. *A Mine of Meaning: Ma'din ul-Ma'ani*. Translated by Paul Jackson. Louisville, KY: Fons Vitae, 2012.

———. *In Quest of God: Maneri's Second Collection of 150 Letters*. Translated by Paul Jackson. Anand, Gujarat, India: Gujarat Sahitya Prakash, 2004.

Margoliouth, David. *Mohammed and the Rise of Islam*. New York: G. P. Putnam's Sons, 1905.

Martin, Ralph P. *2 Corinthians*. Word Biblical Commentary 40. Dallas: Word, 1986.

Martyn, Henry. *The Journal and Letters of Rev. Henry Martyn*. 2 vols. Edited by S. Wilberforce. London: R. B. Seeley and W. Burnside, 1982.

Massignon, Louis. *The Passion of al-Hallāj: Mystic and Martyr of Islam*. 4 vols. Translated by Herbert Mason. Princeton: Princeton University Press, 1982.

Mayer, Farhana. Introduction and Notes to *Spiritual Gems: The Mystical Qur'ān Commentary Ascribed to Ja'far al-Sādiq as contained in Sulamī's Haqā'iq al-Tafsīr from the text of Paul Nwyia*. Louisville, KY: Fons Vitae, 2011.

Mayer, Toby. "Theology and Sufism." In *The Cambridge Companion to Classical Islamic Theology*, edited by Tim Winter, 258–87. Cambridge, UK: Cambridge University Press, 2008.

McAuliffe, Jane Dammen. "An Introduction to Medieval Interpretation of the Qur'ān." In *With Reverence for the Word: Medieval Scriptural Exegesis in Judaism, Christianity, and Islam*, edited by Jane Dammen McAuliffe, Barry D. Walfish, and Joseph W. Goering, 311–19. New York: Oxford University Press, 2003.

———. "The Tasks and Traditions of Interpretation." In *The Cambridge Companion to the Qur'an*, edited by Jane Dammen McAuliffe, 181–209. New York: Cambridge University Press, 2006.

McCurry, Don. *Healing the Broken Family of Abraham: New Life for Muslims*. Colorado Springs: Ministries to Muslims, 2001.

McGuckin, J. A. "The Strategic Adaptation of Deification Among the Cappadocians." In *Partakers of the Divine Nature: The History and Development of Deification in the Christian Traditions*, edited by Michael J. Christensen and Jeffrey A. Wittung, 95–114. Grand Rapids: Baker Academic, 2007.

McNamara, Martin. *Targum and Testament Revisited: Aramaic Paraphrases of the Hebrew Bible* (2nd ed.). Grand Rapids: Eerdmans, 2010.

———, trans. *Targum Neofiti 1: Exodus and Targum Pseudo-Jonathan: Exodus*. The Aramaic Bible 2. Collegeville, MN: Liturgical, 1994.

McQuilkin, Robertson. "Lost." In *Perspectives on the World Christian Movement: A Reader* (3rd ed.), edited by Ralph D. Winter and Steven J. Hawthorne, 156–61. Pasadena, CA: William Carey, 1999.

McVicker, Mary. "*Matam* and Emerging Vitality: Community, Ritual and Commemoration in a South Asian Muslim Sect." In *Jesus and the Incarnation: Reflections of Christians from Islamic Contexts*, edited by David Emmanuel Singh, 113–26. Oxford: Regnum, 2011.

Menzies, Glen. "Pre-Lukan Occurences of the Phrase 'Tongue(s) of Fire.'" *Pneuma: The Journal of the Society for Pentecostal Studies* 22.1 (2000) 27–60.

Merkur, Dan. "Stages of Ascension in Hermetic Rebirth." *Esoterica* 1(1999) 79–96.

———. "Unitive Experiences and the State of Trance." In *Mystical Union in Judaism, Christianity and Islam*, edited by Moshe Idel and Bernard McGinn, 125–53. New York: Continuum, 1996.

Michel, Thomas F. *A Christian View of Islam: Essays on Dialogue*. Maryknoll, NY: Orbis, 2010.

Milik, J. T. "Problèmes de la Littérature Hénoquique a la Lumière de Fragments Araméens de Qumrân." *Harvard Theological Review* 64 (1971) 333–78.

Moffett, Samuel Hugh. *A History of Christianity in Asia: Beginnings to 1500*. Maryknoll, NY: Orbis, 1998.

Mojaddedi, Jawid A. "Getting Drunk with Abū Yazīd or Staying Sober with Junayd: The Creation of a Popular Typology of Sufism." *Bulletin of the School of Oriental and African Studies* 66.1 (2003) 1–13.

———. "Kašf al-Mahjub of Hojviri." *Encyclopaedia Iranica*, Vol. XV. Edited by Ehsan Yarshater, 664–66. New York: Encyclopedia Iranica Foundation, 2011.

Moore, Edward. "'Likeness to God as Far as Possible': Deification Doctrine in Iamblicus and Three Eastern Christian Fathers." *Theandros* 3.5 (2005). Online: http://web.archive.org/web/20080104090654/http://www.theandros.com/iamblichus.html.

Moore, G. F. *Judaism in the First Centuries of the Christian Era: The Age of the Tannaim*. Cambridge: Harvard University Press, 1954.

Morin, Harry. "Sufism and 'the Beloved.'" *Intercede* 28.3 (2012) 1, 4–6.

Murray, Robert. *Symbols of Church and Kingdom: A Study in Early Syriac Tradition*. Cambridge: Cambridge University Press, 1975.

Muck, Terry C. "John Wesley's Eighteenth-Century Contributions to the Twenty-First-Century Theology of Religions." In *World Mission in the Wesleyan Spirit*, edited by Darrell L. Whiteman and Gerald H. Anderson, 93–101. Franklin, TN: Providence House, 2009.

———. "The Third Moment of Muslim Witness: John Wesley Had It Right." *The Asbury Journal* 61.1 (2006) 83–95.

Muck, Terry, and Frances S. Adeney. *Christianity Encountering World Religions: The Practice of Mission in the Twenty-First Century*. Grand Rapids: Baker Academic, 2009.

Murata, Sachiko, and William C. Chittick. *The Vision of Islam*. St. Paul, MN: Paragon, 1994.

Musk, Bill. *Kissing Cousins? Christians and Muslims Face to Face*. Oxford: Monarch, 2005.

Nasr, Seyyed Hossein. "Sufism and the Perennity of the Mystical Quest." In *Sufi Essays*, edited Seyyed Hossein Nasr, 25–42. Albany, NY: State University of New York Press, 1973.

Neusner, Jacob. *Judaism: The Evidence of the Mishnah*. Chicago: University of Chicago Press, 1981.

———, trans. *The Talmud of Babylonia: An Academic Commentary 12: Hagigah*. Atlanta: Scholars, 1994.

———, trans. *The Talmud of Babylonia: An Academic Commentary 22: Baba Batra*. Atlanta: Scholars, 1996.

Newman, N. A. *The Early Christian-Muslim Dialogue: A Collection of Documents from the First Three Islamic Centuries (632–900 AD), Translations with Commentary*. Hatfield, PA: Interdisciplinary Biblical Research Institute, 1993.

Newsom, Carol A. trans. *The Dead Sea Scrolls: Hebrew, Aramaic and Greek Texts with English Translations. Vol. 4B: Angelic Liturgy: Songs of the Sabbath Sacrifice*. James H. Charlesworth and Carol A. Newsom, eds. Tübingen: Mohr Siebeck, 1999.

———. "'He has Established for Himself Priests': Human and Angelic Priesthood in the Qumran Sabbath *Shirot*." In *Archeology and History in the Dead Sea Scrolls*, edited by Lawrence H. Schiffman, 101–20. Sheffield: JSOT Press, 1990.

Nicholson, Reynold A. *The Idea of Personality in Sufism*. Cambridge: Cambridge University Press, 1923.

———. Preface to *Kashf al-Mahjub* by ʿAlī ibn ʿUthmān al-Hujwīrī. Accord, NY: Pīr, 1999.

———. *Studies in Islamic Mysticism*. Cambridge: Cambridge University Press, 1921.

Nickelsburg, George W. E. *Jewish Literature Between the Bible and the Mishnah*. Philadelphia: Fortress, 1981.

Ninomiya, Ayako. "To Whom Do You Belong? Pīr-Murīd Relationship and Silsila in Medieval India." *Kyoto Bulletin of Islamic Area Studies* 2.1 (2008) 47–56.

Nizam ad-Din Awliya. *Morals for the Heart*. Translated by Bruce B. Lawrence. New York: Paulist, 1992.

Nwyia, Paul. *Exégèse Coranique Et Langage Mystique: Nouvel Essai Sur Le Lexique Technique Des Mystiques Musulmans*. Beyrouth: Dar el Machreq Éditeurs, 1970.

Odeberg, Hugo, trans. *3 Enoch, or The Hebrew Book of Enoch*. New York: Ktav, 1973.

Orlov, Andrei. *Divine Manifestations in the Slavonic Pseudepigrapha (Orientalia Judaica Christiana 2)*. Piscataway, NJ: Gorgias, 2009.

Orlov, Andrei, and Alexander Golitzin, "'Many Lamps are Lightened From the One: Paradigms of the Transformational Vision in Macarian Homilies." *Vigilae Christianae* 55 (2001) 281–98.

Osborne, Grant R. *Revelation*. Baker Exegetical Commentary on the New Testament. Grand Rapids: Baker Academic, 2002.

Otto, Rudolf. *The Idea of the Holy*. Oxford: Oxford University Press, 1958.

Outler, Albert C. Introduction, Commentary and Notes on *The Works of John Wesley*. Edited by Albert C. Outler. Nashville: Abingdon, 1985.

———. Introduction to *John Wesley*. New York: Oxford University Press, 1964.

Papan-Matin, Firoozeh. *Beyond Death: the Mystical Teachings of ʿAyn al-Quḍāt al-Hamadhānī*. Islamic History and Civilization, vol. 75. Leiden and Boston: Brill, 2010.

Parry, Donald W., and Emanuel Tov, ed. *The Dead Sea Scrolls Reader 3: Parabiblical Texts*. Leiden: Brill, 2005.

Parshall, Phil. *Bridges to Islam: A Christian Perspective on Folk Islam*. 2nd ed. Atlanta: Authentic, 2007.

Perrin, Nicholas. *Thomas: The Other Gospel*. Louisville: Westminster John Knox, 2007.

Peterson, Galen. *The Everlasting Tradition*. Grand Rapids: Kregel, 1995.

Philo. *Philo of Alexandria: The Contemplative Life, the Giants, and Selections.* Edited and translated by David Winston. New York: Paulist, 1981.

———. *The Works of Philo.* Loeb Classical Library, 10 vols. Edited and translated by F. H. Colson and G. H. Whitaker. Cambridge: Harvard University Press, 1929–1953.

Pilch, John J. *Flights of the Soul: Visions, Heavenly Journeys and Peak Experiences in the Biblical World.* Grand Rapids: Eerdmans, 2011.

Pinault, David. *The Shiites: Ritual and Popular Piety in a Muslim Community.* New York: St. Martin's, 1992.

Plato. *Phaedrus.* Translated by Christopher Rowe. London: Penguin Classics, 2005.

Plested, Marcus. *The Macarian Legacy: The Place of Macarius-Symeon in the Eastern Christian Tradition.* Oxford: Oxford University Press, 2004.

Power, Bernie. "More Missiological Thoughts on 'Strangers on a Train.'" In *Jesus and the Incarnation: Relfections of Christians from Islamic Contexts*, edited by David Emmanuel Singh, 202–10. Oxford: Regnum, 2011.

Price, James L. "Qumran and Johannine Theology." In *John and the Dead Sea Scrolls* (2nd ed.), edited by James H. Charlesworth, 9–37. New York: Crossroad, 1990.

Pseudo-Macarius. *The Fifty Spiritual Homilies and the Great Letter.* Translated by George A. Maloney. Mahwah, NJ: Paulist, 1992.

Quiñónez, Jorge. "Paul Phillip Levertoff: Pioneering Hebrew-Christian Scholar and Leader." *Mishkan* 37 (2002) 21–34.

Quispel, Gilles. "The Syrian Thomas and the Syrian Macarius." In *Gnostic Studies II*, edited by Gilles Quispel, 113–21. Istanbul: Nederlands Historisch-Archeologisch Instituut te İstanbul, 1975.

Quraeshi, Sameena. *Sacred Spaces: A Journey with the Sufis of the Indus.* New Haven, CT: Peabody Museum, 2010.

Qushayrī, Abū 'l-Qāsim. *Al-Qushayri's Epistle on Sufism.* Translated by Alexander D. Knysh. Reading, UL: Garnet, 2007.

———. "Interpreting Mystical Expressions from the *Treatise*." In *Early Islamic Mysticism: Sufi, Qur'an Mi'raj, Poetic and Theological Writings*, edited by Michael A. Sells, 99–150. New York: Paulist, 1996.

———. *Principles of Sufism.* Translated by B. R. von Schlegell. Berkeley, CA: Mizan, 1990.

Rabbani, Wahid Baksh. Translator's Preface and Notes in *The Kashful Mahjub. "Unveiling the Veiled": The Earliest Persian Treatise on Sufism* by Syed Ali bin Uthman al-Hujweri. Kuala Lumpur, Malaysia: A. S. Noordeen, 1997.

Rahimuddin, Muhammad, trans. *Muwattā' Imām Mālik.* Lahore, Pakistan: Sh. Muhammad Ashraf, 1985.

Rakestraw, Robert V. "Becoming Like God: An Evangelical Doctrine of Theosis." *Journal of the Evangelical Theological Society* 40.2 (1997) 257–69.

Ramm, Bernard. *Them He Glorified: A Systematic Study of the Doctrine of Glorification.* Grand Rapids: Eerdmans, 1963.

Redman, Judy. "How Accurate Are Eyewitnesses? Bauckham and the Eyewitnesses in the Light of Psychological Research." *Journal of Biblical Literature* 129 (2010) 177–97.

Renard, John, trans. *Knowledge of God in Classical Sufism: Foundations of Islamic Mystical Theology.* New York: Paulist, 2004.

Renard, John. *Friends of God: Islamic Images of Piety, Commitment, and Servanthood.* Berkeley: University of California Press, 2008.

Riddell, Peter G. "Islamic Variations on a Biblical Theme as Seen in the David and Bathsheba Saga." *Vox Evangelica* 27 (1997) 57–74.

Riley, Gregory J. *Resurrection Reconsidered: Thomas and John in Controversy.* Minneapolis: Fortress, 1995.

Robinson, Francis. "Education." In *The New Cambridge History of Islam*, edited by Robert Irwin, 497–531. Cambridge: Cambridge University Press, 2010.

Robinson, Neal. *Christ in Islam and Christianity.* London: Macmillan, 1991.

———. *Discovering the Qur'an: A Contemporary Approach to a Veiled Text.* London: SCM, 2003.

Ronning, John. *The Jewish Targums and John's Logos Theology.* Grand Rapids: Baker Academic, 2010.

Rowland, Christopher. "Apocalyptic Visions and Exaltation of Christ in the Letter to the Colossians." *Journal for the Study of the New Testament* 19 (1983) 74–78.

———. *The Open Heaven: A Study of Apocalyptic in Judaism and Early Christianity.* New York: Crossroad, 1982.

Runia, David T. "Philo of Alexandria." In *The First Christian Theologians*, edited by G. R. Evans, 77–84. Malden, MA: Blackwell, 2004.

———. Review of Philo, *The Works of Philo: Complete and Unabridged.* Translated by C. D. Yonge. Peabody, MA: Hendrickson, 1993.

Sādiq, Ja'far as-. The Qur'anic Commentary Attributed to Ja'far as-Sādiq. In *Early Islamic Mysticism: Sufi, Qur'an Mi'raj, Poetic and Theological Writings*, edited and translated by Michael A. Sells, 75–89. New York: Paulist, 1996.

———. *Spiritual Gems: The Mystical Qur'ān Commentary Ascribed to Ja'far al-Sādiq as contained in Sulamī's Haqā'iq al-Tafsīr from the Text of Paul Nwyia.* Translated by Farhana Mayer. Louisville, KY: Fons Vitae, 2011.

Sandmel, Samuel. "Parallelomania." *Journal of Biblical Literature* 81 (1962) 1–13.

———. *Philo of Alexandria: An Introduction.* New York: Oxford University Press, 1979.

Sands, Kristin Zahra. *Sūfī Commentaries on the Qur'ān in Classical Islam.* London: Routledge, 2006.

Sanneh, Lamin. *Disciples of All Nations: Pillars of World Christianity.* Oxford: Oxford University Press, 2008.

Sappington, Thomas J. *Revelation and Redemption at Colossae.* Journal for the Study of the New Testament, Supplement Series 53. Sheffield, UK: Sheffield Academic, 1991.

Sarrāj, Abū Nasr as-. "The Book of Flashes (Kitāb al-Luma')." In *Knowledge of God in Classical Sufism: Foundations of Islamic Mystical Theology*, translated by John Renard, 65–99. New York: Paulist, 2004.

———. *The Kitāb al-luma' fi'l-Tasawwuf of Abū Nasr 'abdallah b. ''Ali al-Sarrāj al-Tusi.* Edited by Reynold A. Nicholson. Leyden: E. J. Brill, 1914.

Sarrió Cucarella, Diego R. "Iglesias en tierra de Islam: La Mas'alat al-kanā'is de Ibn Taymiyya." *Collectanea Christiana Orientalia* 5 (2008) 287–324.

Saunders, Ernest W. "The Colossian Heresy and Qumran Theology." In *Studies in the History and Text of the New Testament*. Studies and Documents XXIX. Edited by Boyd L. Daniels and M. Jack Suggs, 133–45. Salt Lake City: University of Utah Press, 1967.

Savage, Timothy B. *Power Through Weakness: Paul's Understanding of the Christian Ministry in 2 Corinthians.* Society for New Testament Studies Monograph Series 86. Cambridge: Cambridge University Press, 1995.

Schäfer, Peter. *Hekhalot-Studien.* Tübingen: Mohr-Siebeck, 1988.
Schechter, Solomon, and M. Seligsohn. "Jose Ben Halafta." In *The Jewish Encyclopedia*, vol. 7, edited by I. Singer, 241–42. New York: Funk and Wagnalls, 1904.
Schiffman, Lawrence H. *From Text to Tradition: A History of Second Temple and Rabbinic Judasim.* New York: Ktav, 1991.
Schimmel, Annemarie. *Deciphering the Signs of God: a Phenomenological Approach to Islam.* Albany, NY: State University of New York Press, 1994
———. *Islam in the Indian Subcontinent.* Leiden: E. J. Brill, 1980.
———. *Mystical Dimensions of Islam.* Chapel Hill: University of North Carolina Press, 1975.
Scholem, Gershom. *Jewish Gnosticism, Merkabah Mysticism and Talmudic Tradition.* New York: Schocken, 1965.
———. *Kabbalah.* New York: Meridian, 1978.
———. *Major Trends in Jewish Mysticism* (3rd ed.). New York: Schocken, 1973.
Seevers, Boyd. "Remembrance." In *Dictionary of the Old Testament: Wisdom, Poetry and Writings*, edited by Tremper Longman III and Peter Enns, 643–47. Downers Grove, IL: InterVarsity, 2008.
Segal, Alan F., "Conversion and Universalism: Opposites that Attract." In *Origins and Method: Toward a New Understanding of Judaism and Christianity. Essays in Honour of John C. Hurd*, edited by Bradley H. McLean, 162–89. Sheffield, UK: Sheffield Academic, 1993.
———. "Paul and the Beginning of Jewish Mysticism." In *Death, Ecstasy and Other Worldly Journeys.* Edited by John J. Collins and Michael Fishbane, 95–122. Albany, NY: SUNY Press, 1995.
———. "Paul's Religious Experience in the Eyes of Jewish Scholars." In *Israel's God and Rebecca's Children: Christology and Community in Early Judaism and Christianity*, edited by David B. Capes et al., 321–43. Waco, TX: Baylor University Press, 2007.
———. *Paul the Convert: The Apostolate and Apostasy of Saul the Pharisee.* New Haven: Yale University Press, 1990.
———. *Rebecca's Children: Judaism and Christianity in the Roman World.* Cambridge: Harvard University Press, 1986.
———. "The Risen Christ and Angelic Mediator Figures in Light of Qumran." In *Jesus and the Dead Sea Scrolls.* The Anchor Bible Reference Library. Edited by James H. Charlesworth, 302–28. New York: Doubleday, 1992.
———. *Two Powers in Heaven: Early Rabbinic Reports about Christianity and Gnosticism.* Leiden: Brill, 1977.
Sells, Michael A. "Bewildered Tongue: The Semantics of Mystical Union in Islam." In *Mystical Union in Judaism, Christianity and Islam*, edited by Moshe Idel and Bernard McGinn, 87–124. New York: Continuum, 1996.
———, trans. *Early Islamic Mysticism: Sufi, Qur'an, Mi'raj, Poetic and Theological Writings.* New York: Paulist, 1996.
Shahîd, Irfan. *Byzantium and the Arabs in the Fourth Century.* Washington, DC: Dumbarton Oaks Research Library and Collection, 1984.
Sharif, Ja'far. *Islam in India, or the Qānūn-i-Islām* (3rd ed). Translated by G. A. Herklots. London: Curzon, 1972.
Shepherd, Michael B. "Targums, the New Testament, and Biblical Theology of the Messiah." *Journal of the Evangelical Theological Society* 51.1 (2008) 45–58.
Siddiqi, Abdul Hamid, trans. *Sahīh Muslim* (rev. ed.). 4 vols. Delhi: Kitab Bhavan, 2004.

Singh, David Emmanuel. "Christology as an Alternative Islamic Theological Structure." In *Jesus and the Cross: Reflections of Christians from Islamic Contexts*, edited by David Emmanuel Singh, 187–200. Oxford: Paternoster, 2008.

Singh, N. K. Munabbih, Wahb b. (664/5–832). "Yemenite Historian." In *Encyclopaedic Historiography of the Muslim World*, edited by N. K. Singh and A. Samiuddin, 677-84. Delhi: Global Vision, 2004.

Singh, Sundar. *Wisdom of the Sadhu: Teachings of Sundar Singh.* Edited by Kim Comer Farmington, PA: Plough, 2007.

Smith, J. Z. "The Garments of Shame." *History of Religions* 5 (1966) 217–38.

Smith, Margaret, trans. *Readings from the Mystics of Islam.* Westport, CT: Pir, 1994.

———. *Studies in Early Mysticism in the Near and Middle East.* Oxford: Oneworld, 1995.

Smith, Morton. "Ascent to the Heavens and Deification in 4QM^a" In *Archeology and History in the Dead Sea Scrolls*, edited by Lawrence H. Schiffman, 181–88. Sheffield: JSOT, 1990.

———. *Jesus the Magician: Charlatan or Son of God?* Berkeley, CA: Ulysses, 1998.

Snyder, Howard A. "John Wesley and Macarius the Egyptian." *Asbury Theological Journal* 45.2 (1990) 55–60.

———. "The Missional Flavor of John Wesley's Theology." In *World Mission in the Wesleyan Spirit*, edited by Darrell L. Whiteman and Gerald H. Anderson, 62–73. Franklin, TN: Providence, 2009.

———. *The Radical Wesley and Patterns for Church Renewal.* Downers Grove, IL: InterVarsity, 1980.

———. *Signs of the Spirit: How God Reshapes the Church.* Grand Rapids: Zondervan, 1989.

———. "What's Unique About a Wesleyan Theology of Mission? A Wesleyan Perspective on Free Methodist Missions." Presentation, FM Missions Consultation, Indianapolis, IN, October 11–13, 2002.

Soltes, Ori. Z. *Mysticism in Judaism, Christianity and Islam: Searching for Oneness.* Lanham, MD: Rowman & Littlefield, 2008.

Sozomen, Salaminius Hermias. "The Ecclesiastical History of Sozomen." In *The Nicene and Post-Nicene Fathers, Second Series*, edited by Philip Schaff and Henry Wace, 2.179–455. Grand Rapids: Eerdmans, 1890.

Spener, Philip Jacob. *Pia Desideria.* Translated by Theodore G. Tappert. Philadelphia: Fortress, 1964.

Starr, James. "Does 2 Peter 1:4 Speak of Deification?" In *Partakers of the Divine Nature: The History and Development of Deification in the Christian Traditions*, edited by Michael J. Christensen and Jeffery A. Wittung, 81–92. Grand Rapids: Baker Academic, 2007.

Stewart, Columba. *"Working the Earth of the Heart": The Messalian Controversy in History, Texts and Language to AD 431.* Oxford: Clarendon, 1991.

Stoffels, Joseph. *Die Mystiche Theologie Makarius des Aegypters.* Bonn: Peter Hanstein, 1908.

Storey, C. A. *Persian Literature: A Bio-Bibliographical Survey*, Vol. 1, Part 2. London: Luzac, 1972.

Streeter, B. H., and A. J. Appasamy. *The Sadhu: A Study in Mysticism and Practical Religion.* London: Macmillan, 1922.

Stroumsa, Guy G. "Mystical Descents." In *Death, Ecstasy and Other Worldly Journeys*, edited by John J. Collins and Michael Fishbane, 139–54. Albany, NY: SUNY Press, 1995.

Subhan, John A. *Sufism: Its Saints and Shrines*. Piscataway, NJ: Gorgias, 2009.

Sulamī, Abū 'Abd al-Rahmān Muhammad ibn al-Husayn al-. *The Subtleties of the Ascension: Early Sayings on Muhammad's Heavenly Journey*. Translated by Frederick S. Colby. Louisville, KY: Fons Vitae, 2006.

———. *The Way of Sufi Chivalry*. Translated by Tosun Bayrak al-Jerrahi. Rochester, VT: Inner Traditions International, 1991.

Suvorova, Anna. *Muslim Saints of South Asia: The Eleventh to Fifteenth Centuries*. Oxon and New York: Routledge Curzon, 2004.

Svendsen, Stefan Nordgaard. "Allegory Transformed: The Appropriation of Philonic Hermeneutics in the Letter to the Hebrews." PhD diss., Biblical Studies Section, Faculty of Theology, University of Copenhagen, 2007.

Swanson, Mark H. "Arabic as a Christian Language?" Presentation, Christian-Muslim dialogue in Yogyakarta, Indonesia, July 1998. Online: http://www2.luthersem.edu/mswanson/papers/indonesia%20Arabic.pdf.

Swartz, Michael D. *Mystical Prayer in Ancient Judaism: An Analysis of Ma'aseh Merkavah*. Tübingen: Mohr-Siebeck, 1992.

Synan, Edward. "The Four Senses and Four Exegetes." In *With Reverence for the Word: Medieval Scriptural Exegesis in Judaism, Christianity, and Islam*, edited by Jane Dammen McAuliffe, Barry D. Walfish, and Joseph W. Goering, 225–36. New York: Oxford University Press, 2003.

Tabarī, Abū Ja'far al-. *Tārīkh al-rusul wa al-mulūk*. Ed. Stanislas Guyard and Michael Jan De Goeje. Leiden: E. J. Brill, 1879–1901. Quoted in Nadia Maria El Cheikh, *Byzantium Viewed by the Arabs*. Cambridge, MA: Harvard Center for Middle Eastern Studies, 2004.

Tappert, Theodore G. Introduction to *Pia Desideria*, by Philip Jacob Spener. Philadelphia: Fortress, 1964.

Taylor, John V. *The Go Between God: The Holy Spirit & the Christian Mission*. New York: Oxford University Press, 1972.

Tillich, Paul. *A History of Christian Thought*. New York: Touchstone, 1972.

Tommasi, Chiara Ombretta. "Ascension." In *Encyclopedia of Religion (Second Edition)*. Edited by Lindsay Jones, 1.518–26. Farmington Hills, MI: Gale Cengage Learning, 2005.

Toy, Crawford Howell, Carl Siegfried, and Jacob Zallel Lauterbach. "Philo Judæus." *The Jewish Encyclopedia*, Vol. 10. Edited by I. Singer, 6–18. New York: Funk and Wagnalls, 1905.

Trimingham, J. Spencer. *Christianity Among the Arabs in Pre-Islamic Times*. London: Longman, 1979.

———. *The Sufi Orders in Islam*. Oxford: Oxford University Press, 1971.

Trotter, I. Lilias. *Between the Desert and the Sea*. London: Marshall, Morgan and Scott, 1937.

———. *The Way of the Sevenfold Secret*. 4th ed. Cairo: Nile Mission, 1933.

Tucker, Gordon. Commentary to *Heavenly Torah as Refracted through the Generations*. New York: Continuum, 2006.

Tucker, Ruth. *From Jerusalem to Irian Jaya: A Biographical History of Christian Missions*. 2nd ed. Grand Rapids: Zondervan, 2004.

Tuell, Stephen S. "Divine Presence and Absence in Ezekiel's Prophecy." In *The Book of Ezekiel: Theological and Anthropological Perspectives*, edited by Margaret S. Odell & John T. Strong, 97–116. Atlanta: Society of Biblical Literature, 2000.

Tustarī, Sahl b. 'Abd Allāh al-. *Tafsīr al-Tustarī*. Trans. Annabel Keeler and Ali Keeler. Louisville, KY: Fons Vitae, 2011.

Tuttle, Robert G. *Mysticism in the Wesleyan Tradition*. Grand Rapids: Francis Asbury, 1989.

Urban, Linwood, and Patrick Henry. "'Before Abraham was, I Am': Does Philo Explain John 8:56–58?" *Studia Philonica* 6 (1979-1980) 157–95.

Uždavinys, Algis. *Ascent to Heaven in Islamic and Jewish Mysticism*. London: Matheson Trust, 2011.

Van der Horst, Pieter W. "Hellenistic Parallels to the Acts of the Apostles (2.1-47)." *Journal for the Study of the New Testament* 25 (1985) 49–60.

Vander Werff, Lyle L. *Christian Mission to Muslims: The Record*. Pasadena, CA: William Carey, 1977.

Vickers, John. Introduction to *The Journals of Dr. Thomas Coke*. Nashville: Kingswood, 2005.

Victorinus. "Commentary on the Apocalypse of the Blessed John." In *The Ante-Nicene Fathers* 7, edited by Alexander Roberts and James Donaldson, 344–63. Translated by Robert Ernest Wallis. Buffalo, NY: The Christian Literature, 1886.

Von Denffer, Ahmad. *'Ulūm al-Qur'ān: An Introduction to the Sciences of the Qur'ān*. Leicestershire, UK: The Islamic Foundation, 1994.

Vuckovic, Brooke Olson. *Heavenly Journeys, Earthly Concerns: The Legacy of the Mi'raj in the Formation of Islam*. New York: Routledge, 2005.

Walfish, Barry D. "An Introduction to Medieval Jewish Biblical Interpretation." In *With Reverence for the Word: Medieval Scriptural Exegesis in Judaism, Christianity, and Islam*, edited by Jane Dammen McAuliffe, Barry D. Walfish, and Joseph W. Goering, 3–12. New York: Oxford University Press, 2003.

Walls, Andrew F. *The Missionary Movement in History: Studies in the Transmission of Faith*. Maryknoll, NY: Orbis, 1996.

———. "World Parish to World Church: John and Charles Wesley on Home and Overseas Mission." In *World Mission in the Wesleyan Spirit*, edited by Darrell L. Whiteman and Gerald H. Anderson, 138–150. Franklin, TN: Providence, 2009.

Wasserstrom, Steven W. "Jewish Pseudepigrapha in Muslim Literature: A Bibliographical and Methodological Sketch." In *Tracing the Threads: Studies in the Vitality of Jewish Pseudepigrapha*, edited by John C. Reeves, 87–114. Atlanta: Scholars, 1994.

Watson, Charles R. *What is this Moslem World?* New York: Friendship, 1937.

Watt, W. Montgomery. Review of *Exégèse Coranique Et Langage Mystique: Nouvel Essai Sur Le Lexique Technique Des Mystiques Musulmans*, by Paul Nwyia. *Bulletin of the School of Oriental and African Studies*, University of London 35.2 (1972) 427.

Wesley, Charles. *A Collection of Hymns, for the Use of the People Called Methodists*. Ed. John Wesley. London: T. Cordeux, 1820.

Wesley, John. *The Bicentennial Edition of the Works of John Wesley: Sermons* (4 vols.). Ed. Albert C. Outler. Nashville: Abingdon, 1985.

———. *Explanatory Notes upon the New Testament*. New York: Lane & Tippett, 1847.

———. *John Wesley's Sermons: An Anthology*. Edited by Albert C. Outler and Richard P. Heinzenrater. Nashville: Abingdon, 1991.

———. "Of Macarius," *A Christian Library*, vol. 1., 1819. Online: http://wesley.nnu.edu/john-wesley/a christian-library/a-christian-library-volume 1/volume-1-the-homilies-of-macarius/.

———. *A Plain Account of Christian Perfection: The Annotated Edition*. The John Wesley Christian Perfection Library. Edited by Mark K. Olson. Fenwick, MI: Alethea in Heart, 2005.

Winston, David. Introduction to *Philo of Alexandria: The Contemplative Life, the Giants, and Selections*. New York: Paulist, 1981.

———. "Was Philo a Mystic?" In *Studies in Jewish Mysticism*, edited by Joseph Dan and Frank Talmage, 15–39. Cambridge, MA: Association for Jewish Studies, 1982.

Wintermute, O. S., trans. "Apocalypse of Zephaniah (First Century B.C. –First Century A.D.)." In *The Old Testament Pseudopigrapha, Vol. 1: Apocalyptic Literature and Testaments*. Ed. James H. Charlesworth, 497–515. New York: Doubleday, 1983.

Witherington, Ben III. "*Preparatio Evangelii*: The Theological Roots of Wesley's View of Evangelism." In *Theology and Evangelism in the Wesleyan Heritage*, edited by James C. Logan, 51–80 Nashville: Kingswood, 1994.

Wolfson, Elliott R. "Forms of Visionary Ascent as Ecstatic Experience in the Zoharic Literature." In *Gershom Scholem's Major Trends in Jewish Mysticism: 50 Years After*, edited by Peter Schäfer and Joseph Dan, 209–35. Tübingen: J. C. B Mohr, 1993.

Woodberry, J. Dudley. "Contextualization Among Muslims: Reusing Common Pillars." *International Journal of Frontier Missions* 13.4 (1996) 171–86.

Wyes, Kate, ed. *From Shore to Shore: Liturgies, Litanies and Prayers from Around the World*. London, UK: SPCK, 2003.

Young, Frances. "Inner Struggle: Some Parallels between John Wesley and the Greek Fathers." In *Orthodox and Wesleyan Spirituality*, edited by S. T. Kimbrough, 157–72. Crestwood, NY: St. Vladimir's Seminary Press, 2002.

Zahniser, A. H. Mathias. "The Doctrine of the Incarnation Supports the Christian Use of the Qur'ān 'for Example of Life and the Instruction of Manners': A Proposal." In *Jesus and the Incarnation: Reflections of Christians from Islamic Contexts*, edited by David Emmanuel Singh, 31–45. Oxford: Regnum, 2011.

———. *The Mission and Death of Jesus in Islam and Christianity*. Maryknoll, NY: Orbis, 2008.

———. *Symbol and Ceremony: Making Disciples Across Cultures* Monrovia, CA: MARC, 1997.

———. "Wesleyan Synergism and the Dialogue with Muslims." In *World Mission in the Wesleyan Spirit*, edited by Darrell L. Whiteman and Gerald H. Anderson, 227–34. Franklin, TN: Providence, 2009.

Zhukovsky, V. A. "Persian Sufism: Being a Translation of Professor Zhukovsky's Introduction to His Edition of the Kashf al-Mahjūb." Translated by Sidney Jerrold and E. Denison Ross. *Bulletin of the School of Oriental Studies* 5.3 (1929) 475–88.

Zizoulas, John D. *Being as Communion*. Crestwood, NY: St. Vladimir's Seminary Press. 1985.

General Index

A

Aaron, 41, 71, 102
Abbās, 219
Abbasid Caliphate, 152
'Abd Allāh Abū Ansārī, 197
'Abdallāh ibn Mas'ūd, 161
'Abdallāh Muhammad, 234
'Abd al-Qādir al-Jīlānī, 170
'Abd ar-Rahmān Jāmī, 199
Abraham, 39, 41, 61, 69, 77, 210
Abū 'Abd al-Rahmān Muhammad ibn al-Husayn al-Sulamī, 156, 167–69, 197
Abū al-Husayn al-Nūrī, 170
Abū Bakr al-Kalābādhī, 4, 157–58, 167–68, 185, 191, 197, 219–20
Abū Bakr al-Shiblī, 157, 195, 209–10
Abū Hāmid al-Ghazālī, 4, 7, 16, 156, 162, 177, 184, 190, 205
Abū Hanifa, 222
Abū Ja'far al-Tabarī, 148, 158, 161, 163
Abū 'l-Fadl Muhammad ibn al-Hasan al-Khuttalī, 195
Abū'l Hasan al Husrī, 195
Abū'l-Qāsim al-Junayd, 156–57, 168, 171, 175, 181, 192, 195, 204
Abū'l-Qāsim al-Qushayrī, 7, 16, 155–57, 180–81, 187–89, 197–98, 204–5, 208, 236, 247
Abū Najīb Suhrawardī, 177, 202
Abū Nasr al-Sarrāj, 157, 186–87, 197
Abū Sa'īd Ahmad ibn 'Īsā al-Kharrāz, 171

Abū Tālib al-Makkī, 155, 161
Abū Yazīd al-Bistamī, 173–74, 204, 218, 233
Adam, 95–96, 98, 104, 125–26, 174, 210
   prelapsarian, 95
   Heavenly, 138
   Second, 109
Aher, 55
'Ajamī. See Habīb al-'Ajamī.
Ajmer, 196
Akiva, 52–53, 55, 79
alastu, day of, 174, 185, 215
'Alī ibn Ismā'īl al-Ash'arī, 206
'Alī ibn 'Uthmān al-Jullabi al-Hujwīrī, x, 7–8, 14, 16, 171, 182, 192–99, 201–11, 213, 215, 217–19, 221–29, 231–38, 240, 243–44, 247–48, 254
allegorical, 39, 44, 163, 169
   conceptions, 49
   exegesis, 38–39, 160, 209, 247
   explanations, 204
   methodology, 146
   understanding, 40
Ana l-Haqq, 178–79
Andrae, Tor, 2, 9–10, 151–53, 177, 247
Andrewes, Lancelot, 113
Anglican, 7, 14, 16, 112–13, 116, 241, 248
annihilation, 171, 182–83, 207, 209–10, 212, 215, 218, 222
anthropocentric, 67, 81, 83, 111–12, 146, 217, 225–26

anthropomorphism, 49, 51
antinomianism, 179–80, 246
　radical, 156
Apocalypse of Zephaniah, 72
Apocalyptic and Merkavah, 25,
　27–29, 35, 52–57, 61, 63–64,
　69–70, 72
Apocalypticism, 29, 32–33, 54
Apocalyptic Visions, 70–71
apostles, 38, 72, 80, 150, 227
Arabic, 2, 7, 16, 19, 149, 156, 158, 164,
　175, 178, 196, 198, 204–5, 207,
　216–17, 238, 256–58
Arabs, 147–49, 198, 227
　pagan, 149
　poets, 153
　pre-Islamic, 153
Arberry, A. J., 153, 155, 171, 174
Arndt, Johann, 91, 113–14, 116, 138
Asad, Muhammad, 3, 163–64, 167
ascension, 6, 9, 13–14, 19, 23–25,
　27–30, 34, 36, 38, 40–41, 43,
　45–48, 50–53, 55–57, 59–65,
　68–70, 77, 80, 89, 92, 95, 97–98,
　105, 109, 111–12, 144–45, 147,
　163–65, 167, 169–71, 183, 188,
　192, 194, 217–18, 220–221, 231,
　237–40, 243–44
　ecstatic, 48
　elements of, 30, 46
　individual's, 35
　Hellenic, 14, 145
　indigenous, 87
　ritualized, 70
　self-powered, 57
　shamanistic, 69, 106
　spiritual, 19, 170, 206, 222
　to the stars, 27
　technique, 37
asceticism, 25, 48, 70, 93, 95, 115, 125,
　157, 222, 244
Ashʻarite, 205–6, 219, 222
Askari, Syed Hasan, 199–201, 203
Athanasius, 13, 133–34
atonement, 133–35, 140
ʻAttār. See Farīd al-Dīn ʻAttār.
Augustine, 17–18, 101, 112, 125–26
Aulén, Gustav, 74

Aune, David E., 69, 71–74, 76–77
authority, 64, 72, 76, 86, 150, 166,
　188, 226
　decisive, 149
　early Jewish Rabbinic, 51
autohypnosis, 251
Awn, Peter, 159, 167, 184, 218–19
ʻayn al-jamʻ, 176
ʻAyn al-Qudāt al-Hamadhānī, 177,
　217

B

Baghdad, 157, 176, 191–92, 195
baptism, 86, 100
baqāʼ, 10, 168, 170–73, 177, 179, 181,
　209, 215, 218, 226, 244, 246–48
bāqī, 209, 247
Barrett, C. K., 45
Barthélemy, Dominique, 56
Barton, James L., 251
Bātinīyya, 156
batn, 161
bat qōl, 69
Bauckham, Richard, 28, 61–62,
　72–77, 82–84, 127, 233
beauty, 5, 28, 54, 62, 99, 106, 168, 182,
　186, 190, 209, 224, 230, 233
　spiritual, 6, 90
　unspeakable, 5–6, 90, 99
beholding, 84, 87, 168–69
beliefs, 11, 18, 52, 111, 175, 187, 192,
　207, 211, 227–28, 238
believers, 12, 66–67, 71, 86–87, 106–
　7, 115, 118, 128, 137, 141, 143,
　166, 184, 187, 206, 209, 213, 220,
　224–26, 229, 232–35, 242–43,
　245, 248–50, 252, 255, 258
Bell, Richard, 4, 150, 152–53, 254, 257
Ben Azzai, 55, 166
Bengal, 8, 129, 172–73, 191–92, 200
Ben Sirach, 23, 27
Ben Zoma, 55
bidʻa, 156–57
Bihar, 8, 193, 199–202
bilā kayf, 219, 222
Bistāmī, see Abū Yazīd al-Bistāmī
blessing, 57, 118, 147, 197, 205, 218,
　226, 230, 236, 245, 257

blood, 68, 98, 175, 253, 259
  ransomed with his, 76
  sacrificial, 74, 259
Borgen, Peder, 40–42
Böwering, Gerhard, 28, 154, 161, 171–72, 185–86, 188–89, 196–97
Boyarin, Daniel, 45
Brainerd, David, 129
branches, 131, 136, 173, 200
bread, 47, 182, 253
  nourishing, 46
  true, 253
  unleavened flat, 259
bridges, ix, 43, 55, 251
  potential, 247
Brock, Sebastian P., 97
Brodie, Thomas L., 67
Brown, Raymond E., 62
Brownlee, William H., 71
Bruce, F. F., 70
Bū ʿAlī Qalandar, 200
Buddhism, 10, 154, 173, 201
Burns, Stuart Keith, 68, 97–98, 102–3, 109
Byzantine Empire, 148–49, 151–52

C

Cairo Geniza, 55
Campbell, Ted, 114–15, 125
Carey, William, 119, 143
centrifugal, 241
centripetal, ix, 241
chanting, 184, 190, 236, 250–51, 258
  audible, 154, 235
  contemplative, 158, 182, 232, 236
characteristics
  blameworthy, 181, 247
  consistent, 34
  praiseworthy, 181, 247
Chariot, 23, 28, 45–46, 53–54, 56, 69, 71, 220
Charles, R. H., 73
Charlesworth, James H., 60, 62–63, 74
cherubim, 23, 31, 34, 45, 90
Chittick, William, 166, 185–87, 206
Christ, ix–x, 1–2, 4–6, 8, 10–14, 16, 18, 20–21, 24, 26, 28, 30, 32, 34, 36, 38, 40, 42, 44, 46, 48, 50, 52, 54, 56, 58, 60–62, 64–66, 68, 70, 72–76, 78, 80, 82, 84–92, 94–100, 102–6, 108–10, 112–16, 118, 120–22, 124, 126–36, 138–40, 142–50, 152, 154, 156, 158, 160, 162, 164, 166, 168, 170, 172, 174, 176–78, 180, 182, 184, 186, 188, 190, 192, 196, 198, 200, 202, 204, 206, 208, 210, 212, 214, 216, 218, 220, 222, 224, 226, 228, 230, 232, 234, 236, 238, 240–42, 244, 246, 248, 250, 252, 254, 256, 258
  ascended, 109
  crucified, 85
  describing, 104
  exalted, 75
  followed, 129
  the fullness of, 140
  glory, 88
  humiliated, 75
  knowledge of, 84
  power for healing, 106
  reign, 76
  rest, 93
  resurrection, 86
  sacrificial death, 77
  See also Jesus
Christensen, Michael J., 115, 117–18, 139
Christian
  ascetic and mystical tradition, 92
  Byzantine tradition, 185
  consensus, 57
  contexts, 176, 220
  ideas, 160
  influence, 153–54
  Interaction, x, 90–91
Christian communities, 91, 120, 146, 148–49, 160, 250
Christianity, x–xi, 2–3, 16–17, 23, 25, 55–58, 81–82, 91, 121–22, 127, 131, 133, 137, 145–49, 150, 153–54
Christian Perfection, 10, 117–18, 124–25, 138–40, 240
Christians, x, 1–3, 12, 16, 28, 32, 51–52, 56, 82, 85, 100, 102, 119–21, 127–28, 141–42, 144, 148–54, 175, 207, 230, 251

Christlikeness, 136
Christocentricity, 81, 86–87, 89, 112, 177
Christology, 4, 60, 75, 77, 99, 177, 179
  of divine identity, 28
  second-Adam, 211
church, 11, 102, 113, 122, 133, 140, 150
  early, 9, 20, 104, 112–13, 138, 146
Clement, 72, 112, 116–17, 182, 244
Coke, Thomas, 119, 129
Collins, Kenneth J., 112, 115–16, 137, 139
Colossians, 70–71
  Controversy, 70
  Mystics, 70
  opponents, 78
  Syncretism, 70
commands, 36, 63, 67, 100, 170, 186, 227, 229–30
commentary, 8, 45, 52, 72, 75, 136–37, 167, 169, 195–97, 202, 219
  classical, 158
  fundamentalist, 159
  legal, 158
  symbolic, 159
communion, 5–6, 80, 90, 99, 107, 117, 125, 176, 246
  ineffable, 140
  unspeakable, 108
community, ix, xi, 2, 12, 21, 35, 51, 64, 80, 114, 119, 121, 130, 146, 167, 169, 230, 237–38, 241–42, 250, 252–57
  believing, 66, 91, 118, 242, 250–55
  emerging, 243, 256
  eschatological, 64
Community of Sūfī Believers in Messiah, 248
condemnation, 96, 208–9
  popular, 208
  strong, 156
congregational prayer, 137, 213, 242, 249–50
contemplation, 32, 35, 42, 47, 103, 187, 191, 212, 219, 222–23, 232, 245
contextualization, ix–xi, 14–15, 27, 203

conversion, 15, 80, 85, 104, 152, 172
  and universalism, 86
Corpus Hermetica, 25, 60
corruption, 82, 133, 135
covenant, 175, 253, 259
  primordial, 174, 215
creation, 9, 38, 48, 53, 61, 73, 118, 123, 125, 135, 170
Creator, 9, 23, 61, 117, 123, 161, 179–80
  likeness of his, 123
creatures, 9, 73, 95, 107, 117, 166, 174, 178–80, 234
crucifixion, 62, 75, 85, 96, 131, 140, 177–78, 253
culture, x, 11–12, 24, 136, 142
  new, x, 12, 138
  receptor, 15
Cumming, Joseph L., 206
Cup-bearer, 22

D

dance, 48, 184, 190–91, 200, 235, 250
Daniel, 31
darkness, 43, 88, 93, 96–97, 100–101, 131, 153, 246
  powers of, 96–97, 102, 105, 222
Dātā Ganj Bakhsh, 192, 196, 235–37
David, 210, 218
Davila, James R., 19, 24, 33, 47, 145, 183, 240
Dead Sea Scrolls, 26, 34–37, 54
death, 16, 18, 55, 59, 62, 74, 85–86, 96–97, 107, 117, 127, 129, 132–34, 138, 143, 176–77, 181, 183, 196, 202, 209, 217, 221, 225, 246–48
  atoning, 138
  dying before our, 172, 248
DeConick, April D., 6, 18, 24–25, 28, 54, 60, 62, 64, 79, 85, 94–95
Dehqani-Tafti, Hassan, 145
deification, 30, 82, 99
deliverance, 104–5, 135, 184, 253
descent, 24, 26, 53, 78, 255
  inner, 170

development, 1–2, 11, 13, 15, 25, 27–28, 57, 69–70, 92, 112, 128, 153, 199, 244
devotee, 9, 23, 85, 98, 101, 103–5, 108, 240
devotion, 4, 10, 19, 114, 129, 137–38, 160, 170–71, 181, 205, 212–13, 236, 251
  inner habitual, 236
  music, 258
dhāt, 168, 206, 224
dhikr, 154, 184–89, 191, 229, 234, 236, 245, 250–52, 257–58
dhikr al-hadra, 188
dhikr al-Qur'ān, 236
dhikr jalī, 186, 251
dhikr khafī, 186
dhikr qalbī, 186
dialogue, 2, 13, 16, 121, 129, 153, 220
direction, 5, 31, 91, 95, 99, 121, 161, 188, 230–31, 249
discernment, 115, 233
disciples, ix, 6, 44, 52, 60, 62, 64–67, 78, 87, 89, 147, 149, 188, 191–92, 197, 201–3, 211, 213, 217, 220–22, 226, 229, 231–32, 236, 259
discipleship, 2, 14, 21, 108, 128, 131, 220, 241–42, 251
divine, 18, 27–29, 33, 40, 43, 46, 49, 53, 57, 62, 79, 82, 84, 89, 97–98, 102, 108–9, 115, 117, 154, 164, 172, 181, 189, 220, 227, 232, 237
  assistance, 133
  attributes, 204
  beauty, 224
  command, 228
  ecstasy, 97–98, 103, 109
  energy, 121, 124
  essence, 176, 224
  glory, 52, 79, 126
  grace, 175
  identity, 30, 62
  illumination, 216, 233
  image, 126, 130
  immanence, 33
  inspiration, 254
  knowledge, 207
  law, 180–81

divine nature, 23, 84, 132
  aspect of the, 43
  partakers of the, 81, 84, 113, 125
divinity, 30, 101, 107, 218
  exalted, 52
  radiant, 178
divinization. *See* theosis
Donner, Fred, 152–53, 177
Dörries, Hermann, 9, 92, 97
doxa, 5, 28, 64, 66, 84, 86, 88, 100–101
dreams, 22, 24, 46, 50, 62, 159, 167, 198, 258
dukrānā, 154
dwelling-place, 5–6, 72, 77, 90, 99, 187
  eternal, 63
  throne of God, 6, 90

E

Eaton, Richard M., 192
ecstasy, 33, 173, 176, 203, 210, 237
  prolonged, 176
  spiritual, 48, 175, 218
ecstatic, 24, 103, 208
Egypt, x, 25, 44–45, 209, 253
El Cheikh, Nadia Maria, 148
elders, 71–73, 216, 253, 256, 259
Eliade, Mircea, 19, 24
Elijah, 28–29, 52–53, 57, 225
Elior, Rachel, 34
empowerment, 64, 112, 126, 137, 146, 183–84, 226
Encratics, 93
Enoch, 26, 29–31, 35, 46, 51–54, 57, 61, 64, 69, 78, 145
  ascension of, 31, 52
  literature, 25
  transformation of, 61
Ephesians, 70, 76, 86, 94, 107, 124, 136
Ephrem Syrus, 100, 116, 182
Epiphanius, 149
Epistola Magna, 92, 94, 101, 106–7
Ernst, Carl W., 8, 153, 157, 170, 176, 185–86, 190, 195–96, 205
Eschatology, Christian, 79, 81, 95
Eskola, Timo, 28

esoteric, 156, 162, 207, 209
  knowledge and power, 24
essence, 18, 32, 41–43, 61, 84, 115,
  146, 163, 168, 172, 175–76,
  206–7, 224–25, 233, 235
  veil of, 205
Essenes, 34, 70
Eucharist, 137, 232, 240, 242, 249–50
Evagrius, 101
"An Evangelical Mysticism," 10, 117
evangelism, 13, 119, 121, 138, 142,
  147, 242, 251
evil, 27, 96, 105, 125, 134, 136, 151,
  254
exegesis, 159, 162, 191, 204, 206, 211,
  214, 243
  Christian, 28
  classical, 211
  esoteric Qur'ānic, 28, 211
  exoteric, 28, 162, 211
exegesis, ta'wīl-based, 160
Exodus, 28, 41–42, 44, 47, 50, 57, 71,
  73, 76, 78, 86–87, 101–2, 151,
  167, 172, 218, 259
experience, ix–x, 18, 22–23, 25, 42,
  48, 57, 79, 81, 103, 141, 143, 145,
  159, 174, 179, 181, 183, 189, 196,
  201, 203, 212, 219, 225, 231, 233,
  245, 249
  apotheotic, 57
  collective, 81
  conversion, 30
  ecstatic, 173
  emotional, 103
  spiritual, 207, 222, 237–38
  visionary, 48
exposition, 160, 212–13
eyes, 3, 5–6, 20, 37, 42, 48, 55, 72–73,
  75, 90, 97, 99, 115, 120, 164,
  168–69, 209, 214, 216, 222, 228,
  244
  full of, 73
  inner, 222
  physical, 167, 210, 219
  spiritual, 167, 210, 219
Ezekiel, 5, 23, 25, 27–32, 34–35, 53,
  61, 69, 71, 73–74, 76–77, 99, 243
  Merkavah, 99, 243

Ezekiel's vision, 5, 31, 34, 69, 99,
  145

F

faith, x, 2, 10–13, 17, 23, 51–52, 55,
  66–67, 82–83, 85, 87, 91, 96–97,
  109, 117–20, 124, 126–29, 131–
  32, 136, 138, 140, 143, 147–48,
  152, 170, 192, 211, 221, 227–28,
  233, 242, 246, 248–50, 255–58
  communities of, 241, 244
  community of, 143, 147, 242–43,
  245, 254, 256
  covenant, 2
  embracing, 212
  grace-enabled, 227
  indigenous, 147
  living, 137
  relationship of, 6, 62
  victorious, 130
Fakhr al-Dīn al-Rāzī, 177
fanā, 10, 168, 170–75, 177–79, 181,
  183, 188, 207–9, 215, 218, 222,
  226, 244, 246–48, 256
  fanā' fī Allāh, 20, 188, 219, 222
  fanā' fī'al-rasūl, 20
  fanā' fī'al-shaykh, 19
  fanā' yi kulliat, 207–8
fānī, 171–72, 209, 247
Farīd al-Dīn 'Attār, 175, 182, 199
fasting, 24, 93, 205, 230–32, 249, 254,
  259
Father, 6, 42, 60, 62–66, 68, 76, 86, 93,
  105, 107, 116, 124, 134–35, 140,
  148, 174, 199, 255
fellowships, 98, 106–7, 240, 251–53,
  256–57, 259
Fifty Spiritual Homilies, 6–7, 92,
  98–99, 101, 103, 107, 111, 115,
  126
fikr, 184, 191–92, 235, 250
fiqh, 191
Firdausīyya, 201–2
Fletcher, John, 10, 117, 121, 124, 129,
  135, 146
Fletcher-Louis, Crispin H. T., 70
flight, 23, 47–48, 98, 221–22, 257
Flint, Peter, 36–37

General Index   291

folk religion, 137, 203, 213, 252, 256
   Evangelical, 213
foreshadowing, 37, 175
   possible, 36
forgiveness, 72, 140
Fossum, Jarl E., 18–19
freedom, 4, 87, 103
   great, 215
   human, 123
   religious, 150
Friedlander, Shems, 183, 190
fulfillment, 6, 179
   legitimate, 63
   ultimate, 13
fullness, 32, 74, 112, 119, 121–22, 130
Furnish, Victor Paul, 87

G

Gabriel, 166, 187
Gairdner, W. H. T., 121, 154
"The General Deliverance," 123
"The General Spread of the Gospel," 119–20, 127, 142
ghair al-makhlūq, 248
Gharīb Nawāz. *See* Moʻīnuddīn Chishtī
ghazal, 21, 252
Ghazālī. *See* Abū Hāmid al-Ghazālī
Gine, Pratap Chandra, 50
glory, 3–6, 23, 27–28, 34, 36, 42, 53–54, 62–65, 73, 84–88, 90–91, 93, 95, 97, 99–101, 103, 105–7, 109, 119, 123, 126–27, 140, 145, 164, 178, 198, 225, 230, 243, 249, 255
gnosis, 19, 117, 169, 227
Gnosticism, 29, 32–33, 54, 116
goal, 9, 19, 24, 35, 65, 81, 98, 108, 126, 174, 213, 240, 246–47
   attendant, 126
   final, 175
   spiritual, 215
   ultimate, 50, 114
God, ix–xi, 1–14, 16–34, 36, 38, 40–52, 54, 56–58, 60–86, 88–110, 112–20, 122–38, 140–48, 150, 152–58, 160–64, 166–90, 192, 194–202, 204–59
   dissolve into oneness with, 117
   enthroned, 73
   fear of, 121
   imitating, 82
   invoking, 189
   knowledge from, 170
   likened to, 49
   love, 140
   mission, 111, 113, 115, 117, 119, 121, 123, 125, 127, 129, 131, 133, 135, 137, 139, 141, 143
   omnipresent, 189
   proof of, 219
   seeing, 231
   trusting, 106
"gold from the dross," 115
Goldziher, Ignaz, 148–49, 156, 198
Golitzin, Alexander, 5–6, 9, 25, 64, 88–89, 92, 99–101
gospel, ix–x, 4, 6–7, 11–12, 15, 35–36, 45, 60–68, 75, 80–81, 83, 88, 90, 92–95, 119–21, 127–29, 138, 142, 144, 148–49, 151, 182, 243, 251
grace, 6–7, 10, 13, 62, 67, 84, 90, 93–94, 98, 100, 103–5, 109, 112, 116, 118–19, 122, 126, 131–33, 135–38, 141–42, 144, 146–47, 183–84, 193, 195, 217, 223, 225, 227, 229–30, 232–35, 237–38, 240, 242, 245, 248–50, 252–53, 255
   convincing, 136
   divinizing, 141
   empowering, 59, 125, 224
   inward, 137, 248
   justifying, 138
   responsible, 13, 142
   sanctifying, 93, 136
   uncreated, 112, 253
"The Great Assize," 138
The Great Letter. *See Epistola Magna*
Gregory of Nyssa, 7, 94, 114
Gregory Palamas, 92, 176
Gregory the Great, 66–67
Griffith, Sidney H., 152
Grillmeier, Aloys, 61
Grosseteste, Robert, 161

292 General Index

Gruenwald, Ithamar, 25, 27–29, 32–33, 35, 52–57, 61, 63–64, 69–72
guides, 6, 13, 20, 48, 67, 90, 190, 200, 213–14, 223, 229, 238–39

H

Habīb al-'Ajamī, 198
hadd, 161
Hadīth, 155, 161–62, 164–67, 170, 185, 187, 189–91, 223, 231–32, 237
hadra, 184, 189–90, 192, 235, 250, 252
Hagigah, 53–55, 79
hajj, 176, 233–34, 249
halaqa, 184, 191–92, 237–38, 250–51
Hallāj. *See* Husain Ibn Mansūr al-Hallāj
Hallājīs, 208
Halperin, David, 53–54, 56, 69, 71
halqa. *See halaqa*
Haq, Muhammad Enamul, 172–73
haqīqa, 19, 170, 204, 207, 211, 214
harf, 161
Hasan al-Basrī, 196, 198, 256–59
hashmal, 53–55, 79
Haywood, Thomas, 7, 108, 139
hayyōt, 54, 72–73, 79
healing, 3, 13–14, 37, 104–7, 110, 112, 118–19, 126, 131–35, 141, 146–47, 193, 240–42
　metaphor, 105, 112, 133
　model, 118
　motif, 193, 226
　spiritual, 105
　theme of, 105, 107, 135
heart, xi, 3–4, 24, 37, 63, 66, 80, 88, 92–94, 100, 102–4, 124, 126, 129–30, 132, 135–36, 140, 155, 163–65, 167, 169–70, 186–89, 191, 197, 208, 210, 213, 220–21, 225, 227–28, 231, 233–34, 236, 249, 254
　lover's, 233
　prayer of the, 185
　saintly, 229
heavens, ix, 3, 6, 21–22, 24, 28, 30–31, 36, 45–53, 55, 62–63, 69–73, 75, 77–79, 85, 89, 94–95, 122, 127, 135, 140, 158, 163–64, 166, 170, 216–17, 219
　door standing open in, 69
　two powers in, 45, 57, 146
Hebrew Scriptures, 27–29, 44, 56, 62, 72, 210, 242–43, 251
Heitzenrater, Richard P., 112
hekhal, 55, 71, 80
hekhalōt, 6, 35, 55, 58, 62, 71
　literature, 24, 29, 33, 46, 55, 165
Hekhalōt, Merkavah ascent, 24
Hekhalōt Rabbati, 24, 54, 63, 72
hell, 104, 156, 231
Hellenic, 22–27, 70, 79, 81, 92, 109, 240
　apotheosis, 175
　Christianity, 149
　context, x, 23, 38, 45, 82
　influences, 26–27, 44, 79
　and Jewish ideas, 40–42, 50, 57, 81, 83, 87
　mysticism, x, 47, 90–91, 111, 142, 194, 240
　paganism, 81
　Shamanism, 89
Hempton, David, 129–30, 143
henôsis, 19–20
heresy, 39, 43, 207
Hermeneutics, Medieval, 158–59, 161
Hermeticism, 25, 32
Heschel, Abraham Joshua, 51–53
hesychist prayer, 154, 185
hijāb-i-ghaynī, 205
Hilarion, 147
Hillel, 44
Himmelfarb, Martha, 30, 51
Himyar, 148, 151
Hinduism, 120, 173, 201, 204
holiness, 3, 93, 99, 114, 117, 126, 198, 221
　communal, 142
　corporate, 92
　holiest, 54
　personal, 112, 114, 141
　true, 123–25
Holy Ghost. *See* Holy Spirit

Holy Spirit, 5–6, 59, 66, 72, 78, 80–81, 84, 90, 92–93, 95–100, 107–8, 112, 116, 118–19, 124, 130–32, 135–36, 139–43, 145–46, 148, 240, 242, 246, 252–53
Homilies, x, 5–6, 73, 80, 90–93, 95–100, 102–9, 115–16, 122–23, 126, 132, 134, 139–40, 182, 246, 248, 253
Horovitz, Hayim S., 52, 57
Horovitz, Josef, 165
Hosier, Harry, 129
Hoyland, Robert G., 152
Hūd, 214
Huda, Qamar-ul, 192, 235–38
Hujwīrī. *See* 'Alī ibn 'Uthmān al-Jullabi al-Hujwīrī
hulūl, 175–76, 178, 208–9
Hulūlīs, 208
humankind, 4, 8, 14, 29, 43, 60, 82, 95, 102, 118–19, 122–27, 130, 133, 136, 158, 166, 174–75, 178, 185, 207–8, 210, 215, 219, 241, 254–55
　creation of, 123, 132, 147
　glorified, 61
　image of God in, 13, 97, 118, 133–34, 146, 240, 242
humility, 86, 130, 152, 179, 209
　great, 178
The Hundred Letters, 8, 194, 203–5, 212, 214–16, 219, 221, 224–26, 229–35, 245, 249, 254
Husain Ibn Mansūr al-Hallāj, 174–80, 208–9, 224
hymns, 35, 132, 139–40, 252
　of Charles Wesley, 138

I

Iamblichus, 79
Iblīs, 166
Ibn A'tham al-Kūfi, 148
Ibn al-Fārid. *See* 'Umar ibn 'Alī Ibn al-Fārid
Ibn al-Husayn al-Sulamī, 148, 155
Ibn 'Arabī, 158
Ibn 'Atā' Allāh al-Iskandarī, 186, 189–91

Ibn Hisham, 148
Ibn Ishāq. *See* Muḥammad ibn Isḥāq ibn Yasār ibn Khiyār
Ibn Karrām, 154
Ibn Kathīr. *See* Ismail ibn Kathīr
Ibn Taymiyya. *See* Taqī ad-Dīn Ahmad ibn Taymiyyah
Ibrahim. *See* Abraham
Idel, Moshe, 27–29, 32, 46, 56–57
idolatry, 102, 174–75
Idu'l Fitr, 255
iftār, 256–57
ihsān, 187
Ihya' 'Ulūm ad-Dīn, 156, 190
image, 4, 14, 19, 23, 25, 33–34, 44, 53, 84–85, 87–89, 95–97, 100, 102, 110, 122–25, 127, 130, 132, 140, 147, 153, 156, 241
　glorious, 64
　mental, 188
　moral, 123
　restored, 141
image of God, 4, 8, 23, 45, 61, 95, 112, 116, 119, 122–25, 127, 130, 132–33, 135–36, 192, 226
Imām Mālik. *See* Mālik ibn Anas
Imam Muslim. *See* Muslim ibn al-Hajjāj
īmān, 170, 227–28
Imru' al-Qais, 153
incarnation, 13, 15, 70, 131, 133, 143, 175–76, 194, 208, 251, 255
India, 1, 8, 120–21, 131, 173, 193, 196, 199, 202–4
indigenizing principle, x, 11–12, 14, 23, 33, 38, 50, 58, 68, 87, 90, 112, 146, 157, 163, 205
ineffability, 18, 41
initiation, 69, 114
innovation, 157–58
　unacceptable, 156
insān kāmil, 248
intercession, 168, 202
intermediary, 45, 226, 245
interpenetration, 108
interpretation, 35, 38, 73, 156–63, 167, 204–6, 212, 235, 237, 244
　allegorical, 38, 49

interpretation *(continued)*
  literal, 167
  spiritual, 219, 229
intimacy, 24, 30, 58, 66
intimate ultimate, 66
intoxication, 102–3, 172–73, 175, 179, 210, 214, 218, 246
  spiritual, 103, 109, 204
invitation, 203
  pastoral, 222
Iqbal, Muhammad, 196
Isaac, 31, 35, 52, 54, 182
Īsā al-Masīh, 27–29, 37, 71, 73–74, 76, 79, 87–88, 106, 216, 248, 257–59
Īsā followers, 255
Isaiah, 27, 31, 61, 69, 78
Ishmael, 46, 72, 148
Islām, 3–4, 9–10, 16, 43, 121–22, 147–55, 157–58, 164, 166, 170, 176, 180, 185, 205–6, 211, 229, 251, 255
  mystics of, 1, 181–82
  orthodox, 163, 180, 196, 206, 227, 231
  required practices of, 229, 248
Islamic Mysticism, ix, 2, 20–21, 106, 144, 159, 182, 235
Islamic orthodoxy, 146, 155–56, 204, 238
Islamic tradition, 7, 160, 237
Ismail ibn Kathīr, 159
isrā', 163–65, 167
Israel, ix, 28, 44, 52, 61–62, 72, 74–77, 79, 88, 127, 233, 253, 259
Isrā' īliyyāt traditions, 151

J

Jackson, Paul, 8, 199–203, 211, 214, 229
Jacob, 44
Jacob's dream, 165
Jaeger, Werner, 94
Ja'far al-Sādiq, 159, 162, 168–69, 172
Jalāl al-Din Rūmī, 178–79, 182–83, 190
jamā'at, 257
jamāl, 28, 168
Jerusalem, 100, 143, 163–64, 166, 231

Jesus, ix–x, 2, 4, 6, 11, 13, 16, 24, 28, 35, 51–52, 58–69, 73–75, 77, 79–80, 94–97, 106, 108, 119–21, 127, 131, 133–35, 138, 142–44, 146–47, 150, 154–55, 175, 177–78, 187, 208, 214, 216–17, 225, 233, 240–42, 244, 248, 250, 253–57
  and the Dead Sea Scrolls, 36–37
  in Islam, 251
Jesus-followers, 250–52
Jesus Prayer, 185
Jesus' words, 64, 216, 245
Jewish, 12, 27, 29, 32, 40, 45, 89, 99, 149, 151, 165, 183
  ancient, 11, 14, 26, 178, 194
  ascension, 27, 34, 164, 243
  communities, 17, 22–23, 38, 56, 216
  customs, 148
  exegetical thought, 160
  Gnosticism, 32
  influence, 32, 70
  Literature, 26, 30–32, 82
  medieval, 162
  shamanistically-oriented, 98
Jewish and Hellenic ascension, x, 14, 47, 90–91, 142, 145
Jewish Christian, 55, 57
Jewish Mysticism, 2, 5, 7, 9, 13, 27, 29–31, 33, 46, 57, 65, 67–68, 80, 99, 163
Jewish numerology, 55
Jewish Pseudepigrapha, 151
Jewish tradition, 25, 27, 32, 44, 46, 48, 69
Jews, 32, 38, 56, 114, 230
jihād, 184, 230, 255
jihād akbar, 254
jinn, 166, 188
Johannine writings, 14, 62, 81, 106
John, x, 6, 45–47, 51–52, 60–69, 73, 75, 77, 112, 128, 133, 135, 146, 175, 183, 233, 243, 245, 255, 258
John Cassian, 186
John's Gospel, 6, 11, 46, 59–60, 65, 68–69, 85, 89, 216, 251
Jose Ben Halafta, 52

journey, 26, 30, 60, 77, 103, 145, 167,
169–70, 214, 217
  inner, 170
  miraculous, 164
  spiritual, 167, 218
joy, 22, 42, 67, 93, 97–98, 100, 108,
127, 130
Judah ha-Nasi, 44
Judaism, 17, 26, 28, 33, 50–51, 63
  apocalyptic, 81
  biblical, 57
Jude, 82–84
Junayd. *See* Abu'l-Qāsim al-Junayd,
156–57, 168, 171, 175, 181, 192,
195, 204
justification, 104, 114, 118, 131, 136,
141

K

Kaaba, 214, 220, 231, 233, 249
Ka'b al-Ahbār, 151
Kabbalah, 32, 53

Kanagaraj, Jey, 35, 43, 45–46, 60, 62,
66–69, 72–73
Karamustafa, Ahmet, 153, 156–57,
176, 195–97
Käsemann, Ernst, 81, 83
Kaŝf al-Mahjub. *See Kashf al-Mahjūb*
Kashf al-Mahjūb, 7–8, 171, 194,
196–99, 202–3, 207, 211, 217–19,
222–23, 227, 229, 235, 237
kāvōd, 27–28, 52, 64, 67, 86, 101
Kee, H. C., 30
Keener. Craig S., 30, 45, 60–67, 78–79,
87–88
kerygma, 12, 128
khānqāh, 153–54, 201–2
Kharrāz, 171
Khidr, 225
Khwaja Ma'rūf Karkhī, 232
kindness, 97–98, 168
king, 33, 36, 43, 60, 67, 88, 94, 98,
104, 107, 226
kingdom, 21, 63, 76, 93–94, 97–98,
130, 135, 202, 216
Kitāb al-Fanā', 171
Kitāb al-Futuwwah, 148, 155

Kitāb al-Luma', 156–58, 187, 236
Kitāb al-Mubtada, 151
Kitāb al-Ta'arruf, 156, 191, 197, 220,
236
knowledge, 3–4, 18–19, 33, 41–42, 53,
65, 83, 88, 118, 121, 137, 150–51,
153, 163, 201, 206–7
  esoteric, 210
  useless, 207
Kohler, Kaufmann, 44–46

L

Lahore, 8, 192–93, 196, 199, 235
lamb, 73–76, 78, 132, 253
  crucified, 74
  sacrificial, 131
Lambdin, Thomas O., 68, 93
lamp, 3–4, 102, 153
lam yūlad marratayni, 217
language, 5, 15, 30, 32, 40, 47, 49,
56, 59, 61, 63–64, 69, 73–74,
76–78, 80–81, 84, 87, 92, 94–95,
97, 99–101, 109, 132, 138–39,
145–46, 149, 174, 179, 182, 225,
232, 241–43, 246
  indigenous, 97, 109
  native, 258
language of mutual abiding, 67
language of mutual seeing, 67
language of union, 99, 146
Latā'if al-Mi'rāj, 167, 169
law, 39, 48–50, 53, 73, 87, 130–31,
134, 163, 175, 180, 203, 207, 214,
220, 230
lawh al-mahfūz, 158
Lawrence, Bruce B., 8, 201–3
leaders, 114, 192, 230, 249
  developing, 128
Lee, Hoo-Jung, 116
Levey, Samson, 55, 69
light, x, 1, 3–6, 24, 47, 55, 59, 72–73,
84, 88, 90, 96–97, 99–100, 102,
104, 107–8, 111, 121, 131, 135,
159, 166, 197, 204, 212, 215, 217,
220–21, 227, 233, 236
  hidden, 103
  ineffable, 97
  spiritual, 246

light verse, 4, 152
likeness, 5, 13, 20, 30, 85–86, 95, 109, 125–26, 136, 189, 249
literal meaning, 2, 160, 211
literal sense, 100, 117
literature
    apocalyptic, 27, 77
    earlier Syrian, 109
    interpretive, 158
Litwa, M. David, 87
Living creatures talking fire, 54
logos, 38, 43–47, 49–51, 53, 61, 68
lookout point, 161
Lord's Supper, 253
Lossky, Vladamir, 13, 125
lote tree of the boundary, 164, 166
love, 33, 48, 62, 64–67, 82, 95, 98, 102–4, 106–8, 116–17, 122–24, 126–28, 130, 135, 137, 140, 155, 165, 174–75, 179, 209, 222, 228–30, 232–33, 236, 246–47, 253, 255, 257
Lover-Beloved relationship, 106, 112, 233
Luke, 79–80, 87, 91
LXX, 28, 64, 79, 82, 86–88

M

Ma'aseh Bereshit, 53
Ma'aseh Merkavah, 35, 53, 55, 57, 71, 79
Macarian Great Letter. See *Epistola Magna*
Macarian Homilies, 5, 7, 9, 16, 88, 91–94, 98, 100–104, 106, 112–13, 115–16, 130–31, 134, 139–40, 142, 146, 182, 241, 243, 245
Macarius of Egypt. See Macarius-Symeon
Macarius-Symeon, 5–6, 9, 12, 14, 16, 60, 73, 80, 88–109, 111–12, 116, 119, 122–23, 126, 130, 132, 134–35, 137, 139–40, 146, 182, 220, 224, 239–40, 246, 248, 253
    use of *doxa*, 101
Maddox, Randy, 13, 125–26, 131, 141–42
magic, 24–25, 27, 33, 35, 65

Maḥmūd al-Ḥaqq Siddīqī, 20
Majnūn-Laila love poems of pre-Islamic Arabia, 204, 233
Maktūbāt-i Sadī, 8, 194, 199, 202–3, 211, 214, 216–17, 224–25, 229–30, 232, 235. See also *The Hundred Letters*.
malakūt, 170, 234
malfūẓāt, 8, 200
Maloney, George A., 9, 92–94, 185
manifestation of God, 224, 233, 249
Manṣūr al-Ḥallāj, 175, 212, 224
Margoliouth, David, 150–51
ma'rifa, 19, 169–70, 180, 227–28
Martyn, Henry, 1, 10, 129, 144
Ma'ruf Karkhī, 232
Mary, 155, 207, 225
Masekhet Hekhalōt, 55
Massignon, Louis, 175–77
Matthew, ix, 76, 94, 137, 209
Mawlawīyya order, 183, 190
Maximus, 18, 92, 151
Mayer, Toby, 153–56, 169, 175, 206, 219
McAuliffe, Jane Dammen, 158–59, 161
means of grace, 16, 147, 184, 191, 226, 228–30, 235, 248–50
Mecca, 149–50, 163–64, 166, 201, 231, 233–34
Mechiltā de-Rabbi Ishmael, 52, 57
meditation, 5, 42, 53, 137, 172, 191, 201, 234, 249–51
    contemplative, 235–36
    extended, 5, 88
    silent, 251
memra, 44–45, 74
Menzies, Glen, 54, 78–80
mercy, 37, 67, 180, 213, 223, 227, 259
merkavah, 5, 25, 27–29, 32–35, 45, 52–58, 61, 63–64, 69–72, 81, 145, 220
    accounts, 61
    discourse, 33
    and *Hekhalōt* and practices, 58
    inverted, 79–80
    literature, 34, 46, 61, 69, 74
Merkavōt Kəvodo, 71

General Index   297

multiple, 55, 71, 80
Mysticism, 32, 52–53, 243
   speculation on Ezekiel's vision, 54, 99
   system, 6, 27–28, 33–34, 53, 60, 65–66, 99
   visions, 64, 78
Mesopotamia, 9, 26, 92
Messalians, 9, 91
Messiah, ix, 28, 36, 49, 58, 74–75, 78, 86–88, 127, 144, 147, 175, 233, 243, 246, 248, 252–55
   descended, 241
   promised, 37
   in Sūfī contexts, 241
metaphor, 4, 15, 74, 79, 84, 96–98, 103–4, 106, 135, 169, 182, 187, 221, 227, 247
   creative, 102
   legal, 133
   literary, 224
   recurring, 182
metaphysical, 4, 18, 172, 181
Metatron, 46, 52, 61
Methodism, 1, 9, 92, 114, 127, 129–30, 132, 143–44
   community, 120, 127
   connections, 129
   early, 1, 114
   leadership, 113
   "methodists of the east," 1, 10, 253
Middle Platonism, 61, 81–82, 84
miracles
   extraordinary, 65
   performed, 148
miʿrāj, 163–67, 169–70, 183, 188, 218–19, 221–22
   accounts, 165, 169
   spiritual, 219
   tradition, 218
mirror, 4, 186, 188, 197, 218, 221, 225, 245
   reflective bronze, 85
Mishkât Al-Anwar, 4
Mishnah, 44, 51, 53
mission, ix, 2, 13, 15–16, 21, 111, 113–15, 117–19, 121, 123, 125, 127, 129, 131, 133–37, 139, 141, 143, 150, 241–42
   centrifugal, ix
missional, 10–11, 13, 118–19, 123, 127, 131–32, 136, 140
missionary, 136, 144, 251
   pioneering, 250–51
models, 42–43, 46, 135, 142–43, 169, 178, 208, 212, 243, 256
   anthropocentric, 126
   general, 256
   holistic, 13
   prophetic pilgrim, 142
modes, 49, 154, 160, 236
   final, 236
   inner, 236
Moffett, Samuel Hugh, 131
Mohammed. *See* Muhammad
Mohammedanism. *See* Islam, 121
Mohammedans. *See* Muslims
Moʻīnuddīn Chishtī, 196
Mojaddedi, Jawid A., 7, 197, 204
monastery, 4, 201
monks, 3–5, 91–92, 147–48, 150–53, 186
morality and piety, 124, 172, 181, 187, 213, 247
Moses, 17, 28–29, 41–43, 46–47, 51–53, 56–57, 61, 87, 101–2, 131, 167–69, 172, 187, 210, 218, 225, 233
   ascension, 41, 46, 53
mosque, 20, 150, 189, 191, 198, 220–21, 257
movements, 33, 49, 58, 170
   emerging Rabbinic Jewish, 27, 51
   gnosis-centered Christian, 57
   growing, 157
   included, 22
Muʿallaqāt, 153
Muhammad, 10, 19, 21, 149–53, 158, 160, 165–69, 171, 178, 185, 187–90, 201, 210, 214, 218–19, 223, 236, 253
   character, 168
   companions, 197
   hearing, 151
   mission, 214

Muhammad *(continued)*
  mystical experience, 164
  practices, 201
  sobriety, 218
  states, 166
  superiority, 222
  vision, 167, 219
  wives, 167
Muhammad al-Mayhanī, 222
Muhammad bin Tughlaq, 201–2
Muhammad ibn Isḥāq ibn Yasār ibn Khiyār, 149–50, 165–67
mujāhada, 184, 222–23, 244
mukhamāt, 163
murāqaba, 187–88, 235, 245
Murata, Sachiko, 166, 185, 187, 206
murīd, 188, 237–38, 257
murshid, 188
  eternal, 248
Mūsa, 168, 236, 259
mushāhada, 169, 187, 219, 222–24, 226, 244–46
music, 184, 189–90, 205, 228–29, 235–38, 250, 258
  distinctive, 236
  elements of, 190, 200
  indigenous-style, 251
  perfect, 48
Musk, Bill, 252
Muslim community, 146, 148, 153, 155–57, 176, 195, 205, 254–55
Muslim ibn al-Ḥajjāj, 165–66
mutashābihāt, 163
muttala, 161
Muwaṭṭāʾ, 166
mysteries, 5, 8, 18–19, 32, 68, 71, 75, 81, 99, 140, 156, 190, 236
mystical experience, 18, 23, 33, 40, 43, 85, 181, 183
mysticism, 2, 8–10, 13, 17–18, 23, 26, 33, 35–36, 38, 43, 45, 50, 57, 60, 62, 66–68, 72–73, 89, 91, 111, 115, 130, 146, 158, 160–61, 173, 202, 217, 242, 247
  ancient, 15, 64
  apocalyptic, 30
  ascension/vision/transformation, 78
  ecstatic, 48
  frivolous, 117
  healthy, 118
  non-Merkavah, 57
  pantheistic, 117
  philosophical, 42
  relational, 47
  speculative, 117
  traditional, 65
  unhealthy, 23
  wise, 12, 117
mysticism of infinity, 9, 23
mysticism of personality, 12
mysticism of union, 12, 14, 24, 33, 108, 180
mystics, 1, 6, 18, 30, 33, 35, 57, 81, 169–70, 174, 178, 201
  devout, 81
  earliest Jewish, 85
  spiritual food of the, 186

N

Naaman, 135
nafs, 183–84
nafs al-ammāra, 206
nafs al-lawwāma, 206
nafs al-mutmuʾinna, 206
Nag Hammadi texts, 32
Najīb al-Dīn Firdausī, 201
Najrān, 148, 150–51
  Christians of, 150
Nakshbandhīyya, 190
namāz, 228–30, 233
Nasr, Seyyed Hossein, 239
nations, ix, 43, 75–76, 78, 88, 119, 121, 133
nearness, 218, 221
nekyia literature, 26
Neoplatonic, 19–20, 109, 153
Nestorians, 207
Neusner, Jacob, 51, 53–55, 72
Newsom, Carol A., 54, 71
New Testament, 12, 36, 51, 56, 59, 61, 69, 81, 89, 94, 106, 137, 242–44, 251, 258
Nicholson, Reynold A., 8, 153, 178–79, 182, 195–97, 203, 205, 246
Nickelsburg, George W. E., 26, 31

Nizam al-Din 'Awliyā', 200, 213
Noah, 214
Nwyia, Paul, 159

O

obedience, 66–67, 170, 219, 227–28
observation, 17, 50, 75, 92, 155, 209, 214, 228, 249
Odeberg, Hugo, 46, 61
Odes of Solomon, 25, 60, 63, 73, 101, 107, 109
Olah HaShabbat, 34, 70–71, 77
Old Testament, 26, 75, 87, 100, 113
"On God's Vineyard," 127
oral teaching, 183, 217
orders, 2, 30, 72, 101, 105–6, 160, 173, 180, 197, 201, 211, 246
orthodoxy, 201, 205, 235–36
Otto, Rudolf, 17
Outler, Albert C., 114, 136–37, 244

P

Pakistan, 192–93, 235, 251
palaces, 6, 31, 34, 67, 71, 104–5, 156. *See also hekhalōt*
pantheism, 173–74, 179, 183, 246
Paradise, 156, 166, 189, 209, 231
Paradosis, 55
PaRDeS, 55–56, 160, 165
Parshall, Phil, 251
participation, 13, 75–76, 84, 89, 98, 107, 116, 125, 142, 187–88, 218, 245
participators, 98–99, 107
passions, 25, 83, 101, 105, 108, 246
  lustful, 84
  spiritual, 106
path, ix, 2, 19, 124, 170, 206, 208, 214, 223, 236, 239
  guided, 19, 171
  shamanistic, 78
  uniform, 160
path of illumination, 19, 170
Paul, 4, 9–10, 30, 42, 56, 59, 65, 71, 75, 83, 85–88, 109, 246–47
  theosis in, 85

peace, 24, 55, 97–98, 107, 130, 140, 149, 187, 189–90, 221, 225, 235
  final blessing of, 230, 249
  greetings of, 221, 257
  soul at, 206
pearl diver, 131, 182, 247
Pentecost, 78, 79–81, 89
perfection, 40, 108, 114, 116–18, 131, 212, 239, 244
perichoresis, 108
Perrin, Nicholas, 67
Persian, 2, 7–8, 19, 26, 156, 178, 194, 196, 198, 204, 224, 228, 230
  apocalypses, 26
  commentary, 171, 220
  influence, 26
  language, 8
  Literature, 8, 169, 196, 204
  Poetry, 145, 226
Pesikta Rabbati, 88
Phaedrus, 24–25, 48
Phemion, 148
Philemon, 70
Philo, 22–23, 38–50, 56, 58, 60–62, 68, 145, 240, 243
  allegorical exegesis, 39
  commentary on Moses' conversation, 42
  interpretation of Abraham's vision, 61
  Logos, 44–45
  mysticism, 42
philosophers, 23, 48, 196
philosophy, 2, 12, 38, 42, 50, 75
Philo's writings, 40, 42–43, 45–46, 56, 68
Photis, 92
Physician, 105, 131, 133
Pia Desideria, 114
Pietism, 14, 91–92, 112, 114, 116, 241
pilgrimage, 196, 202, 230, 233–34
pilgrim principle, x, 12, 14, 34, 47, 50, 58–59, 68, 81, 83, 87, 90–92, 144, 146, 155, 157, 163, 195, 205, 207, 228, 237–40, 243, 250, 256
pillars, 78, 220, 229–30, 232, 248–50, 253

pīr, 2, 19–21, 170–71, 188, 211, 229, 248, 256
A Plain Account of Christian Perfection, 10, 125, 138–39
Plato, 24, 39, 82
Platonic, 25, 38–39, 44, 47–48, 50, 83, 214, 243
Plested, Marcus, 9, 92, 113
polemics, 41, 51–52, 56
  doctrinal, 113
  pointed, 32
  rabbinic, 52
power, 3, 12, 25, 33, 41, 44–45, 49–50, 54, 57, 64–65, 67, 72, 81, 84–86, 88–89, 95–97, 101, 103, 105–6, 108, 112, 115, 121, 134, 136, 139, 141, 164, 176, 181, 194, 206, 217, 223–24, 231, 233
  sanctifying, 13, 98, 112
praise, 55, 71, 73, 77, 80, 190, 232, 236, 251–52
prayer, 3, 20, 35, 95–96, 98, 125, 147, 150, 166, 178, 186, 188–89, 196, 198, 202, 219–20, 228–33, 249, 252, 257–58
  chanted, 232
  continual, 186
  internal, 230
  introductory, 205
  liturgical, 228–30, 248
  ritual, 229
  set, 189
  sunset, 198
  supplicatory, 186
prayer leader, 198, 230
prayer liturgy, 219
prayer of union, 220–21
preparatio evangelii, 121, 138
prevenient grace, 13–14, 118–19, 122, 124, 135–36, 138, 141, 146–47, 192–93, 226, 240–42
proclamation, 7, 103, 119, 131, 138, 142–43, 146, 242
promise, 37, 66–67, 76–77, 84, 113, 141, 164, 250
prophets, 27, 31, 41, 155, 162, 166, 168–69, 186, 210, 212, 214, 218, 221–22

propitiation, 133
prostrations, 230
Pseudo-Macarius. *See* Macarius-Symeon
purification, 140, 170, 228
  inward, 228–29
purified soul, 225
purity, 24, 67, 103, 209, 213–14, 220–221, 247

Q

qalb, 161, 170, 228
Qānūn-i-Islām, 203
qawwālī, 236, 258
qibla, 188, 231, 249
  original, 231
  true, 234
Qisas al-Anbiyā', 151
Quispel, Gilles, 94
Qumran, 30, 34–36, 54, 58, 62, 70, 145
  and Johannine Theology, 64
Qur'ān, 2–4, 9, 28, 121, 146, 150–53, 156–65, 167, 170–71, 177, 185–86, 190–91, 195, 203–8, 211–13, 223, 229, 236, 242–44, 251–52, 254–55, 257–58
Qur'ānic Commentary, 158–59, 172
Qushayrī, see Abū'l-Qāsim al-Qushayrī
Qūt al-Qulūb, 155

R

Rabbani, Wahid Baksh, 8, 195–97, 205, 219, 222
Rahmāniyya, 189
Rajgir, 201–2
Rakestraw, Robert, 85
Ramadān, 249, 251, 253–57
Ramm, Bernard, 28
realization, 19, 119, 170, 183, 208
  progressive, 125
reason, x, 22–23, 49, 52, 70, 82–83, 91, 95–96, 103, 117, 134, 141, 176
recitation, 229, 232, 236, 251

redemption, 68, 70, 104, 109, 116, 121, 131
regeneration, 135
regulations, external, 170
reification, possible, 77
reincarnation, 177
relationship, 9, 17, 23, 26, 33, 39–40, 47, 65, 67, 86, 95, 106, 109, 113, 122, 127, 143, 161, 202, 206, 210–11, 227–28, 231, 240, 245, 248, 252, 255
  abiding, 248
  living, 114
  loving, 47, 65, 68
  transforming, 221
  true, 33
religion, 32, 117, 124, 133, 136, 148, 150, 155, 158, 170, 235
religious obligation, 179, 246
religious ordinances, 219, 228
remembrance, 154, 185–88, 235, 251
  unceasing, 185
  of God, 3, 186–89
remez, 162
Renard, John, 156, 158, 197, 199–201, 218
renouncing self-interest, 209, 247
repentance, 87, 136, 212, 228
  describing, 212
  expressing, 212
  sinners to, 51, 135
repetition, 154, 185–86, 212
response, 27, 29, 36, 41, 51, 56–59, 65, 85, 94, 138, 146–47, 151, 162, 174, 238
  inner, 211
  practical, 211
  rational, 82
responsibility, 105
  human, 125
restoration, 8, 95, 104, 112, 116, 119, 126–27, 130, 132–35, 146, 242
restoration of all things, 13
resurrection, 59, 74, 83, 86, 98, 143, 147, 156, 161, 174, 177, 190, 211, 248
Revelation, 8, 29, 57, 59, 61–62, 69–78, 89, 99, 156, 160, 171, 182, 194–98, 204–9, 218–19, 222–24, 227–29, 232, 234, 244, 247–48, 254
  Book of, 69, 71–73, 76–77
reverence, 168, 219
revival, 112, 120, 122
righteousness, 37, 83, 100, 123–24, 130–32, 213
Risāla, 155–56, 197–98, 236
ritualized prayer, 184, 250
rituals, 19, 24, 33, 35, 80, 137, 184, 187, 192, 229, 250–52, 254–55
  commanded, 228
  devotional, 190, 235
  distinct, 184
  fast-breaking, 256
  performed, 240
  puratrix, 252
  thanksgiving, 203
  theurgic, 20
  washing, 228
Robinson, Neal, 149, 158, 191
Ronning, John, 74
Rowland, Christopher, 67, 70–71
Rūmī. *See* Jalāl al-Din Rūmī
Runia, David, 38, 43–44
Rūzbihān al-Baqlī, 162

S

Sabbath Sacrifice, 34, 54, 71, 145
sacred text, 28, 38, 40, 158–59, 195, 204
sacrifice, 52, 62, 74–75, 98, 131, 178, 256
sacrificial death, 73, 78
  atoning, 77
sacrificial rescue, 259
Sadhu Sundar Singh, 23–24
sages, 44, 52–53, 58, 169, 201
Sahīh Muslim, 165–67, 187, 231
Sahīh Bukharī, 232
Sahl al-Tustarī, 158–59, 161, 223
sahw, 172, 179, 204, 218, 246
saints, 8, 71, 127, 153, 181, 184, 186, 192–93, 196, 199, 202–3, 218, 222
  widely-venerated Sūfī, 196
sakīna, 189–90

salāh, 228–29, 258
Salminius Hermias Sozomenus, 147–48
salvation, 10, 13–14, 19, 62–63, 72, 104–6, 111–12, 114, 118, 124–27, 131–33, 135–36, 141, 146–47, 163, 170, 186, 189–90, 227, 240–42, 245
samā', 182–84, 189–91, 200, 228, 236–37, 250, 252–53
sanctification, 1, 3, 13–14, 102, 112, 114–15, 117–19, 121, 124, 131, 133, 136, 138, 140–41, 143, 146, 177, 192, 226, 240–42, 249, 253
Sandmel, Samuel, 42–43, 45
Sands, Kristin Zahra, 161–63, 206
Sanneh, Lamin, 147, 149
Sappington, Thomas J., 70
Sar-Torah, 63
Satan, 93, 121, 166, 221
Savage, Timothy B., 87–88
Savior, 83, 111, 131–32, 134
Schäfer, Peter, 33
Schimmel, Annemarie, 2, 9, 19–20, 23, 151, 157, 170–72, 174–75, 179, 185–89, 196, 201–2, 234, 245
Scholem, Gershom, 18, 24, 31–33, 53, 65, 99
"Scriptural Christianity," 141–42
scriptures, ix–x, 9, 28–30, 32, 38–40, 47, 49, 55, 59, 81, 109, 116–17, 128, 132, 134, 137, 148–49, 158, 160, 181, 240–43, 250–52
Second Temple Judaism, 23, 35, 44, 57
Sefer Hekhalōt, 61
Segal, Alan F., 9, 13, 23, 29–30, 35–36, 40, 43, 45–46, 49–50, 57, 68, 70–71, 81, 84–86, 111, 119
self-abasement, 75
self-abnegation, 75
self-accusing soul, 206
self-annihilation, 10
self-control, 49
self-denial, 24, 148
self-disclosure, 168, 236
self-effacement, 216
self-effort, 6, 62

self-forgetfulness, 231
self-humiliation, 127
self-knowledge, 6, 62
self-mortification, 207
  ascetic, 222
self-perishing, 178
self-righteous, 229
self-subsistent, 43
self-surrender, 223
Seligsohn, M., 52
Sells, Michael A., 159, 162–63, 165–67, 171, 177, 180–81
šel šāmayyim, 72
separation, 80, 169, 180–81
Sepher Hekhalōt, 46
Shabastiary, Mahmoud, 145
shahāda, 233–34, 236, 249
Shahîd, Irfan, 149
shaikh, 19, 188, 195, 201, 214, 216, 226, 229, 237–38
  perfect, 226
Shaikh Najīb al-Dīn Firdausī, 200
Shaikh Yahya Manerī, 199
shamanism, 19, 24, 33, 49, 53, 65, 111, 145, 183–84
  anthropocentric, 58
  syncretistic, 57
shamanistic, 24, 47, 59, 65, 85, 145, 147, 183–84, 192, 217, 223, 225, 244–45
Shams al-Dīn, 211
Sharaf al-Dīn Manerī, x, 7–8, 14, 16, 193–95, 197, 199- 205, 207, 209, 211–27, 229–38, 240, 243, 245, 248–49, 254
  arrival in Delhi, 200
  discourses, 8
  exegesis, 213
  exposition on repentance, 212
  guide, 200
  malfūzāt, 8, 217
  metaphor, 230
  tomb of, 202
  understanding of *tajallī*, 224
Sharafuddin Manerī. *See* Sharaf Al-Dīn Manerī
Sharh-i-Ta'aruf, earlier, 196–97, 220

sharīʿa, 19, 163, 170, 179–80, 204, 207, 211, 214, 219, 246
Shekinah, 77, 81, 100–101, 190
   glory of the, 100
Shrines, 184, 196, 236
sifāt, 168, 204, 206, 224
silsila, 197, 202
sin, 8, 55, 93, 96–98, 103–5, 112, 115, 120, 122, 124, 131–36, 140, 175, 198, 212, 246
Singh, Sadhu Sundar, 24, 109
sirr, 236
Snyder, Howard A., 13, 16, 116, 118–19, 123, 126–28, 132, 136, 140–41, 241
sober, 103, 122, 130, 175, 179, 204, 214
sober intoxication, 48, 102–3, 122
   idea of, 49, 103
Solomon, 25, 60, 63, 71, 74, 107
songs, 20–21, 34–35, 54–55, 70–71, 73, 145, 252, 258
sorites, 82–83
soteriology, 99
   therapeutic, 118
soul, 5–6, 20, 22–24, 27, 33, 39–40, 47–48, 60, 85, 88, 90, 93, 95–100, 102, 104–8, 112, 115, 122–24, 130–33, 135, 138, 140, 143, 145, 154, 172, 184, 202, 206, 213, 215, 220, 224, 228, 239–40, 245–46, 253
South Asia, 7–8, 20, 151, 172, 184, 193–96, 202–3, 229, 236, 238, 251–52
Sozomen. *See* Salminius Hermias Sozomenus
speculation, 49, 51, 54, 61, 68, 155, 158, 202
   philosophical, 4, 117
Spener, Philipp Jakob, 114
spirit, 4–6, 23–24, 37, 66–68, 72, 78–80, 85, 87, 90, 95–100, 102–3, 108–9, 113, 121, 124, 136–37, 139–41, 143, 145, 167, 176–77, 182, 185, 190, 196, 209, 216, 219, 223, 225, 236, 242, 244, 246–48, 253

Spirit-empowered Christian life, 87, 140–42
spiritual director, 2, 188, 213, 216, 226, 229, 249
spiritual exercises, 24, 80, 229
spiritual guidance, 199–202, 214, 226, 235, 248
spiritual *jihād*, 249, 254
spiritual life, 195, 206, 228, 231, 238, 252
spiritual power, 102, 188, 192, 196
spiritual rebirth, 63
stage
   early, 33
   final, 1
   first, 69
   previous, 173
Starr, James, 81–83
state, 18, 102, 104, 107, 119–20, 122, 125, 131, 135, 155, 169, 172–75, 185, 199, 208–10, 218–19, 226, 236
   abiding, 218
   constant, 103
   ecstatic, 237
   lost, 119
   natural human, 170
   perfect, 122, 125
stations, 168, 170, 221
Stewart. Columba, 92
Stoicism, 25, 38, 44, 50, 81–82, 84
strength, 6, 37, 62, 98, 126, 140, 182, 214, 255
strengthen, 36, 206
study circle. *See halaqa*
Subhan, John A., 184, 196
subsistence, 206, 208, 211
   eternal, 168
Sūf, 19, 157
Sūfī-background believers, 14, 253
Sūfīs, 1–2, 4, 8, 10, 12–13, 16–17, 129, 144, 153, 155–57, 159, 161, 163, 169, 171, 174–76, 179, 184–85, 187, 191–92, 196, 201, 207, 215–16, 221, 227, 233, 235–36, 238, 240, 245–46, 250, 252, 254–55

General Index

Sūfism, 1–2, 7, 9, 12, 14, 19, 21, 28, 145–47, 149, 151–57, 159–61, 163–65, 167, 169–73, 175–85, 187, 189, 191, 193, 195–98, 201, 203–9, 213, 216, 222, 227, 235, 237–38, 240, 246, 250
  ascension and vision mysticism, 147, 244, 248
  authority, 192, 196, 203, 205, 236
  believers, 17, 186–87, 192, 248
  chivalry, 155
  classical, 8, 14, 156, 173, 192, 195, 235, 240
  commentaries, 154, 158–63, 206, 211
  communities, 13–14, 21, 153, 155–57, 163, 184, 190–91, 235, 239, 242, 249–50, 253
  devotions and ritual, 192
  exegesis, 146, 161–62, 171, 211, 244
  historic, 144, 153, 195
  initiation, 157
  intoxicated, 173, 175, 179, 200
  orders, 2, 10, 153–57, 160, 170, 173, 179–80, 183–84, 187–89, 192, 197, 201, 215, 242, 245
  orthodoxy, 11, 205
  practices, 8, 155, 169, 183, 190, 200, 235
  saints, 7, 16, 155, 159, 171, 195, 197–99, 203, 205, 217, 222, 232, 238, 240, 250
  sources, 48, 154, 171, 176, 180, 186–88, 226, 235, 241
  stories, 153, 181–82, 204, 225, 243, 248, 252
  teaching, 1–2, 8–9, 11, 16, 156, 174, 179, 199, 203–4, 207, 217, 236, 243–44, 246, 248, 251
  terminology, 2, 170, 222, 248
  theology, 16, 146
  ultimate goal of, 7, 10, 179, 215, 245–46
  union with God, 163, 247–48
sukr, 172, 179, 204, 218, 246. *See also* Sūfism, intoxicated
Sulamī. *See* Abū ʿAbd al-Rahmān Muhammad ibn al-Husayn al- Sulamī
Sunnah, 121, 160
Sunni Islam, 155, 158, 167, 206, 228, 230, 235, 240, 254
Suvorova, Anna, 195, 199
Svendsen, Stefan Nordgaard, 39, 44
Swanson, Mark H., 152
Swartz, Michael, 33, 35, 55, 57, 71, 80
sweetness, 47, 103–4
symbolism, 39, 66, 159, 164, 182–83, 190
Symeon the New Theologian, 9, 92
syncretism, ix–x, 27–28, 32, 173, 254
  un-critical, 82
synergism, 105, 125–26, 195, 223–24
synthesis, 15, 133, 135
synthesizing, 45
Syriac, 7, 97, 100, 154, 182
Syrian monastic movement, x, 9, 60, 88, 131

T

tāʾat, 227–28
Tabarī. *See* Abū Jaʿfar al-Tabarī
Tabātabāʾī, Muhammad Husayn, 159
tabernacle, 100–101, 134
table, 104, 231–32, 249, 257
Tadhkirat al-Awliyāʾ, 199
Tafsīr al-Tustarī, 158
tajallī, 168, 175, 224, 226, 245
tajallī rabbānī, 224–25, 245–46
tajallī ruhānī, 224–25
Talmud, 46, 53–55, 72, 74
Tamhīdāt, 217
Tannaim, 44–45, 51–53, 56, 82–83
Tappert, Theodore G., 114
Taqī al-Dīn Ahmad ibn Taymiyyah, 159–60, 162
Targums, 44–45, 69, 74, 86, 100
Tārīkh al-rusul wa al-mulūl k, 148
tarīqa, 2, 19, 170, 184, 202, 214
tasdīq-bil-qalb, 227
tawhīd, 170, 206
taʾwīl, 159–63, 204, 243–44, 248. *See also* Sūfism, exegesis
Taylor, William, x, 143

temple, 27, 35, 71–72, 96, 100, 106–7, 166
   eschatological, 31
Testament of Levi, 30, 69
Tha'labī, 151
theology, x, 11, 20, 60, 91, 111, 113, 115, 117, 119, 121, 123, 125, 127, 129, 131, 133, 135, 137, 139, 141–43, 156–57
   missional, 118
theology of mission, 13, 15, 114, 134, 241
theophany, 28, 46, 50, 64, 77, 101
theosis, 5, 10, 13, 20, 25, 50, 81, 84, 87, 106, 114–15, 117–18, 125, 130–31, 138–39, 141, 241–42
therapeutic idea, 126, 131, 134
theurgy, 19, 27, 35, 60, 63
Thomas, x, 6, 67–68, 85, 92–95, 101, 108
throne-chariot, 5, 27, 34, 145
throne room, 6, 24, 31, 62, 69–70, 220, 230
tongues, 39, 43–44, 54, 78–79, 132, 149, 186, 198
   divided, 78
   fiery, 54–55, 78–81
   primary, 158
Torah, 29, 45, 63, 81, 87, 145, 243
traditions, 7, 13, 17–18, 27–28, 31, 34, 38, 53, 58, 71, 92, 100, 117, 153–54, 157, 160–61, 183, 203, 205, 217
   apocalyptic, 18
   biblical, 17, 34, 101, 151
   early Wesleyan, 7, 10
   hekhalōt literature chariot, 34
transcendence, 17, 39, 43, 179
   utter, 61
transfiguration, 5, 25, 88
transformation, x, 9, 12–15, 19, 29–30, 36, 40, 46–47, 50, 52, 59, 63–64, 81, 84–85, 87, 92, 95, 97, 103–4, 109–12, 119–20, 126, 142, 144, 146, 163, 165, 183, 194, 217, 226, 238, 240, 242–44, 251, 256
   angelomorphic, 70

communal, 119
Enoch, 46
gradual, 107
mysticism, 14, 23, 59, 89, 239–40
ontic, 29
perfecting, 226
transformed soul, 21, 224
transitional point, 31
translatability, 158
translation, 3, 7–8, 15, 17, 22, 35–37, 55, 57, 69–70, 80, 93, 101, 108, 139, 148, 159, 167, 178, 196, 217, 219, 244
translation model, 15
translation principle, Walls, Andrew, 15, 146
Trimingham, Spencer, 147, 153–55, 160, 170, 173, 183–84, 187–89, 192, 245
Trinity, 124, 143
Trotter, Lilias, 250–51
True Christianity, 91, 113–14
Tughlaq. *See* Muhammad bin Tughlaq
Tustarī. *See* Sahl al- Tustarī
Tuttle, Robert G., 115
two bow lengths, 218

U

unbelievers, 4, 88, 106, 114, 166
union, ix–x, 1–2, 4–14, 16, 18–20, 24–26, 28, 30, 32–34, 36, 38, 40, 42, 44, 46, 48, 50, 52, 54, 56, 58, 60, 62, 64–66, 68–70, 72, 74, 76, 78, 80–82, 84, 86, 88–89, 92, 94–144, 146, 148, 150, 152, 154, 156, 158, 160, 162–64, 166, 168–76, 178–82, 184, 186, 188, 190, 192, 194, 196, 198, 200, 202, 204, 206, 208, 210, 212–16, 218, 220–22, 224–26, 228, 230, 232, 234, 236–42, 244–48, 250, 252, 254–58
   abiding, 122
   ascending, 4
   attained, 10
   complete, 24
   ecstatic, 122, 185
   goal of, 19, 171, 176

union *(continued)*
  grace-empowered, 246
  inward, 13, 142
  living, 130
  perfecting, 147
  process of, 135, 141
  progressive, 19, 143, 171, 257
  radical, 183
  sanctifying, 110
  seeking, x, 236, 239
  transforming, 97, 100, 146, 183, 192, 235, 242–43, 245
unity, 64, 70, 80, 148, 174, 181, 213, 234–35, 253
  absolute, 17, 170, 234
  compound, 17
  ontological, 64
universe, 25, 42, 46, 61
Unveiled Faces, 4, 59, 61, 63, 65, 67, 69, 71, 73, 75, 77, 79, 81, 83, 85, 87, 89
Upanishadic Hinduism, 173
Urdu, 8, 21, 194, 222
urs, 20–21, 192, 202, 235–38, 252, 256

V

veil, 4, 86–88, 100, 117, 164, 168, 197, 205, 217, 225, 235, 245
Vickers, John, 119
Victorinus, 72
vigilant awareness, 187, 245
vision, 5–7, 9–10, 22–24, 27, 29–31, 35, 40, 47, 51, 54, 56–57, 59–60, 63, 65, 67–72, 76–77, 87, 89, 92, 98, 117–18, 147, 163–64, 167, 183–84, 187, 192, 217, 219, 222, 228, 231, 236–37, 243–44, 258
  beatific, 187
  chariot, 24
  direct, 222, 236
  ecstatic, 48
  inner, 245–46
  prophetic, 26, 28
  spiritual, 100, 169, 219
  throne-room, 69, 77
  transforming, 85, 145
vision mysticism, x, 11, 23–24, 27–28, 30, 34, 47, 51, 54, 58–60, 63, 67–69, 79, 81, 85, 91, 106, 111, 145–47, 241
vision of God, 6, 46, 67, 71, 84–85, 167–69, 219, 222, 244, 254

W

Wahb ibn Munabhih, 151, 153
wahdat al-shuhūd, 184
wahdat al-wujūd, 175, 184, 246
Walfish, Barry D., 161
walī, 2, 19, 188
Walker, Dale, 37, 82, 214, 231
Walls, Andrew, x, 11–12, 14–15, 17, 54, 112, 119, 238–40
  indigenous and pilgrim principles, 14, 23, 47, 50, 58–59, 83, 91, 109, 112, 144, 155, 180, 195, 225, 228, 237–40, 242
Wesley, Charles, 111–12, 132, 138–40, 146
Wesley, John, x, 7, 9–14, 91, 110–43, 147, 184, 192, 195, 224, 239–41, 243–44, 248, 250
Wesleyan, 143
  anthropology, 126, 133
  concept of prevenient grace, 141
  concepts of salvation, 141
  missiology, x, 13, 16, 141
  revision of Macarian Homily, 134, 139
  sanctification, 114–15, 117
  Spirituality, ix, 13, 241
  Synergism, 192
  synthesis, 141
  theology of grace in conversation, 141
  use of Christian antiquity, 115
Whitefield, George, 128
Winston, David, 43, 48
wisdom, 11, 22, 24, 45, 47–49, 71, 83, 118, 131, 225
witness, 2, 12–13, 81, 114, 118, 126, 136, 142, 174, 180, 220, 244, 252, 254–55
  biblical, 15, 119, 213, 244
  unity of, 184
witnessing, 169, 180–81, 219, 234, 244

women, 2–3, 20–21, 125, 150, 191, 209, 252, 255–56
Woodberry, Dudley, 249–50
worship, 3, 17, 35, 57–58, 61, 70, 73–76, 78, 125, 137, 164, 180, 223, 228, 235, 240, 242, 250–52, 257
  angelic, 61, 70
  eternal, 75
  monotheistic, 73
  obedient, 184

Y

Yose, 52–53
Yusūf 159, 209, 257

Z

zāhir, 161
Zahniser, Mathias, xi, 16, 66, 150, 192, 209, 243–44
zahr, 161
zakāt, 233, 249
zamzam, 166
zĕkā' (Aramaic), 74
Zhukovsky, V. A., 7, 195, 197
Zia al-Dīn Simnanī, 200
zikr. *See dhikr*
Zizoulas, John D., 80, 176
Zoroastrian traditions, 25, 165

www.ingramcontent.com/pod-product-compliance
Lightning Source LLC
Chambersburg PA
CBHW050622300426
44112CB00012B/1610